SCRIBNER REPRINT EDITIONS

# DOMINATIONS AND POWERS

---

*Reflections on Liberty Society and Government*

---

*by*

GEORGE SANTAYANA

320.5
S233 d

AUGUSTUS M. KELLEY • PUBLISHERS
*CLIFTON 1972*

118887

First Published 1951
(New York: Charles Scribner's Sons)
Copyright 1950, 1951 by Charles Scribner's Sons

Re-Issued 1972 By
Augustus M. Kelley · Publishers
Clifton New Jersey 07012
By Arrangement with Charles Scribner's Sons

. . . . . . . . . . . .

ISBN 0 678 02775 7
LCN 75 158153

. . . . . . . . . . . .

All rights reserved. No part of this book
may be reproduced in any form without the
permission of Charles Scribner's Sons.

PRINTED IN THE UNITED STATES OF AMERICA
*by* SENTRY PRESS, NEW YORK, N. Y. 10013

# PREFACE

MANY years ago, in the second volume of *The Life of Reason*, I drew a sketch of human society inspired by the ethics of Plato and Aristotle. I was then a judicial moralist, distinguishing the rational uses of institutions and deciding which were the best. If now I submit to the public some subsequent thoughts on the same subject, I do so with a more modest intention. I have become aware that anyone's sense of what is good and beautiful must have a somewhat narrow foundation, namely, his circumstances and his particular brand of human nature; and he should not expect the good or the beautiful after his own heart to be greatly prevalent or long maintained in the world. Plato and Aristotle spoke with authority for the ancient city then in its decline; their precepts are still pertinent to the art of government; but they hardly consider non-territorial powers, such as universal religions, nor the relation of the State to the non-political impulses of human nature. What to them seemed absolute and permanent was in fact relative and temporary.

Circumstances from the beginning had prepared me to feel this limitation in all moral dogmatism. My lot had been cast in different moral climates, amidst people of more than one language and religion, with contrary habits and assumptions in their political life. I was not bound to any type of society by ideal loyalty nor estranged from any by resentment. In my personal contacts I found them all tolerable when seen from the inside and not judged by some standard unintelligible to those born and bred under that influence. Personally I might have my instinctive preference; but speculatively and romantically I should have been glad to find an even greater diversity; and if one political tendency kindled my wrath, it was precisely the tendency of industrial liberalism to level down all civilisations to a single cheap and dreary pattern. I was happy to have been at home both in Spain and in New England and later to have lived pleasantly in England and in various countries frequented by tourists; even happier to have breathed intellectually the air of Greece and Rome, and of that Catholic Church in which the world and its wisdom, without being distorted, were imaginatively enveloped in another world revealed by inspiration. All this was enlightening, if you could escape from it; and I should have been glad to have been at home also in China and in Carthage, in Bagdad and in Byzantium. Had that been possible, this book would have been written with more elasticity. It is a hindrance to the free movement of spirit to be lodged in one point of space rather than in another, or in one point of time: that is a physical necessity which intelligence endeavours to discount, since it cannot be eluded. Seen under the form of eternity, all ages are equally past and equally future; and it is impossible to take quite seriously the tastes and ambitions of our contemporaries. Everything gently impels us to view human affairs scientifically, realistically, biologically, as events that arise, with all their spiritual overtones, in the realm of matter.

Still, a man cannot sit above the clouds and have no prejudices. That would be to have no heart, and therefore no understanding for the glories and the tragedies that he talked about. We cannot help caring; there must be pangs and tears in this business; and of all the claims the heart must surrender, the first is the claim to insensibility. I have my likes and dislikes, of which I am not ashamed. I neither renounce them nor impose them. I simply recognise them to be personal in me, traditional, or otherwise accidental; and my endeavour is not to allow this inevitable bias of temperament or of position to distort my view of the facts, which include the perhaps contrary temperament or position of other people. Let them, I say, be themselves and fight their own battles and establish their own systems. In any case these systems will not be permanent; and where they sin against nature nature will take her revenge.

My own sympathies go out to harmony in strength, no matter how short-lived. The triumph of life lies in achieving perfection of form; and the richer and more complex the organism is that attains this perfection, the more glorious its perfection will be and the more unstable. Longevity is a vulgar good, and vain after all when compared with eternity. It is the privilege of the dust and of the lowest and most primitive organisms. The gods love and keep in their memories the rare beauties that die young. I prefer the rose to the dandelion; I prefer the lion to the vermin in the lion's skin. In order to obtain anything lovely, I would gladly extirpate all the crawling ugliness in the world. Yet the love of beauty, in an intelligent creature, runs over into concern about the causes and the enemies of the beautiful, into a study, therefore, of those *Dominations and Powers* in whose train the beautiful lives, and in whose decline it withers. Moreover, as the beautiful is a mark of vital perfection, and life everywhere, if it can, perfects its movements, there is potential beauty of all sorts latent in the world; and the Power or Domination that roots out one beauty, plants another; so that through the tears of the historian there often comes a smile, and the evening of one civilisation is the morning of another.

This is the moral light in which I am accustomed to see the world. Neither historical investigation, therefore, nor political precepts are to be looked for in this book. All that it professes to contain is glimpses of tragedy and comedy played unawares by governments; and a continual intuitive reduction of political maxims and institutions to the intimate spiritual fruits that they are capable of bearing.

GEORGE SANTAYANA

February
1951

# CONTENTS

## PRELIMINARIES

| | |
|---|---:|
| Title and Subject of This Book | 1 |
| The Sphere of Politics | 3 |
| Naturalism | 6 |
| The Roots of Spirit in Matter | 10 |
| The Agent in Politics Is the Psyche | 14 |
| Whether Naturalism Is Irreligious | 17 |
| Composition and Plan of This Book | 22 |

## BOOK FIRST
### THE GENERATIVE ORDER OF SOCIETY

### PART ONE
#### GROWTH IN THE JUNGLE

| | |
|---|---:|
| Chaos and Order | 33 |
| The Birth of Liberty | 35 |
| Primal Will | 37 |
| Needs and Demands | 41 |
| Liberty Lost | 44 |
| Vacant Freedom | 46 |
| Logical Liberty or Contingency | 49 |
| "Liberty of Indifference" | 52 |
| Captive Spirit and Its Possible Freedom | 55 |
| Vital Liberty | 57 |
| Necessary Servitude | 60 |
| Servitude to Society | 64 |
| Servitude to Custom | 67 |
| Natural Selfishness and Unselfishness | 71 |

## CONTENTS

Slavery   73
Transition from Custom to Government   78

### PART TWO
#### ECONOMIC ARTS

The Birth of Art   87
Claims and Conflicts of the Arts   92
Ambiguity of "Spirit" in the Arts   96
The Ethos of Agriculture   97
Domestic Morality   102
Ideal Monarchy   107
Moral Vicissitudes of Monarchy   111
Independence and Fusion among the Arts   118
Intrinsic Values of Government   121
Psychology of the Directive Imagination   125
Radiation of Political Life   128

### PART THREE
#### THE LIBERAL ARTS

Play   135
Music   138
Words, Words, Words   140
Language and Ideas Symbolic   143
Mythical Domination of Ideas   145
Economic and Liberal Interests in Religion   148
The Dependence of Morality on Religion   155
How Religion May Become Political   160
Liberal Arts Liberate Spirit   168

### BOOK SECOND
#### THE MILITANT ORDER OF SOCIETY

### PART ONE
#### FACTION

Wars of Growth   177
Wars of Imagination   179

## CONTENTS

Private Judgment Ignorant but Inescapable — 184
Militant Mind — 189
The Mirage of Politics — 194
Propaganda — 198
Vicissitudes of Faith — 202
The Disappearance of Chivalry — 204
Realpolitik — 208
The Sentimental Bandit — 212
The Ravages of War — 215
The Secret of Tyranny — 220
Revolutionary Liberty — 223
Alien Domination — 225
Dominant Crime — 227
Distinction between Crime and Madness — 231
Ruling Madness — 233
The Paradise of Anarchy — 236

### PART TWO
*ENTERPRISE*

Degrees of Militancy — 245
The Romance of Enterprise — 247
The Middleman in Trade — 249
Moral Effects of Trade — 254
Radiation of Enterprise — 261
Instability of Compound Units — 267
Domination as an Art — 271
Dissolution of the Arts — 275
The Decline of the Great Powers — 278
Natural and Artificial Allegiance — 281
Militant Religions — 284

### BOOK THIRD
THE RATIONAL ORDER OF SOCIETY

The Status of Reason in Nature — 295
Relativity of Knowledge and of Morals — 300

| | |
|---|---|
| Masks of Vice and Virtue | 303 |
| Relativity of Reason in Politics | 307 |
| Rational Authority | 310 |
| Rational Reforms | 315 |
| Rival Seats of Authority | 321 |
| Utility of Government | 325 |
| The Irony of Government | 330 |
| Confusions about Progress | 334 |
| Public Opinion | 341 |
| Spontaneous Democracy | 344 |
| Absolute Democracy | 348 |
| Moral Unanimity Impossible | 352 |
| Restricted Democracy | 355 |
| The American "Melting-Pot" | 359 |
| No Fixed Ideal of Society | 362 |
| Equality Not Conducive to Peace | 365 |
| Mystical Equality | 366 |
| Representative Government I  Only Generated Organisms Can Live or Think | 370 |
| Representative Government II  Moral Representation in Nature | 373 |
| Representative Government III  Moral Representation in Society | 376 |
| Representative Government IV  Should It Obey Public Feeling or Public Interest? | 382 |
| Representative Government V  Actual Functions of Parliaments | 384 |
| On the Subjects and Objects of Government | 391 |
| "Government of the People" | 395 |
| Who Are "The People"? | 397 |
| "Government by the People" I  How Possible | 402 |
| "Government by the People" II  Psychology of Agreement | 405 |

| | |
|---|---:|
| "Government by the People" III<br>    Ethics of Compromise | 410 |
| "Government by the People" IV<br>    Acquiescence | 415 |
| "Government for the People" I<br>    First Aims Proper to Government | 421 |
| "Government for the People" II<br>    Governments Cannot Serve All Interests | 425 |
| "Government for the People" III<br>    Rational Limits of Government | 431 |
| Liberalism in a Thankless World | 436 |
| War vs. Order | 438 |
| Suppression of War | 440 |
| False Escapes from Domination | 445 |
| The Price of Peace | 447 |
| Many Nations in One Empire | 449 |
| Through Whom Might Wisdom Rule the World? | 453 |
| The United States as Leader | 456 |
| Conclusion | 461 |
| Index | 467 |

# CHAPTER 1

## TITLE AND SUBJECT OF THIS BOOK

THE words *Dominations* and *Powers*, here taken for a title, are not meant to be synonymous and the reduplication rhetorical. The celestial hierarchy from which I borrow these names was composed of orders of spirits, marshalled in a host, where each rank and even each individual has a special nature and office.[1] I therefore take *Dominations* to signify something distinct and more complicated than *Powers*; and the relation between them forms the subject of this book.

All dominations involve an exercise of power, but, as I understand the terms, not all Powers are Dominations. Nor does the difference lie in the strength or prevalence of the influence exerted, so that any irresistible power could be called a Domination simply because it was irresistible. On the contrary, if a power prevailed pervasively, like the atmosphere or the force of gravity at the surface of the earth, so that life had arisen and taken shape under that constant influence, this power would not exercise any domination but would be a prerequisite for the development of every sort of free life in that world.

In other words, the distinction between Dominations and Powers is moral, not physical. It does not hang on the degree of force exerted by the agent but only on its relation to the spontaneous life of some being that it affects. The same government that is a benign and useful power for one class or one province may exercise a cruel domination over another province or another class. The distinction therefore arises from the point of view of a given person or society having initial interests of their own, but surrounded by uncontrollable circumstances: circumstances that will at once be divided, by that person or society, into two classes: one, things favourable or neutral, the other, things fatal, frustrating, or inconvenient: and all the latter, when they cannot be escaped, will become Dominations.

---

[1] Colossians I, 16. Thrones or dominions or principalities or powers.

A moral relation of this sort is naturally elastic. Often a creature that has grown up healthily under one set of powers finds itself suddenly cast into the arms of another set, as when at sea a landsman falls overboard. The salt water is at first a terrible tyrant over him, although not a tyrant over the fishes. And if the landsman survives, becomes a sailor, and builds himself a boat to be a second, more fish-like body to dwell in, he may gradually learn to live at sea almost as if at home, and to use the winds and tides for new purposes of his own devising. His foundations and resources will have been enlarged, and the inhuman powers of the sea will have become occasionally friendly and even serviceable to him, without ceasing to be irresistible.

Physical necessity and fate, when not conceived superstitiously, are therefore the true and only sure foundation for living at ease. They become Dominations only by accident, when we happen to be fit and prepared for something else, or have set our hearts on the impossible, so that all natural conditions seem to us intolerable. The play of political forces and demands is naturally complex and often hidden. Both the governed and the government are variable, drifting from one habit or one notion to another, without much foresight or self-knowledge, the people wishing to reform the government, the government wishing to reform the people, and neither party being able to reform itself.

Meantime nature, in the midst of these blind currents and continual partial catastrophes, manages to bring many happy possibilities to light; and approaches to harmony appear, here and there for a time, between the formative impulse of life and the balance of ambient powers. It is these vital achievements that essentially interest me; but it is only in passing that I can hope to point to them or stop to describe them. My subject here is rather the circumstances which, in each case, enable these fruits to mature, or perhaps nip them in the bud. I am concerned with the fortunes of potential *Virtues* in the hands of *Dominations* and *Powers*. For there was also an order of angels called *Virtues*, a name that I shall sometimes use to signify something presupposed in both power and domination, and of fundamental importance. By *Virtues*, as opposed to *Powers* and *Dominations*, we might understand spirits having only a vegetative or lyric life, perfect in themselves, and not addressed to exercising any influence over other beings. Unwittingly, no doubt, their existence would count in the order and movement of the world, and might be its greatest beauty; they might be the flowers in that garden. In mankind the corresponding virtues would be such gifts as health, wit, or poetic inspiration; they might even include pure intelligence and kindness. Yet in merely mentioning kindness and intelligence, we may notice how close virtue comes to being, by accident, a power. In fact, life itself is intrinsically a virtue in the body that possesses it; so that a great store of virtue is presupposed in any capacity to exercise power, not to speak of exercising domination. Human society owes all its warmth and vitality to the intrinsic virtue in its members. Yet in politics we do not dwell on the physical or spiritual life of individuals. Therefore I do not mention *Virtues* in the title of this book, which treats of politics and not, save indirectly, of the whole philosophy of life and spirit. But without coming often upon the mention of fundamental or ultimate *Virtues*, I hope the reader may feel them always silently hovering over the pages.

## CHAPTER 2

### THE SPHERE OF POLITICS

IN POLITICS the philosopher is spared many a pitfall that he might walk into in physics and biology; his field is limited to human affairs. He need not trouble himself with truths deeper than conventional truths. He has to consider real events and real forces, which are all physical, even when they have a mental and moral accompaniment. In this sense he is a man of science, with the responsibilities of an inquirer after the truth, and not, in intention, a composer of historical romances. Yet his contact with the facts need not go deeper than the contacts which other people have had with them, or may have on other occasions. In this sense his field coincides with that of the historical novelist or literary psychologist. He is composing a drama as it might have been lived. But there is this difference: that his interest, if he is not a party man, is not chiefly emotional or centred in the episodes of the drama itself, as glorious or pitiful; his interest is philosophical and passes from the picturesque surface of those experiences to the causes and conditions that brought them about.

That these causes are all physical is an assumption, or rather a tautology in a naturalistic philosophy. History goes on in the material world, which existed before history began, and by its natural biological developments made history possible. Human beings spring from the earth and still depend on the earth not only for sustenance but through the agency of a thousand accidents which the changing fertility and quick overpopulation of the earth have occasioned. Yet to climate, poverty, and tribal rivalry the reactions of various men are not identical. Whatever pressure the geographical background may exercise, it would not have produced specifically human societies if men were not physically men, and if their biological, racial, and personal development were not what their inherited nature had made it. The environment fosters and selects; the seed must contain the potentiality and direction of the life to be selected.

I say that human beings have sprung from the earth. I was not present to observe the event; but it is a general presumption of naturalism that men were not let down ready made by a rope, as Lucretius puts it, from heaven. They sprung somehow from the earth: not that in any fallow field, as the earth now is, men would in time grow out of the ground afresh, like thistles; but that in the early plastic state of the planet, shot through by who knows what stellar and ethereal radiations, the potentiality of life, and of all sorts of life, lay dormant.

Every sort of creature, every sort of government, will spring up out of the earth, if circumstances only allow it. "Earth" here humbly represents the infinite possibilities of Being, reduced at each point by previous local accidents to a particular arbitrary form, with certain limited powers of transformation. In politics we may assume as roughly constant the physical order of nature and of human nature. All climates and all peoples are not similar; and neither the climates nor the nations, though slightly modifiable perhaps by industry, can be changed or equalised by a theory. Their character must be observed and accepted as it is, together with whatever tendencies to transformation that character may exhibit spontaneously. There are periods of integration, conquest, dominion; there are very brief periods of intellectual and artistic glory; and there follow long eras of confused and monotonous hibernation of the spirit.

Revolutions, in historic times, occur in and by human beings rather than by virtue of external cataclysms. Human beings form part of the material world, their seed carrying over a specific physical organisation, as much as the seed of any plant. In each case the psyche is specific and inherited, without excluding casual variations, from the psyche of each of the parents. This new personal psyche determines all a man's powers and passions, and his taste or capacity for this or that form of association. Circumstances will encourage, re-shape, or suppress these propensities; but without the richly charged individual soul, or the souls of a thousand kindred individuals vibrating in unison, circumstances would continue to compose an empty stage, and a landscape without figures. They become political circumstances when human ambition begins to move amongst them, and to enlist them in its service. Society will then become whatever the psychic disposition of its members may tend to make of it.

A materialistic interpretation of politics need therefore not be especially climatic or economic or Malthusian, but may take account of those important circumstances in letting loose or suppressing the various instincts and powers of human nature. The initiative of individuals and the contagion of their words and actions must not be excluded; although the persuasions and tumults that sweep through society from such sources are more devastating than fruitful if they do not indicate a happy intuition of that which circumstances, at that moment, render possible and appropriate. Human impulses convulse society, but human necessities construct it.

Nor does a materialistic interpretation of politics exclude a moral judgment upon it, or even a mystical flight beyond such a judgment. Each psyche, in proportion as it is integrated and possesses a rational will, each society in proportion as it is self-justified, necessarily sets up its ideal to be the measure of all values for its own conscience. Anything else would be mere confusion and looseness of soul. This judgment need not prevent an intellectual comprehension of the contrary or irrelevant interests of others; but such clear self-knowledge, in counselling the needful exclusions or even wars in the face of what is alien, only reaffirms the morality proper to oneself. This morality is the ultimate expression of one's nature, by which one lives and is different from nothing; and its moral fervour goes hand in hand with physical vitality.

Sometimes, in exceptional and reflective natures, the distraction and the triviality of life, even of healthy life, become oppressive, and a sympathy with the goods pursued by contrary moralities renders one's own morality pathetic and almost remorseful. Then a mystical aspiration, renouncing everything for the love of everything, may overflood the mind. Victory or prosperity for one's own people or one's own civilisation will no longer seem an ultimate or unqualified good. It will be counted, if attained, among the flowers of the field, that to-day bloom and tomorrow wither, only manifesting, in one arbitrary form, the universal impulse in matter towards all sorts of harmonies and perfections. Then all the other harmonies and perfections, not attainable here, perhaps not attained anywhere, will come crowding to the gates of our little temple. And the spirit will be tempted to escape from that particular sanctuary, to abdicate its identity with the society that bred it, and to wander alone and friendless, to be the lover of all climates and the friend of all friends.

The same materialism that justifies ferocity in the jungle may thus breed impartiality and abnegation beneath the stars. But whatsoever may be bred in one place or justified in one person, nature remains elsewhere as free as it ever was to be original, or to prove constant: constancy, where it establishes itself, being as natural and as contingent as change. The imperative of nature is categorical enough, but it is omnimodal. So when this imperative, without ceasing to be categorical, is seen to be private, and relative to some special predicament, a sense of the endless fecundity of nature lifts somewhat the incubus of ferocious Will from the spirit, and softens almost to sadness the vital necessity of being oneself.

## CHAPTER 3

### NATURALISM

THAT mankind is a race of animals living in a material world is the first presupposition of this whole inquiry. I should be playing false to myself and to the reader if I did not assume it. All my thoughts, even the most speculative and sceptical, move quite happily on the basis of public sanity, custom, and language. These conventions are not miraculous revelations of the truth, but they are the only available avenues towards it. I should not wish to be a philosopher, if that meant being a prophet with a message. I am content to stand where honest laymen are standing, and to write as I might talk with a friend in a country walk or sitting at a tavern. Otherwise I should be undermining the conventional assurance that my readers exist at all, or that the reported historical facts exist about which I am writing. I assume that here are the sun and the stars set far above us, and the earth beneath, with the sea a little beyond, and all the sea-routes leading to islanded nations scattered about the globe. I assume that these lands have been inhabited by many peoples now extinct or unrecognisable, regarding some of which we have historical records; so that their moral experience was the beginning of ours, is intelligible to us, and often, when pondered, renders our own experience intelligible.

If here I assume these current beliefs without further argument, it is not because it has never occurred to me to question them. I have questioned them perhaps as closely as any man ever did; and I should admit that a radical sceptic may reject all claims to knowledge beyond the fact that, at this moment, some particular appearance or feeling is present to him. To me, from childhood up, the intuition that life is a dream has been familiar and congenial. But this sentiment misses half the lessons that such a dream may convey and that might enrich it. By passively watching and reshuffling those apparitions, imagination may gather an elegiac wisdom: the dream was joyful, it was horrible, it was lovely, it was sad. Intelligence, however, may make a deeper and more sweeping response to ambient influences than can the highly selective eye or the largely non-representative ear. The psyche in developing this organ of synthesis and comparison, the intellect, could not resist forming the notion of some underlying connecting process that should ignite at certain junctures into this scattered illumination: a process that should go on uninterruptedly both beyond the images observed and beneath the emotions felt. Later perhaps such a notion might prove to be a discovery in regard to all objects that not only appear like dreams or are heard like the thunder, but can be seized, broken, or kept, since these are found to have an inside and to serve to make certain other lasting objects. Then, by acting on the assumption that everything in our waking dream has some discoverable backing of this traceable material kind, we may gradually confirm our first instinctive insight, when by trusting it we can change the course of our dream, clarify its confusion, and dispel its terrors.

The human mind, being full of designs and desires, naturally attributes moral causes to events and, in the absence of natural science, tends to believe in magic, sorcery, and omens. Economic arts and mechanical inventions have driven belief in these moral causes from technical industries, but not yet from politics, history, or philosophy. In these humanistic subjects little but designs and desires occupy the stage, and are worked up into romantic adventures, tragic dramas, and above all into eloquent outpourings of one's own thoughts and denunciation of those of the enemy: for life at this level is felt not as a growth or a vision, but as a conflict of ambitions. No wonder, then, that moral forces seem here to explain events, without themselves having any need of explanation. To feel a passion, or to understand it sympathetically, was to know one of the ultimate springs of personal and social action and of political institutions.

It happens, however, that these potent passions are favoured or defeated not only by one another but by circumstances; and the question arises for the philosopher how he should conceive this interplay of moral and physical forces.

Magic and sorcery, with divination which perhaps becomes faith in inspiration and in revealed truth, all readily interpret what might seem physical accidents as visible signs of hidden moral powers, superhuman or infra-human, but in both cases animated by desires or designs. How should any living being do otherwise when it is these passions that absorb his attention in action and that justify that action in his eyes and measure the degree of its success or failure?

Speculatively, indeed, it is possible to construct the complete system of a universe composed exclusively of moral forces abetting or thwarting one another; but such a world is too remote from the soil of politics to require attention here. Most of the critics of naturalism retain their animal faith in the physical theatre of life, into which, however, they wish to insert their own moral energy, and perhaps other spiritual forces as continual remodellers of matter. This is an old and familiar conception, but its very naturalness renders it treacherous. For if mind moves body and mixes everywhere with it, how is it distinguishable from the energy of matter itself? Those who wish to emancipate spirit from the dark currents of matter should summon it to escape and deny matter; or like the Indians and the Platonists, they should avoid all intimate contact with it and revert as far and as soon as possible to some unruffled, luminous, eternal paradise, such as they catch glimpses of even on earth in their supreme moments.

But this is not at all what modern moralists understand by spirit. Spirit for them is nothing if not a motor; it need not so much as move matter; its vocation is endlessly to move, transform, and explore its own "problematics." Now this is exactly what universal nature seems to a naturalist to do for itself. Yet nature, if we study instead of inventing its methods of evolution, proves to be no mad enemy of repose. When anywhere it can fall into a trope or rhythm that can be maintained, it maintains it, as we see in the solar system; and it is that enveloping and not unchangeable constancy established in the conditions of life that has permitted life to take shape in us, and to evoke in us a spirit that is not mad but serene and fed by the constancy of form which it can observe in the world and can introduce into its own language and logic. Yet these cases of equilibrium which enable life and spirit to arise within us are by no means perpetual. Their insecurity, in the case of our persons and institutions, obliges nature to resort to most circuitous and elaborate ways of restoring the forms of living things, and of societies, since these forms continually lapse, in what we call death or dissolution.

Anyone who, in his zeal for the honour of life, order, and spirit, turns his back upon naturalism as if it would destroy those supreme goods, seems to me to have completely misconceived their existential status. Life and spirit are not the cause of order in the world but its result. In empty space or in deserts life and thought of our sort, and such as concern politics, could never have arisen; and the Platonic hierarchy of Ideas could never have become a scale of needs, hopes, or wonders for a living being or a civic society. Those ideas and even the dramatic aspects of earthquakes and floods would have remained unrealised possibles, without any intrinsic value or moral importance. The very interest and formal authority that attach for us to logic and mathematics do not inhere in their necessity and unchangeableness when once their terms are distinguished, or in the cogency of their ideal relations. All that realm would be a wilderness of dead tautologies did not some of those Ideas become incarnate in a matter that being open to all formations is irrevocably wedded to none yet, so to speak, a libertine in love with all. The impulse which, through an inner ripening, causes a man's fancy to take a particular turn, leaves it nevertheless subject to other casual influences and inclined to run wild; so that life, incarnate, becomes a struggle for life and a conflict with enemies and temptations. It is this drama that lends to such Ideas as figure in it their moral colours, and raises the logical relations between those Ideas into sublime decrees and insidious pitfalls of fate.

It is therefore the tightness with which any particular form or hereditary trope has seized upon some nucleus of matter, and the luxuriance with which that form can extend its tentacles into the surrounding multitude of variable influences, that determines the *virtue* of that incarnate spirit and the degree to which its dominion may be extended and its enthusiasm aroused not only for the triumphs of its bearer in society but for the spiritual or poetic affinities which it may have discovered in the ideal world. For imagination as much as sense must be guided by organs and habits fit to feed on circumstances; so that spirit, in that incarnation, may dominate a wide field of natural truth and yet escape from it into the freedom of ideal creations, as from the stress of earthly passions under the spell of music.

## CHAPTER 4

### THE ROOTS OF SPIRIT IN MATTER

THAT in the heart of matter there was always a germ of spirit seems to me as much a truism as it would be to say that in a grape-seed lies the potentiality of the vine, the vine-leaves, and the grapes that actually grow out of it. "Potentiality" does not signify the pre-existence of eventual things; it signifies only the existence of the conditions which, according to the process of nature, will bring those things about. I smile at the acrobatic logic of Leibnitz, who convinced himself that *little* feelings and ideas must exist in every minutest particle of cosmic substance. Anaxagoras had reasoned in that way in his qualitative atomism, thinking that metamorphosis must be as impossible in nature as in the realm of essence. But eternal self-identity is proper to essences precisely because they are not elements in the existing or living world, where everything is unstable, unnecessary, and arbitrarily original. The fertility of matter is proper to its function as the substance of a thoroughly irrational groping, self-devouring process, which only by chance, or in certain abstract aspects, settles down for a season into constant or calculable order.

As to the emergence of ideas and feelings, it seems to occur only in animals endowed with locomotion; for in a medium full of dangerous and of edible objects, such animals are able to avoid their enemies and to pursue their prey at a distance, anticipating eventual contact and preparing for it to their own advantage. The whole vital endeavour of the organism is thereby directed upon ulterior and absent events. Yet some absent events, for an animal, are not without a present effect, since impressions survive and are capable of being reproduced in some measure by internal stimulation. Three currents then meet in animal life: the passive vegetative process of the quiescent organism; the call of the external lure or threat that arouses action; and the organic revival of old reactions akin to that which is now imminent. To this remarkable complex of tensions between vital, absent, and distant agents, alarm, desire, and perception seem to correspond in the spirit.

If, according to the nebular hypothesis, what is now the earth was once a part of the sun, the potentiality of the spirit now awake in me existed then in the substance of the sun, or in whatever stellar influences may have rained down subsequently upon this planet. The firmament, as we watch it and measure its silence by the rhythm of our heart or lungs, seems a finished and unchangeable marvel; yet it is shining, burning, and speeding influences in all directions; and there is no knowing how many things more wonderful than our own wonder it may yet produce. Spirit is stupified in us by its limitations. Each of our moments thinks all others dead or unborn, yet in eternity, in its true being, no moment is ever anything but present.

When we come down from Leibnitz to Einstein we may catch a more intimate glimpse of the inner bond between matter and spirit.

"Matter," as I conceive the term, points to the principle of natural existence, or "being-in-the-world." Matter determines, for any ideal form, its relations in space and time, its duration and disappearance. Einstein, however, if I understand him, tells us that the principle of existence is Relativity itself. Now relations may be of two different kinds. They may be logical and necessary, as between ideal terms, each intrinsically definite, definable, changeless, and complementary to all other ideal terms, in the peaceful realm of essence. Or on the contrary, relations may be material and accidental, as between things and animate creatures, jostling and devouring one another in the world. That relations of this second sort are the principle of existence had occurred to me in my mathematical ignorance simply by reflecting on the doctrines of Plato and Heraclitus. For essences (or ideal and definite forms of being) become temporary qualities of an existing thing or passing event when, in contempt of their eternal relations to other essences, they find themselves irrelevantly crowded together, usurped by matter, or flashing out and extinguished irrationally in the flux of thought. Einstein casts his theory in other terms; yet he says something that by chance coincides with a point that is crucial in my thinking. Relations are between terms; and these terms, for him, are ultimately pure mathematical centres where cosmic relations cross and combine. The centres have no substance of their own, as had the monads of Leibnitz, which would have ceased to exist if they had stopped thinking or dreaming or at least positively sleeping. But for Einstein no positive intrinsic existence belongs to these centres. Their essence is to be *possible* foci for all dynamic influences in the universe; for though the net of these lines is describable mathematically, they are, for Einstein, paths of energy, and the warp and woof of nature.

This seems to me remarkably parallel to what, in my view, is the potentiality of spirit in the heart of matter. Each point that becomes a centre for tensions from the whole cosmos had no prior existence, substance, or individuality, but is distinguishable only by the range and quality of the influences that meet in it, and passing through it, play as if from that centre upon the surrounding world. Just so I should conceive spirit, essentially a merely possible locus for surveying the universe, to be actualised and individuated only as particular material tensions meet and form a centre for further diffusion of energy. An animal organism has this sort of functional unity. So long as it is alive it can react on things distant, past, or future and thereby evokes spirit. Spirit here will be diversified by feelings and images determined by the range of influences to which that organism is then responsive.

Yet even if not reacted upon perceptibly, *all* cosmic influences are really playing upon that centre at every moment; and in like manner *all* possible feelings and thoughts are always potentially open to spirit, in its proper nature and capacity: but here and now it will enact only such and so much dramatic experience as the sensibility of its organism can evoke. For it is only the limited development of tentacles or of telepathic organs that concentrates psychic attention on a particular field. Thus the acquired organs of spirit, natural or artificial, determine its experience-in-act at each point and at each moment; yet the potential experience of spirit remains everywhere infinite in extent and variety. This happens precisely because, as Einstein suggests, a "centre" in the physical world is in itself something notional, non-existent, and unsubstantial, and can begin to exist and to be individuated only by virtue of the specific physical processes whose centre it has become.

Spirit accordingly when it arises in animals perceives in each case only special images and endures specific passions; its vision and interest spread as far as the prospect happens to be disclosed to the organism, or retained and recomposed within it; and the passions sweep over the spirit, in the measure in which the stress of life in the psyche can discern its objectives. The storm passed, however, spirit reverts to its native repose and potentiality. It has no self, save the intrinsic capacity of all centres of life to resist, to perceive, to attract, and to imitate one another.

It might seem, then, that spirit is in one sense the first-begotten child of nature, if matter has an unlimited potentiality of reacting upon or adopting its scattered transformations dramatically. Yet spirit, in its actual birth, is on the contrary the very Benjamin of nature; since before it can arise, many complicated possibilities and harmonies must first be realised in the bodies of animals and in the world surrounding them. For only then are the dumb tensions of physical life merged in a single vital act such as is hypostatized in memory or foresight; while blind impulse recognises and transcends itself in moral reflection.

## CHAPTER 5

### THE AGENT IN POLITICS IS THE PSYCHE

There is a double force in repeating the old axiom that man is an animal. In the first place we confirm our initial naturalism, and place man among the wonderfully various living creatures that feed, fight, and reproduce themselves on the surface of the earth. But there is a second implication in that axiom that is no less important. An animal has inward invisible specific springs of action, called instincts, needs, passions, or interests; and it is only in relation to these psychic springs of action that Powers and Dominations can be distinguished. The criterion in politics is moral; and the agent in politics is not man as he appears to the senses, but an inner proclivity to action and passion that animates him, and that I call the psyche.

The word "psyche" is simply the Greek for "soul"; but the authority of Aristotle and other technical reasons justify us in giving it a very different meaning from that which the word "soul" has acquired in Christian or Platonising minds. The psyche is not a spirit separable from the body, like a ghost or an angel: it is the life of the body, as the naturalist may observe it, or as he may observe the life of a plant. Anything that lives, reproduces itself, and dies has a psyche; and in saying so we do not in the least prejudge the question whether plants are "sensitive." They are sensitive in the sense that they observably turn to the light and revive and flourish when watered; but whether in doing so they develop something like what we call feeling is an insoluble question. Have we ourselves feeling when we grow? We grow best in sleep, as babies do; but have we feeling when sound asleep? It is a question of private and subtle intuition; the important point is that the psyche in us is capable of waking up, and of doing many skillful things in the presence of external accidents, such as dodging a missile or catching a ball. That animal psyches have feeling, not always but normally when they are awake, is known to each man in his own case, and instinctively and dramatically felt by him in the case of others: a sentiment that reflection will justify, in view of the kinship and similarity between all human organisms, and even between all types of animal life; although here our sympathetic intuition grows vague and, if we attempt to make it definite, as in fables, becomes purely fictitious and comic.

This topic, which might seem academic and speculative, is of great moment for the understanding of politics, especially in the present era. The literary philosophy and the psychological novels which have been dominant in modern times assume, if they do not teach, that thought is something substantial and self-developing; that it has no origin or milieu except in other thoughts; and even sometimes that the evolution of this ideation in a vacuum is itself guided by dialectic. Nothing could be better calculated to keep politics in a fool's paradise of verbal reasoning. Fortunately the contemporary growth of exploration, commerce, scientific discovery, and mechanical industry has kept ideological governments in genuine contact with reality, and prevented them from being entirely useless or pernicious.

Thus two concomitant yet strangely different streams would seem to compose human life: one the vast cosmic flood of cyclic movements and sudden precipitations, in which man has his part like other animals; and the other, the private little rivulet of images, emotions, and words babbling as we move, and often hiding underground in sleep or forgetfulness. Political ideologies are attempts to collect these private murmurs into a chorus, so loud and imperative as to drown the concert of universal nature and turn it into an obedient accompaniment to the human voice. But human voices are hopelessly discordant; they express separate movements and tendencies in the natural development of the human psyche; and even where a certain unison exists in these social transformations, they are usually so vapid and so perturbed that the civilisation of the next epoch will begin by condemning that of its predecessor, and reverting, for inspiration, to the animal impulses of the race or to fresh opportunities offered for action in the material world.

Here a crucial circumstance may be noticed. The contradiction and futility of human wishes and ideas appear only from the point of view of an egotistical mind. Planted in your personal presumptions and demands, you find reality foreign, irrational, and intolerable; and you would gladly persuade yourself that it is an illusion, and of no consequence in proportion to the myths that pile themselves up, like the clouds from Sinbad the Sailor's bottle, in your inspired mind. Yet these plans, these illusions, are congruous with the great process of nature, which is as minutely fertile and full of waste as it is vast and monumental. The psyche is a marvel of organisation and teleology, innumerable processes combining to keep the body alive and to reproduce it. And this is no exclusively physical or automatic complication: automatic and physical though it be, it is also, and for that very reason, vital and potentially conscious. When that potentiality becomes actual, we have a spontaneous overtone and moral expression, such as pleasure and pain are, for psychic achievements and psychic impediments or revulsions; and the coherent fictions of the poet or prophet are the same thing in an elaborated and articulate form. There is nothing in nature *like* these moral or sensuous fictions; but there is necessarily in nature some contact or nexus which those fictions express and report. Regarded as free transcripts, as poetic symbols, they are therefore perfectly true to nature. In ordinary perception and sane language they reveal the relevant relations of things to the psyche in suitable but variously original signs.

A poet walking through the fields and hearing the larks in the sky may well cry: "Hail to thee, blithe spirit, bird thou never wert!" The lyric poet, like the eloquent politician, is a confirmed egotist and attributes objective validity to his own sentiments. If the larks were feeling at that moment what the poet feels, they would indeed be blithe spirits, being invisible and joyful; yet the larks are in fact birds, of whose nature the poet knows nothing, as he knows little or nothing of his own psyche, that he momentarily enacts, and rapturously declares to be all there is. Now it would be ungracious to say that in the singing lark there is probably no spirit. I should be tempted to imagine that he actually *feels* an irresistible propensity to soar and sing at that moment: a more spiritual propensity than if he were flying after something or from something, or were chirping for some particular reason. He is, I should say, in a state of happy excitement, impelled unaccountably to do something which he finds he can do mightily, joyously, and for its own sake. Saint Francis would say that the lark was praising and thanking God for having created him. But the bird, though in some sense a little brother to Saint Francis, would not be naming God or distinguishing in his own little mind any object of praise or thanks: he would be simply singing. And if we asked—as surely he never would ask—what were the causes of this unnecessary effusiveness, we should say that they were the season, the bright morning, the quiet air, the June sun, the sufficiency of food, and the premonition perhaps of love, which supplied his little heart at that moment with superabundant energy.

So I should like to believe also of politicians, that in their ideologies and party principles and public purposes there was a spiritual element; so that without really understanding the actual causes or ultimate results of their speeches they felt exaltation and enthusiasm in uttering them, and love of lovable things. But it is not from what they may propose to themselves ideally that they draw their inspiration; they are in that respect like the larks. Their inspiration comes from their homely interests or dominant prejudices, from the contagion of current language, or from private predispositions. And it is to similar forces in the public that they will owe their influence or their success; I mean, any genuine success in having discerned the possible and profitable direction to be given to public affairs. For the agents, as well as the patients, in politics, are psyches. They change with circumstances and with propensities growing unbidden in men's hearts, and determining their actions and passions. Therefore the turn of events will hang on circumstances other than official intentions; except in so far as officials are perpetual opportunists, and change their principles whenever fortune seems to change its direction.

## CHAPTER 6

### WHETHER NATURALISM IS IRRELIGIOUS

This question is debatable because words in current use have many meanings. Thus naturalism for a pagan is far from atheistic, since it finds room for many gods; and Democritus and Epicurus, though materialists, believed that such gods existed. Jews and Christians, on the other hand, were called atheists for not worshipping the gods recognized by the State; while for them naturalism implies atheism, because it denies the creation and government of the universe by a single God, revealed especially to the Hebrews.

A modern naturalist would seem an atheist also to the pagans, because all reports of deities internal to the universe and interested in the political and moral welfare of any particular nation or particular soul seem to him myths; but they seem myths also to a modern pantheist; and who would dare to call Spinoza an atheist? The Hindus are polytheists, monotheists, and pantheists at once; and the Buddhists, though technically atheists, and denying the existence of souls, are ideally so religious and spiritual that it seems grotesque for a modern Christian to tax them with atheism.

When we broach speculation, especially about pantheism, this question becomes so embroiled that I should not trouble the reader with it here, were it not important for me not to provoke a religious hostility which in the end my conclusions will not warrant. My political principles rest on naturalism: does this mean that they would banish religion? No: they do not tend to banish religion: and it becomes necessary to indicate in what sense they admit and even demand it.

The most brutal form of naturalism is materialism, and I have repeatedly confessed that I am a materialist. Let me start, then, from this extreme position, which more radically than naturalism (which might be poetical) seems to exclude all religiosity. But what, after all, does materialism assert? Not (as a popular impression would have it, especially among the French) that nothing exists except sensations; and not (as another impression suggests) that nothing exists except matter. Ancient philosophers were looking for substance, that is to say for something comparatively simple and lasting, out of which perishable things might be made; and those who were most materialistic thought this substance must be composed of indestructible atoms dancing in a void. That is a pleasant image; yet indestructible atoms are as far as possible from being sensations, or from being everything that exists; for at least the void they dance in must exist too, and also the sensations they cause in us by dancing. Matter is something recondite, which physical science is always studying and conceiving in new, wonderful, and often abstract symbols; but matter is whatsoever in nature, by its motions and tensions, causes all events to take place and all appearances to appear.

A materialist is therefore fundamentally a naturalist, and begins, not with any theory of the essence of matter, but with the natural assumption made by children and poets that he is living in an existing and persisting world in which there are rocks and trees, men and animals, feelings and dreams; yet the philosophic naturalist has stopped to observe how these things change and grow, often passing into one another, and eating one another up: so that they suggest to him the belief that something continuous runs through them, makes them up, or causes them to appear. But the appearances are not parts of the material object, since they change with the distance, position, and condition of the observer; often, too, when no such object exists, as in the case of illusions and dreams. If on examination and in the practice of the arts the naturalist thinks this theory verified, he has become a materialist.

Now in denying immaterial agencies, the materialist does not deny that material agencies may be *at the same time* animated by ideal motives and moral purposes. On the contrary, he asserts that this is often the case. A disease, he says, cannot be either caused or cured by a purely immaterial agent. That would be more than an improbability; it would be a contradiction in terms, since effects would not be effects but chance conjunctions if they were not predictable or amenable to art. The doctor and his medicines or operations are material agents: but the doctor also has ideas and purposes; he may be full of wisdom and charity, and these feelings will be far from irrelevant to the power of his art. They will not be a power added to that of his person and his methods, but they will be the *spirit* in that power. The patient, himself endowed with sensation and sympathy, will feel that spirit in his physician and even in the whole atmosphere of the healing influences to which he is subject. In the physician, goodwill and insight will have been actual facts; if attributed to the ambient influences they will be only poetic fictions bred in the patient's mind. Yet in both cases the world will be bathed for the patient in the light of spirit: not in spite of his materialism, but in harmony with it, and in a way that only materialism can make intelligible.

Suppose now we define religion to be the recognition of the Powers on which our destiny truly depends, and the art of propitiating those Powers and of living, as far as the power in us avails, in devout harmony with them. We should not be friends of religion if we confined it to proclaiming imaginary powers, and living under the real ones in ignorance or despair. A religion worth having must recognise true Powers, however poetical the form may be which that religion lends them; and it must tend to establish peace and sanity in the mind, not fanatical madness. That imagination plays a great part in popular religions, and that fanaticism often invades them, cannot be denied by a materialist; but the fanaticism is often inspired by political motives, as fanatical persecution of religion is also; it is a political rather than a religious vice. Asceticism, on the other hand, has religious motives, and becomes a vice when carried too far; but then the wiser religious authorities themselves condemn it. And the same may be said of the riot of fancy and superstition in some religions. Without killing the imagination that bred religious ideas, theology may interpret them philosophically; and in this the materialist may consistently join. For in his own system imagination is the sphere of all appearances; and for him too everything sensuous, conceptual, and moral is only a symbol for the natural facts.

Materialism is not itself a theology, as are some forms of idealism. Its inspiration and temper are purely scientific and intellectual. But why should so pleasant a thing as science and so vital a thing as intelligence be angry with the world they explore? And they spoil their own work if, with a vehemence which is not naturalistic but political and moral, they inveigh against religion, in the manner of Lucretius or of modern anticlericals. The materialist in his ethics and politics should be a humanist, an anthropologist, and a philanthropist; and is it love of man that prompts the hatred of religion? No. It is insensibility to the plight of man and to all that which man most deeply loves. Modern materialists, I confess, have usually had vulgar and jejune minds; but not so the ancients who were materialists by nature, and not foolishly hostile to popular religion or without religion in their hearts. And they were the only normal materialists, harbouring towards politics, morals, and religion the sentiments proper to a naturalist. They were not deceived by these human passions and inspirations, but understood them and knew the place and the need of images in the world; and when they were poets they sang the praises of the gods with a tender emotion.

So much benevolence may be shown to religion by the intelligent materialist; it is the same benevolence that he feels towards the senses, in both cases delighting in the image without mistaking it for a substance. The substance of both, in his view, will be ultimately the same: namely the Power that brings these images and feelings before the spirit in this order and with this irresistible force. So much he may consistently feel and say without transcending the natural sphere, but still taking the imagination only for a system of signs, to be interpreted as effects produced in the animal psyche by the revolutions of matter within and without that animal.

But this is not the end: for images have other properties and other uses for the spirit beside their value as signals relevant to action. They have intrinsic form; and precisely because they are in a manner illusions, they are originals; ideal objects interesting in themselves. In themselves they are essences without existence. If we pursue reflexion and analysis in this direction we shall see that, not in addition or contradiction to our materialism, but implicit within it, we must recognise form in matter, order in chaos, ideal being in illusion, truth in the history of errors, and eternity in every fleeting drama of time.

Now what materialists have always abhorred in religion is its pretense to be a practical art, its magic, its false miracles, its appeals to animal thrift, prudence, and fear. With the spiritual side of religion they have had little acquaintance. On its spiritual side religion is not a false science but an ideal affection. It does not misrepresent the facts but transcends them. Often where this question touches politics the materialist, being a realist, may feel a natural aversion from the waste, as he thinks it, of faith, sacrifice, and money in keeping up official religions. The natural limitations of human taste and faculty will probably hold him back from developing a religious life in himself. But there would be nothing inconsistent with his materialism if he became a poet, a musician, or a hermit; and his judgments upon existence and the direction of his affection and invention in the ideal sphere might be those of an ancient prophet, as they might be those of a pure artist, without any departure from materialism in his natural philosophy. He might live in moral harmony with the power, the order, and the spirit in the whole universe, and cherish nothing but friendliness towards the traditional religion prevailing in his time and country.

## CHAPTER 7

### COMPOSITION AND PLAN OF THIS BOOK

THE thought of seeing history in the terms of Dominations and Powers came to me soon after I had completed writing *The Life of Reason*. Before the war of 1914-1918 I had set down various paragraphs or short essays on the subject. Others were included in my *Soliloquies in England*, written during that war; but much as the conflict occupied my thoughts from day to day, it left hardly any residuum of greater enlightenment. I soon busied myself with other things; yet sometimes a philosophical argument would ramble into reflections which, on revision, I would take out and put aside under the title of *Dominations and Powers*. A mass of manuscript accumulated in this way during some thirty years. There was therefore no unity of plan, no consecutive development, in my notes, although the guiding intuition remained, and became clearer and clearer with the lapse of years. Finally, however, a more vivid apprehension of the actual impact of Dominations and Powers in the political world was forced upon me by the war of 1939-1945; for I lived through it in Rome in monastic retirement, with the visible and audible rush of bombing aeroplanes over my head, and of invading armies before my eyes. Most pertinent and instructive, also, has been the experience of the after effects of that war. The country where I was living was traversed by two foreign armies nominally friendly to it; one came to defend and the other to liberate it; and both united in pillaging it and leaving it in misery and ruins.

This object lesson in the workings of Dominations under my eyes was reinforced by the reports reaching me from all quarters of a profound mutation in the condition and government of the world: a sudden unification in the control and the fortunes of nations, with a marked conflict between express ideologies. Here, then, were living guides and present occasions for reflection; and all my other proposed labours being completed, I could not help turning to this subject with a fresh interest and the stimulus of new lights. I have therefore undertaken a revision of all my manuscript, expecting to reject much of it, and hoping to arrange the parts that may seem worth retaining in some tolerable order.

The merely physical powers that support or threaten an animal, though fundamental to his existence and fortunes, must be silently presupposed in the study of politics. They may be modified by industry and they may be dramatically addressed in prayer: they cannot be taught how to behave. Physical powers—and I think all power is physical at bottom—begin to figure in politics only when they are exercised by persons forming a society, or capable of forming one. In this study we cannot go deeper than the living human individual, his powers and passions, as they work in society and are modified by it. Our subject matter is man, with an unexplained human nature and an unexplained personal character, but subject to contagion, training, and teaching.

The first powers and dominations to be studied in politics are those on which the individual is most radically dependent, and by which his nature is most radically modified. Now in the human race, the initial helplessness of children and their prolonged immaturity makes the ascendance of parents first and of custom later both inevitable and decisive. Yet the ways of parents are often erratic; and customs, even if stubborn locally, are diverse and arbitrary: so that both parental authority and native ways exhibit Domination in acute forms. Yet this domination is felt to be authoritative and inspires the conscience of the average individual with superstitious as well as prudential fears. Being radical and ingrained, this subjection remains fundamental in most persons and in most peoples; it therefore deserves to be distinguished and studied first. I will gather what I have to say about it under the title of

## The Generative Order

or the order of growth, custom, and tradition.

Now, at first this Generative Order is distinguishable in the general order of nature not by its secret mechanism but by the specific trope which nature here reproduces or tends to reproduce, as it reproduces plants from seeds. Within a specific growth, like that of the human family, we may distinguish fresh complications that disturb or even disrupt the family, and tend to substitute the dominance of a different social unit. Such a complication may arise within the traditional society by creating faction or demanding reform; or it may arise by the superposition of a wider influence or allegiance, as for instance to a new or foreign religion. The characteristic of such a change is that it is deliberate: not due to a variation in unconscious growth or to blind imitation, but prompted by a distinct desire or taste, and establishing express habits or obligations unknown to the traditional society and perhaps hostile to it.

This principle of a fresh social order voluntarily imposed is no less vital than the generative principle, being a part of the same animal life; yet it seems less biological, because potentialities in the psyche now come to consciousness before they are habitually realised in act. There is therefore a contrast, and often a conflict, between the new prompting at work and the traditional convention. Yet these conventions themselves may have sprung from sporting acts as do the games of children. Children do not plan games before they play them; and the adoption by a shrill crowd of a trick, performed tentatively by one small boy, may ensue by instinctive imitation and rivalry, without previous inclination or choice. But when the young crowd set out on a special run, or to do some distinct mischief, the common impulse is a little revolt, a distinct adventure, crossing the round of custom. A new sport may then be established, at once admired by the players, and perhaps regarded by the community at large as highly criminal; so that the ethos of this form of society will be ambiguous: at once highly honourable in its own eyes and deeply detestable in the eyes of others. I will call this therefore

## The Militant Order

understanding that it includes all voluntary associations that cross the generative order of society: not military bands only, but all political parties, religious sects, and parasitical arts.

But which arts are parasitical? Shepherds and husbandmen may say that they alone are profitable labourers, not indeed, by *producing* anything (for nature alone produces) but by assisting nature to produce food for man abundantly and regularly, and always at hand. Itinerant strangers who come telling stories and offering useless trinkets and medicines are parasites who expect to be fed and clothed in exchange for their trash; yet the women and children, who are themselves parasites, love tales and love toys; and when the father has become a rich man he has to humour them. So it is with those wild and lazy black sheep, like Esau, who are impatient at home and run away to the wilderness, and who as soon as game becomes scarce return to steal the sheep and the stores belonging to their industrious family. These truants are not essentially different from the armed bands and the robber barons that eventually settle in caves or castles and become a government and a luxurious society living entirely by the labours of the enslaved peasants. It is true that each bandit and each baron will say that he protects his victims from other bandits and other barons; but that merely proves that parasites have become a plague, and that radical measures should be taken to exterminate them all.

A principle which we may call defensible, since it is often defended, underlies this exposition. It is that man lives by bread alone: therefore every art that does not contribute directly or indirectly to supply mankind with food is a vain art, and those who practice it are parasites. This was a favourite theme for ancient poets: Arcadia, and the Saturnian reign when there were no ships, no commerce, and no luxuries. Yet even agriculture requires instruments; and unless it be in the Garden of Eden, people require clothes and shelter, and furniture of many kinds. Trades must therefore be allowed to exist, at least in the service of rustic life and in its defence. These trades will require special skill and special knowledge; and differences of age and sex, as well as of natural gifts, will establish diversity in the uses that people make of their leisure, and in their tastes and manners. There will appear, therefore, other criteria of excellence, other forms of happiness, besides the virtue of labouring in order to eat, sleep, and breed.

The question will thus arise in what proportion the necessary and the optional arts shall be allowed to develop: the criterion will no longer be merely the contribution made to food, and to the means of enjoying food, but will be some ideal of the free uses to be made of life, when food has been secured, tolerable in quantity and quality. The choice and measure of these other arts, inevitably superimposed on agriculture, determines the *economic order* of society: but as many of these arts, in a material sense, are parasitical yet may be most important for human happiness, I will call it rather

### The Rational Order

In each of these orders mankind exercises its own vital powers either in harmony with the ambient powers of nature or in conflict with them: a conflict which for instance in horticulture is partially a liberation of latent powers in other things, just as the powers of nature, when beneficent, liberate latent powers in man. This alternation of war and of alliance between man and his environment appears in the Order of Generation, but in the Militant and Rational Orders the conflicts and alliances observable are between persons or nations, or, within an individual, between his passions.

It will be in the Militant Order that the interplay of Dominations and Powers will appear most clearly; yet this interplay can never be understood or intelligently judged without remembering the Generative Order which is not merely the earliest, but remains fundamental throughout, lending body to all Dominations and Powers apparently moral. So too without remembering the Rational Order or implicitly appealing to it, nothing human can be justly criticised or appreciated, and politics in particular remain a scramble for place and power without justification. For after all it is the spirit that witnesses and compares all things, and can criticise the Will of that human psyche which is the agent and protagonist in all these dramas.

In choosing this division into three Orders for the arrangement of my materials I am guided by an analytic and moral interest, not by any merely descriptive or anthropological theory. The three orders are interwoven in reality, and while the first may exist without the second or third, as in the vegetable kingdom, the other orders cannot exist without the first; and in human history the second and third are also present throughout. It is precisely for this reason that I wish to contrast them, since Dominations and Powers show their colours within each political or economic system; and the interest that guides the moral philosopher is less to trace the passage of mankind from one type of organisation to another, than to distinguish in each type the good and the evil that it comports: in other words, to disentangle the Powers at work in that civilisation and mark the Domination that one or another of them may exercise over the rest. The Book of Genesis, for instance, describes an earlier society than does the Book of Kings, as is natural; but the interesting thing to observe is not this temporal succession but the survival of patriarchal ideals—including monarchical theism—in a society that has become decidedly militant; and it may be even more interesting in the end to observe how patriarchal ideals not only survive but become again dominant among the Jews in their prophetic period and in their religious influence; while in the Catholic Church militancy and spirituality remain subject to an unconquerable reliance on the generative order, seen in the conception of a miraculous temporal and material universe which there, in theory at least, always dominates politics and devotion.

So too the tragic legends which, more than the religious myths, inspire Greek morality exhibit a conflict between the generative and the militant orders, colouring the rational order that supervenes in Greek philosophy. Allegiance to the generative order, with latent and scarcely recognised economic motives, dominates the issue, and dictates perpetual war, trade, and colonisation, as well as the cyclical changes in the government of cities. Finally with the decline of classic antiquity pure philosophy and religion propose the domination of reason, but to little purpose; since they radically ignore or misrepresent the generative and militant orders that inevitably underlie any spiritual life.

# BOOK FIRST

## THE GENERATIVE ORDER OF SOCIETY

# PART ONE

## *Growth in the Jungle*

# CHAPTER 1

### CHAOS AND ORDER

Chaos is perhaps at the bottom of everything: which would explain why perfect order is so rare and precarious. Even when conquered by form in some particular, chaos revenges itself and proves its fundamental dominance by besieging that form with all sorts of violence or insidious disease, until the form dissolves, and the flux of existence reverts to a nameless continuity.

For if chaos ever exists, and the word is not a mere exclamation of impatience, chaos must have a formal disorder of its own. Any collocation of elements is the collocation that it is; any movement takes the precise course that it takes. But we are human beings thinking in moral terms, and we give the name of disorder to any order in which we cannot recognise the visible essences to which we are accustomed. Chaos is a name for any order that produces confusion in our minds.

Hence we may say paradoxically that a fresh recognition of chaos at the heart of nature may mark an advance in science. It will mark, at least, a closer view of the facts, rendering our preconceptions more consciously human. If study thereafter results in a new conception that seems clear and sufficiently true, we shall say that the order of nature has been more accurately revealed; if we remain perplexed and baffled, we shall at least have become aware of the abyss between our thoughts and their object. As modern astronomy has discredited the visual image of the round heavens, so modern natural history and politics have discredited the ambition of the ancients to legislate for eternity. History is a chaos, if we endeavour to impose our moral notions upon it. If we would find its true order, we must allow it to flow unguided, continually offering fresh suggestions of ideals which it never realises or at last betrays.

The shattering of that hope of the ancients, to build a city on a rock and defy the ages, I think has brought us a real lesson, a valuable discipline to our pride. It has adjusted our wills, in this respect, to the nature of things, which is chaotic, in the sense of being in a pervasive flux, and shifting continually the basis to any moral order erected upon it. This is an old lesson, but ill learned until now: that it is vain to lay up our treasures where moth and rust do corrupt, and thieves break in and steal. Our safe treasures, the objects for us of rewarding love, lie in another sphere; and what existence can offer us is only some image, some suggestion, enabling us to conceive and to define those truly eternal objects. This fact does not render the earth less beautiful, but more so; as art or language is in one sense more beautiful than nature. It is more poignant. Instead of being a dead fact, existence has become an index: it points. Each climate and season bursts into special flowers, which hardly last for a day; but their way of blooming enchants us; we are transported by their scent. Evolution is not performing any set task, much less a task imposed on it for the greater glory of our prophetic minds. Evolution is evolving; it is unravelling itself as it can. And so are our affections.

Nature is well-ordered enough to have produced spirit, yet chaotic enough to have left it free; it is not obliged to copy or to love its antecedents. Before producing spirit, however, a very great constancy had to be established first in the stars, so that an earth might exist with atmosphere and vegetation for animate beings to breathe and to feed upon. Then an inconceivable involution had to be packed into the seed of those animate beings, so that they might be reproduced, and might, in the case of man, acquire arts and traditions. There is therefore a whole cosmos, a whole network of persistent order, presupposed in the existence of spirit. And it is, as it were, a domestic temptation for spirit to worship that parent order, and to idealise it falsely, as if it were a moral order, designed to produce and to protect the human spirit. Here is where the chaos, beneath and within all order, comes in and saves the spirit from idolatry. No: the order of nature is cruel to spirit; it plays with spirit like a cat with a mouse. And, through this cruel discipline, it disenchants the spirit, absolves it from love of existence, from trust in time and in labour, and teaches it to be free, to enlarge its love to a whole hierarchy of perfections, to all the ordered things into which impartial chaos is ready to grow. So that by that very disorder by which spirit is tormented and mortified, it is weaned, it is emancipated, it is directed upon a realm of being where no chaos is possible, because there all essences are inviolate and perfect after their kind; yet where no order is inimical to another order, no beauty to another beauty.

## CHAPTER 2

### THE BIRTH OF LIBERTY

The first act of a new-born child is a cry. His little lungs, useless and squashed hitherto, have now filled with air. They *must* expel it. But the untried bellows has not yet caught its natural rhythm, and makes a feeble, strident, uncertain sound. Such is the first reflex action of free life, the prophetic counterblast to that death-rattle which will be its last exhalation. And this first cry reveals a wonderful power. The child can make the noise that he hears! This is his first assertion of liberty, his first experience of power: a cry.

He finds himself lying on his back in the open. His arms and legs, that used to be curled up and pressed to his body like folded wings, can now be stretched out and wagged. He wags them. This is his second free act: agitation.

But to wag arms and legs, as well as to cry out, is tiring. He feels cold. He feels unhappy. He doesn't know what to do. Things are getting worse and worse. Yet he can still blow; and he bursts out crying again, this time desperately, convulsively, with many tears. This would prove the end of his free career had not nature made the sound of such wailing a potent signal to call his mother and the bystanders to his aid. They pick him up, wrap him up tenderly, fold back his arms and legs into their old places, warm him and sing to him, until he falls asleep and is almost as happy as before he was born.

Such is the history of man's first experiment in liberty.

After it, his sleep is not likely to be absolutely unruffled. He will be pressed too hard here, or exposed too much there; he will be shaken and turned over to no purpose; some loud noises may startle him; or his own vital balance may be upset (for he is now a complete automaton within his skin) and he may grow restless and open his eyes of his own accord.

What he sees is light. If this light is equally diffused, as in a thick fog at sea, the sensation will be much like that of warmth or darkness or duration, a pure feeling, qualitative but inarticulate. More probably, however, the light will be unequally distributed and focussed perhaps at a single point, like a spark. The child's eyes will automatically fix that point, and, if the point moves, they will follow it.

Then something philosophically momentous has happened to that child. He is not merely seeing, he is looking. He is distinguishing the spark from the darker field over which it moves, and he is retracing that movement by a movement within himself. His organism, since it is living and autonomous, can repeat this inner movement after the spark has disappeared. Therefore it can reawaken for the child the image of that spark. The child has proved that he is endowed with intelligence. He can retain a fixed term in thought to mark a lost fact in nature, one on which he need no longer react.

Nor is the eye alone in developing surprising powers. Those arms and legs that wagged so idly, merely to stretch themselves and play, run up against one another or against other things; and it is marvellous how quickly and tightly the fingers will cling to anything suitable that comes in their way, and the toes also, though less successfully. Ah, had this child only been a young monkey! Had he only had a long flexible tail to wind itself round something strong and save him from falling! For be it observed, it is not for the sake of possession that hands and feet are so grasping; it is for the sake of support, for the sake of safety. If no danger threatens, the child relaxes his grasp, drops what he has seized, likes to throw it away. He wants to play with the world, not to acquire and keep it. Burdens would compromise his liberty, and his impulse is to be master.

The mouth, that seemed good only for making a noise, soon comes into contact with solid things also, and discovers a more important vocation. It can suck. It can draw in substance and energy to repair the terrible, perpetual, insidious waste caused by shouting and wagging and weeping and playing; yes, even by living, even by thinking. Liberty needs to be fed.

This is an antecedent necessity which liberty is slow to recognise. The freer a creature is, the more it takes its freedom for granted, and the less it notices the sources of that freedom. Euphoria seems a matter of course; and objects appear as happy creations, like songs or like thoughts; or if any of them proves obdurate and independent, it is recognised as an obstacle or an enemy. Once the obstacle is removed or the enemy devoured, euphoria returns; and it is only later, in reflexion upon much experience, that the obstacle may seem to have been a stimulus and a plaything, and the devoured enemy good food for liberty.

It was the mouth that quite freely and spontaneously uttered the child's first cry in wonder or in terror at finding himself alive; but very soon this same mouth becomes the channel for supplies, which it constantly and urgently calls for from the surrounding world. It takes the place of that umbilical cord, surely never noticed by the sleeping child, that used to feed him in his seclusion, while he grew, took shape, and became himself. Only that now, in the open, the mouth of man can do little to obtain food; it can only chew it and swallow it, when caught and brought to it by those hands and feet that at first wagged in idleness. They will still scamper and beat about with a great waste of energy, as the boy's voice will still shout its shrillest at every turn in the game; yet all this will be but practice and providential rehearsals for serious work to come. Soon arms, legs, and voice will have little energy left for play. They will be kept busy, if not exhausted, in pursuit of food for the mouth, until this disciplined service of liberty will have seemed to abolish liberty and turn it all to hard labour. Yet so long as life endures, liberty cannot die. It only sleeps, ready to awake again on the first occasion.

## CHAPTER 3

### PRIMAL WILL

BIRTH in mammals is inevitably violent, not like the unfolding of a bud or even the hatching of a bird. Chicks step out pert and inquisitive from the broken shell; and there is nothing heavy or helpless about the tumult of the hungry brood in the nest. But the human suckling has had a hard time of it; and that first cry of his, besides uttering alarm at the sudden emptiness and cold that surround him, may also be heaving a sigh at great troubles past, and at the lost elysium, unconscious while it lasted, that somehow looms behind all trials and sorrows. Sweet was that generative euphoria of silent growth, in profound security, more vital and free than any artful or deflected action in a world of accidents.

The first of Newton's laws of motion tells us that all bodies persevere in their state of rest or of motion in a straight line, unless prevented by external forces. This is not what the naked eye sees in the streets or in the fields, nor what happens to us in our customary movements. We tire soon of any one motion, and also of inaction. Boredom, inexpressible boredom, would be our lot if we had to obey that fundamental law of all free bodies; and yet I think that, in spite of the progress in modesty made by science since Newton's day, his proud first law ideally divines the primal spontaneous behaviour of every element of being. Nevertheless, on the scale of human perception and action, those hypothetical elements are unrecognisably fused or interwoven organically, so that the units distinguishable by our senses are compacted of innumerable invisible tensions, arrested impulses, and unstable equilibriums, established by fortune; as if every atom in our bodies were already one of the hungry worms waiting to devour us. Therefore all our large human units, physical and moral, are tragically transitory, and our enacted wills comically cheated by our secret desires; for in society we act as persons with apparent spontaneity and initiative, yet were we really able to have our way, not one of us would persevere, like Newton's free bodies, in the course or in the state in which we actually find ourselves. Our own official wills are often false to our natures, not so much through hypocrisy as through blind habit and gregarious vagueness. Indeed, even those silent and undeviating motions of the heavenly bodies can never move in a straight path, but are tethered to the parent sun by a tyrant attraction.

On the other hand, we must allow that a monstrous liberty to keep forever being or doing the same thing is a vain and unreal demand; the satirical limit of independence. Among living beings such independence is not only not found, but is logically impossible, because life is an exchange of materials and a variation of phases.

It requires to be launched, surrounded, and fed; and the liberty proper to life needs to be fed also. At the same time, this environment and this food must feed and surround something given. There must be a station from which things are viewed, a seed for whose development other things can be noxious or useful. There must be specific directions of growth, at least potential, for the living process to exemplify. Otherwise the emergence of life could never be discerned, nor its progress measured, nor its varieties and perfections distinguished.

This prerequisite lends a fresh importance to the notion of free beings persevering each in its own state or in its own motion. In physics this notion may prove only a useful fiction, but in logic, morals, and politics it becomes a fundamental principle. By it attention is first fixed on anything distinct or definable, on anything right or good. It introduces *The Recognisable* or *Essence*, without which language and thought would be impossible.

For this reason Aristotle (who in spite of realistic observation and judgment was at bottom a disciple of Socrates and Plato) believed that all motion and change were violently imposed; that they were all not powers but dominations. Even the planets, although animated by divine intelligence, did not by nature, or quite spontaneously, repeat their eternal round, nor could the sphere of the fixed stars do so daily, at a frightful speed. They were impelled thus to labour only by hopeless love of something immutable, namely, of eternal mind. This he taught although he was no poet; or rather, because he was no poet, he could believe that utility governed the world, and that nothing could exist save for the sake of something else. In this, as in the Platonic worship of essence, there was tragic wisdom; but it expresses the ultimate religion of spirit, not the primary motive power or Will in nature. It therefore inverts, by a schoolmaster's fallacy, the generative order of life and of society, as if grammars had been written first, and children manufactured afterwards, rather unsuccessfully, to learn them.

In order to trace as faithfully as possible the generative order of things, let me return now to our ideal infant at his second awakening. I say our *ideal* infant; because although I mean to study existence as it naturally expands, I am interested less in the accidents of existence than in its potentialities: an interest that far from being inconsistent with my materialism is inspired by it, since from the point of view of politics, the essence of matter is precisely its potentialities. Our potentialities, for us, are as yet mere ideals, but ideals rooted in the actual movements of society and in the primal Will of man, duly controlled by the material circumstances in which from time to time he may be living. Now it is this primal Will of man that at his second awakening our ideal child is about to discover.

Let us suppose that he awakes gently, not for being rudely shaken or compressed or turned upside down by unknown powers, but having been softly kept warm and troubled by no revolution in his insides, he now quietly opens his eyes, because after all they were made to open. He sees lights, bright spots, vague luminous shadows that drift by and disappear: they dazzle, they tire, they do not satisfy. Somehow, he wants help. His arms and legs and especially his mouth are after something. There is something more real than lights at work within him, demanding something more real than lights outside. He is hungry.

Food, now that he is no longer supplied with ready-made blood from his mother, is his fundamental need. Here his plight and his behaviour demonstrate a radical truth which he does not yet perceive, and perhaps will never quite acknowledge: that he is not free at all, but altogether dependent, since he cannot exist unless supported by other things.

A need is not a good. It denotes a condition to be fulfilled before some natural virtue can be exercised and some true good thereby attained. To feel needs is to feel separated from the good by some unfulfilled prerequisite to possessing it. Therefore the state of that child awaking with a need is an essentially precarious and unhappy state. It need not be acutely miserable. He may merely feel restless, troubled, impatient; but if the requisite mother's breast or nurse's bottle is not immediately offered, he will begin to whimper; and presently, distress being aggravated by its own efforts, he will suddenly change his stops and break out howling with all the might of a concentrated impotence.

The impotence of what? The impotence of primal Will in each creature; an impotence undoubtedly armed with enough internal power to be foiled in its blind agitation, and to devour its own strength in its all-embracing fury. This initial endeavour does not know what would satisfy its need, yet feels overwhelmingly what Hamlet calls a "plentiful lack" in the empty desire to exist.

This, considered inwardly, is the fatal source of spiritual suffering; this and nothing but this is the primal Will in man.[1]

## CHAPTER 4

### NEEDS AND DEMANDS

PRIMAL Will, as I understand it, is not coextensive with the entire automatism of nature. Automatism and Will are indeed akin, and the first always subtends and envelops the second. Will, however, though it does not imply intelligence or premeditation, does imply eagerness to act. For this reason I should not attribute Will to plants, in spite of the precise and persistent order of their growth. Seeds are not impatient; each has its promise within, but none possess the active organs requisite to pursue the realisation of that promise. All wait for the timely assistance of sun and rain, or even of roving insects, to bring them the means of growth and of reproduction. It is animals, with their prehensile and locomotive organs, that are first able to rummage for food and run after mates with a pertinacity as fateful as it is voluntary. A violent sense of urgency apparently fills them during the pursuit, but not for any previous idea of the object or the result. The law of nature at bottom would seem to be that the object should disappear when attained, devoured or forgotten, and that the avid chase should recur for ever, only to keep the ball rolling.

Human life, however, goes through a multitude of phases, many of the earlier subsisting submerged during the later ones and being their foundation. Morally the child is still a mere embryo, destined to enact a drama of adventure in a world that will both fertilise and suppress his native powers. When he cries in his hunger he does not know for what he is crying: he finds presently

---

[1] By the word "Will," written with a capital, I understand the universal movement of nature, even if quite unconscious, in so far as running through a cycle or trope it precipitates a result that seems to us a consummation. When this Will in man foresees and desires some consummation, perhaps impossible, I call it will in the psychological sense, and write the word with a small letter.

that he has recovered the reality, that it satisfies him, restores his peace, allows him to dismiss all questions, and go to sleep again. Yet increasingly there will come placid intervals of wakefulness for looking and loving and exploring. His hands and even his feet will attempt to seize everything. They will cling for a moment to what they seize; but there is nothing profitable in this, as there was when something suitable got into his mouth. The fingers and toes give it up at once, let go, or even toss the vain thing away with something like spite. The child is not yet acquisitive: he is born an aristocrat and a prodigal.

Life seems to require equable support in its beginnings. Before it can begin to live dangerously it must have been deeply sheltered, so that all the buried pregnancy of its seed may become potent in it. So in war, which brings us back to fundamentals, the stronghold half-buried in the earth is at once a home and a castle for the primitive man; later the walled city, always ready to stand a siege. Finally shelter is sought in the mechanism that calls most urgently for peace, because it is most exposed in war, I mean in the tissue of maritime and industrial relations stretched all over the world. It is said that Russian soldiers, in readiness for a severe engagement, arm themselves first with ammunition, then with vodka, and lastly with rations. Ammunition in the militant order corresponds to safety in the order of generation; it prevents the enemy from coming to close quarters by disabling him first, just as ditches and mounds and walls prevent him from doing so by interposing a passive obstacle. Vodka frees primal Will from untoward entanglements, revives courage in the morning, and drowns discomfort and worry at night. Only then, when there is respite from battle, food has its turn.

This is the order, not indeed of vital growth but of rational defence: as we are told in the Gospel not to take thought for what we shall eat and drink, and yet to build our house upon a rock. Safety will not keep us alive, but without a feeling of safety, and the vital liberty that comes with that feeling, life would not be worth living.

But how terribly precarious this vital liberty is! Primal Will assumes it without question, and gets on well enough so long as it demands nothing that the intrinsic tendency towards equilibrium amongst all movements has not provided. So the child finds sooner or later, and in most cases, maternal arms to hold it and breast to

## NEEDS AND DEMANDS

give it suck. The eyes will find light to see, the hands things to play with. In this way established instincts and customs ordinarily find a physical and social world in which they can operate, since that world has, for some time, suffered those customs and instincts to flourish and become a part of its domestic economy.

These natural adjustments between Will and opportunity are, however, loose, conflicting, and variable, so that our trustful child will fall a thousand times and be continually hungry, or hurt, or beaten, or disappointed. As it is contrary to primal Will to reform, it may be checked, driven under, cheated, and misled by false promises, but it can never be changed, if it is truly primal, by opposition, only by internal variation. What may happen is that after long suppression some of its demands may be atrophied, and others diversified into caprices and fashions, that entertain for a while without giving much satisfaction. The primal Will of the psyche is thereby partly inhibited and partly distracted or entrapped. In order to liberate that Will, and allow it to develop congenially, we should have to discover its true latent needs. The true needs of a psyche would be those that, if satisfied, would free that psyche from moral contradiction.

These needs will vary as the psyche grows; and as this growth will be controlled by circumstances, the ultimate needs of a soul are not fully determined by its inherited disposition. We can hardly imagine what the needs of a human psyche might have become had the world miraculously satisfied them all as they came to the surface. As things are, day by day from birth up, total or partial denials will have confronted the psyche. It will have learned, if it is teachable, to be patient and to tread the beaten path. If only the world itself were constant, it might educate that psyche to need nothing but what it finds or can contrive by its own action. Unfortunately, apart from physical catastrophes, the social world is more variable than any psyche can honestly be; so that adjustment to it is impossible to the heart, even if it be achieved, as it rarely is, by the intellect. Some, and probably the deepest and most fundamental of true human needs can therefore never be satisfied. In this predicament the generative resources of nature may veer in various directions. The more stupid animals and the more confident idealists simply persist in their rash endeavour and die martyrs to their first faith. The flightier spirits drop every disappointed hope, to pick up the next for no better reason. The martyr, however, might have been deceived in his innocent faith, and when compelled to give up his mistaken demand, might have discovered his true vocation, perhaps not wholly impracticable in the world and in any case worth dying for. And the cynic, on his part, feeling the ignominy of needs and demands imposed by the flesh on the spirit, all equally gratuitous, might play the imposed game only for sport, laughing at his tyrant fate, and never risking his secret treasure, which would be his scorn of existence.

This distinction between needs and demands has an obvious application to democratic customs when, instead of studying the true needs of the people, their leaders profess humbly to await the expression of popular desires. But the populace has no collective memory and no natural common psyche. Consensus is attained only by talk, in which now immediate advantages, really attainable, are offered to the public in its innocent greediness, and now impossible promises are made to some political sect in its blind enthusiasm. All the demands fostered by political propaganda are thus likely to be vain, some because the object is worthless and would satisfy no true need when attained; others because the true need felt is one of the inopportune gropings of nature after something impossible: a demand which wisdom would outgrow and a prudent education would discourage.

## CHAPTER 5

### LIBERTY LOST

WHEN the young child has discovered his primal Will, which is to feed, to grow, to master and possess everything; when he has learned that his mouth and hands have the power to absorb and to grasp what satisfies that Will, then a terrible counter-discovery awaits him. He had lapsed securely into placid sleep, and when he awoke again he knew perfectly what he wanted. Yes, but how shall he get it? How can it happen that sometimes there is no breast at hand, or that it is covered up or snatched away from him? Is his Will, then, not a power? Is it only a need, only a capacity to call for the well-known good, to cry for it miserably, vehemently, and in vain? No, not altogether: for presently the breast is here once more, the milk flows, and the last slow tears trickle cold down his cheek. *Perhaps* he can have his fill; *perhaps* he can go to sleep again, half comforted. But sleep will never be beatific now; a vague uneasiness will drift through it; he will have his first bad dreams.

The first shock of having his Will disregarded, and his vital liberty smothered and defeated by dark contrary powers, soon subsides into a habitual mood of vague suspicion and injured innocence. Things are wicked, but they sometimes smile, and may become obliging. Other persons—for things all appear to him rather in the character of persons, who please or offend him—ghostly persons, as he begins to distinguish and recognise them, no longer leave him quite helpless. His liberty is not gone altogether: by exercising it he may accomplish a good deal, and get those alien powers to do for him, in part or in time, that which he wishes. He learns that often crying works; also begging. And meantime, if he is a healthy child, he learns something much more deeply satisfactory. By looking at the dog or calling him or patting him, he can make the dog come, or follow, or wag his tail; and by picking up blocks and putting one over another, he can make them stay—for a while—just as he puts them. Here is vital liberty recovered; here is a part of this unintelligible world that behaves as it should.

Education, if the child is teachable and well cared for, ultimately develops another side also. Sometimes, when mother is cross or when pup is naughty, the fault is not wholly theirs. The trouble was that he, the child himself, by chance did the wrong thing, spilt the milk or didn't throw the ball when he pretended to throw it. He was a fool. It's not worth while to indulge useless whims that bring trouble; and it's not worth while to insist on wanting what you can't have. The best way to make things come about as you wish is to learn to like the way they have of coming about of their own accord when you give them a gentle push.

This is one of the first and most fruitful lessons of experience; the great lesson of conformity; conformity with the nature of things, in order to profit by them, and conformity with the will of God, so as to be content with the measure of profit which things, when intelligently exploited, can yield us. This is not, I think, the *ultimate* lesson of experience, because it chokes that fountain of life within each individual which can play freely, in its own ideal way, even when nothing else feeds it. Yet conformity is the method of successful action and art, and it partly saves vital liberty by bending before the denials of fortune, and compromising with them. Uncompromising spirit has only one means of dominating absolutely; to understand the cruel world and to transcend it ideally. This is an escape and an enthronement of spirit vertically; there can be no real victory on the horizontal plane of flux and mutation. *There* there can be only idyllic interludes amidst perpetual quarrels. These the poet and the philosopher may make the text of their meditation, as the musician, more abstractly than the moralist, may draw from their movement impassioned themes for his harmonies.

## CHAPTER 6

### VACANT FREEDOM

WE COMMONLY think of an atom as *free* to move in empty space, since there are no obstacles to impede or deflect its motion; and we say, in our human language, that it can move as it *chooses*, if it has or develops an *impulse* to move. We may, if challenged, discount these metaphors drawn from human life; yet figures of speech often leave behind them metaphysical illusions, when they are imported into physics or mathematics. In this case, for instance, in spite of all critical disclaimers, we may continue to imagine that a single atom in infinite empty space might or might not change its position, might travel at an assignable speed in an assignable direction, and might have constant dimensions of its own by which its trajectory could be measured. Yet in infinite geometrical extension none of these things is conceivable; for in a vacuum there is no intrinsic scale, nor any individuality in the points of the compass. The most elaborate universe might be inscribed in any part of pure extension; and alleged flight in any direction would be indistinguishable from rest or from flight in any other direction at any other speed.

This relativity was well known before Einstein: it was only

## VACANT FREEDOM

Descartes and Newton who seemed to deny it. We experience it personally whenever the medium through which we move remains empty and homogeneous to our apprehension. Sitting in a quiet garden we feel, and morally feel quite truly, that we are at rest; so too lying in a cabin on a calm night in the fastest of steamers. If the scientific observer outside assures us that we are moving at some astronomic rate, this is true only because cosmic space is not empty; material bodies and material currents diversify it, and render it an existing medium. Were there no material bodies and no light-traversed measurable space, and had we no front and back, up and down, determined by our organic structure and functions, no point in that space and no direction or distance could differ at all from any other; and the infinite vacancy that left that atom speciously free would prevent it from ever moving.

This illusion of possible motion in an infinite vacuum reappears in the moral illusion of free action without a definite impulse in an existing world. Agent and occasion must preexist. Even God or the universe, if we attribute liberty to them, would exercise it internally, by the circulation of their substance or the play of their dialectic, without the need or the possibility of any aid from beyond. They would live eternally free and self-sufficing in a vacuum. So we, and probably all animals, when we are young, well fed, and untrammelled, nurse the illusion of self-sufficiency. We think we could live happy if eternally free in a world we might build around us and constantly rebuild, like a happy dream, to suit our secret disposition. This feeling is not too extravagant to be the guiding inspiration of some romantic philosophers, notably of Fichte; and in a less articulate form it underlies much modern sentiment in politics. Reformers when they utter the word "liberty," and peoples when they take up arms in response to that cry, seldom have a clear idea of what they will do with their liberty when they have won it. *Ense petit placidam sub libertate quietem* is the motto of the State of Massachusetts. Once liberty secured, the blue sky will make mankind happy for ever.

I think there is an ultimate spiritual ideal in this illusion, the ideal of heaven or of Nirvana; but this requires us to transcend everything in human nature except intellectual light, and lies beyond the horizon of politics. That which turns vacant freedom into an object of passionate desire may be seen in our ideal child when a little older. He no longer wants his arms and legs to be bundled up close to his body; soon, except when tired or hurt, he struggles against being held or carried and insists on toddling on his small feet, at the risk of finding himself unintentionally sitting down. Never mind! That only screws up his love of independence to ignore the accident, as if it hadn't occurred. Finally he will even scorn to be led by the hand. His joy will be to run faster than other boys, dodge them, or even fight them, to prove that he can do what he likes, and fears nobody.

All this is an evident rehearsal of what we see in politics and in the superficially courteous arts of diplomacy. Fundamentally every vitally integrated tribe, nation, or government, unless in straits, looks on all others as nuisances or dangers, that it would be a relief to get rid of. Their territory ought to be annexed, the inhabitants assimilated, exterminated, or reduced to slavery. A treaty of peace or of commerce is a temporary compromise dictated by necessity or minor convenience. The political ideal remains always infinite, vacant freedom surrounding a chosen way of life. This ideal has been loudly proclaimed by every militant religion, as to-day by the apostles of both kinds of democracy. It was frankly expressed by Virgil for the Romans and by Dante for the Holy Roman Empire; and it is betrayed by the Soviets now in their continual demand for unanimity. In those who dislike to mention it, it persists in a secret unrest and perplexity at the existence of so many millions of blacks and of heathens; while good innocent souls everywhere are irritated at foreigners who do not speak the right language or have the right manners. It is the outsider who suffers some casual discomfort for being out of his element; but the deeper wound festers in the native soul, because it feels morally ignored and contradicted.

The thirst for vacant freedom may nonetheless be a sign of inner fullness, when a people or an art is really able to guide itself better than tradition or tutelage could guide it. In this case the freedom gained in the open would be vital liberty. Then the desired reform, if grafted on the right tree in an appropriate climate, might absorb substance where it had asked only for freedom, and might merge in a united and persistent public life. But more often it is blind constraint that provokes rebellion. A foreign domination seems to be a disgrace or a rival home government a disaster. Then the love of liberty is only a stage name for the hatred of repression, and the reformer, if he succeeds, will be himself a tyrant.

In an ancient and complex society there are bound to be institutions and customs that offend particular persons and particular circles. There is bound, therefore, to be disaffection, more or less general and more or less profound. Yet it is not the fault of a living organ if another organ arises that finds the first an impediment; the established order may reasonably ask why the new experiment is not tried elsewhere, where vacant liberty might surround it and allow it to display all its possibilities. But people cannot choose where or when they shall be born; and the fact that in their own time and country they find much to annoy and impede them seems to them a scandal. The constitution, the habits, the whole past of their nation ought to have been drastically different, so that they might have opened the way to the perfect order now first imagined. Ignorant wills cannot reflect; they cannot consider that it is not any initial wrongness in the established order but an accidental newness in their own demands that creates a discord; and the reformers blame the world for being themselves ill fitted to live in it. The reforming passion in the reformer would like to make a clean slate of society; as Descartes, who had theoretically made a clean slate of the universe, detested the picturesque cities of his day, and thought they ought to be demolished and rebuilt geometrically, like the fortresses of Vauban. Such minds belong to the militant order, and forget that they are themselves slow and groping products of generative nature; as indeed appears in their reconstructions, when these can be built to stand. There is always more in the reformer than his reforming zeal, especially if he is an artist; and there is always more in the world than the vacant freedom that the Will in its blindness had hoped to find.

## CHAPTER 7

### LOGICAL LIBERTY OR CONTINGENCY

There are various kinds or stages of liberty in the growth of things. Logically the most primitive and profound groundlessness lies in the essential contingency of existence. This world is only one of a numberless multitude of possible worlds. Even if in the vain vanity, which the superstitious indulge idly and the scientific man indulges ambitiously, there is a sort of divine terror in these visions of immutable order in events. On the one hand you are thereby encouraged to take risks, to lay wagers, to try experiments. The gambler and the inventor may not only pride themselves on their feats, but may make money by them. Yet here the dark side of the picture may appear. Luck may change, the experiment may fail, the explorer may perish; perhaps the gambler's imaginary sure system or the theorist's universal law may survive their person, and become a superstition in heady circles. In religion it may even become terror of hell or of helplessness before inexorable fate, felt to mock and to crush our inner consciousness of liberty.

A moment's reflection on the logical non-necessity or contingency of all existence should suffice to exorcise the fear of fate, which is a spectre of order, or the fear of hell, which is a spectre of a bad conscience. Unfortunately the sense of absolute contingency often raises another ghost, a fervid claim to "liberty of indifference," which is a spectre of vital liberty. But the order that may prevail in nature, unless we mean to include all time in our survey, may itself be a transitory order; in any case it is evidently such an order in the world known to us, as involves a continual variation and destruction in material things, and utter moral disorder in history. Terror at omens or predictions was simple terror at future accidents, fatal because they will come whatever you do.

## CHAPTER 8

### LIBERTY OF INDIFFERENCE

THE sense of contingency, the feeling that anything that happens might have happened differently, has a frivolous side and also a profound one. The notion occurs familiarly to frivolous clever people who know all sorts of men and countries, and are themselves the sport of miscellaneous alternate desires. If they were stupid and ignorant they would think everything had to be as it

## LIBERTY OF INDIFFERENCE

is at home; that there could be no good language, religion, or taste other than their own. And if they were stupid but learned—not a rare combination—they would incline to think that everything must necessarily happen as the men of science, or the philosophies of history, explain that it happens according to physical or dialectical laws. These pedants ignore two considerations. The first is that these so-called laws are rash generalisations, the dialectics verbal and arbitrary, and the theories of science hypothetical; they are perhaps true only locally, or approximately, or often, or for rough statistical averages. The second consideration is that even if known laws held universally for our known world, this fact would be itself contingent, and other worlds or other ages might be laughing at it, like the immortal gods. On this point the sentiments of worldly sceptics seem to me more enlightened.

Not more enlightened, perhaps, but far more earnest and deep-rooted is the conviction of many conscientious people who are sure that there is absolute contingency in their deliberate choices. Since these choices produce particular actions, which in turn have effects in the world at large, it follows that the whole structure of nature is plastic, and obedient in some measure to the free will of human beings. The crucial point in this view is the clear intuition that the motives and prospects which incline a man to this side and to that were inadequate to explain the sudden decision that finally occurred in him; so that, as he will repeat again and again, it was *he* that made the decision, and not motives of measurable weight or more or less pressing circumstances that made it for him.

I think there is no doubt, in many cases, of the accuracy of such confessions; they are sincere and exhaustive studies in self-consciousness. But what comes to consciousness in different minds comes from different depths and represents wider or narrower fields of acquaintance. Self-consciousness is not self-knowledge; much less does it afford a fair field from which to draw analogies to things in general. Yet in this particular instance I think that intense scrutiny of immediate experience does yield an intuition of a truth; not at all, however, of the truth about the ground or origin of human decisions, but about the *inadequacy* of the conscious arguments crowding and disputing in the mind to cause or justify the decisions taken. With this comes also the intuition of a positive truth, that beneath that loud forum of sophistical pleadings there is a silent judge, *the self*, that decides according to its free will, contingently, and inexplicably. For the close texture of events in nature is what it is by chance; yet what it is by chance determines, according to the occasion offered, what it shall do by nature. The affinities of this self are far more constant and certain than the passing passions or influences that may absorb conscious attention. Therefore the self can check its reasoning fancy; it can repel sensuous suggestions; it can seek dangerous adventures apparently without reason; it can recover its freedom, and reverse its habits and opinions. Moreover, this hidden self is, like every other centre or kind of movement in nature, perfectly contingent in being groundlessly determinate; and to this profound characteristic of all existence self-consciousness bears witness in the conviction that a man is the author of his actions, and that his actions are free.

The consciousness of acting freely, and not by the measured weight of motives or reason, has therefore a natural basis, not only in human nature, but in the essence of all existence. But it is not so that in Christendom this feeling has been interpreted. Instead of fetching man's vital initiative from the very rudiments of life, spontaneity has been attenuated into something non-natural and non-sensical called the "liberty of indifference." With tempting prospects open equally in opposite directions, like Buridan's ass between two equal bundles of hay, the "liberty of indifference" miraculously enabled a man to choose one alternative, for no reason, rather than the other. Since there was nothing in his nature (which he owed directly to God) nor in his circumstances (which he owed also to God indirectly) to determine this choice, God could not be blamed for it if it were contrary to his commandments. Responsible was only the free will which wickedly chose sin, when the motives for sinning and for not sinning were naturally perfectly balanced. The man might then be justly damned or graciously saved, according to the turn taken by his "liberty of indifference."

This is not the place for examining the mythological and conceptual habits of thought that led to this singular conclusion; they are a part of the verbal and imaginative jungle which the exuberant fertility of nature breeds in the innocent mind. And society has done much to aggravate the confusion and the pain of these moral entanglements; for it has imposed codes and logics on minds that had not that natural bent, and loaded with praise and opprobrium, to which the social man is keenly sensitive, the congenital choices of his blind heart.

## CHAPTER 9

### CAPTIVE SPIRIT AND ITS POSSIBLE FREEDOM

THE above analysis applies to the life of spirit, when spirit ignores its station in the material world. This word "spirit" will occur at various crucial points in this book, because politics is a moral subject and it is the earthly fortunes of spirit that, at bottom, are its theme; but the word has many meanings and I had better explain at once in what sense I use it. By "spirit" I do not understand any separate power, soul, person, or deity persisting through time with an individual character, like a dramatic personage. I understand by "spirit" only the awakened inner attention that suffuses all actual feelings and thoughts, no matter how scattered they may be and how momentary, whether existing in an ephemeral insect or in the eternal omniscience of God. Spirit so conceived is not an individual but a category: it is life in so far as it reaches pure actuality in feeling or in thought. All imaginable ideas fall within the sphere of possible spirit, and are open to it by right of its intellectual essence; yet in fact, in you or me, poor spirit may be helplessly humming some old tune, or stupidly watching leaf after leaf fall from the autumn trees. Spirit is the witness, involuntary and unprepared, of everything real or imaginary, good or evil that is ever experienced.

Yet sometimes, militant passion will drive spirit to proclaim the absolute rightness of one casual opinion and the intolerable wrongness of any other. Evidently primal Will is at work here, which is an inexplicable fatality to spirit. The venom of disagreement and the agony of doubt are alike physical, since this rivalry between opinions does not belong to them as pure thoughts. In it looms some obscure predicament of animal life: dumb terror at perhaps being cheated in action, contradicted by facts, ridiculed by tribal clamour, or left alone in a world false to its every promise. And militancy, in which primal Will becomes factious and makes war upon itself, likewise drags the spirit away from its intellectual innocence and monopolises all its light, as in a hooded lantern, to guide it in some fatal adventure.

But let us suppose spirit freed from all such material domination and faced only by the infinite morphology of pure Being. This infinitude is not empty, like that infinite extension which is the conceptual ghost of physical space. It is the infinitude of the realm of essence, chock-full (though without crowding or rivalry) of every form, quality, trait, or distinction by which anything could ever be assimilated to anything else or contrasted with it.

Spirit is pure light, in itself equally ready to fall on anything; and we might think that the choice of its object ought to be left to it, if, as we are supposing, spirit were absolutely free. What, in that case, would it choose? The supposition is mythical, and contrary to fact; yet indirectly both the birth and the triumph of spirit, as we know or can imagine it, suggest what the choice might be. It was not by the spirit's choice at birth, that the child's first cry was, on the whole, a cry of distress. When that cloud had passed, there was perhaps some light, especially some moving light, that led the child's eyes to follow it, not with distress but in vague curiosity and wonder. There was a certain ambushed Will prompting the spirit to look, to notice, to understand. Let us then say, in our myth, that the choice of the spirit would fall on anything, since any essence offers something to observe. Or, by a bold but legitimate inference, let us say that the choice of the spirit would be to fall upon everything, to be omniscient.

Now, we noted that the child, even when he began to look and to grasp voluntarily, and with apparent pleasure, at once lost interest or even tossed the thing away with a kind of spite. It would seem then that, if not spirit, at least that psychic function that evokes spirit, is not directed upon apprehension for its own sake, but chooses the object and sustains attention upon it by force of circumstances that the spirit knows nothing of. And so in regard to the ideal of omniscience. Actual omniscience, such as is attributed to God, is not only beyond the power of spirit in man, but would be fatal to all incarnate spirit; because (not to speak of infinite essence) omniscience in regard to facts would involve present knowledge of the entire past and the entire future of the universe; with all other creatures' wishes as clearly felt as one's own. The man's body might continue to live, but there would be no mind proper to that body, only a dramatic representation in the mind of a universal poet of what would have been his, and everybody else's, experience. And it is indeed, according to the witness of all profound spirits, such a dramatic representation of experience, and not the flux and perpetual injustice of the experience itself, that the spirit in man pursues as its ideal. For spirit, it is only as ideas, as essences, that things can be seen or loved; and it is only as an essence, or as the truth about some fact, that existence can be possessed or retained by a free spirit.

Incarnation, therefore, which seems to imprison spirit in the toils of time, place, person, and circumstance, is in reality the cause of its existence and the necessary prior occasion to any selection of images, feelings, wishes, or ideals that it may encounter. If it were disembodied, its indetermination would not be freedom but absolute apathy and impotence. If it beheld and possessed everything, it would be without movement or preference; in a word, without life: and yet to be the very flower and flame of life is its intrinsic essence. Its proper freedom is liberation, disentanglement, parturition of its inner burden. For the spirit there is no question of *choosing* to be or not to be, or *choosing* this or that fortune or love. Given existence, given fortune, given love, in which the spirit is captive, the problem for it is to digest, to refine, to dominate that existence, that fortune, or that love, so as to become the *perfect* flower, the *pure* flame of that passion. The inner liberty of spirit will not then be vacant, but vital; for it will be the very vitality of its body and of its world here now actualised and become conscious.

## CHAPTER 10

### VITAL LIBERTY

THÁLASSA, *thálassa*, cried the Ten Thousand Greeks when, after a weary march from the depths of Asia, at last they saw the open sea. It is with this sentiment that politicians and moralists cry after vacant freedom. If we examine their words or their ideas we find nothing there but negation or confusion of thought; but we find something decidedly positive if we examine their situation. They cry out for the same reason that makes a young child howl if held down too long or too tightly. They do not know what they want, but they find their condition insufferable. Vacancy, they feel, would be heaven, if only they could get into it.

Perhaps the open sea, with all its hardships and perils, might not have so much gladdened those exhausted adventurers if they had not had memories of ships, of friends, of tight little cities where there were fires and feasts and motherly women to welcome their return. Yet it is hardly the love of home in itself that warmed their hearts. Home had had trials that drove them from it. Their cry is almost as absolute as that of the raging child; it is a cry for escape, for space, for air, for being let alone; a cry for freedom pure and simple, freedom wholly abstract yet unspeakably precious.

But why does this empty freedom seem so full of promise? Why does the sea, a more inhuman element than air that we can breathe or fire that can warm and serve us, why does this blue horizon tempt even the most disappointed traveller? Not, surely, for what he sees in it, but for what he feels potential and urgent in himself. Could he only escape this present constraint, this unnatural predicament, how spontaneously, how richly, would he find a thousand things to enjoy and to do! It is life in him, as in the impatient child, that is aching to expand. The charm of vacant freedom is entirely secondary, borrowed, deceptive. It is vital liberty that the rebel wants, that he needs, that might alone make him happy. But in his inexperience or in his ill fortune he does not know what form that vital liberty would take, and he cries only for the vacuum in which it might take any form it chose. His clamorous love of liberty is almost entirely hatred of compulsion. Liberty for the slave means simply freedom from his bonds.[1]

What, then, will liberty bring to the free man? That is the great question in morals and politics. And the difficulty in answer-

---

[1] There is a subtle difference in the suggestions of the two synonyms, "liberty" and "freedom." The first word is Latin, the second Teutonic. We may notice that of the "Four Freedoms" demanded by President Roosevelt in the name of mankind, two are negative, being freedoms *from*, not freedoms *to*. Had he chosen the word "liberty," he would have stumbled on reaching these desired exemptions, because the phrase "freedom from" is idiomatic, but the phrase "liberty from" would have been impossible. "Liberty" thus seems to imply vital liberty, the exercise of powers and virtues native to oneself and to one's country. But freedom from want or from fear is only a condition for the steady exercise of true liberty. On the other hand it is more than a demand for liberty; for it demands insurance and protection by provident institutions, which imply the dominance of a paternal government, with artificial privileges secured by law. This would be freedom from the dangers of a free life. It shows us liberty contracting its field and bargaining for safety first.

ing it is enormous, because all the external possibilities and all the inner demands that will impel or control that liberty remain unknown or unspecified. Robinson Crusoe had vacant liberty to perfection when he found himself cast on his desert island, but he would have perished of exposure, hunger, and boredom if he had not been richly furnished with mechanical skill and with sufficient instruments, cast up with him from the wreck, to found a new economy. It is such arts, such fields, such instruments that the liberated slave requires for the exercise of his vital liberty; else he must perish, like a fish out of water, for want of a medium fit to entertain and develop his natural powers.

When I speak of natural powers or of primal Will I have in mind nothing immutable or identical in all the members of a particular race or a particular region or epoch. I do not even mean an unchangeable endowment, the prenatal product of sexual fertilisation, which should determine the capacity and possible virtues of each different individual. There is, undoubtedly, a prenatal organism with a determinate compound heredity; but just as the heredity in each individual is a novel mixture of the two heredities of his parents, so the development of that compound heredity will be determined afresh at each moment by the stimulations, inhibitions, atrophy, or redirection which circumstances may impose. In nature all events are fresh products of confluence among various currents, each possessed of its own energy and character, but none predetermining alone the combined result; and whether any of these initial currents survives unaltered in its source or in its movement depends upon the retroactive influence, if any, which that conjunction exerts. Nothing can alter the past; but a plastic organism can hardly help feeling, to its very centre, the effect of the shocks it receives. The natural powers or primal Will of each individual will therefore vary, perhaps infinitesimally, perhaps radically, in the course of their manifestation.

The integrity of a person or of a government is a living integrity; it lies in the *concomitant* wholeness and absoluteness of the Will. Fidelity to the past is not involved in it if the man or the people has undergone a veritable μετάνοια; nor is absolute constancy in this new allegiance to be expected, except in the measure in which the conversion responds to all the ingrained needs and all the relevant circumstances of that person or that people. Fidelity, for instance, to the marriage vow may be demanded of all wise and honourable persons; yet it is impossible that the actual love and spiritual union should preserve the same colour through courtship, honeymoon, parenthood, old age, and separation by death. Natural powers and primal Will are thus elastic; and vital liberty changes its form with the changing phases of life.

This plasticity in the psyche, with its cycle of natural development and its capacity to profit by experience and training, has more than one moral consequence. In some measure, especially in youth and under discipline, vital freedom may leap into the breach, and grow along the lines marked out for it by custom and opportunity; but often the growth of self-knowledge and of knowledge of the world widens the chasm between the mature demands of the Will and the path open to action. That which the world allows and encourages may be the opposite of that which we truly prize, believe, and are competent to do: so that experience, instead of tending to create a harmony between vital liberty and lifelong practice, perhaps closes all the hatches down upon that liberty and condemns the true soul to voyage blind and captive below deck, while pirate circumstances sail the vessel.

It is the frequency of this predicament that leads public feeling in modern times to identify liberty with rebellion. But rebellion at best can only clear away some obstacle to free living. The substance and joy of liberty begin only when the well-integrated powers of the psyche find or establish a world in which they bear their specific and appropriate fruit.

## CHAPTER 11

### NECESSARY SERVITUDE

WE SAY that childhood is happy and charming; we love children as we do flowers, for their trustful helplessness and innocence, sometimes with an admiring pity, sometimes with a rather cruel liking for animal playthings. But for the child childhood is ignominious. He has his pride in his own ways and is overpowered by

## NECESSARY SERVITUDE

sudden trouble; yet in both he finds himself impotent. At every turn he must renounce and obey, ask questions and get no answers. And I speak only of children that are well treated. Childhood is the first necessary servitude of man.

The whole problem of life appears in its essence when a child, animated by primal absolute Will, discovers his physical dependence. And at first, if not his whole life long, he discovers only half of it. He feels checked; he ignores that he himself is derived, conditioned, supported. In recognising the power of the non-ego, he recognises it only as an enemy to be conquered or as an obstacle to be circumvented; at most, as a possible ally to be won over. He cannot recognise it as a formative, sustaining power; much less as an undermining power within himself. He does not suspect the native treachery of those hands and of that heart which are working for the nonce in such lordly unison.

Suppose now that a docile disposition and a sheltered nurture sustain this euphoria in him almost undisturbed. An exhilarating sense of union with nature, with society, and with the gods may turn his youth into a pious festival. He will acquire all the wise virtues, together with a conviction of their exclusive and universal rightness; and he will count on the principles and promises of orthodox politics and religion. Have I asserted that matter cannot be cheated, and that a fair pact made with matter may be relied upon by the engineer? Perhaps it may, on a familiar scale, in the kitchen or the laboratory. The sun will rise in the morning, and the pot will boil if you light a fire under it. But earthquakes and tornadoes are unpredictable; and when you thought you had acquired all wisdom, your correct virtues and orthodoxy may have lost their prevalence, and you may miss the praises and the prizes of the world. You might have done better not to be so docile; and a less favourable climate might have trained you better for trials ahead.

Worldly wisdom—which includes practical politics—must therefore change with the times; and it is not possible to establish a true unanimity between a perpetually changing world and a constant spirit. There is a radical antinomy here: because spirit, even in its most extroverted acts, such as sensation or perception, reaches a conclusion, defines an image, intuits an essence, which becomes a private term for it in retrospect and reasoning. Meantime the flux of nature has flowed on; and were it not for the cyclical character of this flux, which without arresting any existence sustains approximately recognisable forms, mind would be totally incapable of learning anything about nature, its own matrix and vital source. What mind sees in nature is always but a garment: yet nature's children have, in each family, such a family likeness, that a coat made for one brat, when he has outgrown it, will serve for his younger brothers; and it may serve even for his children's children if it was well made of perdurable, ideal stuff.

If this were all, the disparity between the movement of existence and the ideality of thought might seem admirable as well as instructive, as it would doubtless seem to spirits looking down on it from a changeless heaven; but the trouble in our case is that the psyche that kindles itself into spirit in us is itself a part of the flux of matter. It cannot itself be constant to its constant terms, but is continually slipping away from one set of habits to another, modifying its organs, growing old and becoming childish again, not only in decrepit individuals and societies, but in the normal renovation of the race: each generation being compelled to learn its lessons anew, and not to learn exactly the same lessons as its ancestors, but to forget their language and their gods in running after new idols.

This tragedy, which defeats any true education of the psyche by its living contacts, is relieved by the possibility, in civilised states, of retrospective science; so that the learned at least, by understanding this very instability in life, transcend it in speculation, and can discount spiritually the bias of their own age, while putting up with it in daily life and in politics. The consequence of such critical self-knowledge is spiritual self-transcendence, whereby the whole procession of natural events, known and unknown, is ironically congratulated for spinning itself out so variously, with so much vital vim and perpetual youthfulness, while it furnishes man, in his intellectual moments, fresh orchestral themes for his delight and wonder.

The necessary servitude of the spirit in man is thus double: to the great world, and to the animal psyche. The great world conditions psychic life; and the psychic life so conditioned conditions the spirit. When the generative order of nature develops harmoniously, so that the primal Will in any part is not frustrated by the operation of primal Will in its neighbours, the conditions of life, cosmic or animal, do not seem constraints but blessings; and the spirit flowers joyfully in the psyche, as the psyche flowers beautifully in the world. Vital liberty in that case finds all the requisite means of action at hand, and feels no variation in its own demands; it may therefore ignore its dependence on its bodily organs and on their physical and social milieu.

Such egotism, seen by the naturalist from outside, may seem sheer madness; but the psychologist understands and forgives it, since it is the inevitable presumption of a new-born healthy Will. Pride normally indicates conscious capacity. Were the soul humble before it was contradicted and chastised by uncontrollable circumstances, it would be a feeble and empty soul. Humility is strong and profitable only when it is the fruit of experience and of a tragic contrast discovered and accepted between aspiration and destiny. Christian doctrine in this, as in much else, contains a perfect allegory of the truth. We must be born again, before we can enjoy true liberty or enlightened happiness. Our original unregenerate vitality was not madness—as solipsism would be—but only sin; not sin in yielding to any base or unworthy temptation, but that original sin of which Calderón speaks when he says that the greatest trespass of man is that he was ever born. It is the tragic sin of ὕβρις or arrogance, in laying claim, by existing, on whatever we want, when nothing is really ours. The sin does not lie, as superstitious cowardice supposes, in willing this or that which is taboo, but in willing *anything* without leave. Where leave is granted by fate, the love of life and of freedom is normal and noble. The psyche can then run its vital cycle with a happy zeal; and the spirit, from each moral hilltop, can select and fashion an inspired vision of the world.

To primal Will liberty therefore seems a right, and is indeed an ideal that never can be surrendered; so that when this Will, not being altogether extinguished, is forced to compromise with the dominant enemy, it still remains suspended and ready to reassert itself as soon as the hostile pressure is relaxed. Yet in the economy of nature there is no such thing as a right. Existence itself is an unearned gift and an imposed predicament. The privilege of more or less freedom is meted out to individuals and to nations temporally and unequally, not by any ideal justice or law, but by the generative stress of a universal automatism. Primal Will pervades this movement; it is original and central at every point, in every atom or cell; and the confluence of all these impulses, in their physical medium, determines spontaneously the measure in which each may deploy its vital liberty.

## CHAPTER 12

### SERVITUDE TO SOCIETY

THE unfathomable non-ego dominates spirit in a man within and without, fitfully in the world and subterraneously in his hidden passions. To spirit in a philosopher this same non-ego wears a specious unity, to balance his own integrity; and he perhaps calls it the Universe or Fate or, if his imagination is dramatic, he may call it God. But to spirit in the child, with his shorter perspectives, the non-ego is distinctly plural, familiarly active and morally equivocal. It is all foreground, composed of the persons who at each moment feed, carry, coddle, amuse, slap, or abandon him. He is the slave of society. Even material objects, especially his toys, acquire for him a certain personality; they are numinous, like giant trees and migratory birds. And places, no less than persons, may become a refuge filling him with peace and confidence. Still the non-ego remains always dangerous; there is no knowing what its next onslaught may be; and this servitude embitters existence.

Yet society, the necessary cradle of the individual, ought to be agreeable to him. And so, in some ways, the child soon finds it. Other children and all animals attract him; he loves playing and tussling and fighting. But society, as we grow older, imposes on us far more. Other people's gregariousness is overwhelming because it is cumulative. Quantity overpowers, and the irresistible crowd may cut us off from the very society which we might have liked and might have flourished in. The crowd compels us to adopt its language, manners, morals, and religion; and it is a rare freedom in human life when even a slight personal originality in any of these matters—or even in dress—is not crushed at once by universal obloquy and persecution. This is not because the public is wicked but because it is the public—which is hardly its own fault. Society suffocates liberty merely by existing, and it must exist, and all its members are equally its slaves.

The individual may elude the feeling, though not the fact, of subjection to society either by a willing conformity or by a mental reservation. The first is easy to most men, except on rare occasions when their impulses are especially galled; the second is possible only in lucky cases. The secret of it is not so much obdurate self-possession or stoicism as secession; for society is factious and friable. In the name of science or of wit you may venture to lift the hem of religion; supported by a party, you may abuse your country, and may migrate mentally, if not materially, into another world. God, the Church, the ancients, the poets afford so many social sanctuaries to which you may escape from ordinary society.

Parents necessarily exercise authority over their young children and often claim it later; becoming in this way veritable tyrants. But tyrants are seldom free; the cares and the instruments of their tyranny enslave them. The child that cries is your master; and he is your master again when he smiles. Your love makes you work for him, and at the same time besets and belabours him in order that he may turn out not as he wishes but as you wish. He obeys in a perfunctory fashion that is your torment; or if you tame your affection, making it really unselfish (which is hard for a parent), and sympathetically watch over his welfare, you find a double disappointment: for you observe sorrowfully that he does not place his welfare where you place it for him; and later, that he attains neither what you wished for him nor what he wished for himself.

Nature kindly warps our judgment about our children, especially when they are young, when it would be a fatal thing for them if we did not love them. This fond blindness is itself a slavery; a hard slavery, when you think of it, to feel a compulsory and sleepless affection for a perfectly average creature, and this quite apart from any merit or promise in the child; and afterwards to be disgraced by his disgrace, wounded by his indifference, and half killed by his death, if you survive him.

No doubt parents who can sympathise with their children (sympathy is a different thing from love) may make a fresh life for themselves in their children's circle, like the grandparent's life in the chimney-corner; and as the children can elude the consciousness of their slavery, if they are docile enough, so can parents elude the consciousness of their superannuation, if they are self-forgetful: a becoming but difficult virtue in old age.

Thus the necessary servitude of parents comes round to that of children again. Human life is hedged completely round with compulsory sacrifices. Yet they may be made gladly or as we say freely; for to be in harmony with necessity gives us a sense of freedom, which is the only freedom we have.

These compulsions are natural and acceptable, being due to the method of human propagation and the economy of human industry and war. But they are neither logical nor spiritual necessities. That is why subjection to them is true slavery, even if it be wise of us to endure it with good grace. Indeed, there are cases where obedience to necessity is really perfect freedom. It is no slavery for a fish to be compelled to live under water, nor for a man to be compelled to breathe or to walk on two legs. To play the quadruped at first is easier, but before long it becomes more exciting and exhilarating to run about upright. Above all, it is no slavery for a man to love. On the contrary, it is precisely in the first flush of running and loving that the spirit wakes to the joys of vital liberty, and that loveless servitude, by contrast, becomes an odious burden.

What is it that has taken wing and was caged before? What is it in man that can be free or enslaved? A cipher, we know, could be neither: the freedom of nothingness to become anything is not moral liberty. That which feels free in these joyous moments is the total aspiration of a man's animal nature, building up his spirit and becoming conscious in it. This total aspiration is indeed ill defined and ill harmonised; the man's nature is probably chaotic, and his Will divided against itself. Hence his sense of subjection to vice and temptation, and his unhappiness whichever way he may turn. Yet there are limits to this vital disorder, or life would end in convulsions. The fish in its perplexities never pines for mere air, and the man never hates himself for breathing or having but two legs. At the same time there are many faculties that are best exercised in solitude, or over the head of society, in sympathy only with nature and with truth. Nor is it simply a private and speculative side of our being that chafes under social servitude; it is also our social and moral conscience that actual society offends. Local loyalties condemn the spirit to injustice and overwhelm it with the ignominy of taking sides selfishly, for one's self against everybody else, for one's family, country, party, or religion against all others. Is not political man necessarily a fool in his hatreds and a beast in his ambitions? Could there be a greater curse than his forced—geographically, chronologically forced—national allegiances and endless wars? Pacifists are eloquent about the waste of money in armaments and of blood in wars. But blood and money, after all, belong to the earth; they must be spilt in the same fields in which they are gathered. The servile thing is not that we must fight and die—it is noble to accept that physical necessity. The shame is that we do not fight or die under our true colours. We neither assert ourselves with perfect integrity, nor abdicate with perfect content; so that we are enslaved both in living and in dying: enslaved to accidental coercions suffered against the harmony of our total nature, and enslaved to the general order of destiny which we have not the elevation of mind to observe philosophically, and to turn to spiritual uses.

## CHAPTER 13

### SERVITUDE TO CUSTOM

THE primal social bonds, parental and sexual, are intermittent; life may go on when they have snapped. Even hunger and thirst seem assaults of a tyrant as soon as spirit, kindled within the organism, turns it into a transcendental centre from which all surrounding forces are measured and judged. Many of these foreign impacts or attractions are greedily welcomed; yet a living creature is happiest in the interludes when, enriched by those trials, it breathes again in peace. Unfortunately the highest organisms, being the most complicated, bring the most trials upon themselves. So it happens in society where each individual is congenitally a vital centre, yet is aware of neighbours that cross its path and cut off its light. The material obstacles to freedom become less, or are more easily surmounted in society than they would be in solitude; but meantime society has itself imposed a net of duties and prohibitions and petty quarrels that the single explorer or hermit would have escaped. Industry has supplied from the beginning, as it does today, new instruments and fresh occasions for artificial demands and unnecessary subjections. Men and women are braver when so armed and banded together; their servitude to fate has receded into the background, to reassert itself only in the great crises of life; but their joint labours and cohabitation have surrounded them with exactions, compulsions, critics, and spies, and made them the slaves of custom.

Custom arises when some casual public act at a critical moment strikes the fancy, or seems to secure an impressive result. The act thereby forms in the agent and even in the spectators an acquired reflex, so that it spontaneously presents itself to the mind or is unwittingly repeated on any similar occasion. Customs may be superficial and transitory like the vogue of a slang phrase, or may be fused with primary actions, and become an integral part of an established ritual. Much that passes for instinctive and rooted in human nature is merely traditional and could be abandoned or radically varied if a knot of people felt the impulse to do so. The family, monogamous and living each family apart, is raised in Christian ethics to a divine institution; yet it is less instinctive and more an imposed custom for human beings than for sundry birds and mammals; and the fact that the human family forms a life-long bond, whereas in those other animals it is usually limited to the breeding season, testifies to the circumstantial and optional character of this domestic institution. The long childhood of man causes young and helpless children to succeed one another in a numerous family for perhaps twenty years. The nest becomes a home to which in civilised times brothers and sisters remain attached indefinitely by habit and by the dependence, affection, and common possessions that habit has gathered there for them all. Yet this very attachment to the home may bring about its transformation into a more numerous and looser society; because married sons with their families, not to speak of married daughters, may cling to their father and brothers with a political allegiance and co-operation, transforming the original monogamous family into a tribe or clan. Or could a gregarious band have existed first, in which mating was promiscuous and momentary, food-getting and migrations and battles being carried on by a common impulse, with only occasional private quarrels? I am not broaching anthropology for its own sake; possible origins concern me only as moral possibilities. Society may still develop in the direction of any of these systems, as politically it may repeat, on a different scale and under other names, the monarchies, aristocracies, democracies, and tyrannies of classic times. The question for us is how far and in what direction may necessary servitude be sweetened, and vital and spiritual liberty enjoyed, under any of these dominations.

The cruelty of parents is an old and interminable story. It is not a wanton cruelty. They hurt because they suffer, and have been suffering from birth up through the inordinate demands made by everything, as now by their children, upon their labour and patience. Things are not as if we were animals perfectly adjusted to our habitat, with impulses maturing in exact time with seasons and opportunities. We are all born more or less lame and destined to a thousand difficulties and disappointments; our natures are partly diseased, disorganised, incapable, and inconsistent. Moreover, the native liberty that in the parents is so ill-adjusted to new demands is crossed further by the native fatuities of the child, always a rash and somewhat original compound. Old and young, even of the same breed, find themselves at different phases in the vital cycle, and cannot agree in mood, opinion, impulse, or affection. Contact means constraint on both sides, and a hearty unison can seldom be established except amongst comrades of the same age.

If parents are cruel, children are cruel too. They mistake their greater quickness and agility for superior intellect; and they resent the air of omniscience, the closed mind and heart, the blind censoriousness and petulance of their elders; and in their eagerness to make their own way, they show themselves ungrateful, fitful, rash, and often ultimately helpless. It is not only the open prodigal that returns repentant: daily and without acknowledgment, in a thousand small ways, the younger generation falls gradually back into the habits and views of the elder, ready to take the old man's place even before death has mercifully removed him. Mercifully yet probably to the momentary unfeigned grief of the survivors, even though they be the heirs: because beneath their irritations and quarrels, families preserve a deep sense of kinship. Each member is an exemplar, an indelible memory, a secret influence on all the rest; and in burying the father the children measure their own span, feel their own errors and insecurity, and see for the nonce how much they too are pilgrims and helpless strangers in this world.

Endless alternatives are compatible with human nature, which innately is a vague thing; and what determines the choice is accident, on which imperious custom is soon grafted. This custom, when it arises, cannot have been altogether contrary to instinct, and it cannot have proved fatal to the race, where it still lasts; but short of that extremity, there is hardly any degree of constraint, cruelty, and ineptitude which may not characterise custom. The stupid moralism [1] which clings to it is like that which assumes the inevitableness of a given language. Like the respect for language it doubtless represents a certain superstitious conservatism, a certain obsession and excitement about imminent periodic events, like feasts or wars, which men crave as they do the satisfaction of other recurrent appetites. These tense experiences, even when in abeyance, haunt the mind and seem to float suspended over it, like so many gods, whose influence and contagion may sweep down again on men at any moment, and "possess" them. To expect, to experience, and to brood over these wild crises is the deepest part of tribal life.

The savage likes to be a savage. Uniform custom has narrowed his experience, and narrowing experience has warped his imagination, and nothing now seems to him comparable to his apathy, his orgies, and his baubles. The most sordid routine comes to have its charm: the savages and gutter-snipes are not our only witnesses here. The pothouse, the morning paper, the novel, the game of bridge or patience have their devotees among us, and if these people expressed their philosophy (for they sometimes have one) they might say, like the savages: "Let me alone, I am content. Are you happier for all your needless undertakings? I at least should not be." And if good little people can say this, who have crawled into their warm corner, our great private or official criminals say much the same thing in a shriller key: for their principle too is the one on which the savage would defend his cruel rites and debauchery: for they say that one crowded hour, even if crowded with delirious agonies, is worth a lifetime of empty comfort. The childishness, the hardships, and the lubricities of primitive life still have some hold on us; how much more on those whose imagination can picture nothing else!

[1] The word "moral" comes from the Latin *mores*, customs.

## CHAPTER 14

### NATURAL SELFISHNESS AND UNSELFISHNESS

A PHILOSOPHER who understands that moral units, such as persons, are not substances but modes of substance—I mean that they are incidental to a certain movement in deeper things—will not be disinclined to admit any degree of unselfishness to be possible, even to utter self-sacrifice. These unitary roving creatures, whom we suppose to be obviously interested in themselves, have no existence of themselves; they spring from what they know not of, and they enact whatever purposes their unknown source may have put into them together with life. These purposes may therefore be quite other than their own preservation or private benefit; yet if they have clear souls, and are wise, they will find their happiness in their natural function, however disinterested this may be. Since they are addressed to it initially, by the constitution of the seed from which they grow (for I am not speaking of forced sacrifices), they can achieve integrity and happiness only by loving their congenital function, and adoring the ulterior end which their existence serves. There may be animals capable of acting and willing only for the sake of other animals, for whom they pave the way; or they may blindly supply a link in some process itself without a purpose.

Man, however, is not one of these purely instrumental animals. He is a selfish or, as he calls it, a rational creature, and nothing offends him more than to feel himself a slave. Not that he lacks altruistic instincts, very strong in respect to his young children. Even impersonal objects or duties sometimes fascinate his imagination, such as his religion or the glory of his nation and government. But in human nature generous impulses are occasional and reversible; they are absent in childhood, in dreams, in extremities; they are often weak or soured in old age. They form amiable interludes like tearful sentiments in a ruffian; or they are pleasant self-deceptive hypocrisies, acted out, like civility to strangers, because such is in society the path of least resistance. Strain the situation, however, dig a little beneath the surface, and you will find a ferocious, persistent, profound selfishness.

We feel this to be a fault, and I may be accused of misanthropy in describing it: yet it is an integral part of what some moralists think the greatest possible virtue, individuality. The transitive instincts have fallen into a vortex, or tied a knot: organs for self-defence, or parasitical organs, like sports or hobbies, enriching the life of the individual, have grown about the transmissible seed. This integrated system has generated a reflective consciousness; it remembers and forecasts its own career, and the landscapes and passions that solicit it no longer do so absolutely, for the mind surveys or cultivates them deliberately; they are its fond possessions, nursed and brooded over day and night. Even the pre-personal impulses are brought into this personal vortex: the lusty male becomes a husband to be waited on, the father becomes a chieftain, the blind gregarious fighter becomes a deliberate bandit, or champion, or cock of the walk. Even when he still obeys impulses that serve other people, he serves them for the sake of his own pleasure or ambition; and pride and willfulness may gruffly drive him to refuse or to denaturalise the service that his old nature might have prompted him to render.

Man is doubtless surpassed in selfishness by some animals, as by others in unselfishness. The concentration of interest within one's own skin and one's own period of life is perhaps even greater in fishes, without mates or recognised offspring, or in persistent flies without imagination. Man is social even in his egotism, like a government in malicious diplomatic relations with foreign powers. He may retain enthusiasms borrowed from his parents and play fellows, or from the established religion, classical schooling, or code of chivalry perhaps respected by the gentleman. But he serves his present mind, not his total nature, as a politician serves his party prejudices and ideas rather than the interests of the people, which he absurdly assumes to be identical with what is pleasing to his fancy at the passing moment. As to what might prove pleasing to *others* in the long course of their experience, he is incapable of appropriating or of conceiving anything so complex and ambiguous. His own interests, vivid, limited, and passionate, are also sometimes more noble than would be that infinite routine of little burdens and quarrels which occupies the trudging mind.

But the point to remember is this: any ideal enthusiasm, any loyalty to duty or commandment, is incidental in man. It cannot be relied upon. You must fortify it by personal appeals, by wages in this world or the other, by some smiling prospect opened to the

## SLAVERY  73

social conscript. This was long ago discovered by wise religions, which promised the saints heaven and gave the clergy the earth; but foolish governments and philosophies in our day sometimes try to get on without reconciling the individual. The result, sooner or later, is disaster; their constituency deserts them with a wonderfully sharp and sudden revulsion of feeling. Converts, infidels, and revolutionaries have bad memories and worse tempers. To justify their apostasy and heal the wounds it may have caused they require the balm of libelling their past and lording it over their new surroundings. They are the founders of the worst tyrannies.

## CHAPTER 15

### SLAVERY

BEYOND necessary and voluntary servitude, a third kind of servitude is possible, which is involuntary yet accidental. I mean slavery. Nothing could be less involved in spontaneous life than that one man should be merely an instrument in the service of another. Each man is by nature an end to himself, and sufficient unto himself, except precisely where necessary or voluntary servitude has made him subject to other persons and things. But necessary servitude is no slavery, since it provides the means of life and of freedom; and voluntary servitude can never go so far, being voluntary, as to abdicate the privilege of terminating that servitude at will. The slave, by definition, cannot abandon his service, yet the master could normally live without that slave; so that servitude of this kind arises only out of accidental complications in human economy.

The first slaves were captives seized in some raid, as it were prisoners of war, whom the raider might have killed but preferred to keep alive in gangs, to do hard labour in ships or mines, or perhaps singly, if he could trust them, for domestic service. Women and boys would make good slaves of the latter kind.

I will not attempt to trace the history of slavery, now almost extinct; but there was a precedent or accompaniment to this slavery which will probably last forever and which is morally most instructive. There were tamed or domestic animals and beasts of burden.

Animals had at first been hunted in self-defence or for food; but some of them, when captured alive, could advantageously be turned into slaves. For this purpose it was requisite either to tame them or to breed them tame. Now, when an animal is tamed he has been more or less kindly persuaded. We might say that his original vital initiative has been acknowledged, studied, and cleverly turned to the trainer's uses. In one sense his free will has been enlisted, according to the contract-theory of government. His consent to do the trick or the work required has been secured by bribes, blows, or narrowed alternatives in action, establishing acquired reflexes and reliable habits. The animal has learned his trade and become wise; the man is served by the animal and becomes rich.

Cruel as the exploitation of animals often is, there remains a margin in it for sympathy and even for superstition. When the cow and the ox were annexed to domestic economy, religion intervened. The cow, and especially the bull, were worshipped and were sacrificed; and it is difficult to establish, from the animal's point of view, the balance of benefit and injury, degradation and sleekness, involved in his servitude. The cattle in our fields and barns do not now seem to suffer, or to resent their captivity; and the eventual hard labour and slaughter that awaits them may be regarded as no worse than the wounds, famines, battles, and lingering death that might have overtaken them in the wild state.

The danger of passing unreasonable moral judgments in such cases, and in politics at large, comes from not considering how natural and how changing are the criteria of benefit and injury involved in living. Undoubtedly cattle in the wild state would resist and resent being domesticated. Our children, too, often resist and resent education, and many reformers deplore the fact that they were forced in childhood to study Latin. Probably it was wasted on them; perhaps they never learned it; perhaps their gifts and temperaments were naturally such as to demand a different employment. So there may be innately roving creatures in our stables, as in our menageries. Yet would our sympathetic romantic souls justify us in going about enthusiastically opening cages and emptying stables? We need not consider the loss to owners or trainers: they could always be compensated at the public expense by a popular government. But from the animals' point of view, would the paved, fenced, cultivated world outside seem a paradise? Would they not perhaps come sneaking back to their stables and to their cages? There is a time for life in the jungle, namely, when nothing else is possible; and there is a time for tame domestic civilised life, even for the brutes, when the alternative is extinction.

The comparison of the just governor to a shepherd has the authority of Plato as well as of the Old and the New Testament. Yet if the shepherd were, as he must have been in the beginning, the owner of the sheep, his care for the flock would be naturally prompted and limited strictly by his proprietary interests. He would not love sheep at all, but only wool and mutton. Nor does breeding with a view to the superexcellence of these products, as it appears at least in England, always seem to profit the sheep themselves in their health or vigour. They are safe from wolves, but often deformed and helpless in their sodden pastures. It is a fate comparable to that of eunuchs or ladies of the seraglio, or lapdogs or other favourites of tyranny. If some fabulist ventured to put a description of their keeper into the sheep's mouth, it would surely not depict him as a ministering angel, but as a driver, a gaoler, a shearer, and a butcher.

At the same time, if the proprietor of great flocks dwelt at a distance and committed the care of his animals to young and unsophisticated shepherds, the interests and feelings of the latter might well begin to coincide with those of their charges; for the more the flock prospered the less grudgingly the shepherds would be paid and the better spoken of. Probably the butchering if not the shearing would be done out of sight, by less familiar and more hardened officials. Then sentiments of a brotherly nature might indeed grow up between lambs, sheep-dog, and shepherds; especially if any one of these shepherds was himself an unhappy captive, suffering from the same cold and heat, not in England, but amid arid and thirsty wastes, and munching hardly less bitter herbs than his silent companions. Then the half-guilty, half-injured mood of Cain or of Esau might perhaps invade our young shepherd, and might transform him into a militant champion not only of his own freedom to run wild, but conceivably also of the same freedom for his sheep, who likewise might prefer to climb dangerously and browse frugally amid mountain crags rather than to rot in clover.

Very young and tame lambs might indeed say: "What a blessing this is, to be led into green pastures and to a clean trough, and be sheltered at night from the wind in a comparatively warm pen, and kept from thoughtlessly straying by a nice watchful dog always running about me! And what a relief, when my wool is getting hot and messy, to have it kindly cut off quite close with a new, safe and very rapid shearing machine!" When a little older, if he preserves his optimism, the lamb might even add philosophically: "What a blessing, too, to die an almost painless and useful death when still young, and be spared the horrors of old age, when sick wethers become so ugly, filthy, feeble, and smelly!" The brave and happy young heroes of a hygienic communism could not have more orthodox sentiments.

So far I have been considering the domestic slavery of animals from their own point of view; but what is its effect on their masters? In the fourth chapter of *Genesis* we read: "*And Abel was a keeper of sheep, but Cain was a tiller of the ground.*" Now in the course of history the pious victims of aggression are usually the settled tillers of the ground, while the keepers of sheep, nomads given to raiding, are the criminal aggressors. How is it that in this case "*the Lord had respect unto Abel and to his offering; but unto Cain and to his offering he had not respect*"? We might be tempted to reply that the children of Abraham, whose sacred book we are quoting, were themselves keepers of sheep, and ready, with the Lord's blessing, to raid and exterminate the agricultural Canaanites. But modern historians are not lacking who possess and admire the militant virtues, and who tell us that tamers and breeders of animals are morally superior to stupid peasants content to cultivate their inherited plot of ground. Certainly in the beginning it must have been the cleverer and more enterprising members of the tribe who first stopped picking nuts, berries, acorns, and herbs and took to trapping or shooting animals for food. The young of these animals might sometimes be kept as pets, and might breed in captivity. Dogs might become companions and aids in hunting, and horses, above all, splendid creatures to mount. The ethos of the hunter and rider is glorious, compared with that of the kitchen gardener; and it will certainly be the hordes of migratory cavalry that will conquer the lowland peasantry and become lords of the soil as well as of the husbandman. Later, when a feudal society is formed and especially when this society becomes a great monarchy, the peasants will not make bad soldiers in trained cohorts and

## SLAVERY

phalanxes; but they have become conscripts, initially regarding military service as a terrible imposition. Only peasant proprietors, who have much of the masterful freeman in their disposition, still go to war willingly when their possessions are threatened.

All this belongs to the past or is obsolescent; but new forms of mastership and a new form of slavery appears on the horizon. Animals will henceforth be little wanted for tillage or travel; agriculture will be carried on by mechanics, accustomed to town pleasures and belonging to political unions. Everybody, rich and poor, will need to use machines and will like to do so: for a good machine calls forth and satisfies much the same sense of mastery and of judicious action as did riding a good horse: there is the same control to be exercised over a greater physical force, with an even more exact manifestation of your own will and purpose. The natural concomitant reward of virtue, the joy of doing something well, will therefore be at everybody's command at all hours.

For at school, and even in the public nursery and Kindergarten, everyone will have to be carefully watched and encouraged to cultivate and learn to practice, just for sport, the particular lordly art for which he shows most aptitude; and at the proper age he will be assigned to that particular public service. Ample and suitable food will be provided for him and his kind. Thus both the primary needs of human nature will have been duly satisfied, leaving a man's whole mind free and clear for his appointed duties. Exact fulfillment of these will indeed be required of him by custom and law, because laxity in running any part of the vast and delicate engine of universal industry would derange the other parts and cause general inconvenience if not disaster. For we must never forget that among the raw materials of industry one of the most important is man, and even all the atomic and stellar energy as yet wasted would be utterly useless, and would never of itself make the simplest machine, such as a wheel, unless some man had first put it together and still stood by to mend it when it goes wrong. Such is the terrible responsibility that will weigh upon every man, as upon no other creature in the universe. Civilisation will require and must enlist every human being in its perpetual service. To hang back would be treason and would deserve death. There need be no beasts of burden, no masters and servants, no hireling, no speculators; but to the perfect order of society all men, even their leaders, must be slaves in soul and in body.

## CHAPTER 16

### TRANSITION FROM CUSTOM TO GOVERNMENT

LANGUAGE and religion, the family, the gang following a leader, arise of themselves, before anyone has noticed or desired them. How indeed could they have been planned or desired when no one as yet had experience of anything that could suggest such notions? When, however, these things have arisen and perhaps assumed rival forms, attention is attracted to them; the sense of a double possibility, of a compulsion to choose, enables a man to say that the one preferred is *better* than the other. His instinct now operates in the light of ideas; he is conscious of what he is doing; perhaps he plumes himself on his action and boastfully bids everyone observe him (as children do in their feats). He feels a disposition steadily to repeat what he has done, and to demand that others should do likewise: and in this case he would be said to act according to free will and reason and an idea of the best.

Such consciousness of preference, and such orders published to the world to conform to these preferences, are common in societies without government, and may even be made in soliloquy, as in prayers and curses; but the passage is easy from preferences expressed in imperious maxims to the systematic use of force and the establishment of law. All that need be added is a certain countenance from public opinion, and a precedent that the general judgment is to be enforced. Such a precedent is not far to seek; for impulsive men and mobs enforce their wills before they express them in words or even in thought. By the time a law is established, an organ for enforcing it already exists in the strong right arm of the legislator, probably not unpractised in anticipating his legislation by a vigorous use of the cudgel.

Indeed, custom in most communities is far more sacred and unbreakable than law, and some spontaneous authority, chieftain, prophet, or boss is more respected than the government. Political institutions do not serve to establish the ascendancy of rules in society; they serve merely to register this ascendancy or to apply it in detail, or determine it precisely in debatable instances. It is for this reason, doubtless, that politics seem to deal so preponderantly with questions of men and methods; large questions of policy and of human ideals are settled behind the politician's back by the growth of social institutions. The monarchy, the town meeting, the Church, the army, the family, property, justice, all arise and are virtually in operation before a law or an explicit agreement consecrates or defines them; and the history of politics is accordingly reduced almost entirely to the compromises and transitions between ruling interests when they conflict openly and threaten a civil war.

Government is a modification of war, a means of using compulsion without shedding so much blood. Of course this relative bloodlessness of government comes from the aversion to war felt by the person who is coerced, a war in which he might be the only combatant on his side. Save for that apprehension he would resist the police, the tax-gatherer, and the recruiting sergeant. All government is therefore potential war; and if this threat and the ability to use force disappear, government ceases. In the countries, for instance, in which laws are not enforced, there is, to that extent, no government. Those who fancy themselves in power are simply one or more social philosophers editing precepts for the public; the public admires these precepts, and the philosophers' function is fulfilled. But if this academy employs an armed force to arrest and eventually execute or mulct anyone who does not respect their edicts, then they are a government; and to take people prisoners, to kill or despoil them are acts of war. Every government is essentially an army carrying on a perpetual campaign in its own territory; it is always up in arms against actual or possible faction—called illegality or crime.

This does not mean that, in the absence of government, chaos would return. Social pressure, spontaneous unanimity, and cooperation, when they exist, are far stronger forces than force itself: they operate directly, through instincts contagiously set in motion, whereas organised eventual force operates indirectly only, by suppressing spontaneous instinct through fear of punishment—a process full of uncertainty and friction, and never final, since the tendency to rebellion remains in the persons cowed. Government is always an evil and sometimes also a good, as war is. It renders acute for the moment that friction and disarray which it tries to suppress by its brutal agencies. But the cooperative and unanimous action which may be imperfectly secured through government is a good, and may be perfectly secured, in many cases, without government.

Consider, for instance, the prevalence and authority of a language. As everyone is imitative, as everyone likes to understand and to be understood, as defects or novelties of speech, unless meant to instruct or to amuse, seem ridiculous and discreditable, a whole community with one accord will use and cultivate the same language; and this is a thoroughly involuntary, yet contented, uniformity. Language is not, at first and when at its best, a concern of government. But it sometimes becomes so; and it is interesting to observe on what occasions. When, owing to rivalry between several languages, or to the unwillingness of the people frankly to speak their several local dialects, official schools are set up to teach the official language to children, lest they should succumb to another more prevalent way of speaking—then language falls within the purview of government. It becomes compulsory, if official schooling is cumpulsory; in any case, it is promoted by mechanical arrangements, which the government uses force to maintain. And it may be noticed in passing that this interference of government with language, as it is a symptom of social conflict or disease, is also an evil omen for the beauty and cohesion of language itself. It makes of living language a partly dead language; and what a laboured Latinity was at the dawn of modern times, that will all literature in modern languages become if governments insist on an artificial uniformity in the speech of different classes and different regions. The school-board or board-school languages of our great democracies threaten to become self-conscious, affected, cramped, and, because not frankly popular, spotted with horrible barbarisms. Nobody's speech is now either merrily plebeian or thoroughly refined.

A more momentous instance of the same thing is seen in religion. Here social pressure is rather more conscious, as religion, at least in modern times, does not pervade society and thought as language does. The individual more often is tempted to ask: Why should I worship in that way, or worship at all, or believe this story, or conform to this troublesome precept? Yet where a wave of religion sweeps a people, as it often does, it is wonderful what volume and comprehensiveness it acquires: more than human courage and conceit would be needed, in many an instance, to resist it. Yet in all this the government need not have spoken; it need not even have existed. But when incipient imaginings of indocile minds, or the assault of a foreign or new religion, disturb social convention; when altars are profaned and gods denied and cults neglected, then those shocked and made uneasy by these disturbances may put their heads together. The ancient, spontaneous, and occasional practice of punishing the blasphemer, or of sacrificing the man of evil omen, will be revived by acclamation; and lest fresh cases should go unpunished, a tribunal armed with secular powers—a clerical police—is charged with watching over the community. Or the existing military organisation takes over the supervision of religion lest, in the absence of social unanimity and social pressure, some needful part of it should lapse. Religion thus becomes a province of government, an occasion for steady war. Historians may decide, if they can, whether this is a sign of strength or of weakness in religion, when religion of itself seems too weak to dominate society, yet too fierce to allow society to disregard it. A consequence sometimes is that the fanatics are caught in their own trap, since their religion is diverted by the government that protects it to the service of its own interests. Then we have national churches, national philosophies, and cultural missions in the service of trade and of political conquest.

It is much in the same way that social rules relating to crime and to property pass under the aegis of governments and become formal laws. The submission to government is never complete, e.g. property in small articles—so precious to womankind—is not legally controlled within families; and the punishment of many crimes is tacitly left to the art of self-defence, with words, fists, or revolvers. Law sometimes is superseded by the spontaneous actions of judges and juries, pronouncing the legally guilty innocent, or vice versa: then, as in the cases of Dreyfus and Madame Caillaux, strong social instinct or party passion consciously resumes its authority, and disdains legality. It is by no means to be assumed that legality in such a case is the better form of justice. For as in language and religion, so in the matter of crime or property, government introduces an external and often antithetical element. Enactment has taken the place of living social instinct, and the ideals which that instinct projects, which are the sole criteria of justice, may be thwarted rather than helped by that codification. What makes genial illegalities— duels, elopements, honourable perjuries, etc.—dangerous to society is not that they abstract from law—all true morality does so, because it is deeper than law—but that they often express an antiquated or partisan or disruptive ethos; a form of morality doubtless more vital but perhaps more partial than that which the written law has consecrated. Not all the heroic victims of legality are martyrs to a nobler cause.

Since the operation of government is a sort of constant war, it is intelligible that government should assert itself especially when the nation is attacked by its neighbours or takes to the warpath of its own accord. Even the chase fosters leadership and many a rule which—like not shooting foxes—is deeply sacred; but the chase after another set of huntsmen calls for greater concentration of authority, greater discipline, and, what is very significant, a more persistent organization. Hence the general of the army becomes naturally the first king, or the first president. The council of war is the first parliament, the first cabinet, and the first supreme court. War is as impossible without a virtual government, as government without a virtual war.

It must not be supposed, however, that if government were abolished and social institutions remained alone, war would cease; on the contrary, war would become more obvious and more pervasive. The latency of war which we call peace, and owe to governments (where not to chance) would disappear or become rarer; and war would greet us if not in every house, certainly round every corner. To fight is a primitive necessity; life cannot take or keep any definite form without crowding out, crushing, or devouring some other form of life. But there are gentle and violent methods of assimilation, and self-assertion may take the form of attraction as well as of suppression. The weaker life in any case perishes, but it may perish insensibly, by being transformed rather than annihilated. All depends on the mechanism that does the execution; and it is here that the great alternatives present themselves between the various forms of society, authority or political government. People long coerce one another of their private initiative or follow some tradition, before they begin to do so through special military or legal agents. Government concentrates domination in its own hands, and regulates it. It neither originates nor abolishes domination.

It is true that governments continually wage wars of their own, which if society had had no government, or a government of a different sort, would have been avoided—as wars of succession would not occur in the absence of hereditary monarchy. But this (as we shall see) is due to the fact that government is a special organ of society, with a life of its own, and adds to the irritable interests and dangers, as well as to the resources of the society it grows in. While without possessing a hereditary monarchy people could not have wars of succession, they would have wars about whatever other things they possessed; and they could never be safely and altogether at peace unless they possessed nothing, and did not exist.

# PART TWO

## Economic Arts

# CHAPTER 1

## THE BIRTH OF ART

ALL animals seize and crush their food in their mouths or gullets, and many seize it first with their paws and tear it with claws or talons. Now every human infant has a like native impulse and power to seize any small object at hand; and if, when older and stronger, he seizes a heavy stick, he will immensely increase the range and power of his arm to strike a blow. Similarly if he seizes a pointed stone, he may easily break things that defy his teeth. Such sticks and stones are the primitive instruments of human art, and simply extend beyond the living body the functions of teeth and claws.

With this, the human psyche has begun to bring parts of the surrounding world under its dominion. This involves no miracle, no immaterial power. Every psyche, in proportion to the complexity and precision of the powers involved in its seminal heritage, spreads around it a sort of magnetic field; its presence and quality are faintly traceable throughout its environment, like the radiation of smell or of invisible gravity. But this self-transcendent effect of any living creature on its neighbours remains for the most part imperceptible or marked only by a vague tension or, as it were, a shadow passing over things without disturbing them materially. There is needed, for instance, an intense and deeply intentional concentration of a glance to cause a passer-by to feel it, and turn his head; yet not only the force but the motive and spirit of that glance may be sometimes felt strongly, and be a signal for distinct emotions of terror, repulsion, amusement, or attraction. These are psychic reactions to another psyche, which is exerting only an ethereal force, yet one that some children and animals are quick to distinguish.

It is when the psyche uses the human hand that its influence can begin to transform inanimate matter. The first man who wields a stick, the first child who throws a stone, has initiated that use of material instruments which has created for us the immense and overpowering modern mechanism of industry, trade, and war. And this has happened without any miraculous intervention of disembodied foresight or reason. Expert skill in doing what is feasible merely extends the eagerness of the suckling to swallow what is swallowable. It is the need of free exercise for all organs that *initiates* useful arts; their utility, when discovered, flatters the pride of the discoverer, as a stroke of good luck flatters the gamester; for it not only supplies a new resource and increases the powers and demands of the lucky fellow, but convinces him that he has a guiding star or native genius, or a vocation to serve the whole human race. Prometheus, in discovering fire (which the poets call bringing it down from heaven), acquired an undeserved fame for philanthropy. Fire breaks out spontaneously sometimes in the woods, and must have been struck a thousand times by primitive man ferreting in the jungle. Where intelligence and thrift appear is in observing and applying the use of fire in keeping away wild beasts, roasting or (when pots existed) boiling victuals, and in melting metals so as to render them malleable.

These arts have a less pious moral effect than has the practice of agriculture or even of taming and breeding animals. In work upon dead matter nature seems to do less and man feels that he does everything. Bits of stone, wood, or metal in reality condition the character of the service they can come to render to human life as much as do earth and seeds, rain and sunshine; but they do not, like plants, grow of themselves and reach highly articulate forms such as human fancy or labour can never rival. What we call dead matter seems relatively passive and changeless, although this turns out to be a profound error, caused by the blanketing effect of summary human sensations turned upon the object and, for the fool, seeming to define it. But of all the secret agitation and power of wood and clay and even of stone, nothing reveals itself at first except its deadness. You may pick it up, cut it up, throw it about, or heap it together and it will remain, for the most part, as you left it. This constancy of inanimate things on the scale of domestic instruments renders them faithful missiles to use against animals and enemies, or means of bending the wider elements, land, water, and the jungle itself, to human convenience.

The maker or skillful user of tools feels a different attachment to them from that which the farmer feels to his land or his cattle.

## THE BIRTH OF ART

His possessions lend the landlord his dignity; they probably have been inherited, since they form a continuous source of livelihood and a relatively safe nest where an entire life is profitably spent and a family is founded that may grow into a clan. The land sustains its lord, morally no less than materially; so much so that in feudal times the nobility bore the names of their estates and even kings those of their dominions. And it was only a recognition of their position when they learned to love their lands and their families, their castles and tenants, and to feel pride in their worth and welfare. But the pride of the artisan in his art and its uses is pride in himself. His tools are indeed precious, but his use of them is not a duty but a feat, and it is in his skill and ability to make things as he wishes them to be that he rejoices. His distinction, when he is a great master, is not to be called after his works but that his works should be called by his personal name.

Probably the first use made of sticks and stones as implements was in attack or defence or at least in knocking down fruits or any other object out of reach of the hand. This militant or destructive posture appears necessarily in the chase, where the original purpose is to get food: a posture that belongs essentially to war. These two most pressing occasions for using weapons, hunting and fighting, make the manufacture of weapons the most competitive and crucial of arts in human society, and never more so than it is now. The scale and the destructive power of armaments have lately increased so surprisingly that we can see, as if magnified for our instruction, what is the ultimate or fatal function of mechanical arts: namely, to make primal Will in man irresponsible and absolute. There is a fundamentally cruel egotistical joy in plucking, breaking, killing anything. This passion is normally checked and balanced by others; but the greater and swifter the power that mechanical instruments put in man's hands, the greater will be the occasional temptation that will assail him to put this power to the test. And this is socially and morally an omnipotent power, less to produce than to destroy, since physical force can sweep the ground and exterminate the bearers of every moral tradition.

Apart from the present plight of a mechanised world, I suspect that there is a profound duplicity in the destiny which the power of making tools opens up to mankind. Evidently it expands the range and multiplies the instruments of the psyche, so that man in his frail body, becomes the master and reconstructor of everything on the earth's surface. But morally this triumph is a snare. Individually, if bred under an agricultural regimen, the boy with mechanical aptitudes will emancipate himself, become a pedlar, a mountebank, a lion-tamer, a sailor, an explorer, a pilferer, a bandit. The world he moves in will become more and more a human, an artificial world. The more expert he grows in his tricks, the less respect he will have for the matter he works on, and the more confidence in his own abilities. Collectively the class of artisans and mechanics will be festively proud of themselves, jealous of one another personally, like all artists, but animated with much *esprit de corps*, and factious only against men of other professions, and contemptuous above all of peasants and clerics. Having power over society, when society has begun to think their wares indispensable, they will push their corporate claims to the utmost, be turbulent in politics, and ready to impose monopolies and even governments.

All this flows from the economic direction in which the toolmaker or commodity-maker directs his interest. He triumphs by enlarging the sphere of human material possessions, material power, and material demands. His ideal (if he were made articulate) would seem to be to supply everybody with the greatest possible quantity and variety of things; and he, by helping to make these things, would naturally deserve to enjoy any amount of them of the best quality. There is perhaps a dialectical difficulty in this expectation; for if the artisan is fully employed in making one sort of material commodity, it seems that he could hardly have taste or time to enjoy or consume a daily growing number of other luxuries, even if they were socially supplied gratis. His body and his mind would neither need nor enjoy the greater part of them. However, he might have all he wanted, so long as he worked as hard as he could.

But what is "work"? When the first man or boy made his first tool he did so in play, out of curiosity at seeing the way in which long grasses or pliable stems could be woven together to make a basket that would hold pebbles or nuts or berries, and enable him to carry them about. Or he was intellectually fascinated by the transformations that he would cause an object to undergo, and the way in which he could make it imitate something else, so as to astonish or deceive people, and make them laugh. These amusements were voluntary; they were entertaining; yet they were the

## THE BIRTH OF ART

beginnings of mechanical industry. They were also, however, the beginnings of liberal arts. This "work" might well be a free, happy, and enlightening occupation, its own reward, and the product of it might be good, not for being useful but for being beautiful.

There is a sense, indeed, in which the effort to dominate matter materially is, in the Stoics' phrase, "contrary to nature"; not that it cannot be done, and done brilliantly up to a certain point, but that the intrinsic constitution of man and of the world he lives in limits the profitable effects that they can have on one another. Agriculture rewards the labouring man by yielding better and more abundant food for him near at hand, and at the same time developing certain splendid forms of vegetation impossible in the jungle. But the manufacture of instruments renders all sorts of new works possible which may be tempting to the producer, if he can sell the product at a good price, but may be bad for him as an occupation and bad for the misguided buyers as a luxury: acquisitive vice in the conceited inventor; prodigal vice in the others. Cooperative vices may build a Tower of Babel, until the foundations give way, and vain indulgence and vain labour collapse together.

In so far, on the contrary, as making and using instruments can remain liberal arts, "work" is not carried on under external pressure but with a vital liberty, which studies and remoulds matter in sympathy with its own life or in ideal variations upon it, expressing human capacity for conception and enjoyment. This element is primitive and able to pervade economic arts, as well as the whole militant order of society, when work or war responds to a native inclination and is carried on with a masterful understanding of the means employed and of their object. Arts may all be liberal without ceasing to be useful, or when they become useful accidentally; and in a well ordered community few or none of the offices of daily life would lack a spiritual sanction. It is rather "fine" arts that grow pale and empty, as well as ugly, when they are altogether separated from economic and moral uses, and express only caprice, luxury, and affectation. The tyranny of forced labour, in its turn, defeats the moral function of economic art, which is to enlarge vital liberty.

## CHAPTER 2

### CLAIMS AND CONFLICTS OF THE ARTS

Arts are animated by an interest which becomes the criterion of their excellence. This interest may be intrinsic to the action, as in singing; or it may be rooted in some other function of the organism, as in tilling the earth; for in this art little remains of the childish interest in delving for its own sake; all is hard labour for the hands, done to satisfy a lively impulse of the mouth and a radical need of the belly. Casual effects that an idle man's action may have, such as making a slightly meandering path through a field by often walking across it, are signs of his passage; but since his Will in that action was only to cross the field and not to make the path, the path was not a product of economic art, although it may have economic and even legal effects by establishing a right of way.

Society is traversed by paths of this kind: moulds set by casual action for public action, such that, although never intended, they now complicate social existence with a network of needless difficulties and foolish compulsions. An implication of this is that society dominates more than it is dominated. It was not originally a work of art, and education and government have a hard task in trying to make an art of it.

Not all arts are as clear as agriculture in their problem and criterion, but in principle they all rely on some hunger in the psyche, to be relieved by some specific eventual attainment, perhaps only vaguely conceived and easily missed by the groping efforts of inexperienced souls, perhaps under hopeless conditions. Even the primitive husbandman is not sure of success. Some rival may claim his land; the incorrigible jungle may invade it; inundations, drought, or a plague of insects may destroy his crop, or an enemy horde may purloin it. Misfortune, if he has no other means of subsistence, will seem to him the more unjust, the more intelligent and constant have been his exertions. Land, when a man has cultivated it, seems to him his by right, as do all its products. So too do his tools. Agriculture, by virtue of its calculable periodic fruits, excites the feeling of proprietorship with a particular force. It is not only his present property that a wicked enemy threatens to rob the farmer of, but of his father's heritage, of his whole future and of that of his children. He will take up arms, and, if he has no nearer protector, will call on heaven for vengeance with a mounting fervour of devotion.

This intense proprietary passion repeats in a human form the absolute fury with which the bulldog clings to whatever he holds in his teeth. The same feeling, variously qualified, animates all economic art. It overflows illegitimately but intelligibly into the liberal arts also, even into what we call fine art. This happens because the artist and his work are dynamic units in the realm of matter which possess or attract a strong interest in their preservation, or in continued exercise of the rare faculties thus acquired. Such moral units become nuclei for a whole web of interests that seem all the more urgent in that they are precarious. They may lapse in oneself, and when they flare up most vividly they may be denied and opposed by other people.

Here we have a cue, if I am not mistaken, to the vital human side, hidden in the psyche, of all economic arts. The secret economy of an animal organism passes in the political world for an inspiration by ideal ambitions or a dramatic evolution of history according to providential or dialectical laws. History is indeed tragic enough; but why have men such misguided ambitions and inexplicable enthusiasms? That they should ever invent such dialectical laws or devious divine designs is itself evidence of psychic promptings crossing observation and breeding impossible expectations and vain anxieties. Economic arts in particular, which are most closely controlled by the real potentialities of matter, nevertheless deviate in all directions from rational industry, run into the opposite blind alleys of avarice and luxury, and equip militant egotism with instruments for its mad experiments. All this occurs because the motive force in economic labour always remains some offshoot of primitive greed and cupidity. The good to be attained is not seen or imagined; there is at bottom only an indiscriminate impulse to grasp, to keep, and to swallow. This lends demogogues their power, gamblers and speculators their false hopes, and misers a chuckling contentment in their misery.

Anthropologists and economists may trace all the forms that domestic and rural life has assumed; and historians may describe the quick development of civilisation in various times and places, with the long decadence or the sudden catastrophes, due to barbarian conquests or perverse revolutions, that have caused civilisation to decline, often to the point of local extinction. I take a summary knowledge of those things for granted, and limit myself to the side of the subject which touches political morals, or the fortunes of vital liberty in the face of all kinds of alien oppression. And the reader must not expect me to trace the fortunes of liberty historically or eschatologically, as if all were progress towards perfection. Everything in this world, considered temporally, is a progress towards death. True progress is an approach, in favourable seasons, to perfection in some kind of life. It is, in other words, the emergence of *virtue* of any kind, in any place and for any period, out of the play of dominations and powers. Those whose philosophy formulates alleged "laws of history" or "dialectic of events" would call my results "abstract"; and they certainly neglect the infinite miscellany of facts, and regard only interesting classes or types of facts in their interesting relations. Such a consideration of things is what I would call moral, and I am confident that the reader will find my account of history less abstract than that of the historical philosophers. For they attribute events to abstract laws or ideal implications of essences; so that their history is vitiated by a sectarian interpretation of events and by "wishful thinking," and their moral judgment is vitiated by inhumanity and by the worship of success and of endless mutation.

All arts are powers in danger of becoming dominations because, necessarily having organs in the psyche and many of them also instruments in the public world, they are rivals, and each tends to monopolise the energies of life at the expense of other developments or even at the price of life itself. The economic arts, however, just because their instruments and their subject matter are alike physical, are open and honest rivals, and it is easier in regard to them for the critic to conceive the combinations or the alternative sacrifices that they may make, so that each might be developed most completely where circumstances favour it, without impeding the development of the others at other times and places. In other words, a rational peace among economic arts is conceivable and might perhaps be established, if mankind could be governed by a single enlightened and impartial authority. Great economic developments are not necessary to life, if population does not outrun the local means of support. If the simpler economy of one nation were not invaded by the richer economy of another nation, more favourably endowed for the arts prevalent at that moment, all might practise their own industries in peace, and make such exchanges as did not derange them.

I am not professing to offer recommendations on this subject or on any other. Those concerned must speak for themselves if they can distinguish their real needs and powers and are not carried away by needless or hopeless ambitions. The desire, for instance, of those who are naturally different to become socially alike makes for moral suicide, as if cows wished to behave like bulls, or bulls like cows. The generative order of nature is the seedbed of every kind of beauty and virtue; and both can be realised only by fidelity in the growth of the psyche to its own potentialities. Not all these can be realised, nor any of them always, but only as circumstances permit. The virtues that any man or society will actually manifest are therefore always variable; but only those will be genuine that can take root in the psyche, so as to become definite and even hereditary. Uncongenial virtues or opinions that a man may assume for worldly reasons are hypocritical and really, in him, vices. It may, however, be a genuine virtue in someone else, but not when injected into a creature whose natural life it will derange, contravene, and perhaps destroy.

Such fatal experiments are more easily recognised and avoided in material than in moral collisions. For this reason economic arts, though occasionally lost or crippled in some regions, have on the whole maintained or slowly improved their ancient methods until recent times, when these methods have been suddenly transformed by the invention of machinery propelled by steam or electricity. For thousands of years ploughing, reaping, milking, and cooking had preserved their fundamental character throughout the world; and spinning, weaving, and building had varied chiefly on the decorative or monumental side, while mechanically constant in their principles. But meantime in the liberal arts all has been mutation without progress, because no quick material control excluded all physically possible vagaries in language, religion, philosophy, manners, and dress. Edible mushrooms are distinguishable at sight from bad ones; but the poison of vice in conduct, and in government, though visibly damaging and sometimes fatal, seduces generation after generation in their vital innocence and nation after nation in their helpless public fatuity.

## CHAPTER 3

### AMBIGUITY OF "SPIRIT" IN THE ARTS

There is a sense in which life and reason may be said to vivify the arts, but this sense is recondite and remote from the conceit and rashness with which people speak of the "spirit" in history or of "reason" in the universe. It is not at all true that, as Virgil says, mind *agitates* a lump of formless matter and *mixes itself* with the vast body of nature.[1] Mind would have to become matter before it could do that. Nor is it true even in the human fine arts or in eloquence that there is a previous purely mental image that the sculptor's hand or the speaker's words retrace when they are inspired. A deliberate speaker may, in conversation or argument, think of what he will say before he says it; but that thought is itself a form of words coming spontaneously into his mind by gift of his unforeseen vital fertility. The physical agitation issuing in that inspiration is felt strongly in the body, and noticed by the listener. Were that total bodily action wanting there would be no true eloquence, but only the cold recitation of a phrase not then being bred in the man's heart. The good actor must train his pose and features to imitate the gesture of all the passions, so as to seem to feel them: whether he feels them a little or not is immaterial.[2]

Similarly the marble block[3] contains all possible geometrical forms in its pure extension, but only passively and without discrimination, and without predisposition of any sort in favour of any one of them. It is the psyche in the artist, producing all sorts of specific stresses and modifications among the physical impressions it receives, that guides the hand in quite abstractedly hitting upon or fantastically evoking them, and evoking at the same time, and even before, a new evanescent image in the mind; but this dream-image

---

[1] Mens agitat molem et magno se corpore miscet.—*Æneid*, VI, 727.
[2] Cf. Diderot: *Le Paradoxe du Comédien*.
[3] Non ha l'ottimo artista alcun concetto
che un marmo solo in sè non circonscriva
col suo soverchio, e solo a quell'arriva
la man che ubbedisce all'intelletto.
                                       Michelangelo.

the artist will find it difficult to define, retain, or reproduce in his work. What his hand (or his verbal imagination, if he is a poet) supplies spontaneously will form the real starting point and first guide in his inspiration. Round it his expert art may then arrange and rearrange other elements, suggesting themselves spontaneously or habitually, until he has composed a satisfying total design, if ever he succeeds in doing so. This complex and tentative labour of the psyche Michelangelo attributes to the "intellect," following Platonic tradition; but this "intellect" was conceived mythologically as a divine and unchanging life, a pure ideal of the contemplative ecstasy that the artist himself would attain, if he could perfect his every intuition, and hold it unclouded for all eternity.

This ultimate vision of the spirit is not essentially ultimate in time, as if art began with making tools and ended with pure music or religious ecstasy. Spirit, in so far as it is spirit, is pure from the beginning, and the sense of precision and triumph that may escape from a blow well struck, or a dance well danced, is like the widow's mite in the life of spirit: an obscure and forgotten virtue peeping for a moment out of the tangle of animal misery and greed. So the rudest primitive arts, like the elementary passions, throw out glints and sparks of vital liberty glorying in something well done; and the perfection of action, dominating matter, realises the good and the beautiful at every stage. The useful does not possess these virtues for being useful; but the art of devising and executing useful works has a vital virtue of its own, which sheds a modest and healthful rightness and beauty over those works, not for their utility, but for their intrinsic order, as if they were new tribes of animals come by magic to people the magnetic field of the human Will.

## CHAPTER 4

### THE ETHOS OF AGRICULTURE

AT THE root of agriculture we have placed hunger and the avid absolute stubborn Will, not only to devour, but to gather, hold, and guard everything devourable. Such, I think, is the primary impulse that supports all the civilising and civilised attachment to property. That the most brutal of instincts should be the source of all civilisation will not seem a paradox to anyone who understands what life is. This impulse never ceases to be brutal in itself; but a thousand circumlocutions are imposed on it in action; and a thousand refinements of perception and feeling arise in the development of subsidiary organs capable of serving it. Each of these useful organs has a free and liberal life of its own. It does not exist in order to be useful; but if it has not proved cooperative and friendly to the total organism in which it lives, it would not have been propagated with it as an essential part, but would have dropped out, or subsisted only as a burden and a parasite. So the eye and the mechanism that draws the eye to anything bright or moving enable an animal to place and to pursue his prey at a distance; but before doing so the eye must have grown sensitive to physical light, and its inner life, with its cerebral connections, will, under this ethereal stimulus, evoke the *divine sensation* of light, with all the charming variety of colours and the mathematical and aesthetic infinitude of geometrical forms.

Greed in this way, enacted at first only by a rudimentary mouth and stomach in the worm, breeds within and puts forth beyond its skin an endlessly elaborate system of instruments, all internally alive, with each a function and perhaps a joy of its own. The first layer of such outworks is bodily; the second layer is detached materially but in its use and in its form essentially a servant of its master and moved by its master's hand. Then, immaterial in essence and ideal in status, a third layer is formed of images and of moral relations, all deployed and warmed by the central power-station of the human psyche, from which they draw their meaning, and which in turn they enrich with all kinds of sensuous excitements and ideal possessions.

Agriculture displays this process, from the bottom to the top, more clearly than the other arts, because its first steps are the most humble and its last lessons the most certain and sublime. It begins and ends close to nature. It does not allow its derivatives or refinements to seem independent, uncontrolled, or arbitrary. It must always continue to plough the earth, to sow the seed, to watch the harvest ripen precariously according to the weather. The farmer's eyes watch the clouds no less anxiously than the fields; his motive is not star-gazing, yet he learns to distinguish the stars and their movements; he knows how far the conditions of his existence stretch beyond his power of doing anything to control them; and yet his conviction is complete and constantly verified regarding the fruits of his own intelligence, fidelity, and labour. He rises eagerly at dawn; he works all day; and fatigue and food make him heavy and dull in the evening. He remains all his life half stupefied by the monotony and limitation of his life; clever town people think him a dunce; yet his philosophy, with its old proverbs, is sound and comprehensive. He knows the need and justification of both materialism and religion, and their perfect agreement. As for their expression in words, he leaves that to old priests and to young lovers.

It was beside the rural hearth, in rural feasts and by a rustic altar that sound human morals and religion took definite shape. Duties were clearly imposed by the conditions of life and by the precise natural structure of a society, composed of a patriarchal family with its sons, daughters, and servants, all engaged in the traditional service of one household, with no government or institution dominating it, yet running over into kindred households forming a village or scattered over the countryside. All these were bound together by common dangers and misfortunes, blood bonds and blood feuds, in which maxims and standards of fidelity, mutual assistance and condign punishments were traditional. Rooted in the land and in sacred obligations, the mind became conservative with a double strength and wisdom, since its first principles were borrowed from necessity, and at the same time formed a solid nucleus for experience and experiment to weave round that centre a congruous web of law, firmly clinging to the earth by its roots, yet plastic to the winds and the seasons in its branches. Wisdom was fear of the Lord, respect for the conditions of health and prosperity; and with this Lord the people had made a covenant, which would govern their destiny, according to their fidelity to it or their disloyalty.

Every society, however, has its Esau to snap his fingers at home life and at the thrifty Jacob; and even without a positive secession, the wilder son will take to adventure and hunting; and if the love of wealth and domination is not extinct in him, he may learn to train animals, to breed and to domesticate them. I have said something about this, from the point of view of the tamed animals in the chapter about Slavery; here it remains to consider the qualities generated in the tamer, breeder, and driver. About the ethos of shepherds I have also said something in the same place. Commonly the shepherd, even if he has his hut and his nightly bonfire on the mountainside, is only an emissary in an outpost of a partiarchal farm. More distinct, and tending to migration, militancy, and conquest, is the nomad master of cattle, horses, or camels. He prefers the tent or the wagon to the house; he has no temple or shrine, other than perhaps some great stone or mountain that is a landmark for him in the wilderness; and his way of life is possible only in a thinly populated region of desert and sterile plain, where his herds must continually change their pasturage, and from which he is tempted often to raid the fertile lands on his borders. Farsighted, silent, masterful, and abstemious, he appreciates and values in himself the virtues of his mounts: strength, steadiness, sureness, endurance, and swiftness. He is not bored at long days of solitude, or nights under the stars; his thoughts and his songs—for he sings and versifies—are monotonous but pregnant and terse; and his passions, when occasion occurs to excite or to indulge them, are intense, absolute, jealous, and cruel.

Such, at least, is the Asiatic and African type of nomad; but in the North the breeders or hunters of animals, and the seamen, form a different species within the same genus of the primitive dominant man, expert, meditative, and independent. But in the North he is more in need of copious food and drink, with a nebulous intellect, and sentimental melancholy or jovial moods. Strains of these kinds often reappear in stray individuals in the most highly civilised circles in Northern countries; and whole classes, like the British gentry and the American rich, show a marked preference for the country over the town, not only for sport but for residence and companionship; as if immersion in society, which they probably think a duty as well as a necessity, wearied their inner man and they felt an atavistic longing for solitude and the wilds. Their interest in animals, from being sportive, often becomes tender and scientific. They could never have made gods of them, like the dramatic ancients; their gods are vague spirits blowing within them, or perhaps through all nature into new worlds. But there is the same resistance as in Eastern nomads to civilising trammels, material or

## THE ETHOS OF AGRICULTURE

moral, and there is also a comfortless need of profound internal changes, not change merely playful on the surface: as if nature had no fundamental structure, no growth by accretion, and fulfillment in perfections of every kind, but rather a radical indecision and instability, flying from any acquired form as from a prison or a deadly temptation.

Arts, in these persons, have been only a concession to the exigencies of matter, which will hold together and serve a specific purpose only if moulded on definite lines; but there has not been a corresponding articulation in a healthy psyche, fixing its particular goals of progress. Economic arts, here, have therefore always remained servile and ugly, never becoming liberal arts as well. Or if in the elaboration of needlework or of grotesque sculpture, a liberal impulse plays about an essentially useful or superstitious practice the aesthetic element seems never to be separated in the peasant mind from pride in possessing something rich and costly, or pious rspect for something numinous. And it has seemed to me in casual contact with country people, especially in Spain, that the best of their wise proverbs and their enthralling monotonous songs was not wholly native to the soil, but an echo of ancient wailings, Arabian or Gypsy or perhaps ecclesiastical, now adapted to popular taste and to amateur execution. Yet this execution, though unequal, often betrayed the nostalgia of an artistic spirit for the purest tone and the most complex harmony. Such cries, though they may escape the soul anywhere, are not to be attributed to the ethos of agriculture in its practical soundness and hardness. To the rustic, religion speaks of safety; song and dance speak of war or of frisky love; and where there is competition in skill, it is also a competition in courtship. To an agricultural people, mountains and rocks seem horrible, and a beautiful landscape must contain fruit-trees, well-watered meadows, and some convenient copse in the background. When a vocation to some free art arises, as it may, in their milieu, the young man leaves his plough in the field, as the Apostles left their nets by the shore, and accepts the exile and the poverty that face the poet.

## CHAPTER 5

### DOMESTIC MORALITY

REPRODUCTION, like nutrition, is indispensable to an animal race. The economy of sex is therefore no less important in life than the provision of food. The sexual impulse must be strong enough, at certain seasons, to abolish a more prudential selfishness; and special habits and sentiments must be so rooted in the psyches of parents that their offspring may not perish. This, in man, is a serious commitment, whereas in some other species everything is made ready in the young before birth, or very soon after, so that parenthood is not a serious interruption of hunting or migrating or fresh love-affairs. The prolonged childhood of the human race, on the contrary, demands disinterested and probably unrewarded devotion to the young, at least on the mother's part. But the birth of more children, before the first is weaned, fetters the spontaneous affections of the father also to his nest and to his wife. This is the basis of human domestic morality.

Leaving aside the alternative between monogamy and polygamy (an alternative decided by ulterior political conditions rather than by the exigencies of reproduction itself) we may consider the home from the point of view of the child. He begins by being helpless but not will-less, a truly unhappy condition; yet one of the most beautiful harmonies that can arise in nature or in social life comes to his rescue in this plight. The mother, and in some degree the father also, possesses a strong instinct and a heroic determination to look after that child. She supplies him with the milk suitably provided by nature, while protecting him from mishaps, carrying him with her wherever she goes, and helping him to learn to behave as will prove most agreeable and advantageous for him.

This impulse in one person to do for another whatever this other person needs, but cannot do for himself, to divine and to share his secret wishes, and to satisfy them more wisely than he would have done in his inexperience and clumsiness, this is *motherly love* and is like charity in quality but not in scope. Natural brotherly love is not charity at all; for brothers, while better companions as a rule than a parent and a child in play and in adventure, are not naturally sympathetic or self-sacrificing but rather jealous and fault-finding under slight provocation; and this is natural, because they are rivals. It is when not rivals, because of decidedly different ages or temperaments, that the elder may show a fatherly or protective tenderness towards the younger, who will correspond with canine worship and admiration; but this belongs to friendship, the love of the free for the free, rather than to domestic morals.

The lucubrations of Freud about incestuous instincts in infants are of no political moment. Sensual vices can be grafted artificially upon the very young by persons of either sex or any age who are already vicious; but while, as mere sensuality, the effect may survive throughout the victim's life, this sensuality will be diffuse and not concentrated on any person or class of persons. It will not prevent fancy and passion from choosing its normal objects after puberty; and it may provoke, in timid or very haughty tempers, an angry rebuttal of all unsolicited love. Jealousy, on the contrary, provokes murderous impulses towards all rivals, as if they were guilty of insults or theft, which may not be at all the case; and the crimes of jealousy are more often prompted by ambition or offended pride than by infidelity in love. It is when love has become proprietorship and dominion, as in Blue Beards and domestic tyrants, that husbands kill adulterous wives and lovers. This is social vengeance, according to a militant code of honour. When a young lover, who has as yet no conventional rights over his sweetheart or mistress, finds her unfaithful, sadness rather than rage possesses him. It is not his honour, but his conceit or his hope that is mortally wounded, and if he kills anybody, it may be himself; for he feels humbled rather than outraged.

The pre-established harmony between the mother's instinct and the child's wants is less perfect in man than in some other mammals, because it is less automatic at first, and more crossed later by other cares in the mother and by caprice and dangerous gropings in the child. The mother has to undertake to correct as well as to nurse or carry: and an education that is not carried on by example and instinctive imitation (as is education in speech) soon becomes a nuisance both to teacher and pupil. A fundamental sense of union and confidence usually remains, but crossed daily by little episodes of irritation, severe looks, accidents, and tears. The spectre of authority appears behind each human individual that exercises it, and turns him or her into a natural enemy. Only a very timid, submissive, and still vague Will can shape itself exactly according to prescription, and never feel any conflict between service and freedom. The family, and every other form of society, would be slavery but for the suave influence of imitation and custom. "Everybody does this," "nobody does that" become the most imperative, yet the most acceptable, of guides to action. You are checked, thwarted, and harnessed, but you are made safe. Soon you will be proud of your livery, intolerant of any other habit, and ready to die for the red rose or the white.

Prosperous growth in a family or tribe is not what it might be in a flock of sheep. Sheep in a luscious pasture, free from shepherds and wolves, would simply multiply; or, if some variation appeared in the species, it would be only towards greater size and thicker fleeces. All the sheep would get fatter, the rams stronger, the ewes softer, the milk thicker, and the lambs more frisky. The family of a merchant suddenly grown rich might develop among us on similar lines; but I am considering how the primitive family could grow into a more complex moral and political organism, not how it might later altogether dissolve. The primitive human family, even if it lived in the Garden of Eden, would set to work at once to choose a particularly good place for a nest, would spread a soft and sheltered couch, clear a space for a hearth, and dig a hole, to be covered with a flat stone, for a treasure-house and a pantry. Having prehensile hands and agile legs, the young males would soon begin to forage. They would prefer climbing hills and trees, swimming in rivers, and chasing animals, to squatting idle at home. The young women would vie with one another in weaving aprons and arranging feathers, each hoping to make herself more conspicuous than her sisters or her neighbours. While civilisation thus dawned at home, the young men in good weather—for even Eden must have wet seasons—would perhaps silently disperse, one taking to the woods, another to the seashore, both possibly to be lost forever or to return late, sullen and wounded, full of secret knowledge and hidden plans. Next year, perhaps, a girl from another tribe would come back with one of them, carrying a child in her arms.

Soon the family would become numerous and divided into smaller families. Besides daughters-in-law and grandchildren the patriarch might have captives or refugees, become his servants: for even among primitive, scattered, and domestic populations there will be wars and, in wars, prisoners are often the most valuable

## DOMESTIC MORALITY

spoils. These wars may be provoked by militant hordes, living by pillage; but they may also arise automatically and unintentionally between peaceful neighbours. For if the land is fertile, it will soon be overpopulated; families will encroach upon one another, or migrate, and it will be hard in either case to avoid conflicts and feuds. In the jungle there was already a constant silent war of plants upon one another, and of animals on plants, not prompted by militancy but imposed by rivalry in growth: and a living creature cannot be reproached for being alive. Even the religion of charity, which represents the ultimate dictates of experience, wisdom, and sympathy, teaches that the starving have a natural right to seize their part of another's food, which it is a duty to surrender to them. This is feasible and morally satisfying in particular cases and incidentally: but nature cannot allow all species or races to waste away, so that they may share the same fate. Starvation is not naturally a contagious cause of death, but a cause of selection by eliminating the weakest or most passive. Therefore the struggle for life never terminates by the extermination of all; and inevitable war among lovers of peace, though incidentally it encourages militancy in a part of the people, is not itself a sign of militancy but only of some contrariety encountered in innocent growth.

A society based on the family, for instance the Roman, can be strong in war, and constant in it, because its military frontiers, where it runs up against the uncivilised world, are simply the fringe of its moral domestic economy. Rome incorporated what it conquered: and this might have been the beginning of a universal and permanent organisation of mankind according to the generative order of nature, without any intrinsic militancy or willful tyranny. But Rome had met, as its vital economy expanded, races more maturely civilised than itself which succumbed to its government but retained their own ethos, individual and cynical, or individual and mystical, or tribal and militant. All these foreign influences crossed Roman tradition and contributed, with the temptations of wealth and power, to relax Roman virtue at home as well as to prevent it from taking root abroad. There are porcupines and armadillos that have become terribly hostile and overloaded in attempting to defend an innocent life against fate; and they sink under the weight and the drain of their defences.

Had promiscuity and the herd-instinct universally established themselves in the human race, the family might have been reduced to an early episode, of no political importance, in the perilous emergence of one generation out of another. Infants must have had nurses, not necessarily their mothers, to give them the breast or, in civilised times, the bottle. As soon as children could walk and eat, they would have flocked, played, and quarrelled in troops, according to their ages; and in troops they would have been drilled afterwards in whatever arts the government thought proper. This simple regimen, which nature has somehow overlooked, might still be introduced artificially by a radical communism, such as Plato proposed. Such a society would obviate all the life-long dominations and jealousies, as well as the life-long affections, that family life involves; it would also abolish all hereditary classes or possessions, retaining only those necessarily formed by membership in particular trades, arts, or sciences, and by the relative proficiency and authority attained in them. We, with our diversified society, can hardly imagine the interests and the passions that would then agitate the human heart. Would these be only irresistible unanimous gregarious sentiments? Or would the serried ranks of those disciplined multitudes, like sea waves or desert sands, excite only a greater sense of solitude, and a greater spiritual liberty in the private mind? In any case, the family, as we know it, is a conventionalised political institution, not a social necessity.

A consequence of this is that the family has various degrees of extent and cohesion, and involves different, even contrary, standards of virtue. It once had a political authority which it has largely lost; but the bond which at each stage has held it together has always been the same: economic interdependence. The patriarch was a monarch, so long as he held all the property of all his descendants and servants and controlled their pursuits, marriages, and friendships. When, on the contrary, the sons begin to earn their own living and the daughters to choose their own husbands, when nobody expects any important inheritance, and when all the children have been educated in public or boarding-schools, with books, friends, and ideas perhaps unknown to their parents, the kingdom and the power have passed from the patriarch and his traditional family morality to the authority of the social world, its fashions and opinions. A little sentiment, fed on consecrated phrases and on childish impressions, may still add a little glamour to the idea of family and home: but the heart, the mind, the pride of life, and the standard of morals are now rooted elsewhere.

Thus the family and the monarchical order of society growing out of it, the greatest social and moral triumph of simple nature, proves to have been only an insecure and imperfect triumph. That regimen, which seemed to harmonise all duties, interests, and affections in a noble and varied unity, natural and lasting, dissolves as spontaneously as it grew. The morality that it required was too social for the Will in the living individual and too domestic for his intellect.

## CHAPTER 6

### IDEAL MONARCHY

GOVERNMENT being an art, although many labourers may co-operate in carrying it on, only one Will and one intelligence can plan and conduct it; so that in a dialectical sense all government is essentially monarchical. When several architects work at once or successively in building the same monument, either they all follow the designs of their first chief, or the finished work is *one* only physically, because its parts are contiguous, but artistically, like Saint Peter's and almost all cathedrals, is a compound of various designs and of labours differently inspired.

I do not mean to disparage this growth of human works by accretion, or of historical buildings in mixed styles, when each part is genuinely inspired by the taste of its date and author, and all the parts conspire in expressing a common passion for beauty and fitness. No single design can look towards all kinds of excellence; and often compound works and eclectic civilisations are richer and more justly human than any pure embodiment of any single idea. But this happens, I suspect, because our single ideas or unchallenged passions are always unjust to our total nature and express a domination in the soul of one faculty over others that are no less truly rooted there. It is the glory and the torment of human nature to have more budding half-conscious capacities than it can bring to expression together. For that reason the new seems exciting out of proportion to its real merits, and the old dull and irksome in spite of its relative propriety.

Were it possible, however, for a single language to utter all that the soul, at any stage of development, is ready to say, utterance in that single language would alone be legitimate where it was native, and any foreign word a disloyalty and a waste. So if the mind and heart of a monarch could share all the demands of his people, reason and goodness in him would automatically dispose all things for the best. His sense of justice in each case would be better than any law, which is never more than an abstract rough rule not representing exact equity in any single instance. And his policy would be wiser than that of any possible party or assembly, because he would appreciate equally all other men's aims and possibilities, and would see clearly and follow faithfully the best possible path in the given labyrinth.

Such universal sympathy and impartiality is of course an ideal not realised in any mortal; yet relatively to a special function it may be approached, as a father, who may not be without passions and crotchets of his own, may be perfectly disinterested yet sympathetic in guiding and judging his children's interests, much better than they can guide or judge them. For his very pride and lordliness as master of his household will quicken his sense of whatever is for its common advantage. He will, in his own ideal interest, restrain one member of his family and encourage another for the peace and prosperity of his house.

It is this natural gift in the father that has made patriarchal government possible and lasting among pastoral tribes, where war and politics were not too complicated or on too vast a scale for one man to direct everything with sufficient knowledge. And the tradition of such patriarchal government, with its domestic roots and its semi-sacred authority, was often preserved and fortified as much as possible in great hereditary monarchies, both in ancient and in modern times. The monarchs, to be sure, were seldom models of wisdom or virtue; yet everything in their breeding and their position was calculated to support artificially that identity of interests between the ruler and the ruled which existed naturally in the patriarchal household. The wealth and glory of the monarch were inseparable from that of his country; yet two great obstacles to good government subsisted in spite of this identity of true interests. The king might be so frivolous that his own true interests and glory as a monarch might not count with him in comparison with private intrigues and amusements; or his pride and stubbornness in his sovereignty might render him militant in governing his people according to some fanatical notion of his own instead of in sympathy with all their natural and genuine interests. Unfortunately it is not hereditary or absolute monarchs only that are subject to these vices. Popular leaders and popular sects are also subject to them; and we must patiently study the history of each people to understand why they have been fortunate for such brief periods, and have strayed into so many blind alleys.

The almost universal sense of the badness of the contemporary government has, however, a deeper cause than the vices of the governing person or party; discontent with any government is inevitable, because any real government that does not let things merely drift must impose sacrifices, some severe and some universal. The virtue of the ideal monarch would be to feel all these sacrifices keenly and impartially, and to distribute them in the way that would make them most tolerable all round. The sacrifices that are most felt are those that are obvious, like taxes and conscription. It is therefore good politics, though not necessarily good government, that taxes should be indirect and military service voluntary and professional. Obvious sacrifices are least resented when they are habitual, not excessive, and equally distributed. People will still grumble at them, as at bad weather, but will put them down to the nature of things, or the will of God. Yet it is normally these natural scourges, poverty, ill-health, ill fortune, and dreary labour that make the wide unhappiness of man; and it is these beneath the inexcusable scourge of ignorant and wicked governments that an ideal monarchy, like a wise parent, would seek to prevent or to mitigate.

It is here that ideal monarchy, falling back on its natural model, the patriarchal family, paints for us the picture of a society opening the door to all the potentialities of human genius, natural, stable, and decent, and in so far as it was decent, contented.

Monarchy is government by a single psyche, by the organising principle of a living soul. Organisation signifies the cooperative regimen of a great variety of functions, senses, and instruments. It makes possible, by properly timing and spacing those different activities, to make room, without disorder or conflict, for the most various types of life. Society in an ideal monarchy is a many-coloured society. There is vital freedom for the individual, since a wise monarch recognises the inwardness, originality, and secrecy of each actual life; and there is vital liberty for spontaneous association, when persons find themselves cultivating the same arts and developing congruous thoughts. There must be distinct classes, with corresponding privileges and duties; for it is impossible to carry on different trades without acquiring different habits and a different range of ideas; and to live and act together, when people have like minds, is a means of stimulating and deepening the originality of each, and the range of their common intelligence. Classes may sometimes become castes; and it is natural and pleasant that sons should adopt their father's profession. But each individual arises by a fresh fusion of generative elements in new circumstances, and his disposition must be respected and nourished generously under any morally representative government. The dicebox must be fairly shaken before each throw. Careers may be open to talent without destroying the home in which children are brought up according to the means and station of their parents. An ideal monarchy—I am thinking of the East rather than of Europe—would maintain a hierarchy of offices and emoluments, as the Catholic Church does; but it would not allow a hereditary nobility, even if it had naturally arisen, to monopolise the higher posts. These would be given with an eye to the good of the whole people, and of the special service concerned. They would therefore never be given by popular election or party influence.

That monarchy, if good, is the ideal of good government follows from the nature of government, which must be an exercise of intellectual and moral synthesis in a living mind; this can exist only in one person; and it follows also from the possibility of instinctive representation of many children's interests in one disinterested paternal mind, and its impossibility in a collection of many children's minds, each bent on its special interests. In a primitive society of hunters and pioneers where all have similar preoccupations and there is room for all, so that emulations can exist without hostility and cooperation without interdependence, the mind of each comrade may be a good mirror of the common good, and action may proceed by acclamation without breeding resentful minorities or desolate pariahs; but where civilisation is articulated, places limited, and aspirations diverse there is only one way of establishing a relative justice and contentment. This is to compose by political art a moral organisation of society such as nature generates spontaneously in the family and in the patriarchal tribe.

Variety and subordination of arts and functions must be established, and the powerful influence of custom and of pride in special forms of skill, sentiment, amusements, and even dress may be trusted to render the necessary diversity of classes, manners, languages and perhaps religions, a peaceful and contented enrichment of human life.

It is not in the militant Will of any of these classes or opinions that the generative order of society, which produces endless variety, can be reconciled with the peace and order that each type of life or art requires for its perfecting. A superior comprehensive organ must prudently plant and foster such growths as the circumstances favour at each point in each season, while maintaining the fundamental industries and morals on which all liberal arts depend for their liberty. This superior organ can be only a human mind, not incompatible, in its official elevation, with the inevitable imperfection of human beings. But a proper education, a wise selection (not hereditary right) made by the predecessor or by some council rich in experience, besides the traditions of his great office, with its established organs and advisers, might be expected to keep this elective monarch tolerably free from scandal and caprice.

Can such an ideal monarchy ever arise? Alexander the Great caught a glimpse of what it should be; so did Augustus Caesar and perhaps Napoleon. But these were chiefs of militant adventures—as the Popes are too—and not fruits of innocent growth. Their partisan heritage was a fatal handicap for justice and universal sympathy with nature. Life must inspire the control of life.

## CHAPTER 7

### MORAL VICISSITUDES OF MONARCHY

A MOTHER with her brood is a natural form of society: domination by the father seems in comparison accidental. It will arise nevertheless if the father is vigilant over his mate, claims her continued loyalty, and is capable of providing for her and for her young, or at least of defending them. It is ominous to be defended: we shall soon be possessed. There are males indifferent in these matters; they may be ignorant of their fatherhood, and may regard little ones as a troublesome accident to which females are subject for unknown reasons; and they may contemptuously leave their mates and offspring to their own devices or to the jurisdiction of the tribe. Socialism in this respect is very ancient and most convenient for the cock of the walk; it is also very conservative, like all anonymous powers. An inexorably cruel education and cruel neglect sift each generation, killing off the weaklings and imposing the tribal virtues. Patriarchy shows more initiative, a personal mind being keener to perceive special possibilities; and matriarchy is more tender, being quick to protect the weak and to note the ways of individuals.

A sort of matriarchy often survives within the patriarchal order. We find it still in the kitchen, in the drawing-room, and in the nursery. There is also, here and there, under peculiar laws of inheritance, a civilised queenly matriarchy, like that of Penelope. It marks the dominance of the homestead, in which the mother or the grandmother may embody and impose tradition with a greater authority than, in ordinary times, can belong to sons or to husbands. The men are constantly abroad, hunting or fighting, perhaps on distant expeditions, and probably dying young. They came to seem only emissaries, serving from afar the sacred hearth, where the mother keeps religion and wise industry alive from generation to generation. Nevertheless, this quasi-religious matriarchy exists only on sufferance. We must expect that any exceptionally vigorous or long-lived husband or son, choosing to stay at home, will at any moment resume or usurp the government. There can be no real domination by the weak, unless through the imagination, as in theocracies; and the imagination is inconstant. The family, if it is to exist at all as a form of moral government, must be controlled by the father; to give the mother and the children an equal voice, or an actual supremacy, is to surrender the unity of the family, substituting control by society at large, or leaving each individual to take his own course, like a roving animal. Matriarchy would therefore appear to be a convenient and habitual regency, for the benefit of absentee-monarchs, rather than a genuine sovereignty of its own account.

In a well-governed Roman or Christian family this regency has always belonged to the mother within the household; the husband

# MORAL VICISSITUDES OF MONARCHY 113

is supposed to be preoccupied with public affairs, and with making a living; he does well to leave the care of young children, servants, food, clothing, and even religion to the wisdom of his wife. Sometimes, however, when he is a busy-body by temperament, or does his work at home, or has grown old and lazy and cantankerous, he becomes a petty domestic tyrant, always faultfinding and meddlesome. Better if he has to stay all day at home, that he should play the grandfather in slippers at the chimney corner, or sun himself in the garden, frankly letting his wife have her own way and do his thinking for him. Matriarchy makes for peace.

A certain appearance of good order and happiness in some families is due to this cause; but the appearance is treacherous because according to the irresistible order of nature, the nest exists for the sake of the flying birds, not the flying birds for the sake of the nest. Hovering round it and sitting in it may be an occasional duty, but flying from it is the joy of life. Yet when the father leaves all authority in the mother's hands, or in the family as an institution, his own function seems to have become merely instrumental. He is the servant of his wife and children, existing only that they may exist, and working only that they may carry on for ever the routine of domestic life. If he fights, he must justify the war in their eyes; if he goes to the chase it must be only that they may have game for their table. If he studies or theorises, it must be to defend their possessions and their prepossessions. He, whom nature endowed with the energy and intelligence of a master, has become a mere agent or attorney to watch over their interests.

The vigour of a true autocrat depends on a nice balance between the man's personal authority, which protects him from criticism and rebellion, and his competence, which enables him to supervise the detail of government. The ideal dictator should be old but vigorous; he should have done all the things that he commands others to do; he should know his people familiarly, and the names and characters of his servants, yet he should have no favourites, and his own wives and sons should tremble before him. He should be always able to revoke and to exercise personally the powers which, on occasion, he may delegate to others. For this reason, it is important that his dominions should not be too extensive or his government too complex. The secret of his power is that everyone's interest should lie rather in obeying and supporting him than in setting up any opposition, secret or open; if he must have satraps and viziers he is likely to be their victim, or at least their dupe. His palace should still be a tent or a farm-house, where messages may reach him daily from his farthest possessions, and where he may sit in perpetual judgment, distributing orders concerning war and the chase, relations with his neighbours, migrations, bargains, and the care of animals, lands, and crops. He should also, if he is not to be thwarted by superstition and by visionaries, be high priest in his own house.

A mark of truly patriarchal government is polygamy: polygamy, I mean, for the patriarch's benefit, because the people at large can seldom be polygamous. They may be promiscuous, and but loosely tied to any permanent mate; but poverty, with the number of males equal or little inferior to that of females, makes it impossible for every man to monopolise many women. Yet this is the dream, conscious or unconscious, of every truly masculine bosom. Erotic impulse is always young, always dazzled afresh by beauty and excited by opportunity; yet when spontaneous and not grown weary or vicious, it is terribly jealous. The natural masterful male therefore insists on preserving his conquests, and demands fidelity in his wives, without admitting an obligation on his part to be constant to any one of them. So thinks the Oriental monarch, feeling himself absolute; so Mohammed, knowing the heart, encourages himself to feel: so Henry VIII and Louis XIV ventured to act, if not to legislate. And so modern emancipated persons of all classes would like to do, if the modern world left any room at all for genuine freedom of action; but you can't play the whale in a box of sardines.

Polygamy not only gives satisfaction to sexual pride: it protects kingly pride also; it is the ruin of matriarchy. The influence of a favourite sultana may be decisive at a given moment, but is not likely to be permanent; and even when a single queenly wife or mother presides over the harem, the plurality of concubines, their seclusion, and their quarrels leave the master wonderfully free to think and act like a man in the world of men. He is doubly lordly; lord in his own house and, out of his house, lord of himself. By weakening each mother's authority in comparison with that of the common father, this system strengthens the clan. It multiplies the troop of sons and sons-in-law and grandsons; the family becomes an army, the home a castle and almost a city; and the patriarch, if not an absolute lord and prophet in the desert, is at least a great patrician in the State.

Paternal authority is often galling: the child rebels against his elders, screaming and kicking with the most absolute intensity of hatred, long before he can speak. Yet paternal authority generally wins in the end: it secures the sanction of custom, conscience, and affection. How does this happen? Is it because the child soon finds himself happy, and is launched, well instructed, into a free life in the world? Far otherwise. The child soon forgets or seems to forget his impotent rage, because he soon forgets or seems to forget everything; but if he does not retain, deep in his heart, the sense that his parents are his natural enemies, it is probably because he has no depth of heart to retain anything in. They *are* his natural enemies, just as the winds and the sea and wild animals are. They are necessary and useful to him in the same sense. They have instincts of their own—paternal instincts—which he profits by, and without which he could not live. Their affection, their precepts, their possessions are his hunting ground; there he lays his little traps, picks up his worldly experience, and finds stimulus for his dreams. But they are not his friends; they do not understand him nor he them; they do not will anything as he wills it. If occasionally—perhaps in the mother—one ray of real sympathy breaks through the everlasting cloud of anxious fondness and admonishing supervision, it seems a momentary miracle; something as wonderful, as incredible, as dreamlike as if the winds, or the sea, or the wild animals had spoken and answered him intelligibly. The older he grows, the more he grows apart. His friendships, his love-affairs, his musings, his vices, his hopes are all things to be screened from the domestic eye, to be nursed away from home in secret. But home remains home for all that; and parents remain parents. The prodigal, in his extremity, will return to them repentantly, his private will apparently broken; but his more prudent brother had had essentially, in a latent way, the very same history. Only he has tried the length of his tether more cautiously and from the beginning has discovered in domestic authority a force to be exploited, a resource worth all the excitements and hardships of freedom.

What then gives to the patriarch his enduring, unshakable strength? What enables him, even in his dotage, to keep in hand his tribe of grandchildren and great-grandchildren, his host of servants, slaves, and clients, his great possessions, and his absolute personal government? The cause is that every member of this vast family, from the mother down, is daily and hourly in the same situation as the prodigal and his prudent brother; driven to obedience and conformity by the inclemency of the alternative and terrified at the abyss of a bleak, solitary, disastrous rebellion. The patriarch is probably neither better nor wiser than his children; he has no *right* to his dominion; he is merely a centre of crystalisation, round which custom and petty vested interests of every sort have gathered. No one is satisfied; but everyone nevertheless is attached to what crumbs fall to him from the patriarchal table and most jealous of all domestic puppies or alien curs that scramble for more than their customary share. Everyone will conspire to fortify the chieftain's authority in order to bolster up his own; the wives will appeal to him against each other, the daughters against their mothers, the mothers against their daughters, the sons against their servants, the slaves against the slave-drivers, and everybody against the slaves. A distant and tolerably impartial despotism will seem to each of them a guarantee against neighbourly outrages. In any close society it is more urgent to restrain others than to be free oneself. Hence the tendency for the central authority to absorb and supersede such as are local or delegated. Partial autonomy if accepted is only a political compromise, not a spontaneous ideal. That a contant centralisation still goes on is shown by the intolerance of great nations to smaller nationalities within their borders. There is no mercilessness like that of nationalist movements. The people are always for some sweeping plan: it is more remote, more steady, more impersonal, easier to attribute justice to and to idealise. A judge, even if arbitrary, is good to threaten your rivals with; and bad law is better than none. At least it enables you to forecast the risks and issues of your affairs; it offers you guarantees. A judge has a discoverable generic character and ruling motives; his past decisions, by force of personal vanity and inertia, will suggest his decisions in future; and when the public too has come to take his habits of judgment for granted, common law has been born.

The energy of a concentrated autocracy is sometimes enormous. Everyone at home resists the thought of insubordination, while their absorbing patriotism has turned everything abroad into a moral blank. In warlike or raiding enterprises, the ties that bind

## MORAL VICISSITUDES OF MONARCHY 117

the militant nation to its chief are tightened; and since the vengeance of the enemy will fall indiscriminately on this whole predatory people, they must all hold the more desperately together. At the same time, in case of success, the spoils of war, in the form of office and advancement by the leader's favour, will raise his followers to a relative sense of importance if not of eminence. If territories are conquered and the natives made serfs the conquering race will become an aristocracy. Every member of it will occupy a privileged position in virtue of his blood and of his allegiance to his tribal lord and his tribal laws.

This was the basis of feudal monarchies in Europe. The rulers were at first kings of the Franks or Goths or Huns, etc.; they became kings of France, and the rest, simply by extending their possessions, through conquest or marriage, until they came upon a brother king strong enough to resist them. Fortunately the feudal system allowed an elaborate hierarchy of landlords, from the tenant farmer to the supreme and usually theoretical suzerain, with the most picturesque variety of customs, rights, and privileges, so that the monarch with the widest nominal dominion might well be the most gracious and chivalrous and the least oppressed with business. The relations of all these monarchs to one another and to their nobles were survivals of tribal relations and duties; their relations to the conquered natives and to the resident aliens, like the Jews, rested on different forms and degrees of territorial dominion.

When, however, through fusion of the languages and legislation of the two superposed races, and the partial fusion of their blood, the original contrast between them tended to disappear, the ground for feudal monarchy was undermined. The kings were no longer the patriarchs of their aristocracy, nor were the landowners of another nationality from their tenants. How then did the monarchs have hereditary rights to allegiance, or the landlords hereditary rights to the whole revenue of their land? Evidently, when some external power did not suddenly destroy the system, gradual mutations must cause the land to pass to the cultivators of it or to the State, and the monarch, if retained, must fade into a decorative first magistrate of the republic.

So at least an innocent philosopher, expecting people to be rational, might have imagined. But in fact the function of a real monarch has never yet graced the President of a Republic, unless Cromwell can be said to have graced it; yet the exercise of autocratic power is too spontaneous a function in some phases of society for someone not to exercise it unbidden as if by magic. It fell to Napoleon and to minor dictators for short and troubled periods; but it has become almost normal, at least as an ideal, for party leaders. They may be mediocre and shady persons, but so were many hereditary monarchs; and it is not in themselves or for what they do that they triumph: they triumph as demagogues. A demagogue leading a popular party, and far-sighted enough to keep himself in power when once he has seized it, becomes a perpetual dictator. Almost all the real tensions that give strength to a monarchy are repeated in such a drama by an untrained actor in a meaner setting: but the audience remembers nothing better, and can be made to applaud.

## CHAPTER 8

### INDEPENDENCE AND FUSION AMONG THE ARTS

THERE are two chief offices, long performed by parents and elders, that grow into distinct departments of government: to administer justice and to wage war. Ideally an appeal to justice takes the place of some imminent appeal to force, as if the sense of equity in the judges, who may be the crowd present at the quarrel, would bring the virtual force of the community to the rescue of the side that had been wronged. In practice, however, especially when precedents or laws can be invoked to influence the judgment, the sense of justice itself expresses a vested economic or ambitious interest, an established domination, not founded on fairness but on force; so that the force of law appears to the free mind as itself a brutal force. And there is another element of judiciary justice when long established that, without being economic, seems to the free mind an imposition; and this is the element of mere custom or superstition that enters into the traditional law. It may require military force to eradicate this legal tradition; since economic domination, if firmly established, can remake legality, if not equity, in its own interests.

Often, too, the growth of legal justice is cut short and rendered unnecessary by foreign invasion and conquest, which at the same

## INDEPENDENCE AND FUSION

time impose a distinct government, sharply contrasting with the native customs on which a native government would have rested almost unawares.

That all government is an imposition and an evil, and that freedom, empty freedom, is the first and fundamental political good, may then easily become the secret conviction of the natives, even if their foreign rulers have rescued them from many evils incident to life in the jungle. It would require an almost hopeless inquiry into which I cannot enter to trace the ins and outs of arrested evolution and imposed progress in the history of various nations. I must be satisfied with merely pointing out that these mingled currents exist and render unjustified and superficial many local grievances and many rash dogmas that figure in political controversy. The natural growth of society is not rational; it is subject to every evil without attempting to counteract these evils scientifically. Government, however irrational may be the Will that animates it and however regardless of the Will of its subjects, at least is an art in method and in the use of means to its ends. It may be odious, but it affords an object-lesson in the control of events.

That the lessons so offered are seldom or never learned by the government that supplies them through its blunders and vices does not deprive those lessons of their force for the philosopher; but the philosopher has no greater power than the statesman to trace the causes of public events and less opportunity. Plato, no doubt the greatest philosopher who has carefully studied politics, while he has painted admirably the vices of society and of politicians, has proposed only arbitrary ideals and given futile advice, like any other moralist who disregards the vital liberty of nature, and the consequent diversity of attainable goods.

With this premiss, the reader will not expect me to follow Aristotle in declaring that there are three good forms of government, monarchy, aristocracy, and constiutional democracy, in this order of excellence, when they are good; but that when corrupted into absolute or direct democracy, oligarchy, and tyranny, tyranny is the worst and absolute or direct democracy the least pernicious. These would be judicious judgments if at the time and in the place of Aristotle a man were called upon to express a practical preference. The passions of the people are spasmodic and soon divergent, while human nature and tradition survive in them and restore a tolerable balance, as the sea does after the worst storm. The reign of a tyrant is also shortlived, but his vices are professional, and both the occasion and the practice of them become chronic. Yet these types of government, as seen in classic antiquity, change with epochs and races, and ancient judgments become inapplicable. Preferences are themselves expressions of aims bred in particular persons in particular circumstances. A philosopher is a man and has his tastes; but it is not his business to insist on them; rather to abtract from them as far as possible and to exhibit the character and connexions of institutions of various kinds, so as to enlighten the Will of whoever may chance to hear him. To summon others to will what they do not will is as impertinent as it is useless. But an enlightened primal Will sees in the first instance how to attain its purpose without making or inflicting unnecessary sacrifices; and later, having drunk the cup of success to the dregs, the Will may even revise or rescind itself, in so far as its blind demands contradict one another. The contradictions are temporal and local, in that incompatible forms are, in this world, rivals for the same matter. But among the forms themselves there is variety without rivalry. The circle neither envies the square nor wishes to devour it.

The growth of society and the shifts of dominations and powers that underlie it are not to be traced to politics, that is, to the question who governs and by what superficial play of intrigues and conspiracies, of private opinions and public opinion. All this forms the gossip of history, and may be important by accident, because trifling accidents sometimes divert the course or cause the wreck of the ship of State. But the economic and liberal arts raise civilisation above barbarism, no matter into whose hands and by what methods official power may pass from one man or party to another. The weight of such men or parties itself depends on the economic or military forces that they seem to lead but that sometimes support and sometimes betray them. To the foreign militant order that often traverses and deflects a people's heritage, I will turn later. Now it is the economic and the liberal arts that I would consider in their specific functions.

The spontaneous economy of the human race discovers and improves the means of defence and attack, in so far as these seem to contribute to preserve its existence. There is no essential change in the direction of intelligence and art from the rudest contrivances to all the mechanical wonders that now surround us, complicate our lives, and absorb our attention. The so-called domination of mind over matter, which is really the domination of one animal species over its habitat, might become a moral domination of means over ends in that species; and it would become such a domination if the liberal arts did not flourish, as they do, at the same time and profit by the wider field that economic labour opens to spiritual dominion. Not only do manual and ideal arts profit by being practiced together, but even two purely industrial arts render one another sounder and clearer in their principles and theory. As arts they cannot conflict; it is only the persons that practice them that may be rivals for place or reputation in society, and the more so when the art they practice is the same and in the same country; for duplicates can oust one another, but a poet and a sea-captain interfere so little with each other's success that they might even with advantage be the same person.

## CHAPTER 9

### INTRINSIC VALUES OF GOVERNMENT

THE moral pros and cons of government are not confined to utility or oppression; for besides affecting prior and independent interests, government initiates something new. At the very least, it institutes itself; and the mere fact that this new vortex has arisen in the habits of a group of men, introduces among them a new art, a new type of desires and satisfactions. This new art, called government, is not without its specific emotions, which never could have figured in human life if no governments had existed. Politics are a sport like hunting, fighting, and play-acting: they are also a lottery, with big and little prizes. What is called ambition is largely, in the ambitious soul, a tendency to play a part, as in a dream, proudly placing oneself in the centre of thrilling scenes, and impressive ceremonies, full of sound and large gestures, but perhaps signifying nothing. Megalomania inebriates with a sense of greatness, without knowledge of what is great.

The pose, the art, the orderly procedure of government are a human good. They not only flatter the vanity of men at the top, probably tormented all the while with secret worries and fears; the same pageant fills the underlings far more innocently with satisfaction and vicarious pride. They feel they are not altogether ignorant of great affairs; not only what reaches them through the keyhole, or in the antechamber, but the mere sense which reading the newspaper may occasion, that momentous matters are afoot, that clever men are quarrelling about them, and that these clever men are perhaps as little masters of events as is the man in the street. Criticism, satire, and wise shaking of empty heads are certainly privileges that the existence of government propagates generously among the governed, no matter what other benefits it may fail to confer. And here too all is not mere malevolence or complaint; in criticising the government the wiseacre feels himself in the government's boots; he imagines how much better he would have managed; and the honest glow of doing so much good—unfortunately prevented—and of transforming things according to his ideas, gives him the emotion of ruling, without its commitments. No wonder that conversation, in circles where government is familiar, turns continually upon politics.

A rather monotonous trickle of actual authority also flows down to petty officials. These have, no doubt, satisfactions of their own, but rather acrid. They are too conscious of the rather objectionable official immediately above them; and the petty tyrannies they may be able to exercise over the public are no compensation for the narrowness of the sphere to which they must be confined. And often a ministry or office under the government is not a participation in government at all; it is only a place to fill, a routine to follow; and there is more obeying than commanding in the poor clerk's life. Military men (especially when retired, and no longer subordinate), police, and attendants feel themselves more directly channels and representatives of authority: they button up the official uniform with complacency, and bubble over with righteous indignation at the laxity of the times; they whisper the news with trepidation; and they prophesy how things are sure to turn out. You would think they were talking of a race or a prize-fight; but no; they have not a bet on the result, and the issue is only which party shall be next in office, and what words shall be in vogue for a while, without anything else being changed in their personal destiny. Political enthusiasm is a disinterested thing. It is a free gift which the existence of governments makes to the imagination.

In self-governed nations (as the phrase goes) this popular participation in the life of government is more serious. Indeed, the theory of free government is that the people themselves govern, the constitution adopted and the officers elected being supposed to be passive vehicles for the popular will; and in some ancient republics and in modern states, where the referendum is adopted, a majority of the people (or of such part of them as vote) actually do decide particular points of policy. To that extent, in fact, the voters are at the moment a part of the government; whatever breadth of vision or sense of initiative and responsibility they may acquire is simply their share in the directive imagination proper to governments; while it is not impossible that even the official and bureaucratic passions of a governing body may take root in public assemblies. The Greeks, it has been said, spent their lives governing themselves; for the love of listening, speaking, and shouting at the public assembly they would neglect their trades and their families, and in their zeal for a party, a reform, or a war, they would gladly sacrifice the most solid interests of themselves and their country. Thus the corporate governmental egotism which in autocratic and in party governments is so marked and so scandalous may extend also to democracies, proud of being governments too: just as a people of Pharisees, who feel that they are champions of a divine law, may carry on a theocracy no less blighting, and more reckless, than would a few conservative priests.

The meanderings of a bad popular government hardly ever stray so long from the direction of tolerable policy as do those of an oligarchy. Where everybody is a part of the government the aims of the government are more plebeian, and the radiation of political life does not exist—partly because there is no outlying nation to be irradiated, and partly because there is no focus intense enough to spread a dominant magnetic field.

This of course is not true of great *constitutional* democratic races, like those of England, France, or the United States; because in these countries the popular mind is hardly cognizant of the private bodies, foundations, traditions, and vested interests that actually carry on nine-tenths of the national business. What the people decide is at best which of two traditional parties shall govern: but the whole machinery of government, most of the points of policy, and the whole body of law, privilege, and custom is guarded and known only by the official classes. In such democracies there are great *centres* of charity, learning, influence, and fashion; there are professional armies and navies, and a caste of politicians, and there are established or incorporated religions. Hence the life of the people is actually governed and inspired by custom—from occult, unsuspected, uncritical sources of benefit or injury; and the radiation of current governmental life takes place as in an autocracy.

One faculty among others which is stimulated by office is directive imagination. Directive imagination is very lively in children; their day-dreams are full of the times when they shall be princes, and make great gifts, and forgive great offences, and win a great love, and thwart the vast insidious machinations of some baffled fiend. Real life somehow smothers these youthful impulses; and the directive imagination is suspended until the little obsessions of daily business can be laid aside—if they ever can—and then for want of the old childish faith, nothing ensues but moonshine and mere sentimentality. To become actually master, however, reawakens the old impulse. The new-fledged minister is again a child. Again the dazzling scene appears of the feats and triumphs to come. He dreams of speeches applauded, measures passed, elections won, finances restored, fleets and armies equipped and victorious, miles of waste land covered rectilinearly with model cottages, and statues of oneself in a morning coat and a crown of laurel rising in public squares. All this is not wild imagination; it may be realised; and yet soon something is apt to go wrong. Directive imagination is not power: it is only that Nietzschean egotistical folly, the will to rule. This will requires the cooperation of circumstances to become effective. Even an oriental despot, untroubled by colleagues, constituents, or the stubborn routine of departments, finds that all is obstacles on the throne. Great things are about to begin when the Grand Vizier, with a lengthened nose, announces that the treasury is empty or the provincial governors in revolt; and when that wicked Vizier is sent to prison, his virtuous successor regrets to discover that a royal brother, supposed to be safely accounted for, has turned up alive, or that the whole harem is pecking at the new Sultana. Then the directive imagination has to furl its sails a little, and take a new tack; and it may not be long before it comes permanently to anchor.

Nevertheless directive imagination must be taken seriously: it is a dangerous thing. The illusion of creation is one of the greatest of pleasures and is most passionately defended by human conceit. To see things take shape before your eyes according to your idea—

# THE DIRECTIVE IMAGINATION

as may actually happen when the idea is opportune—is an intoxicating spectacle. In that case the idea, being bred in an organ trained and ready to act, can more or less accurately refigure the coming action; just as you can think what you are about to say, and almost hear the words, when what you are about to say is already being rehearsed in your brain.

One of the suspicions hardest to entertain is that what you create, or wish to create, might after all not be beautiful. Therefore all the forces of passion, egotism, vanity, habit, and conscience unite to attach a public man to the line of policy which first attracted him, and to those persons who abet him in it. This prepossession he calls loyalty to his party. Whatever concessions his directive imagination may have to make, whatever feathers his ideal may moult, he will continue in his partisan course as swiftly and irrevocably as a launched torpedo. A party in power is a blind engine, incapable of redirecting itself, and carried forward by the pledged and mortgaged imagination of all its members. It is not only the public that is then in danger of ruin, but the members of the government themselves, whose private interests subsist, of course, beneath their political intoxication; and the more honest and self-forgetful they are, the more apt they will be to defeat their own residuary interest, as well as that of others, in their visionary zeal for their political nostrums.

## CHAPTER 10

### PSYCHOLOGY OF THE DIRECTIVE IMAGINATION

MAN is a plastic, suggestible, histrionic animal. He can act many extravagant parts. He can become the slave of any one of many notions, passions, or habits; but the notion, passion, and habit of governing is only one of them. In order to submit himself and his community to some plausible political regimen, the simple voter will pursue, just like a tyrant, the most disastrous enterprises and bonanzas. He will play the politician and the demagogue at his own expense. Meantime, however, he will glow with activity and vanity, he will enjoy his power, and vote himself largesses and credits at his own cost. And he will acquire the gifts and lights of a governing class. He will be able to make good speeches, maintain an argument, penetrate to a principle, disguise a fact, or at least repeat a mouth-filling maxim. If he fools himself, he will not be easily fooled by anyone else. And if ever he discovers his folly (as is not probable) he will never be driven to cut his own throat, as do despairing heroic patriots and entrapped tyrants.

This difference in the depth of political passion in great souls and in little shows how accidental that passion is. On the other hand it is contagious, and the rabble will catch it and be swayed by it for a moment; but it takes root and becomes dominant morally only in persons of strong and highly articulate imagination, like those in whom religion can take root and become dominant; for religion too is easily diffused and histrionically popular, but seldom transforms or even touches the radical motives guiding a man's life. Therefore, when the orthodox language and morality of an articulate religion or polity is imposed by custom or law, it becomes perfunctory for the public at large; and only a special school of art and literature expresses that orthodoxy, while the lay and jovial cynical mind vents itself as far as it can in popular forms. Then learned and choice minds that study only the high lights of history may be deceived by the tragic masks which dramatic imagination substitutes for foolish faces.

So when Nietzsche, for instance, substituted for Schopenhauer's phrase *The Will to Live*, the phrase *The Will to Dominate*, he gave, I think, an entirely false place and importance to the directive imagination. Primal Will is unconscious and initially indeterminate; and Schopenhauer, under this psychological metaphor, meant and described the true process of universal genesis. But Nietzsche was a professor of Greek, and also inherited the hectic traditions of a romantic and militant Germany. He dreamt of a transcendental spirit, with a perfectly conscious and lordly will, assuming a vital liberty of action as well as thought, as if in the real world Will could conquer and possess all things by despising them. That, as Schopenhauer knew, is a moral fable: and the heroes of Greek legend, in so far as they gave free rein to their vital liberty, came heroically but miserably to grief; because Will, in so far as it would cope successfully with Circumstances, must respect Circumstances, and cultivate such arts as Circumstances allow and render fruitful. Spirit is the fine flower of the World as Will, and must respect the rest of the World of Will in order to enjoy it as Idea.

# THE DIRECTIVE IMAGINATION

We may perhaps interpret Nietzsche on his German side in a way consistent with his Greek wisdom by taking him for a "heroic pessimist" after the manner of Kant according to Vaihinger. Transcendental spirit, according to this view, should have the courage to assert its absolute vital liberty in the face of Circumstances. It will perish materially, but it will triumph morally, in its pride. The Will to Dominate will pronounce all things to be nothing, in so far as they refuse to be dominated. Egotism, idealism, and absolute liberty, though short-lived, will thus be indomitable.

In its origin the directive imagination marks the momentum of economic art; the organism finds itself able and happy to play with Circumstances, and the impression left by these tentative successes in the past rises again in anticipation of what may be done when a fresh occasion of the same sort appears. But imagination applies to the present an expectation based on the past; it may prove prophetic, if the two occasions are really similar; but it is not directive dynamically. That which is directive dynamically is fresh, direct, accurate attention to the development of the current action; and readaptation of this to changing opportunities. The result will be a new impression, probably modifying the prophetic expectation at first aroused. If the imaginative momentum is strong, the lesson that the new occasion offers may be missed; the action will repeat the former successful action, which in consequence may be fruitless in the new cause. In successful art the directive imagination remains cautious and docile: if it continues to dominate and to reject correction, action becomes precipitate, misleading, and a source of failure in real dominion.

It is in a humanistic atmosphere, where the circle of action is limited (as in a single household or where literary and religious conceptions veil the face of nature) that the directive imagination controls the psyche and professes to control the world. It prevails in government more than in war or trade, because the contact with corrective reality is more remote in councils and debates and proclamations than in campaigning; and it prevails in the minds of women more than in those of men; for though women deal constantly with domestic economy and behaviour, it all appears to the mistress as a matter of obedience or disobedience to her prescriptions. She is acutely conscious of the failure of her directive imagination to dominate her house and her social circle as much as she thinks it should; but she has only feeble lights, not social or religious, to make visible the non-human and non-domestic order of things. She can be very intelligent, but only in humanistic terms. It is not wonderful, therefore, that to command, to exercise authority, seems sometimes to be her ruling passion. Her imagination is cold and weak when it attempts to picture things that transcend the interests of her heart; and though these interests often passionately transcend her personal fortunes, they never transcend the field in which her heart might see all its wishes realised.

In traditional morality and political reform the directive imagination, not content or not able to be dominant at home or in a man's own life, becomes universally militant. There is a curious contradiction or ambiguity in this. Propaganda is altruistic, in the sense of being meddlesome and intent on securing what it thinks the welfare of others; but it does not consult others in distinguishing their welfare; it defines this *a priori* according to its own sense of what others ought to like. It is therefore in its generative principle purely egotistical, and in its application cannot distinguish between being beneficent and being tyrannical.

Here, however, all depends on support from a deeper principle. People may be ignorant of their own good and cramped by vices and errors so that they choose, if let alone, the direct path to their own misery and despair. If the militant prophet, then, knows people's nature better than they know it themselves, and if he has at the same time a truer view of their circumstances, his apparent tyranny is an act of charity, and rational even if by accident, in some instance, it proves vain. Primal Will and Circumstances, not the man's wishes or the reformer's prescription, determine the true interest of each person. And this is also the criterion by which the genius or folly of the directive imagination would be determined.

## CHAPTER 11

### RADIATION OF POLITICAL LIFE

EVERYONE would spontaneously regard the existence of poetry and painting as an advantage to a nation; yet neither for the sake of any material or practical utility, nor because the lives of the painters and poets had been particularly admirable. In fact, to dwell much on either of these points (as Plato did) would show a bias against the fine arts: for both their material utility and the happiness of their votaries are, if anything, negative quantities.

It is rather the radiation of painting or poetry in the lives of ordinary people that makes up its chief value to society by awakening human interest in a thousand inspiriting things remote from the routine of existence.

Now, political life radiates in the same way. The past politics of a nation make up its history—something which the most absolute democracy can no longer affect by its vote; yet this history supplies all the points of pride, all the stock maxims and heroes, and most of the aims which guide any man's political feeling and opinion. What is called patriotism is most often a radiation of political life. The love of country is neither the love of material goods which the native government may secure better than other governments—the opposite being always the case in all countries but one; nor is it a sense of participation in the management of one's government with the consequent interest in its continuance. It is rather a feeling of pride, anxiety, ardour, and pugnacity, aroused by the idea of the government exercising or extending its authority in striking ways—by conquest, by noble foundations, by growth of public wealth and the arts, by the opportune vindication of justice. The attachment which people feel to their language, religion, literature, and manners is often reckoned in their love of country as much as their attachment to the soil and aspects of their native land. It would be better if we had another word to designate such appreciation of national possessions, which a foreigner might share, according to his lights: for the word patriotism suggests not a moral attachment but a political passion, an animal will enlarged to cover the whole social organisation of which one forms a part. Ideal allegiance might extend even to extinct civilisations. The Helleniser may love ancient Greece more intensely than he loves his native land; yet ancient Greece cannot arouse his patriotism. His partiality for the ideal possessions of another people can only express his personal taste; it is not a participation in the corporate interests of a living institution, such that he might share its destiny and appropriate emotionally its triumphs and defeats, as a patriot must.

Now, whether this passion of patriotism is a good thing either for states or for individuals is an open question. The answer would probably be dictated by the same ethical conclusions that would pronounce the passion of love, or earthly life itself, a good or an evil. Like other passions patriotism, in its effect on the individual, is a source of anxiety, bitterness, conflict, self-sacrifice, pride, delight, and malevolence; it quickens the speed of life, enlarges its joys, and multiplies its heroisms and its crimes. Theft and murder when dictated by patriotism are no longer sordid or unavowed. They have a public motive and stimulate public sympathy, without thereby becoming less noxious to the victims. A moralist who judges by results will still condemn them unflinchingly: but a moralist who judges actions by their tone and temper, by the *virtù* of him who does them, will think that patriotism redeems and transforms these acts of violence. But he will not convince his rival moralist; who, far from condoning these crimes for being inspired by patriotism, will unhesitatingly condemn patriotism for having inspired them.

In its public operation, too, passion has an ambiguous value. There is a swiftness, an instinctive sureness, a fine intensity about passion that seems to make it a desirable accompaniment for all life; and if a government can enlist passion in its service, it may count on a brilliant and dramatic career. Yet those political institutions, like commerce or the administration of justice, that normally arouse no public passion are not perhaps less well managed than is the executive government; and if all political functions had been carried on dispassionately it is very probable that they would have been fulfilled more steadily and more accurately. Passion, in driving a nation faster, may drive it afield. Patriotism, like the government it radiates from, may become a vice.

Loyalty to monarchs, at certain times, has been a powerful sentiment; and its operation is quite independent of its utility. Not that the claims of a monarch, even of the infant heir to a crown, may not be representative of very great moral interests. They may stand for a whole way of living and feeling, such as the feudal system was, on which innumerable personal and poetic goods may be inextricably grafted: as perhaps a cavalier, in seeming so irrationally devoted to an unworthy liege and an obsolete legality, was very rationally devoted in reality to himself, to the only life he could lead joyously, and the only world in which he could lead it.

In oriental societies (if we exclude religion, which is often their chief government) the advantage of being governed may be almost reduced to the splendours of the monarch, his court, and his works. In ancient Babylon, the vast city walls and the temple in its seventh architectural heaven must have enlarged the hearts of the inhabitants; and the Egyptians, gazing on the Pyramids, must have learned something of the feeling of mountains, as gazing on the desert, they surely learned something of the feeling of the sea. The mere fact that they possessed monarchs evidently supplied them with rich themes for legend and poetry, as well as many a pageant for the eye. But this participation on the part of the public in the life of absolute monarchs is distant and non-political; it might be set down perhaps as a sort of artistic religion, a show for which they paid a perhaps exorbitant price, as we do gladly for our operas, dramas, and ballets.

The extraordinary passion shown in the United States at the national conventions that select candidates for the Presidency should not, in theory, be regarded as a radiation from the art of government but as a part of that art itself; each party is "getting up steam" to propagate its policy and to choose the chief magistrate who shall carry it out. But in reality little of that irrepressible steam goes to propel the formidable locomotive already full of fuel and pointing to the line on which it is to run. Almost all the hot vapour bursts out in shrieking geysers of abstract enthusiasm that are their own excuse for being. The results of government will appear later, and God knows what they will be: but the excitement, the pride, the glory of governing comes now and here. The point is to break the record in the number of people shouting at once, in the excruciating loudness of their shouts, and in the length of time—twenty minutes, thirty minutes, forty minutes—that they can keep on shouting. The effort will prove how intense can be the zeal of free men in their self-government, how glorious the sense of being harnessed all together to the triumphal car that will crush all possible opposition. So the intoxication of victory is felt before the victory and drowns all clear notion of what the victory was really meant to bring.

In fact the issues that separate the two leading parties in the United States since the Civil War have never been momentous; all is a question of local colour, geographical or moral. When it comes to important definite measures both parties move in the same direction, though perhaps at different speeds, or with more or less clearness of outlook. The Republicans rather represent the North, and vested interests; the Democrats rather the South and the proletariat; but both feel the same momentum of enterprises already on foot and commitments already accepted. Such a fundamental unanimity is no doubt a sign of a genuine and healthy democracy, where differences that come to the surface regard only alternative means to ends that are silently presupposed or remain conveniently nebulous.

This happy innocence might be expected to remove all occasions for political passion; but on the contrary it seems to favour a certain youthful or sporting licence and rivalry and debate, for the fun of it; this will work up an intensity of conviction which normally you might not know that you had; and yet you really have it, as any crisis will prove that comes to put it to the test. That the stakes in these occasional debates and elections may be trivial, far from preventing noisy demonstrations, leaves the field open to them, as a feast does to fireworks. It is only a corrupt gamester, playing for money or pledging sums that he cannot pay, who sits dumb and sinister, watching the roulette or the cards; your pure enthusiast will shout himself hoarse at a football match without having bet on the result, and will enlist for a colonial war without asking what it is about.

Thus boisterous demonstrations, even strikes and riots, may be true radiations of public interests into private passions: passions with mock objects, but with real grounds in the disposition of a body and a mind hungry for exercise and excitement. In some, in the speculative or artistic, this overflow waters the imagination, and the life of governments and armies breeds epics, tragedies, novels, and philosophies; while for others the vital stress of action alone proves contagious, and they will shout and fight for a government far more heartily than the ministers and generals, troubled and disconcerted as these must be at every turn in the maze of thought, and thwarted at every step in the maze of action.

## PART THREE

### The Liberal Arts

# CHAPTER 1

PLAY

THE realm of organic matter, in which human society flourishes, is automatic: each part has its own movement, but depends on circumstances for carrying it out, so that each rehearsal of its spontaneous tropes differs from the preceding. Even vital impulse often veers from its initial direction, falling into a different rhythm, learning to rely on new contacts and supports.

And it is not merely an adaptation to circumstances that ensues. Certain contacts and certain new internal fusions may positively fertilise the psyche, initiating there a new trick, or an unexpected excitement. The primary instincts themselves may be modified in this way, as by the conflagration that produced the first roast pig, or like the accidental caresses that may first have awakened or fixed or redirected a child's sexual inclinations. But in such cases the momentum of ordinary routine is likely to override chance impressions and to impose conventional habits, only slightly modified by special circumstances or endowment. Animal life and mind are terribly generic, even in man.

There is, however, a vast elusive margin of idle impressions and budding impulses bred by the play between maturing organisms and casual stimulations. Vivid marvellous realms open out in the fancy, as we see in dreams, in which what waking sense would call miracles and waking reason absurdities do not surprise, but engage the credulous psyche profoundly in fictitious predicaments. Some of these dreams may take root and become an incubus that recurs from time to time with the same burden in endless variations. But the most obvious and pleasing evidence of this by-world is found in the play of children. How much easier, how much more interesting, how much more friendly they find the worlds they invent than the world they are condemned to live in! And nothing could be simpler or more harmless than some of these games. What an entertainment it is to whistle! What an excitement, what a victory, to walk on the top of a garden wall! What an absorbing task to toss and catch a ball, to build sand castles, or to play with marbles! And the psychology of these tastes is not hard to decipher. The young psyche is wound up; it is full of untried or half-exercised powers. But the conventional human world is out of scale with these abilities. It is simple mechanisms, it is other young animals, that give them a chance. The grown-up world is all dark dominations; the play world is the paradise of powers.

Such overflow of unemployed vitality into idle invention is by no means confined to childhood or to dreams. It goes on unheeded during all waking life, as the stars go on shining all day invisibly. For life has an inner fountain and hidden waters. What modern idealists call "experience" represents only a superficial selection or bubbling up of certain feelings or images evoked frequently or powerfully by subterranean currents both in the animal psyche and in the outer world. These few orthodox images and feelings, floating down the cosmic stream, in themselves have no more substance or power than the heretical images and feelings in dreams, or in children's fictions; but they are signs of more important movements in the world; their ideal qualities may therefore serve as terms in useful knowledge.

Words in particular, which in themselves are idle music, like whistling, serve for summary signs of familiar objects and events; but this utility they acquire gradually and only externally, except for the element of mimicry that there may be in uttering them; and prior to their utility, and superabundantly developing it, words have a spontaneous euphony, prosody, and syntax of their own, like arabesques. It is when sound abandons the servile function of signification, and develops itself freely as music, that it becomes thoroughly vital and its own excuse for being.

Free play, however, no matter how spontaneous and purely mental it may be, always exercises and modifies the organism of the player, and also that of any possible witness. It is a rehearsal of life by the psyche, when immature or unemployed, as are children's games and the sports of young people; and from a political or economic point of view, some competitive sports and games are evidently good training for the senses, the muscles, the temper, and the habit of cooperation.

Some games and some sports, however, have a quality in common with hunting. Often they imitate the chase, which in real life is not primarily a sport but a form at once of food-finding and of war. It is war on animals. The intrusion of a militant element into the life of play, which is essentially free and ought to be liberal, forms one of the darkest chapters in the life of reason. It infects with care, with ill-will, and with deception what ought to be a realm of pure art. Yet ideal constructions and liberal arts, which suffer this infection, return good for evil, and immensely enhance and ennoble the whole militant order of society. I will therefore leave this subject to be touched upon in the analysis of militancy, where it shows its beneficent side.

Economic hatred of waste, become a passion, persecutes play, sport, ceremony, and all the spontaneous homage that life pays to its own gracefulness and generosity. Such hatred assimilates play to vice, gambols to gambling, jollity to drunkenness, love to folly, and religion to ignorant fear. And no doubt industry suffers from play in the quantity of its products, perhaps as much as it gains in their quality. It is a nice and open question for the rational moralists to balance this account; but the economists should remember that life itself is play, and utterly needless for making the planets go round the sun. It is only the free exuberance of forms springing up for no reason on the earth's surface that sets their hard duties on industry, commerce, and morality, because exuberance is dangerous to itself. What it breeds here may destroy what it was breeding there; and it is not on earth that all the possible and budding kinds of unnecessary trees and animals can live prosperously and amicably together. Conflict, domination, rebellion, suppression cannot die out altogether: this the very exuberance of *natura naturans* forbids. Yet freedom can destroy itself only partially, since the victorious earnestness that would suppress it is itself play of the same freedom in another direction; and the more successful the economist may be in dragooning human energies in his cause, the more surely, from within, a play of variations, luxuries, and caprices will mock his victory. Only external material cataclysms or failure of supplies could kill the generative power that, pressed and compressed as it may be by circumstances, is pressed and compressed only because it is spontaneously intent on play.

## CHAPTER 2

### MUSIC

Music comes to birth in idleness, and it can fill idleness with refined peaceful emotions, apparently about nothing. Emotion is indeed independent of the objects to which it may be attached, but never independent of the movement that produces it. Old poets were never tired of celebrating the music of brooks and birds; and it was often through delight in mimicking natural sounds or the cries of animals that men, and especially mocking boys, discovered and began to train their vocal powers. They found that by some precise contortion of their mouths or throats, they could crow for fun as the cock apparently felt obliged to crow in order to publish his dignity as a husband, or challenge his rivals to mortal combat. Crowing was no joke to him, but it was a joke to his human mimic. Mimicry, though it be imitation, is not flattery, rather ridicule: because the mimic can reproduce the airs of his models and parody their seriousness and self-importance without being pledged to any of their physical or moral commitments. The parrot that can reproduce our language so tartly, with scanty vocal organs and nothing to say, gives us the most humiliating proof of the mechanical detachable character of our elocution; also of how accidental the conjunction is of signification with words. Speech is primarily vocal music, and its development in euphony, inflections, and prosody, though intertwined with modes of signification, has its own principles and beauties, never to be disregarded in civilised eloquence.

The liberal character of music, the fact that it belongs preeminently to the vital liberty of art, divorced more radically than the visual imagination from preocupation with matters of fact, appears especially when music is instrumental; and its source is then discovered experimentally. This source is measure in motion. Nothing then could respond more absolutely to physical conditions; yet these conditions, though material, are vital, since the material instrument must vibrate; and this vitality and its various modes have a rational measure, though not at all a particularly animal or human or moral essence: the movement must beat time to specific cosmical rhythms. The horizons of music are all its own, boundless, free, ultrahuman; yet its heart is human enough, because the life of the psyche also is bound to measure and time. The whole of nature is full of repetitions, some steady and perpetual, others variable in span and volume, like storms, or subject, like the seasons, to anticipate or retard a little, according to other accidents, their periodical return. And in these large meters innumerable finer ones are included, among which are human measures of the heart, the passions, and the ages of life. It is to these vital analogies in the period and volume of change that sound appeals in music; through these it diffuses the atmosphere of the various passions without representing their occasions; and the technical precision of its own medium, when artistically developed, lends to those climates of passion a non-natural form, so that the passions themselves seem to be rendered metaphysical and unworldly, all their ardour and trepidation being embodied in the apparently bodiless torrent of sound. The torrent is not bodiless, however, nor is the organ bodiless that re-echoes it in the psyche; but the realm of sound being invisible, and all its mighty events evanescent, there is a romantic or mystical or supernatural air about it, especially for those to whom music is not technically intelligible but only a sensuous stimulant or sedative. Yet the technical varieties of musical composition form an inexhaustible treasury of possible delights. Music used to be felt rather as an accompaniment to words or to dramatic passions or to stirring events: but now it seems almost a profanation to dwell on those human occasions; and pure music, in its own sphere, has become the most transporting of the arts, and the one most sincerely appreciated, even by the general public. It is therefore a signal proof of the unexpected fertility of the generative order in the liberal dimensions; for all this science, all this art, all this unfeigned pleasure and exaltation, comes to us, as it were, from nowhere, serves us for nothing ulterior, and yet seems to us the elixir and finest flower of the spirit.

## CHAPTER 3

### WORDS, WORDS, WORDS

*Great is the power of words,* says Homer, *words will make this way and that way.*[1] Like other coventions, language takes root in the organism, develops there a life of its own, and by its inner tensions or accidental entanglements, distorts the facts it professes to report or sways the feelings which the facts would naturally arouse, so as to create artificial and heady passions. Language is the great instrument of fanaticism. A critic of politics finds himself driven to deprecate the power of words, whilst using them copiously in warnings against their influence. It is indeed in politics that their influence is most dangerous; so that one is almost tempted to wish that they did not exist, and that society might be managed silently, by instinct, habit, and ocular perception, without this supervening Babel of reports, invectives, laws, arguments, and slogans. But in that case human society would have ceased to be human; and before considering further the political misdeeds of language, I wish to make my bow to it and apologize briefly to the muses for being compelled to speak ill of them.

*In the beginning was the Word:* and Faust (or Goethe) showed little understanding of the subject when he found it impossible to prize the Word so highly. A word, by the intuition it evokes, arrests a meaning or essence; arrests precisely that form in any phenomenon which is capable of being recalled or repeated; and unless phenomena had assumed or suggested some such form, and presented a definite character, they could never have appeared; they could neither have been nor have seemed to be in any way distinct from one another. The Word, in this its logical force, is therefore prior logically to any fact or feeling or perception, and may truly be said to have been in the beginning.

Moreover, this formal element in things, making them what they are, makes also the specific language of imagination. It spreads out infinite spaces through which spirit may wander, uttering here one word and there another. This play of signs and sounds may

---
[1] The hexameter is Matthew Arnold's.

become reflective, organising memory, legend, poetry, and science. In this ideal direction language, with its grammatical creations, forms one of the fine arts, and does not figure among political dominations and powers. Liberal arts are relevant to government only as the whole realm of spirit is relevant to physical life, by witnessing it and supplying it with a moral excuse for being. The material utility of language as a code of signals is obvious; but such a rattle is in itself useless, if not positively evil, unless it proves good and self-justifying intrinsically; and it never can do this except by so perfecting its material and useful functions as to rise, in the very act of fulfilling them, into the realm of spirit.

So much for the intrinsic and ultimate function of words in giving free expression to the spirit, and forming a sacred poetry or liturgy in which life celebrates its existence. There remains what concerns us here, the intervention of language in affairs, partly to expedite them, and partly to complicate and confuse them by substituting words for things, and duties for benefits.

Language is one of the most powerful influences to which a group of men can be subject; yet little in language is rational: almost everything is arbitrary and conventional. To make vocal sounds and to employ signs are both instincts; but no particular language is instinctive. Particular languages are social *institutions*. For various reasons, probably trivial, certain sounds and certain ways of arranging them (which we call grammar) become habitual in a particular tribe; the young out of the infinite noises that they make, learn to repeat and retain those they most often hear. How casual that instituted language is, how arbitrary and blindly selected is the grammar it embodies, appears in the Babel of languages which arise wherever intercommunication is suspended; also in the rapid variation of any dialect not used for ritual or for inscriptions. The vocal instincts that language is built upon are infinitely vaguer, more plastic, more rich in possibilities, than is any particular language; and the necessities or utilities subserved by society (almost the same all over the world) are far sharper and less ambiguous than the meanest language: for language if fit only musically to express feeling is all metaphorical in describing material fact, which mathematics can do much better. Hence any current language leaves the gift for language unexhausted and unsatisfied, poetry breaking its wings pitifully against that rigid cage. At the same time any language gives of things only one of an infinite number of possible renderings, all meant to be identical in deliverance and therefore each provokingly arbitrary in that special linguistic flutter which distinguishes it from the rest.

So truly, however, is habit a second nature that very soon the casual peculiarities of a current language seem indispensable to it, and essential to any speech or thought; so that the existence of foreign tongues seems at first incredible, then ridiculous, and to the end displeasing; and there is nothing in which absurdity looms more obvious and enormous than in solecisms and verbal slips. Later, when reflection sets in, it hardly corrects this prejudice of habituation; on the contrary, grammar is often sublimated into logic, and logic into physical or divine necessity, so intimately can the threads of the narrowest convention be woven into the texture of mind.

Yet this idolatry of language is no mere foible for the satirist to deride; it is as truly a window opening on the fields of free imagination. Each language has its special euphony, as every string or wind instrument has; and its peculiar genius casts over the whole world, which men survey and conceive chiefly through verbal description, a distinctive grammatical and poetic colour, a mode of vibrating and rhyming which only those who use that language can discern in things.

In this case of language we may see clearly how a social institution may be grafted upon an instinct, how it may satisfy and yet strangely limit that instinct, and how it may find a practical use and may yet be terribly cumbrous, wasteful, and misleading. If this can happen to a social institution like speech, which is based directly on bodily impulses, and points largely to visible things, how much more may we not expect it to happen to institutions which are political, seated in no visible organ and pointing to no visible object? We must expect government, when it arises, to be, like language, spontaneous, arbitrary, partly useful, largely redundant, and sportive, excluding almost all the original potentialities of its organ, yet realising one of them and giving to social existence a special form, acutely vital, terribly exclusive, and highly prized for its own sake. For it is in this way that each language, with its written and its latent poetry, becomes a precious heritage, and one of the chief elements (as we see to-day) of union and of division among nations.

CHAPTER 4

LANGUAGE AND IDEAS SYMBOLIC

The psychological sphere is functionally moral, consciousness marking a *success* in organic life; [1] but the whole machinery of this moral triumph is physical. Language, for instance, and its social function are physical complications, vocal, economic, and historical: and even the spiritual function of language, yielding music and truth, can be exercised only through that physical medium. Words should therefore not be blamed for being only words, symbolic and wholly unlike their objects. Rather they ask to be used freely, with sympathy towards the genius of words; so all the better, through the plastic network of their sound and syntax, something of the structure of things may be revealed.

I say this in apology for the fact that in some parts of this book I use such phrases as ruling ideas, inspiration, or moral influence. Such expressions might seem inconsistent with my materialism; they are not so if understood to describe the dominance through language of a physical agency—an imposing personality, a phraseology, an institution—over simpler human forces. The more intimate operations of the human organism either escape attention altogether or, like digestion, pregnancy, or ripening puberty, are felt only in a vague change of mood, or conceived only indirectly and deceptively behind the name and character of their obvious results. So in politics, which is not an exact science, the terms used can have only a conventional and dramatic truth. Even in what ought to be physics we are often reduced to the same rude symbolism. The family doctor, looking through his spectacles at a slight eruption on the skin, and pronouncing it *eczema*, will confess if he is candid that this is only a Greek word substituted for the Latin word eruption. He is merely naming the visible fact, the surface appearance. To trace the underlying physiological and chemical processes may be impracticable and not necessary for taking some general precautions or giving some relief. So the eruptions

[1] Pain, and every sort of impatience, mark a *vital failure* or difficulty; but sensibility to that difficulty or failure is a *moral success*. The organism and the spirit are quickened thereby and made alive to their condition.

and up-boilings of human society doubtless have economic and physiological causes which a complete historical science might trace; but the forces that created animals and still govern them are not on the animal scale; and the public can observe only gross surface events, and express them in dramatic language. Desire, ambition, hatred, and love are the loose emotional categories by which actions are first discriminated; and the refinements by which speech may eventually describe human motives, for instance in Shakespeare, never escape from the same region of spontaneous fiction and verbal fancy.

Seeing, then, that the dynamic texture of events, both in ourselves and in the world, escapes observation, we are reduced to naming those superficial features or rhythms which most strike the eye and focus the emotions. The dramatic nomenclature of politics must be accepted, not as revealing a magic world in which some spiritual nebula evolves into material events, but only as the inevitable verbal symbolism by which material events are distinguished and interpreted in the human imagination. A more exact science of life, if we pursued it, would pay for its truth by its abstractness. If it were possible to obtain accurate statistics of human conduct, such information would be irrelevant to the dramatic experience of life, whether private or public; and that mechanical skeleton of history would need to be clothed with the rhetoric of passion and intention before we could recognise it for our familiar world. After all, that which interests the moralist is the phenomenology of spirit; the rest is only the architecture and mechanism of his stage and his stage properties. The play he watches and judges on that stage is a tragic fable, saturated with rival illusions, and spoken in verse.

Illusions form a second reality which may be described with truth. Ideas, however fantastic, grow out of their occasions, and are natural symbols for them. In the proper and widest sense, ideas are *prophetic*. They speak for the Lord, for the dominant power making itself felt in the present, reverberating in the past, and preparing the future. It is no illusion to feel that our words and thoughts are inspired; they really flow from the dynamic process of nature which they describe or forecast; they have some true value as oracles and omens. Their existence is testimony; and they convey knowledge, however partial and qualified, of the course of the world and of their own destiny. This signification of ideas we may admit and retain without any lapse into superstition; and the ordinary idolatrous way of speaking about ideas, purposes, and laws as if they were powers is not only excusable but admirably poetic, if we have the good sense not to press it into a dazed worship of images and words.

## CHAPTER 5

### MYTHICAL DOMINATION OF IDEAS

THE WORD "idea," being in common use, has various meanings in various connections. Etymologically the word means an appearance to sight; but even this is ambiguous. For an appearance may be conceived as a picture composed of various parts or elements, or it may be treated experimentally, as a stimulus, or as an indication of something else to be found or done. A mere stimulus, however, would not be an idea: it is not an idea that makes one sneeze. Nor would an idea be an index to something else without the help of an impulse not ideal in oneself which I call animal faith. The word idea directs our attention only to sight, and in seeing or even in looking we are scarcely aware of any movement within ourselves that should render vision a biological activity, rather than an absolute and placeless revelation. If instead of vision we had first examined sound, which in its purity is at least as aesthetical as light, we should have felt, especially when the sound was that of our own cry, that a strong commotion in us and a violent effort in our chest and throat produced that sound, and gave it lodgment and meaning in the life of nature. Were seeing more often accompanied by being dazzled or blinded, and looking by being intensely lustful or frightened, we should be less inclined to say that sight could reveal nothing but a patch of coloured light, not to speak of celestial essences recalled by a banished soul.

The latter mythical notion, once launched by Plato in his poetic prime, has the spiritual value proper to the deliverance of any trance. That which pure vision can actually report is always an ideal figment composed by the organs of vision and saturated by the moral force of that active function which those organs exercise. This figment or visionary idea turns the haphazard impressions made by the material stimulus into a single somewhat definite term for thought. Vision has thereby endowed the object encountered with a recognisable aesthetic character, clear and distinct enough to serve memory and cursory science in the description of that object and of its distribution in the world.

We speak of ideas carrying themselves out; but that is a loose figurative way of speaking, which only a most idolatrous idealist could mean literally. Ideas are never carried out unless there is *somebody* to do it for them; they are but images in the mind of the aspects that events may come to wear. In the mind the idea is a memory, a perception, or a prophecy: in nature the idea is a pattern or trope exemplified by *growing* into them, by *taking* that shape: the ideas are introduced into nature by the processes of nature. And this is notably the case when we, by our arts, introduce the variation. Intuition will not perform the miracle; work must perform it. The tongue must move; the audible conventional word must come to the lips, and reach a ready ear; the hands, with tools or plans in them, must intervene to carry the project out. Art is a material proficiency; inspiration a material impulse, flooding and surprising the mind.

I do not mean that art or inspiration are *only* material. They are seen, felt, reviewed, prefigured, enjoyed by the spirit. But I mean that the spirit can never possess, much less communicate, such a revelation unless a material occasion and a material endowment exist capable of arousing that inspiration and exercising that art. There is no art without artists, no inspiration without flesh and blood to gather and express it.

This would appear clearly even in soliloquy, when the mind withdraws as much as possible within the circle of its memory and fancy. Why had I this particular and probably ridiculous career? And why do I remember and ruminate over it, and only in scraps? Why do I conceive certain other possibilities or impossibilities that somehow interest me? Why do I care for the things that I care about, often painfully, when, not caring, I should be spared so many pangs? And, in a word, why am I myself—the very last person I should have chosen to be? And whence do I fetch this deeper criterion, by which I judge my actual self to be so alien, so accidental, and so unimportant?

Perhaps the reader, applying these reflections, suitably moderated, to his own person, will reply that he has a conscience, and

## MYTHICAL DOMINATION OF IDEAS

judges himself and all other facts by the self-evident criterion of right and wrong, goodness and badness. But that is only a habitual verbal screen for his animal and social impulses; and I am sure that, with a little patience, both he and I might discover the chief circumstances that had determined us to be as we are, and perhaps to wish that we might have been different. These are natural, animal, human circumstances. Our souls are created souls; and the great flood of earthly life that has cast them up determines at once what they shall be and the effects they shall have, or shall wish to have, on the world they move in.

Thus ideas take shape, and point to action in particular directions, only because the organs of perception, imagination, and action have been already spontaneously adapted to the objects that normally surround them. Such organs are the human eye and ear, the hand and the tongue, the digestive and sexual apparatus, with their periodic impulses; and such, for the body politic, are the primary institutions of family and tribal life, of agriculture, domestic handicrafts, and barter. Proficiency or virtue in these matters will depend partly on steadiness, on unswerving adherence to the modes of action already established and expected, and partly on cleverness, on alacrity in taking advantage of particular openings and opportunities, always in the service of the interests already dominant. Evidently fresh intuitions, fresh laughing emotions, will go with this cleverness, and old words and old affections with that tradition. Ideas and sentiments in verbal psychology and verbal morals will figure as the *causes* now of steadiness in conduct, now of successful initiative; but in reality a firm settled temperament is requisite in the one case, and a mobile hair-trigger temperament in the other. The character of the ideas occurring to a man is due to his own character, their action to his action; and the effects said to be produced in the world by an idea flow from the causes by which the idea was itself produced.

An idea will do perfectly well for a sign of the powers at work in a man or in a society, provided the critic can estimate the depth to which the roots of that idea run in the world. For a literary physics, that regards all causes as merely series of associated ideas, any sign will be as much a cause as any other; and it would be arbitrary to say that a dog's mouth waters at the physical presence of food but not at the spiritual presence of the image supposed to fill his consciousness; both being equally antecedents, both would be equally causes. But this is literary psychology, and literary physics. The spiritual antecedent is introduced poetically, and is undiscoverable by the experimenter, except perhaps in his own person, and then imputed to the dog by dramatic analogy; and it would be only by some further physical observation that the justice of that analogy could ever be tested. The two antecedents are not, therefore, on the same plane in respect to evidence. An even greater contrast exists in respect to derivation. Physical causes are not associations established in any mind but movements generating one event continuously out of another; there is an uninterrupted flux of measurable and traceable events, a transformation of the same objects rather than an association of independent images. A son is not related to his father by mere similarity and contiguity: he is born materially out of his parents, not pinned on to them by the genealogist. He may be spurious; and no amount of pinning ideas together in his mind or in other people's minds would then render him legitimate.

The growth of ideas too is spontaneous and may take any direction and reach any development for which a physical basis can exist not fatal to the organism; and within the limits of tolerable health and sanity ideas may vary indefinitely with the sensibility of races and with their traditions, industries, and way of living. Yet, beneath the tangle of doctrines and passions the ultimate control will be exercised by physical forces, in which the disciplined forces of individuals and nations must be included. The issue may be charged with all the insights and spiritual refinements imaginable; but these refinements would be neither possible nor inwardly impassioned and exalting if they were not proper to a race of animals living in a material world.

## CHAPTER 6

### ECONOMIC AND LIBERAL INTERESTS IN RELIGION

THE interplay of economic and liberal arts is well exemplified in religion. To the crude naturalist it may seem that magic and primitive cults are wild economic experiments which myth and dogma afterwards are invented to justify. The blank mind, dazed by some image and obeying some impetus, tries all sorts of tricks and mouthings, on the chance that they may work some wonder, as the prestidigitator and the medicine man do; and if any real virtue can be attributed to that performance, or to that apparition, these are retained, called up, or re-enacted in fear and trembling whenever the occasion suggests them again. Superstition then attaches itself to all the terrors of life, and adds the terror of omitting some prayer or some ceremony that might supernaturally dispel them.

Religion would then be, like alchemy and astrology, merely a hasty error in science. But religion, even superstition, has a positive side; and when the religion is not one in the truth of which we have a personal stake, that positive side is easy to distinguish and to admire. It is moral truth or familiar human predicaments dramatically expressed in fables. The parables in the Gospels are avowed instances of this; not avowed but not less poetical are the traditional metaphors that represent the moral economy of society and the force of natural law as the personal government of a celestial Monarch. These metaphors were not wholly transparent even to the minds that first employed them; they came as revelations of sublime facts. The Vow of Jacob in the 28th chapter of Genesis, 10–22, is a matchless example of this:

> "And Jacob . . . lighted upon a certain place and tarried there all night, because the sun was set; and he took of the stones of that place, and put them for his pillows; and lay down in that place to sleep. And he dreamed, and behold a ladder set up on the earth, and the top of it reached to heaven: and behold the angels of God ascending and descending on it. And, behold, the Lord stood above it, and said, I am the Lord God of Abraham thy father, and the God of Isaac: the land whereon thou liest, to thee will I give it, and to thy seed; and thy seed shall be as the dust of the earth, and thou shalt spread abroad, to the west and to the east, and to the north, and to the south: and in thee and thy seed shall all the families of the earth be blessed. And, behold, I am with thee, and will keep thee in all places whither thou goest, and will bring thee again into this land: for I will not leave thee, until I have done that which I have spoken to thee of.

"And Jacob awakened out of his sleep and he said: Surely the Lord is in this place, and I knew it not. And he was afraid, and said, How dreadful is this place! this is none other but the house of God, and this is the gate of heaven. And Jacob rose up early in the morning, and took the stone that he had put for his pillows, and set it up for a pillar, and poured oil upon the top of it. . . . And Jacob vowed a vow, saying, If God will be with me, and will keep me in this way that I go, and will give me bread to eat and raiment to put on, so that I come again to my father's house in peace; then shall the Lord be my God; and this stone, which I have set for a pillar, shall be God's house: and of all that thou shalt give me, I will surely give the tenth unto thee."

The whole religion of Israel is contained implicitly in this passage. The Lord is the power that governs the world, and men's fortunes in it. This is not in itself a religious conviction but a summary recognition of what a philosopher might call the nature of things. The Lord becomes the God of Abraham, Isaac, and now of Jacob in so far as he protects them and enters into a covenant with them. This establishes a moral and tribal religion. And the visionary and ceremonial side of religion is not neglected. Revelation, and the promise of protection, of local dominion, and of universal moral authority and honour, come in a dream: it is conscience and ambition that together inspire this faith. And even ritual and ecclesiastical privilege are established. A stone, raised into a monument, is sanctified by being anointed and becomes the promise of the Temple; and tithes are promised to support it and its priests. And this Vow of Jacob is renewed later by the Prophets with a significant variation. Jacob will be true to the Lord as to his God, if the Lord protects him. The Prophets said that the Lord would be true to Israel if Israel was true to his Law.

This inversion is not a contradiction of the original expression but a complementary view of the same relation. It would be a grave error to suppose that, because Jacob's Vow, in the curt form given it at the end, makes religion a purely economic art: therefore there is no religion in it, but only a calculation of profit. That such a promise of profit should be dreamt of, and warmly accepted as worth trusting, manifests a religious mind, just as the reforming

# INTERPLAY OF INTERESTS IN RELIGION

zeal and conscientious scruples of the hedonist manifest a moral disposition. What the calculating hedonist lacks is not morality but nobility and strength of feeling. So what a pure economic religion would lack would not be faith or piety but only spirituality. So although Jacob's Vow is not spiritually inspired, its religious background, form, and tendency are full of religion. With his head upon a stone, he dreams of heaven, conceives help awaiting from there, and vividly composes the aspect and the language of the Lord, speaking with favour to his servants. This is a most religious vision, and the seed of the most fertile religion that has ever existed. It was not spiritual at first, being politically very strong; but it became spiritual later, and it generated other religions even more spiritual than itself.

This development is natural, because fear, faith, and obedience, such as an economic religion instils, bend the psyche into conformity with the conditions of its life. Vital liberty, under such discipline, tends not only to coincide more nearly with opportune action, but to develop ideal interests, such as science, and other liberal arts that can flourish without any direct conflict with reality But to flourish without feeling any domination crossing your path is to obey, and thereby to develop, your inmost, freest, most disinterested powers; it is to live in the spirit. Your compulsions have become your choices and your limitations your virtues.

The chief virtues of spirit are intelligence and sympathy. These represent, in human terms, the initial interdependence and perpetual equilibrium of all the parts of nature. Thus spirit, though in act the ultimate and perhaps most thinly scattered phase of existence, *in potentia* always lay prepared at the root of things.

The liberation of spirit, though most heroically found in religious holiness, is therefore to be found also in a thousand other places and forms. Anywhere rhythms proper to action may survive action, and may form self-repeating tropes. What at first was a passive sensation may become a temporal perspective, called expectation or memory; or if its narrative interest endures when its temporal moorings are lost it may become a story, a dream, or a myth. The thrust of external events or the very confusion and fatigue of thinking is bound before long to cut short all free speculation. Spirit dips under, sleeps, or becomes a diffused sensorium under the patter of facts. This is its fate in what the world calls good fortune and fair weather. There are worse dangers, physical suffering, unhappy turns of fortune, moral conflicts or disasters. But while, at their best, human affairs may capture spirit and drag it along with them, it never can rest in them. Existence only mocks the mind, save by virtue of ideal and emotional characters that spirit discerns in it. The complete art of living would therefore be economic in its actions for the sake of being wholly liberal in its enjoyments.

Apply this now to religion, and the superstitious side of it becomes simply an error in economics. The prayers for rain, the sacrifices for good crops or for victory in war, the penances or benefactions offered as propitiation for sins added up like debts, are wise and prudent measures if the dogmas about divine laws and punishments are true. We should then be preventing disasters that would otherwise have overtaken us in this life or in another temporal and eventful life that was to follow. But why are such penitential exercises supposed to propitiate Heaven? Or why was Heaven imagined to exist at all and be an ally of the police in keeping order in our civil society? Because order has a beautiful as well as a useful side, and so have all the civic virtues; so that in appealing to God for help in these matters, or in preserving the health and life of those we love, or even of our crops, ships, and gardens, we are abandoning for the moment the economic arts that are proving insufficient for our good, and invoking the sympathy of God, because we believe that he loves the ideal goods that we love, and may work a miracle, if necessary, to save them for us.

Here the confusion with economic arts is abandoned for an explicit substitution of a liberal art—the discrimination and love of the good in all its forms. Now, religious faith regards the good as a miraculously physical power, and if this belief is an illusion, the pious practices invoking that miraculous power are vain economically. Yet even then they are not vain spiritually, because they quicken in us a clear view of the good attainable and a comprehensive sense of the volume and overwhelming splendour of things perhaps unattainable for the moment but profoundly congenial to the latent aspirations of our nature.

I should therefore venture to disallow, in all religions, the economic motives which they appeal to in promising heavenly and also earthly rewards for obeying their precepts. These precepts may be wise or harmless in themselves; but if obedience to them is only a means to secure something different or contrary, as if fasting on earth procured a banquet in heaven, neither the discipline nor its purpose is in the least religious, even if it was a religious authority that discovered the prospect of that feast and the divinely appointed conditions for being invited.

Is it not evident that a celestial banquet, for a religious mind, can be nothing but a metaphor, pathetic if not satirical, representing precisely the beauty and peace of frugality and forgetfulness of cravings and passions? Asceticism is something forced, and therefore insecure, unless it be a refuge and happy relief from indulgences that are insatiable, always fretful, always oppressive and remorseful. Religion begins when in the midst of its agonies and self-enslavements the Will is arrested, hears an unexampled music, drinks a water that cancels the possibility of thirst. Yet in all this suspension of what the world calls life, we see and understand and accept the world as we never could accept it before, in its wholeness, in its fleeting suffering, and in the eternal beauties and truths which in each phase it can reveal to a poetic spirit.

I would not quarrel about words or prescribe beforehand what forms the human imagination should take; it is the only competent judge of its own products. And if a positivist tells me that all in religion that is not economically wise is absolutely foolish, I leave room for his position; no other could come within his horizon, if he is absorbed in the accidental excitement and adventure of living, with his tastes as they happen to be and his circumstances as he finds them. And I leave room also for other positivists who use a pious language, and say that the fear of the Lord is not only the beginning or principle of wisdom but the whole of all religion: it is indeed the essence of piety that regards gratefully and obediently the conditions by which life may be preserved or in harmony with which life should be perpetually recast. It is not contrary to classic usage to see religion chiefly in that light, as an economic art or method of survival.

Yet religion has another side, which arrests the eye of disinterested reflection. What is it that survives when fishes are transformed into reptiles or reptiles into birds? One is the continuity of transmitted substance and life: in order to live and multiply the original creatures have abandoned their shape, their habitat, their powers, their temper, and doubtless the quality of their feelings. Something of them has survived materially, as something always must, but nothing has survived morally. Now in man, and doubtless in some measure in all living creatures, what the Will strives to preserve and to manifest more and more completely and clearly is the *form* of life; the continuity of substance in changed form is not, for them, survival but corruption and horrible decay. The man whose pleasure is to melt away in the universal flux into something always different and unforeseen is not essentially human because he banishes intellect, the capacity to arrest and distinguish forms. His arts, however complexly organised, can never be liberal. They must always be economic, not in the sense of finding means to a given end, for that would imply a clear intuition of both, but in the sense of always taking the path of least resistance, obeying the drift of destiny and piously becoming no matter which of God's creatures.

There is in fact something trustful in such self-surrender and something humble in such equal regard for all kinds of things. Yet there is also something slack and destitute about having nothing to defend, something unmoral in loathing nothing. What a moral nonentity is this existence that will not limit or define itself for fear of ceasing to exist, this lump of *materia prima!*

Such doubtless is the substance variously moulded by nature and later by man; and in politics we might imagine such a formless raw material of society, a proletariat, all children of both sexes swarming in one immense orphan-asylum, left to invent, if they could, a new language, a new morality, and a new religion. But would they ever be anything but a troup of monkeys screeching together? The tentative discrete arts of man were not born in this way. They leapt separately here and there in different directions like streams down the hillsides, liberal and bold before they could be useful. But the forms they assumed in play found uses in action; these uses then deepened and complicated their channels, as embankments and bridges formalise rivers and make the incidental glory of their maturity, as cascades and music made that of their rustic youth. So religion too is steadied when it becomes moral, and morality is liberated when it becomes spiritual.

# CHAPTER 7

## THE DEPENDENCE OF MORALITY ON RELIGION

"The old humanity," writes an historian of Islam, "had been killed by the new religion." This is what always happens. True morality, the adepts of each religion tell us, is dependent on their particular faith; the morality that may have preceded, or that may survive, can only be a false morality. If some unbelievers are virtuous it is by a fortunate inadvertence or kindliness on their part; they ought logically to indulge every passion, for if our faith is vain we are of all men the most wretched. This was said by Saint Paul in view of a young Christianity turning away from the world and watching for the second coming of Christ in the clouds; but the same segregation and the same risk are inseparable from any enthusiastic religion, even from the pantheism or romanticism of the enraptured unbeliever. He, too, is the most wretched of men, if his faith is vain; because he has alienated almost all human sympathies, and become a hater of the real world, for the sake of some vain pose, or empty fanaticism. And when he discovers his predicament he may think the bottom is knocked out of the world and may bitterly cry with Saint Paul—too late, alas, for his own person—that nothing remains but to eat, drink, and be merry.

This contention might seem singular, when we consider how much older human morality is than any of the religions on which it is said to be founded; and yet this contention is sincere, and in some sense justified by daily experience. Not only does the decay of religious faith let loose all sorts of moral licence, but the inevitable rebellion of the passions, noble as well as base, against any external control, is often the secret cause of infidelity; because people wish to be free to do as they like with a good conscience. People always do as they like; but while they are believers, they must confess that they have sinned; whereas by the easy method of discarding their faith, they can have their fun and call themselves virtuous.

Undoubtedly the principle of rational morality is utterly independent of each and of all religion, and rather inimical to any special gospel; because rational morality coordinates all interests and all types of value, whilst each new gospel attributes a unique and final authority to one type of value and to one passionate interest. Nevertheless each religion is the source and only sanction of a special morality, coloured and heightened by that special enthusiasm; so that each religion, from the point of view of human reason, carries with it a moral heresy. To undermine that religion is to undermine this bias in morals; a bias which custom or ignorance or narrowness of temperament causes believers to identify with morality itself.

For instance, it would undermine Jewish morality to doubt that the Ten Commandments were written by the finger of God. For then there would be no harm in breaking the Sabbath, and everyone would soon do so, unless he happened to like the observance. Everyone would also commit adultery when tempted if not deterred by prudence or by some contrary private allegiance. For a man on rational grounds may resist a weak temptation; but resistance becomes irrational when the temptation is stronger than the love of all other things including life itself. The function of religious commands is precisely to load the dice, to load them with mystical authority and disproportionate fears, so that no temptation should overcome the force of the official precepts. The conformity thus secured is often more verbal than practical, more intellectual than moral; but even then a convention and a public conscience may be created coercing human nature in the individual, and overawing his private reason.

Now, it is a curious assumption of religious moralists that their precepts would never be adopted unless people were persuaded by external evidence that God had positively established them. Were it not for divine injunction and threats everyone would like nothing better than to kill and to steal and to bear false witness. Undoubtedly, there is little integration or integrity in most men's characers; there is only habit and a plodding limitation in life and mind; and if social pressure were not added to lack of opportunity disorderly lives would be more common than they are. But decency, at least verbal decency or conventionality, establishes itself automatically in human society; a relative decency of course, according to the age and breeding of the circle concerned, but a decency very sharply enforced, since nothing is more intolerant than club opinion.

These spontaneous and local codes coerce the individual, but they claim no divine authority. On the contrary, one of the most powerful means of exercising moral pressure is to impose a very special code, avowedly that of only one class or country or profession. The contrast to legal and public standards is often a chief part of this private allegiance; the excitement and danger of being lawless are merged in a sense of superior privilege and enlightenment. Pride, vanity, *esprit de corps,* secret oaths, backed by the intense viligance and quick vengeance proper to secret societies, can work up the special conscience and zeal of party men almost to madness; and the isolation of the conspirator from the rest of society binds him the closer to his gang.

It has been in this atmosphere of mystic isolation, secret conspiracy, and fervid union that religion has sometimes taken shape; and perhaps the claim to divine revelation and divine sanctions has simply given mythical form to the absoluteness of the party conscience. Surely, without faith in the divinity of their inspiration, the propaganda of the early Christians, with the asceticism and martyrdoms ensuing, could never have been so prolonged; and the conventional but peculiar commandments of a religion, after it has been long established, may be nothing but the fossils of that living inspiration which filled it in the beginning. If a religious morality is to become that of society at large—which original Christian morality was never meant to be—it must adapt its maxims to a possible system of worldly economy; and the more successfully it does so and seems to become the inspiration of an entire nation or age, the more its specific organisation will assume a worldly and formal character. An irrational, inspired, specific moral zeal will still glow at the centre; but its light and heat will fade in diffusion, and be variously intercepted and refracted in the surrounding field. The orthodox morality of the Church will have become almost rational morality, or human orthodoxy; and the special inspiration of new moral heresies may attack it, as it attacks the ordinary morality of the world. There will then be two sorts of religious morality invading human life, and tending to transform it; first, the original special inspiration at the heart of the established religion, an inspiration still alive at the centre, though hardly felt at the circumference; and secondly, any fresh inspirations descending upon individuals or upon sects, and tending to infuse a new special morality, at once into the world and into the Church.

This is what has happened in modern Christendom. Catholic

mystics, from time to time, have renewed the original eschatological and ascetic morality of the early Christians, with new warnings to the world that the end, with a fearful judgment, is at hand; also that the salvation of mankind must come by supernatural means, transporting the elect into a supernatural celestial kingdom. At the same time Protestant reformers, transcendental idealists, revolutionary politicians, and humanitarians of all sorts, have kindled each his fresh focus of moral illumination and propaganda; sometimes partly coinciding with the old slumbering Christian fire, but more often arising by spontaneous combustion in some entirely different quarter.

I need hardly say that Christian morality has never ruled the world. It could never do so unless it turned the world into a monastery; and the extreme interest and picturesqueness of Christendom come precisely from this perpetual interplay between a religion at once prophetic and mystical and the old and new secular passions of mankind. Christian chivalry and Christian art were lovely but unstable and barren hybrids born of this union; and the moral chaos through which the world is now passing marks the efforts, perhaps ineffectual, of the invalid to dismiss his physician, and to forage for himself again in the universe as if he were a free and healthy animal.

Health and freedom, however, if recovered against the lingering domination of Christianity, may reserve some surprises to the modern mind. The modern mind is liberal and romantic; but a state of society and a discipline of the will inspired by pure reason would be neither romantic nor liberal. It would be sternly organic, strictly and traditionally moral, military, and scientific. The literary enemies of Christianity might soon find reason to pine for that broad margin of liberty and folly by which Christianity, in merry Christian times, was always surrounded. They could have played the fool and the wit to better advantage under the shadow of the Church than in the social barracks of the future; and a divided public allegiance, half religious and half worldly, might have left more holes and cracks for fancy to peep through than would the serried economy of reason.

When any social convention is relaxed, there is a flutter of loose living, and human vices, before hidden, venture to come out into the open; yet the decay of a religion, or of any marked social discipline, far from undermining the general principle of morality, sets that principle free and permits human morality to become rational and normal. At least such would be the result if no new religion or special social constraint came presently to fill the room of the lost convention. It would hardly be fair to say, except perhaps in the single instance of Greek ethics (and even this had many shades from Athens to Sparta) that the new religion killed the old humanity, because there was never a sane and perfect humanity dominating the life of men; the new religion probably kills nothing but old superstitions or old conventions no less partial and perhaps less noble than itself. Public morality is always a more or less chaotic thing, with many a foolish custom and compulsion woven into its texture; and a new religion, or a new social enthusiasm, however extravagant, is at least something somebody has consciously chosen and preferred to all other things: something capable of being loved, even if incapable of being attained or of producing happiness. Perhaps the rooted prejudices and vices of mankind can be overcome only by some prophetic reformer himself largely deluded; and we should never know the scope of our own nature, or its possible harmonies, if we did not yield to each of our passions in turn, and count the scars of those experiments. In this comparison and reflection, after the fray, we may draw the outlines of what would be, for us, a life of reason; it would be the art of satisfying our compatible inclinations in the midst of our inevitable circumstances. If special religions have disturbed this rational morality in its formation, they have done so by misrepresenting our real circumstances, or ignoring our necessary inclinations; imposing instead some morose and windy passion, or some false hope. Yet these passionate errors, since they are errors, have no firm roots or consistency, and float somewhat ambiguously, even when prevalent, over the hard realities of life; and meantime they may have served, by their first impact, to plough up the ground in some fertile spot and awaken the mind there to its true vocation.

## CHAPTER 8

### HOW RELIGION MAY BECOME POLITICAL

It is hard for any man to speak for others in the matter of religious life: human endowment seems to differ profoundly in this respect from individual to individual. Yet it is in these obscure and uncontrollable reaches of religious imagination that the claim to universal conformity has been most boldly put forth, not without some partial sporadic successes. One great religion calls itself explicitly the Catholic, and several others believe themselves no less exclusively well fitted and necessary to every soul; whereas in political government, which deals with situations so much better known, and interests so much less dubious, no universal system has yet been born alive. One reason for this anomaly is doubtless that religion in its systematic theories coincides with a pursuit or announcement of truth, and impinges on the sphere of history and science and philosophy; studies which being explicitly directed upon the description of the existing world, necessarily aim at cogent conclusions, which everyone ought to accept. Yet it is safe to say that religion originally had a different outlook, and floated in a medium quite other than truth or the aspiration after truth; so that in a religious system of the universe it is easy to distinguish what religious inspiration has assumed from what observation or reason may have discovered.

Religions are social, but religion is private. The sources of religion in the soul lie in the sub-soil far beneath the surface of social and moral needs, and even beneath the whole experience of a natural world; they lie in that unused residuum of life which the animal soul still feels within itself after social institutions and intellectual conventions have hemmed it in. Indeed, the most characteristic function of religion would seem to lie in lifting the soul out of its earthly environment altogether and bringing it into an imagined commerce with supernatural things. But by the irony of fate this heroic means of escaping convention becomes at once conventional and compulsory. The human soul is anxious, agitated, and ignorant; she cannot wait for confirmation of any reports first coming to hand; she dare not neglect any casual suggestion, any mystic

# HOW RELIGION MAY BECOME POLITICAL

impulse, however irrational, that reaches her in her distress. The omens she reads everywhere, the fancies and dreams that visit her, pass for facts and forces not to be neglected: terrible divine dangers, or divine helps, more important than any calculable agency. Thus groping anxiety glides into random experiments, these into fixed rites, and these again into sacred laws, disobedience to which is death. Religion has then been reduced to an art, ostensibly necessary to social welfare; it has been swallowed up in authority, in mock science, and arbitrary law; it has become the most tyrannous element in that hostile, hopeless world from which it has come to deliver us. Religious impulse is therefore always rebelling against its own creations, the positive religions, even more violently than against the dogmas of science or the stupid moralities of the world.

What, after all, is the mystical soul after? Is any soul so modestly poetical as to be satisfied with awakening and possessing in idea, like a sort of music, the good things denied it by the real world? Such an aesthetic and sentimental entertainment for idleness is not what we call religion. In religion there is always a certain urgency, a certain assimilation of the ideal to the real; in other words, what the mystical soul is after is commonly to find some secret power behind actual events, some pleasing extension of them, or some means, not so laborious or inadequate as human effort, to secure well-being.

Religion so conceived would differ from science and art only in method, not in aim. Seeing that an adequate view of the conditions of well-being could not apparently be furnished by vulgar experience, some rarer and privileged approach to the ruling facts would be desired. The motive would be the ordinary desire to live and prosper, the ordinary interest in discovering dangers and opportunities. Revelation, intuition, moral postulates, or whatever the means might be, would then serve merely to disclose magically the latent constitution of the universe, for our more prudent guidance; and religion would be merely the practical recognition, on that magic authority, of the actual situation in which we find ourselves, a situation which vulgar experience might not be able to discover, but which in fact controlled our earthly destiny, and our possible destiny beyond the earth. It is interesting to observe that even the pessimistic faiths, that look to absorption in the Absolute, are not content to preach withdrawal from an existing world not worth living in, but rather teach (at whatever expense of sophistry) that this world and our life in it are illusions, and that only the Absolute is a fact. So rooted is the demand of religious people that religion should not be a free choice made among ideals by each musing soul, but rather a way of life imposed on all by the objective nature of things, and enforced by the most dreadful sanctions.

Now, if religion had arisen later than science, or had always been built upon a scrupulous prior collation of all human knowledge, this claim on its part to bring us into harmony with hidden but real things would have had no political consequences. For all mundane action and judgment would have been determined before religion intervened; in fact religion would not have intervened at all; it would have supervened only, to adjust our relations to alleged interests lying wholly beyond the range of science, politics, or public morals. Without admitting in theory that it touched only imaginary objects, such a religion would have practically conceded that this was the case; and it would have made little or no difference to society what religion a man embraced, or whether he embraced any. At most the religious man might face the common mundane business in a somewhat different spirit, according to his type of religion; he might be more cheerful and buoyant than the mere worldling; or more scrupulous and solemn, or more detached and disillusioned. But his views about trans-mundane things would not touch his opinions or his rules of conduct in respect to this world.

Such a situation has been actually approached in Protestant countries, and especially in the United States. The whole foreground of life is filled with activities carried on in a common hearty national spirit, including the social activities of the various Churches themselves; all the wheels are turned by one central motive power of enterprise and good-will; and it makes little difference what dim metaphysical landscapes may be reputed visible out of this or that religiously painted window. The operatives are too busy each at his machine to look afield, and too fatigued and mastered by their week's work to be much stimulated or deeply convinced by what they hear of on Sundays; unless, indeed, the preacher eulogizes enterprise, public spirit, and domestic affection.

Such a state of affairs, however, is most exceptional and, judged by what prevails and has always prevailed in the world, it might well be said to neutralise all religion and politely turn it out of doors. For religion is in fact much older than science, or than lay government and law; it is much older than the mechanical arts. It prejudged every question of cosmology, history, morals, and manners long before investigation or private judgment began to operate at all. Undoubtedly it has assumed new forms from time to time, in response to secular cross lights, or to fresh religious inspirations, perhaps more consonant with some later state of knowledge or of feeling. But these very reforms, being often the conscious work of one man, are if anything more systematic and unyielding than religious tradition, and if they do not regulate all social and political questions they at least establish principles and lay down specific laws which virtually prejudge the whole field of government.

It should be observed that, if a systematic religion is true at all, intrusion on its part into politics is not only legitimate but is the very work it comes into the world to do. Being, by hypothesis, enlightened supernaturally, it is able to survey the conditions and consequences of any kind of action much better than the wisest legislator. It also can probe the heart (being the voice of primal Will) better than any momentary and conceited introspection. It can accordingly lay down with assurance the course of conduct that can lead men to save their souls, by so ordering their lives that they may avoid all false passions and ambitions, help one another in what it truly profits a man to undertake, and develop the capacities of their nature in the right and possible directions. Now, all this is precisely what wise legislation and good government profess to do: so that the spheres of systematic religion and of politics far from being independent or incommensurable, are in principle identical. If they do not wholly coincide in practice, the reason is that a religious prophet may, out of contempt or prudence, leave many details of life unregulated; and on the other hand political constitutions may be little more than by-laws for men in office, expedients for reconciling a few powerful interests, rather than complete regimens for human economy. Yet only in view of a complete ideal economy can any piece of legislation be justified in its principles or in its tendency. The empiricism and opportunism of politicians without ideals cannot absolve a government from the duty of considering and furthering the ultimate welfare of its subjects. And that precisely is what a systematic religion also undertakes to do, claiming to know by inspiration the conditions of life and the needs of the soul; and if you honestly accept this religious system you cannot, without the most shameless frivolity, be guided by anything else in your politics.

This truth seems mouldy and distasteful to thinkers of the liberal school, whose notion is to divide human economy into a number of disparate activities, family life, trade, morality, art, science, religion, government, none of which is to interfere in the least with the others. The human mind would then resemble a well-kept menagerie, where each wild animal of a distinct species lives in a separate cage. The absurd proposal would never have been put forward had not liberals (much to the credit of their hearts) been earnestly occupied with freeing certain particular interests felt to have been unduly subordinated—such as the material well-being of slaves and labourers, elementary education, commercial enterprise, and private philosophies and religions. But they had not at first the coherence of thought nor the moral courage to see that if these particular objects were so good, it must be because man had a vocation quite different from that which the Christian Church had supposed, and lived in a world otherwise constituted— with no heaven or hell in it, for instance. All this, when duly observed and thought out, would impose the programme of the Renaissance and the Revolution—that is, the re-establishment of Christian nations upon a pagan basis. To this conclusion the parties that were once liberal have in fact come in those countries where politicians think, or care to look where they step.

The word politics has a nobler and a meaner sense, and it is only in the latter that most people use it. It may mean what relates to policy and to polity—to the purposes of human cooperation and the constitution of society—or it may mean what relates to the *instruments* of policy only, as for instance to the form of government or to the persons who shall carry it on. Now, the most thoroughly political religions—the Hindu, the Jewish, the Catholic, the Mohammedan—disdain to enter the latter field. Having laid down the principles of politics in the higher sense, and supplied maxims for personal conduct, they leave the means of enforcing the law to circumstances. If God fixes the values, Caesar may be allowed to coin the means of exchange. This way of abandoning civic government to its own caprice is not due to any hesitation on the part of religious authorities to meddle with practical details. The book of Leviticus and the Koran conclusively prove the opposite. But we should remember that in the places where these religions took shape law and government were in a rudimentary stage; righteousness, the spirit in which men should treat one another, the rules which a patriarch should impose on his household, covered most of the problems of organised life. As for the kings and armies that might periodically sweep the world and levy tribute in it, their operation was not more amenable to precept than that of the weather. God no doubt sent these military scourges as he did tempests and floods, to chastise his disobedient children; but precepts as to how this wholesome castigation should be inflicted formed no part of his law. Righteousness might flourish quite as well, if not better, under those external visitations; it could not attempt to control them. If now and then a pious man found himself on the throne, his casual judgments, like those of Solomon, might show forth his wisdom, not, however, his policy; for it is not written that the wise Solomon was expected to do for mankind anything except build the Temple, and display his glory before them like a peacock. A man of God might by chance be a hunter and might rival Nimrod; yet God was not therefore expected to give commandments for the chase; no more for the royal sport of hunting mankind, or breeding them in the national preserves.

It was such a feeling of the hopeless brutality and nonmorality of government that made it possible for religious legislators to ignore it. Hence the complete life of Hindus, Jews, Catholics, and Mohammedans may very well be lived under an alien despotism, provided this does not attempt to be a thorough government, but leaves to the various religions the regulation of morals, manners, marriage, education, language, and all works of imagination. In these conditions the Jews have lived long: Hindus, Catholics, and Mohammedans are now largely and may soon be entirely in the same case. They will form a state within the state: but that complication is possible only when one of the two authorities, or both, abdicates its noblest and most vital function—to govern life.

Ancient Greece is the most political nation that ever existed, and the position of religion there is very interesting. That element in religion which was supposed to affect the public welfare—oracles and local rites—was altogether identified with policy and law. The speculative part, which we should call belief, was on the contrary abandoned almost entirely to the caprice of poets. Not that the caprice of poets was itself conceived for a moment to elude the political sphere: ethics, as Aristotle says, is a part of politics, and the inspiration of poets, though in its source it might be irresponsible and Dionysiac, was by its presence and tendency one of the threads which the legislator's skill loved to weave into the life of a perfect commonwealth. Therefore the inspirations of poets and philosophers did not escape the public censor, or even the courts of law. But the question was: will this Pythagorean philosophy or this Euripidean drama or this Socratic disintegrating criticism tend to dissolve the moral life and strength of the city? Are new stories about the gods likely to offend the powers that have hitherto protected us, or perhaps to derange the sane mind in our healthy body? The religion of the Greeks, in the earnest Hebraic sense of the word religion, was their politics. Mythology and worship they took seriously only when these seemed integral factors or agencies in public life. If we like to say that they wisely left religion free, we shall (in so far as this is true at all) be pointing out that they thought free religion frivolous, a lot of old wives' tales, or old men's hobbies; otherwise they would most surely have built it into their states, or built their state upon it. If we prefer to say that their religion was wholly political, a matter of legal sanctuaries, public feasts, and national hero-worship, established in the supposed interests of health or victory, we shall only be pointing out in a different way that what was truly sacred to the Greeks was the whole body of influences that can render civilised life noble and good; influences which they beautifully pictured in the forms and worships of the gods.

In spite of all this, it is possible for religions morally very powerful to be quite non-political; Buddhism and Protestantism are there to prove it. Protestantism has indeed been often entangled in politics but only by accident; it had to fight its way to freedom, to disengage itself from its own trammels or to suppress the gay religions and the gay manners that shocked its consecrated austerity. Protestantism has also had a great influence on politics indirectly, through the type of character it has developed—upright, sober, self-confident, thrifty, unctuous, and unintellectual. But in its essence and tendency Protestantism is non-political; not that, like Buddhism and other monkish religions, it turns away from the world, but rather that it presents the whole world to each man as an instrument for his education and discipline. He is to live the life of the world, conscientiously no doubt, but heartily, and his religion is to separate him as little as possible from it. In strictness one might say that the ultimate Protestant ideal is to have no outward or specific religion at all—no priests, churches, theology, Scripture or Sabbath, and indeed, no God. This position has not been reached by most Protestants, but I think that the nearer they come to it the more Protestant they are. It is the position of the great German idealists, who have brought the Protestant spirit to its perfect and most speculative expression. And these idealists are, in a large way, very industrious, very professional, and very worldly. Their religion encourages them to be so, for it teaches them that the world is a stage into which they are sent to play their part, and all sorts of parts have to be played, since the play is to be infinite. The more zest they can put into their work, the better. It is not the results or the pleasing incidental effects that matter, but only the training and education which the experience brings: for it is all only solemn play-acting. The play need not contain any religion, for religion is to act the play well. It need not contain any peace, for peace is to feel that you have done your duty. It need not contain any happiness, because the only happiness is the intensified will to go on playing this game for ever.

It is obvious that such a subjective and metaphysical religion might have nothing to urge in favour of particular institutions or customs; theoretically it can accept and digest them all. In practice, however, German idealism has framed a historical picture of the entire education of men, or rather of God, which is a sort of criterion for judging the progress of institutions. This progress is made to culminate in an apotheosis of romanticism, of Germanism, and of this idealism itself as the true religion. Driven out of the door, political religion thus comes in again at the window in the form of a religious philosophy of history, religious nationalism, and even religious war. The reason is, perhaps, that Fichte and Hegel were German patriots; a less local idealist might turn into incidents what they regarded as culminations, and might extend their curiously snug and circular panorama of the world. He might then approach politics with a free hand, as far as his religion went; and his religion would not need to be political because he would have outgrown religion, except for his idealistic motive in condescending to live. In Nietzsche this transformation actually occurred. His religion of the *Uebermensch* is a fantastic romantic version of Greek aristocracy.

## CHAPTER 9

### LIBERAL ARTS LIBERATE SPIRIT

The intuition of Walter Pater that all the arts aspire towards the condition of music may be clearly illustrated and in a sense corrected by the case of architecture. Architecture is a fundamentally economic art and more dominated than any other by its materials, its costs, and its practical uses. Yet its chief masterpieces have been always temples and palaces, triumphal gates and monumental tombs: edifices that a cynic might pronounce to be scandalously useless. Royal vanity and pious zeal have evidently taken possession of these means of expressing their militant passions and of giving to their social dominations the powerful help of wearing an imposing and bewildering aspect. The Pyramids of Egypt, the Temple at Jerusalem with its vast courts and bastions, the colossal statues and crowded tiers of grotesque sculptures in Indian temples, all show an extreme anxiety to outdo oneself at once in sacrifice and in display; thus turning architecture, like everything else, into something to throw away on one object of consuming passion. What could have happened to the utilitarian craft of house-building that it should be classed in this way among luxuries and treasures?

Useful structures are seldom imposing unless vast; and then, on acquaintance, they become hateful. The liberal element does not enter into economic works at the bidding of patrons or public, but through adaptation and sympathy established between the workman and his task. This adaptation is itself partly economic, smoothing and straightening materials so as to render them manageable and better able to fit together. But the straightening defines and assimilates various forms, and the smoothing gives polish and kindles fresh colours; so that under his hands the artizan's labour mingles constant gratifications with its inevitable difficulties, and the product becomes an object of pleased contemplation and pride.

The eye itself by a native gift is an artist that has to paint pictures in order to convey facts. Smell can teach animals to react suitably on things without any such graphic creations, which are the first toys that nature makes for the mind. Even in science such graphic fictions are misleading; for it is only the dynamic effects of objects that matter economically, and the attribution of aesthetic qualities to them is an illusion, and the first of myths. Yet it is this pictorial accompaniment that endears, from childhood, the world to the spirit.

Never will these appearances catch the eye more quickly, or suggest more variations possible among them, than when they present themselves spontaneously in the artizan's own work. Every detail in construction, like the projection of beam-ends under the eaves, suggests, and is finished off to imitate, the head of a dog or lion; or the jutting eaves themselves, as in China, are curled into a scalloped cornice. In favoured climates the walls themselves might discard those dead spaces not essential to their stability and become loggias or arcades; or a far-sighted economy might substitute stone piers for inflammable wooden props; the central piers, and ultimately even those at the corners, would become somewhat thicker cylinders; and thereby the basis would be laid for the greatest glories of mature architecture, peristyles and cloisters, traceries and balustrades; and, when the principle of the work had been discovered and applied, vaults and domes.

Meantime in communal works, serving the other chief need of society, safety from raids and sieges, city walls and scattered castles, both in town and country, produced unintentionally the most massive and picturesque of effects. The roughness and forbidding blankness of the walls and towers only heightened, by contrast and breadth of setting, such grated gates or windows as might be indispensable; and these offered splendid occasions for the boasts of heraldry to defy the enemy and reassure the citizen with an ever-watchful guard of stone monsters.

A passion for plastic and decorative art was let loose by these opportunities offered unwittingly by the harsh necessities of existence; and a marriage of war and play, of religion and magnificence gave imagination freedom while feeding it on vital and tragic themes.

Now, does this marriage of the artistic impulse with moral and political powers, while it gives to liberal arts a prominent part in society and in history, run counter to that aspiration towards pure music, which Walter Pater divined in them? I think that in that great enrichment there does lie a great temptation. What happens to a hermit when he is made a great abbot or bishop happens to the pure artist when he figures as a wit or a prophet in the popular mind. And when sensitive connoisseurs reacting against this enslavement and worldliness in official art look for pure models, they find them only in interludes, or first sketches, or irresponsible play of minor episodes, happy phrases, or intricate arabesques that peep in the corners of the approved academic masterpieces. It is the artist's soul that they find there; and they encourage the young artist to defy the great world, and trust his personal rebellious fancy.

In the history of Gothic architecture we may trace the fortunes of free imagination, aspiring towards the condition of music, conquering and dazzling a militant society and a militant Church, and then suddenly failing, leaving its greatest monuments unfinished, or patched and half-disguised by a sudden passion for the ruins of classic antiquity and the rational government of all human affairs. In this reaction of the lay world against tradition reason was not based on solid science but on impatience and ambition in superior persons. The types of art so revived or invented had the variety and brilliancy of fashions. The middle ages, as they grew rich and urban, had become increasingly subject to bold fashions in dress, in romantic fiction, in poetry, and in architecture. This was a symptom of a hybrid heritage, racial and political, which bred contrary tastes and rendered many charming Gothic inventions sterile and short-lived. That is a natural characteristic of liberal arts that lack an economic or traditional foundation, and it persisted in the free manners and thoughts of the Renaissance, making its successive phases and styles, down to our times, as inconstant and arbitrary as the more naive fancies of the middle ages had proved before.

Inspiration comes from the heart, and is always initially as blameless and courageous as life itself. This is its inalienable privilege; but it is born in ignorance, and cannot count either on permanent youth for itself or on a place for it in the world. A later fashion, essentially perhaps less authentic, could therefore replace it, especially as the society that dismissed it had not only its new tastes, but its modern science and politics to back it. The perfect scorn with which the seventeenth century treated everything mediaeval was an economic scorn; and the new architecture with its regularity, symmetry, and quiet dignity, embodied good sense and good order no less than the rational appeal of its human scale and private convenience.

The lesson to be learned from architecture may be applied to the other arts. Consider music itself. The physical vehicle of sound, gross vibrations of the air, is far less swift and subtle than that of light radiating throughout cosmic space; and this circumstance renders vision a much better means of information than the arts of sound, music and language, in that music hardly informs at all, and language, in informing, greatly overloads and distorts the truth. Therefore spirit, although intelligence is one of its chief functions, suffers horribly from the snares of language, while soothed by its music; and in pure music, free from the sophistry of words, it finds the vital echo of its potential experiences in their emotional urgency and colour, without the irrecoverable and distracting detail of their accidental occasions. For the flight of time tends to carry the lessons of time away with it; but the organic tropes of music are rich in recoveries and repetitions, and can themselves be repeated by faithful memory and tradition; not that the spirit cares for the temporal longevity of anything, but that it sees, especially in music, the precipitation of life falling into recognisable cadences, and reaching its natural climaxes with the glow of triumph in the peace of silence.

All the arts, even the economic arts when they become personally liberal, serve the spirit in this way, by instinct, not by intention; for the intention of the artist, even of the musician, is normally directed upon some technical problem, proper to the task assigned and to the phase of art dominant at the time. This predestined service rendered to the spirit has two sides: on the side of the art in its political status, this service is what is now called "creation"—that is, originality acceptable to the public, and capable of being incorporated in the living traditions of the art. On the side of the spirit, which is essentially a witness and not an agent, this service is liberation from the obstacles or the inner confusions that may have been rendering spirit, in some adventure, bound and not free. The spirit is, in each man, a phase of his psychic life, in which love or intelligence has become self-transcendent, disinterested, and lost in its ideal object. Will, as Schopenhauer would say, has been eclipsed, and the Idea has come forward and filled the stage. But the Idea here is seen, it is lived; so that there is still a living intuition, perfectly temporal and human, that brings that essence for the moment into the light of day. And this light of day, for the spirit, is pure; it adds no date or place to the eternal form conceived but sees and loves it for its intrinsic beauty and perfection. In feasting the spirit on this its congenial food, the arts liberate it from what it felt as exile or captivity, and allow it for a moment to be itself.

# BOOK SECOND

## THE
## MILITANT ORDER
## OF SOCIETY

# PART ONE

*Faction*

# CHAPTER 1

WARS OF GROWTH

AT THIS point it may be well to remind the reader that the three Books into which this work is divided, like the distinction between Dominations and Powers itself, are not to be taken for separate natural processes, such as history or natural science might distinguish; for all events arise according to the Generative Order of Nature, whether by involuntary growth or by militant or rational action; and all liberal arts, materially considered, form a part of the economic articulation of society. The distinctions which I establish are made in view, not of any distinct forces imagined to be at work in the world, but in view of the different *moral results* generated by the concourse of all natural forces. Politics are a part of morals, as morals, for a philosopher like Aristotle, are a part of politics; both are names for the human physiognomy that natural life acquires at certain junctures, or for the natural conditions that cause that moral physiognomy to change. So the material process by which a man makes an axe, when he uses it to fell a tree, becomes an economic art; but if he uses it to kill a wild beast or an enemy, the axe, without ceasing to be a product of economic art, becomes a weapon and an instrument in the arts of defence and destruction. How easily the moral function of industry can be transformed in this way, suddenly and on a vast scale, recent wars have shown us, when great works and whole populations have been turned from manufacturing locomotives and motor-cars to manufacturing bombing aeroplanes and tanks.

So when I distinguish a Militant Order of Society I mean to separate, in the sphere of politics and morals, the love of reforming the world from the total mutation that the world is always undergoing. All action, all economic art, exerts force and has effects; but this does not render all action or all economic art militant. Even destruction, even war, is not always inspired by a militant spirit or meant to impose a domination; it may be unintended destruction or purely defensive and unwelcome war. There is primaeval war in the jungle, before arts arise at all; the stronger plant intercepts the rays of the sun and sucks up the moisture needed by its weaker neighbours; and this is not malice on its part but the Will to Live. So populations overflow their borders, or are driven by hunger to migrate in vast numbers, submerging or pushing away the natives; and though the most decisive and terrible wars come in this way, sometimes, as in North America, the intruders could make themselves at home with a calm conscience and hardly leave the natives time to protest.

The colonists in both North and South America were indeed all militant; they all went forth to acquire new lands, or perfect independence, or to amass gold, or to convert the heathen; but this varied militancy was not military except by accident. The incidental destruction of primitive or of barbaric cultures was not the dominant aim, but rather the need of space for the body and for the spirit as it is for flora and fauna in the jungle.

Perhaps man the maker of weapons preceded man the maker of tools for agriculture or house building. Those cave-dwellers who, we are told, allowed many centuries to pass before they changed their habits, hunted large wild beasts for their food; which suggests ferocity as well as efficient weapons on their side. They must then have been decidedly militant and aggressive; yet they simultaneously practiced liberal and religious arts, if their admirable drawings were meant, as is said, for talismans to attract their prey or, who knows? by a kind of sympathetic invocation to entice them and bring them to sacrifice themselves to save the souls of their worshippers. We do not know in what guise or in what order spiritual lights may flash into the lives of other beings.

Economic and military uses often coincide in the arts. The roof and walls that keep out the weather also protect from wild animals, and in a castle, moat, bastions, and keep serve also for fish-pond, granaries, kitchens, chapel, chambers, and hall. And defences are not useful only for defence; they attract the lovers and the arts of peace into their precincts, until the castle becomes a palace and its outworks a town.

Existence itself, since it involves continual lapse and renewal of forms and relations, is essentially a blind and involuntary war. This Heraclitus long ago asserted, Lucretius insisted on, and Darwin perceived afresh. It should never be forgotten by anyone who does not wish to be deceived about this world and about the place of life and morality within it.

This universal passive war, though it is cruel, is blameless. We may occasionally shudder at existence, but while we exist and wax in strength, we must harden ourselves to suffer sacrifice and also to impose it. Construction involves destruction of the state of things that preceded. It nips in the bud, or in the flower, all the values that the previous state might have developed. They must dip under, and wait in the abyss of nonexistence for some future wave, more favourable to them, to bring them gloriously to the surface. Meantime that wealth of missed possibilities, or crushed virtues, is balanced by this fresh growth—one of those many possibilities—which was actually brought forth by our action: a growth that must not be grudged its moment of victory nor reminded too often that in the act of coming it has begun to go.

An ephemeral organism, like the tiny male of some insects, that had only one possible function would be spared all moral vacillation or dispersion; it would fly its bridal and tragic flight with absolute fixity of impulse and courage. But when, in a human psyche, an approach to such concentration goes with a clear sense of obstacles in its way and of contrary impulses in other people, the master passion, that would like to be absolute and to dominate the whole world, becomes hostility and hatred towards all dissenting forms of existence. Then war becomes intentional, self-righteous, and fanatical; and the spirit of such war is what I call militancy. It is not unintended and open to chivalry, as is the great war of life; it is blind to its own accidental bias and to the equal legitimacy of all existence; it thirsts to destroy its enemies and to see nothing in the world except its own likeness.

## CHAPTER 2

### WARS OF IMAGINATION

INSTABILITY in the human psyche, more than exhaustion of the soil or changes of climate, keeps history moving; and even when, as in this twentieth century after so many mechanical inventions, an immense mutation occurs in the equipment of industry, very little is decided in respect to politics or morals. All races are quick to learn the new arts. Europe by taking this blind lead has lost its leadership, since tool-making is precisely the field in which younger or less martial nations can easily prove its equals. And in this mechanical melting-pot, all the more passionate traditional enthusiasms of the different nations become confused and ashamed of themselves, or are revived hectically, with a desperate self-consciousness. Social epidemics, political fashions, wilful philosophies spread and collide, not always merely in the mind. Primary needs and passions are enlisted in the service of the most baseless dreams, as if by some verbal shibboleth human nature could be transformed.

Even material well-being may be jeopardized by material development. Economic security is not attained, and moral simplicity is lost; thus the greatest material progress may only expose the poor to foolish ambition, the very canker that has always eaten up the heart of the rich. The more equal and similar all nations and all individuals become, the more vehemently will each of them stick up for his atomic individuality. When men accepted as a matter of course the station and the prospects assigned to them by tradition, not only had they a certain natural pride in the arts, costume, and pleasures of their class, but they felt that they figured in the great procession of classes and arts and dignities that formed the variegated carnival of this world: so that their littleness seemed honourable and homelike, and integral to the greatness and glory beyond. But when all are uniform the individuality of each unit is numerical only. Independence is cheerless, when universal freedom and chaos oblige you to decide the most important questions afresh and by accident; and association is profitless, when the whole world beyond you is as ignorant, as helpless, and as undecided as you are yourself.

Rebellion against nature is bound to fail; yet it is free nature within us that rebels against incorporated nature: *natura naturans* against *natura naturata*. This contrast would be verbal and merely a contrast in points of view, if nature had only a single nucleus of life and a single direction of development. This seems necessarily the case to a pantheistic cosmology. When the universe is conceived as having passed (perhaps an infinite number of times) from a germinal to a fully developed phase, *natura naturans* will be a name for that universe conceived as a total unit and *natura naturata* a name for the same universe conceived as a manifold of parts. The manifold will simply pay out in successive bits what the unity held tied up in its purse: nothing will be lost and nothing added. In such a world there could be no failures, because only the omnipotent Will would originate any action; and enthusiasm, if that could exist, would be the vital glow of doing perfectly that which each was inspired to do, like a rapt musician improvising.

In reality, life has many centres and divergent developments, so that *natura naturans*, or what it would be natural for any organic thing to become, is very far from being identical with what, under accidental circumstances, that thing actually grows into. Failure, at least partial failure, is therefore everywhere; and there is really no such thing as *natura naturata*, in the sense of native potentiality realised, but only *natura denaturata*, or a jumble of potentialities all more or less distorted and baffled.

Thus the formal perfection of the universe, as completely expressing its own nature and laws, covers a moral chaos, in which the vital nature or law of each thing is defeated and turned into a maimed and monstrous caricature of what that thing was capable of becoming.

For this reason the folly of the enthusiast may sometimes be wiser than the wisdom of the world. He will perish; but the wisest man dies in the end, perhaps a little dulled and vulgarised by his possessions, successes, and length of years. And in perishing prematurely the enthusiast may have revealed a hidden possibility, an unsuspected germ of order in the *natura naturans*, prefiguring unexampled beauties perhaps not always destined to be nipped in the bud.

Militancy is therefore not absent morally from what politically passes for peace. Mrs. Grundy is militant; so are all missionaries and politicians; so are most philosophers. Militancy is even found in writing what is called history. In poetry it is incidental, since fury of a different colour may be expressed by the same poet in the next effusion; and the total spirit of the greater poets is not militant. There are nine Muses, and they are not expected to quarrel but to dance together. In polite society there is a good deal of envious or satirical militancy amongst rival leaders and fashions. Snobbery is militant when it is a desire to climb and not merely an innocent admiration of unattainable greatness. In families and between friends also there is a good deal of unreasonable insistence on dominating one another. The people we care for most give us the most trouble. Social enemies are easily ignored or avoided; but who shall deliver us from our families and from our habits? It is we who cannot deliver ourselves from them. To stick to them is almost always the lesser mutilation of our primal Will.

For even in each individual there is often a civil war, in which a new passion militates against an old circle of interests, or where in turn the old interests, alarmed, raise a storm of protests and insults against the intruder. Yet mere existence hardly gives custom a right of possession, and habit insensibly varies of itself, until it is opposed not by accidental, unintentional lapses but by open defiance and contradiction. Yet by this defiance and contradiction a convention that was originally quite peaceful and complacent may become constitutionally and furiously militant, as happens to dogmatic moralities and religions when rebellions arise in their own camp. When, however, a not too moralistic sage like Goethe finds two souls, alas! dwelling in his breast, it by no means appears to him that either of them need be wicked in itself; the only trouble is that he loves them both and finds them, alas! incompatible.

Here we see the roots of militancy laid bare by a poet uttering his genuine sentiments with a philosophical frankness, suffering and yet not condemning the cause of his suffering. Are not all objects of desire necessarily desired, as the Scholastics said *sub specie boni,* under the guise of the good? How then should any of them be intrinsically evil? And why should primal Will, which by loving them all is the common father of their goodness, ever disown any of them? Ah, it never would, if it were the primal Will of a free and absolute spirit. But then it would be divine, infinite, and immutable. To exist in this temporal and self-transforming world it must become incarnate in an animal psyche, which has a limited range of possible loves, a limited predetermined circle of friendly powers to feed and to serve it, and an unlimited abyss of unknown indifferent or destructive powers ambushed beyond. And this incarnation, be it observed, is no intrusion on the part of spirit into the world from a foreign sphere; it is a development of that extensible sensibility which in every atom receives and returns the radiating energy of every other atom, manifesting this sensibility in its motion and fate, but not usually able to feel those ambient forces or to picture them in its imagination.

Now, imagination, which includes distinct perception, anticipation, and memory, requires an organ making the same total reaction on all the radiating energies that may meet in it. The organ must be an organism where different reactions can occur to different influences, and can be *learned*, so as to occur spontaneously by mutual stimulation between the parts and functions of that organism both after the stimulus lapses and before it recurs. Life in such a complex organism can therefore be guided internally as well as externally; and it can undergo imaginative as well as environing influences and conflicts.

An ambiguity which plays a great part in politics may then overtake vital liberty. Emotion and conduct much guided by imagination seem to be more inwardly and loftily inspired than when guided only by physical predicaments or economic prudence. On the other hand, imagination presents a private, highly coloured, passionately biased picture of facts, of advantages, and of possibilities. It inclines a man often to folly and sometimes to crime. Wars of imagination are therefore odious to a sober statesman; and yet the leaders and the motives of such wars have something heroic about them, something of a militant conscience wrecked for aiming too high. I think, however, that militancy does not indicate a higher morality than the common, but only a harder luck. There would be no conflict betwen ideals or between tastes if each found a good field in which to be realised. There would be none between the two souls of Goethe if they were not in the same human breast, with the same accidental circumstances and short life. But the material person has perhaps none of the gifts or opportunities that his dreams would require for fulfillment, each in turn and to perfection. Or he covets material goods that are already in the possession of others, whom he therefore wishes to remove from the world; and the original ideal and special excellence of his chosen objects will not redeem the injustice of his attack upon the man who has the good luck to possess them. There can be no conflict between one good and another within either, or between the two seen by an impartial and disinterested spirit; but each becomes evil in the sight of the other when both animate or covet the same matter.

The source of militancy does not lie, then, in the diversity of possible goods, which would be an ineffable joy to pure spirit; it springs entirely from the indecision or self-contradiction of animal Will in pursuing distractedly incompatible goods at the same time in the same place. Incarnation limits spirit, if it would remain at peace, to be content in each case with the special virtues which its organs and its world are capable of realising.

## CHAPTER 3

### PRIVATE JUDGMENT
### IGNORANT BUT INESCAPABLE

THE maxim that every man is the best judge of his own interests recommends itself by its simplicity and its air of honest good sense. It can nevertheless be seriously questioned, and its meaning, on reflection, may seem ambiguous. Are a man's interests those of his body only (which he might be expected to feel) or do they include those of his family, his friends, his enterprises, his "honour," his "soul," or his "country"? And if such ulterior interests are included, does he remain the best judge of what is best also in those perhaps infinite careers? Or are we to understand that he cares and works for these remote results inasmuch only as he expects them to react favourably on his own peace and comfort, and that he is indeed the best judge of how they may be brought to do so?

Perhaps, however, the democratic mind can dismiss these difficulties without needing to solve them. A man may not always eat and drink what is good for him; but it is better for him and less ignominious to die of the gout freely than to have a censor officially appointed over his diet, who after all could not render him immortal. So we might urge that while we certainly have neither the lights nor the strength of will to act always for the eventual good of all whom our conduct affects, yet it is better that we should blunder freely in love, in politics, and in religion, than that we should follow the prescriptions of external authorities, dubious authorities at best, which might save us a few knocks, only to lead us and the world, in their ponderous organised blindness, to the most hideous catastrophes. The art of governing mankind is difficult: until a true master of it is found, we may well prefer to try experiments ourselves, and run our chances in detail, like the

# PRIVATE JUDGMENT INESCAPABLE

other animals who love their perilous life of instinct and ancestral freedom.

A man who is wilful and opinionated like a child may know at each moment what he wants. At bottom he always wants to have his way. But if you ask him why he chose that particular object at that moment, he would be nonplussed. Why he wants it, how long he will want it, and how satisfied (and for how long) he will be when he gets it, are scientific questions which only his doctor, or his guardian angel, could answer for him.

Nor is it enough for us to know what we want; the crucial points are whether the present circumstances render it obtainable and whether we have the means of securing it. On both these points, in the political field, the ordinary man thinks little and gets that little wrong.

In a civilised society, in which history and science are cultivated and where government has accumulated experience and information regarding the management of affairs at home and abroad, there will be plenty of "authorities" to tell the average man what he should think and attempt to do, if he wishes to prosper; but these authorities, in a liberal age, will be many, often technical, and at odds among themselves. An outsider, who either is a comparatively will-less sceptic or who is bred in some intolerant sect, might suppose that loose individuals would be distracted by so much diversity of doctrine; but no: life-long observation has taught me that what happens in such a case is rather that sectarianism flourishes, and that each self-confident authority or sudden fashion attracts plenty of adepts for whose temperaments or circumstances that solution, at least for a moment, becomes a refuge from apathy and a social bond. The perplexed mind and empty heart thus find a congenial occupation, protected by an encyclopaedic ignorance.

Private judgment preserves this radical ignorance no matter how much learning there may be woven into the doctrine that it adopts. Even the experts in each of those sciences often preserve a blank mind as to its significance; but if their science is physical at least they know well the experiments and the alternative expectations they have been intent upon. This detail, in which theory comes into contact with fact, necessarily escapes the layman; and he may not even imagine that he understands the popular maxims or formulas by which the public are impressed. Perhaps the experts themselves may be—as many are when I write these words—what are called Logical Positivists; and in that case they publicly warn us that they themselves learn nothing by their science, except the minimal words to which it may be reduced or the most abstract algebraic formulas, better than deceptive words, that indicate relations without suggesting images.

Images, however, are the most precious of realities for the sensualist, the painter, and the poet; while the musician rivals the mathematical physicist in constructing with pure sounds a human echo for inhuman things. Yet music, as far as I know, has never attempted to direct politics; the only points where it is fused with action are war, love, and religion; and here music brings to light an elementary rhythm or euphoria in processes deeper and more intimate than what vision can represent or science describe. If the other senses, sight, touch, smell, and muscular tension when it grows conscious in pleasure or pain, could develop their intrinsic variety into progressions and harmonies as vital as music, they would expose their essential ideality as plainly as music exposes it. In becoming the material of a liberal art, each of those classes of sensuous phenomena would proclaim its pure subjectivity and its remoteness from the sphere of physical existence and economic art; while the hidden physical instrument that, in each case, produced that phenomenon would become as familiar to us as are the bodily and instrumental sources of music.

How then does it come about that in daily life pictorial and mathematical ideas do not mislead us as dreams do, when those ideas, too, intrinsically, are the very stuff of dreams? Because hereditary life, when it takes the form of an animal psyche, by adapting action to external occasions begins also to evoke internal feelings and ideal images; so that, in so far as these feelings and images vary with those occasions, they become an ideal record of that action, and of those occasions. This record we call memory or knowledge, since it is mental in itself yet signifies material events; and with the growth of economic arts imagination learns to reproduce the history of remote occasions not from anyone's memory but in ideal perspectives centred in the animal life of supposed witnesses. Many of these pictured histories are only dreams, expectations, or myths; the degree of their significance is correspondingly various; and there is far more illusion or mere imagination in human thought than there is truth. Yet truth is still sought and partly found in so far as thought is not lost in centrifugal fictions.

## PRIVATE JUDGMENT INESCAPABLE

It is always true at least in assuming that there is truth to be sought. If this assumption were false, knowledge would be impossible, since perception and expectation would have no intended objective, but be non-indicative sensations. Life imposes faith when it imposes action; and it justifies that faith in so far as its promise is somehow fulfilled. To that extent our mental language is normal and innocent, though subjective.

The more, therefore, a man's attention retreats into speculation, and judges not according to custom or instinct, but by questioning and comparing his precise ideas, the more at a loss he will be; and either become a sceptic in theory, abandoning himself in practice to convenience and usage; or else, finding some of his ideas and feelings stronger or more pleasing than others, he will confirm himself in these and dismiss all others as false or wicked. The faith by which he lives will in either case be a perfectly ignorant and groundless assertion either of a convention or an inspiration; a plunge by which laughing nature eludes an intellectual suspense incompatible with action and with moral determination.

It is to this ignorant and spiritually dangerous course that private judgment would condemn us all, if we readily exercised it. But we seldom do so; and it is only in the decadence of political unity and traditional virtue that the few commit this intellectual suicide. Meanwhile the many run like sheep before this or that shepherd, stampeded by his shouts or hounded by his dogs.

Nature would never have suffered imagination to become so dominant if in itself waking sensation had not been as evanescent and harmless as dreams are during sleep; but waking fancy in its moral significance is a symptom not, like dreams, of organic waste but of organic reaction and ready adjustment to things at a distance. And this distance is not only spatial, such as is spanned by the animal sense of smell, hearing, or sight, but also a temporal span backwards in memory and in man often forward also, when the psychic preparation for appropriate action enables us to foresee and to plan probable events or elaborate undertakings.

This is the greatest feat, as far as we know, that the generative order of nature has ever accomplished. The teleology visible in all self-repeating processes, where the beginning of each phase or beat is pregnant with the end, here becomes rational art; for here a living being produces a result that it had actually preconceived and desired. Sensibility, intrinsically merely an aesthetic overflow of organic life, now has acquired the moral dignity of intellectual and emotional accommodation with nature or with the "Will of God."

Such a development of sensibility into intelligence repeats at another level that power of budding into something new which vegetative life displayed when it generated feeling. Intelligence too is something unprecedented in quality and entirely unforeseen; yet it remains relevant to its physical occasions both in distribution and in momentum. For like feeling, but more sparsely, intelligence realises in some degree a living ideal of logical and dramatic complexes: dynamic formations that the flux of existence, in spots, may fall into automatically.

The most intelligent of men, therefore, possesses only human images and concepts, taken from a casual point of space and time with a casual sensibility and moral bias. His knowledge is an ideal figment, painted with his vegetative oils and dramatised by his private passions. This is just as true of conservatives, who cannot conceive that the authority they recognise could be wrong, as of the most inspired prophets or rebels. In either case an absolute conviction can be nothing in its physiological actuality but a wager made by a sudden fatality, rich perhaps in eloquent justifications, but absolutely ignorant of its dumb sources in the self. Being alive a man cannot help breathing, seeing, feeling, and acting in one way or another, without any original ultimate reason for existing, feeling, or acting as he does. Once caught in the vortex, his momentum becomes in his eyes its own reason for being; and so does their momentum for all other things and all other persons.

Can there, then, be no such thing as wisdom? And without prior credentials, may not wisdom bring a sense of security and peace, not based on arguments, but on placid participation in the generative order of nature?

Yes: but since all things, even the most insane, arise according to that order, we must reduce our criterion to the political standard, if we would discover the secret of relative soundness in opinion. Private opinion in an independent observer who has had much contact with nature or with economic arts is likely to be sound, though partial; but public opinion, though it arises by contagion from private opinion, grows abnormal in the exclusive climate of hearsay, exaggeration, misunderstanding, and artificial excitement. For in society opinion is ignited by opinion, fanned by controversy, and fed by internal combustion; so that the more fiercely it blows the less relevant it becomes to its original causes or its ultimate effects. If on the contrary, some competent individual has been able to found an institution which will embody his convictions, however simple, and will perpetuate a way of life, however special, that institution, if it takes root, will produce not public opinion in the air, but settled habits and attachments in a group of men, who may become the nucleus of a distinct civilisation. Not all mankind will adhere to this one system, nor all individuals in any one region; and the wisest civilisation cannot, if definite, be at once changeless and vital. Yet it can be a civilisation with its appropriate insights and virtues.

Private judgment will still remain the seat of the original choices embedded in any moral institution; and it will be also the seat of each pupil's choice in his fidelity to it or his rebellion. And both the founder's and the disciple's judgment will be ignorant, not totally indeed at the points where it touches reality, but in regard to the extent and the literalness of its truth even there. Knowledge, if it means more than dumb feeling, looks to some existent or ideal object; but the terms of this knowledge are necessarily ideal in any case; so that in taking ideal terms to describe existence, all knowledge of facts implies a literal and immeasurable ignorance, mitigated by a constant possibility of verifying a virtual knowledge of environing powers in terms of their effects in human life, material and moral: which involves an intimate dramatic knowledge of the virtues and evils of that life itself.

## CHAPTER 4

### MILITANT MIND

LIBERAL arts are liberal in their spontaneous growth and free function; yet in their organs and conditioning circumstances, they remain portions of the universal automatism of nature, and in this capacity they may become militant. In fact their very liberality, which gives them a self-justifying moral independence, exposes them to presumption, as economic arts having clear uses are not exposed. A sober shoemaker is too well aware of the utility of his art to abandon making shoes for making stilts and selling them as superior boots. Stilts are toys; and it should be, if anything, the toymaker who might be tempted to advertise and falsely impose his wares, not as toys, but as things essential to human safety and dignity. And this is just what happens to the essentially liberal arts of language and poetry, when logicians become metaphysicians and poets religious prophets.

Religion in its pure essence might itself be a liberal outgrowth of morals, as is friendship; it might be spiritual friendship with all Will, rejoicing in nature's kinship with man and respecting its superhuman authority and freedom. Morals, however, are an economic discipline by which the human psyche learns to accept the conditions of life, while transforming them as much as possible in its own favour. And religion originally was no doubt a desperate experiment in controlling events beyond human control. Yet I suspect that religion contained, from the beginning, an incipient element of delight and terror at the miracle of things and at the plight of oneself in their midst and at their mercy. Fear, which is economic Will in a quandary, thus unites in religion with transport, which is liberal intuition in a trance. But both fear and free imagination are wild; they both evoke extravagant visions; and when these visions are at all constant and imposing, they pass for true. True, profoundly and threateningly true, the prophet is sure that they are; yet the people are lamentably ignorant of them, and the wicked leaders of the people flout those momentous truths as nonsense. Then religion, in love with itself, becomes militant.

The militancy of religion is justified in so far as real forces are conciliated or real dangers escaped by the moral discipline which its recommends; and on this stout stem of felt saving power many liberal arts and graces may be grafted.

A more special but more blatant case of unjustified militancy is that of sophistry, or thought and knowledge perversely abstracted. Knowledge is a hit in the play of universal faith, and thought the shaft which it launches. When a chick, just out of the eggshell, pecks at the first bit of something seen on the ground, that act of faith may be deceived in its casual occasion, if the bit is a pebble and not a berry or a grain or an edible insect; but the chick is not deceived in the generic cognitive function of pecking with which its psyche is endowed. It will peck again, and soon learn to distinguish at sight the choice bit from the useless pellet.

Now, I am convinced that the trained chick, like the trained child or workman, never confuses appearance, whether deceptive or trustworthy, with reality; for the veracious appearance is not veracious in itself; it might be seen in a mirror or in a dream; but it is veracious only because it comes from the sort of thing that can be eaten or less directly turned to the uses of some economic art. What the reality may be in its substance, if such a question arises at all, is a matter of vain speculation. The object encountered may, if examined, present many new appearances; but all that our knowledge of it will ever yield pictorially will still be an appearance, or information about some condition under which the appearance is elicited.

That which for a living being distinguishes reality in anything, in contrast to each and all of its appearances, is that he encounters it, may move, keep, or transform it by the work of his hands, or be swept away by it and perhaps destroyed, even when, like the wind, it is invisible. The reality exists in the same sense and in the same sphere as does his own body, known to him primarily and perpetually, not as a vapid, impotent image observed but as a vital agent inhabited: a fighting agent in that continuous dynamic sphere which is the real world.

Common sense and natural science, in so far as they succeed in tracing and calculating the continuous dynamic process beneath appearances, simply adopt and refine the chick's adventure in animal faith, which is re-enacted in every perception and expectation and is verified in every successful action or piece of work. But in man imagination is extraordinarily fertile and redundant. He does not see only with his eyes open; when he shuts them he often sees the same things again—although they are not there—or sees other grotesque and inconstant images, that agitate him and arouse his anxiety no less and perhaps more than in waking life; so that between his sane ideas he has others; and even when the control of reason on the whole keeps his beliefs and actions appropriate to his real environment, a cloud of half thoughts and faint, irrelevant visions floats through his mind, and sometimes fills the scene, so that he forgets (as when tipsy) where he is or what conduct is in order. Quiescent instincts and capacities may profit by this relaxed mood to inspire all sorts of fancies, not wholly absurd, since those potentialities in the psyche find in them a visionary satisfaction. Moreover, a man's waking fictions flourish as his night dreams hardly can do in their evanescence. Day-dreams may be recalled, developed, corrected; they may become plans guiding hope and ambition; or they may be given out as true stories, myths, or revelations. On them not one dreamer only, but whole races, may feast their hearts and enlarge their imaginary world and their imaginary importance and powers.

When fabulous history or fabulous religion becomes militant, the passion which they evoke is not a mere obsession with words or images, although these have a magic of their own, as appears in the cult of names and of pure poetry and music. The militant motive is rather political; and imagination helps only to render this motive clear and communicable in the very act of rendering it, in most cases, fantastic and disastrous. Sometimes, however, the power of words or images serves to arouse enthusiasm for a secretly rational aim; and false beliefs may nerve the Will to profitable actions.

There is, moreover, a disinterested, though not unprejudiced cult of images and words among sceptics and psychological empiricists and it sometimes becomes fantastically militant not because they love words or images (for they are not poets) but because they hate to bow to any alien power or admit the existence of any hidden thing.

I have said that this speculative militancy by negation, though disinterested, is not unprejudiced. Emotionally, among the Greek Sophists and the modern psychological sceptics, a sense of outrage rankled at having been deceived, oppressed, and imprisoned by tradition; and their revenge was to deride tradition, bringing in all the proofs that the natural philosophers had begun to give of the fictitious character of myths and of all moral and political conventions. But they hardly reckoned with their host. The human psyche had not composed those myths by dint of arguments or alleged proofs, but had woven them almost unawares, letting imagination and human feelings of dramatic truth suggest and develop the vital secrets that might lie beneath the surface of events. There had been, at least in early Greece, no militancy or fixity in these traditions. A great liberty had been allowed to poets and philosophers in devising their theories and expanding their fantasies. The very exuberance of these ideas proved how innocent they were and how studious and fertile the minds were that bred them. *But*, cried the

# MILITANT MIND

knowing Sophists, *those ideas are false!* And they could quote old Xenophanes (who was no Sophist) who had said that if they had had hands, horses would have painted the gods like horses, and oxen like oxen.

This truth was an important acquisition in criticism and self-knowledge; but unfortunately the dominant tradition in ancient science stopped there and retained images of sense, as if they were primary and absolute facts, identical with the constituents of the physical world. But in fact the sensations and ideas of man are as much products of human nature and figments evoked by the reactions of human organs as are the fictions of poets and prophets; only that they arise more often in response to contacts with external forces, and therefore follow the movement of the real human environment more closely than do dreams or irresponsible reveries. Blind to this fact, both ancient and modern critics have made a metaphysic out of appearance, and have thought themselves enlightened for being deceived only by the most artificial of illusions.

Perceptions are indeed not illusions if taken, as active life takes them, for *indications* of external facts and forces, as language is when used in giving names or commands; but they become illusions, as all thought and language does, when substituted for the external and dynamic conditions of human existence and action. Feeling and imagination at the same time constitute an inner music, which in times of leisure and reflection can be developed into an ideal world of various dimensions, logical, aesthetic, and mythical. These visions are like dreams in their status and unsubstantiality, but superior to dreams in two respects; for since they occur in waking hours, when a man is firmly adjusted, physically and morally, to his real physical surroundings, he cannot mistake his ideal objects for material things; and since, being awake, he can be coherent and steady in his ideas, he can notice and verbally record their intrinsic qualities and essential ideal relations. Logic and painting, mathematics, grammar and music, can thus form new and wonderful other worlds; worlds clearer and surer than the naturally existing one in their ideal texture. Why, then, grow militant and pretend to control or to replace the physical chain of events? It is the ideal originality and purity of appearances, in their existential dependence on material forces, that gives them all their superior virtue.

The patter of words and the drift of ideas meantime have a

double moral function, first, to express human passions and aspirations, as in poetry and religion; and second, to indicate the occasions on which those passions and aspirations find their satisfaction or their discomfiture. When both these functions are well performed, in no matter what verbal or sensuous imagery, the psyche has won a great prize in what we call genius; but when the Will, no matter how violent or eloquent, flies off at a tangent from the orbit of cosmic and social revolutions, all its tragic thunder becomes madness. Mind, then, by denying its material dependence and professing to rule the world, dishonours the ideal originality which, if content to be humble, makes the pure glory of existence.

## CHAPTER 5

### THE MIRAGE OF POLITICS

THE political firmament is not peopled by obviously impossible monsters, like the old signs of the Zodiac, but only by slightly enlarged and vaporized copies of the very images and grammar current in the economic arts; so that everything in the politician's mind represents the real world, except his politics.

It is history, I think, when critical and disinterested, that can help us to trace the real forces of nature and of human nature that have determined events and to distinguish them from political or religious "philosophies" of history. The real forces leave their mark in customs and institutions. If we could trace the complete material history of events and monuments, we should possess a dumb show or pantomime that would irresistibly suggest many a plausible myth about the feelings and thoughts that might have animated that spectacle. Such a modern dramatisation of other times would probably be romantic and baroque; its chief value would be to express our own spirit. This would tinge our understanding even of any surviving words and monuments of the past; but at least in their material form the relics were integral parts of it, even though the words may have been lies, and however falsely we may interpret the feelings that they then conveyed.

Suppose that by a sort of ventriloquism we could now draw

from the past only an echo of our own passions; yet even such imputed feelings might deceive us less about that buried world than at the present moment our feelings deceive us about our own times. For in that other historic case we should be simultaneously conceiving people's actions and the issue of those actions; so that, being in possession of a long stretch of physical facts, not veiled by any particular psychological view contemporary with them, we might attribute to those dead actors words and thoughts more appropriate to their predicaments than any that had ever occurred to them; more appropriate perhaps than any that living beings ever enact under stress of the flying present, when we are too intent on passing accidents to remember their causes or foresee their results. Our historical dramas would represent a nobler society than ever existed.

It is only when, as for a dramatist or historian, all the relevant facts are open to inspection, that moral reflection can select special episodes and special threads of relation in the dense tissue of events, and can turn that tissue into a tapestry full of decorative and romantic motifs. For some historians the whole life of the universe then becomes a poetic composition, in which everything is legendary, heroic, and mythological. Others, however, content with the scattered bits of self-revelation contained in literature and in monuments, may truly revive fragments of the moral inspiration that has actually animated mankind. These eclectic historians would not invade the territory of natural science, or add any complementary facts or principles to those for which there is material evidence. Their psychological reconstructions of past or alien life would be aimed rather at correcting and transcending the ignorant interpretations that the public always tends to make of whatever is foreign to it, so as to flatter contemporary prejudice by representing every other epoch as either a stepping-stone to the present culture or else an aberration.

Political philosophy is therefore compelled to flounder in the treacherous waters of passion, rivalries, projects, theories, and interests, most of them only imputed to whole governments or peoples. These are all second-hand, conventional, verbal factors. That which really determines action, and thereby the course of history, is the combined momentum of all the bodies and psyches concerned, which at the same time determines what passions shall be roused in the psyches, with what images of past predicaments, called motives, or of future possibilities, called aims.

This momentum, in individuals and in groups, where it is normally spasmodic and diversified, appears in politics as in religion, in war and in sport, with particular vehemence: but this vehemence only intoxicates, blurring whatever feeble lights the mind might have evoked in those circumstances, if the rush and confusion of those very circumstances, and of the exacerbated Will, had not drowned all clearness. Tragic and comic poets have depicted human life, even at political crises, much more truly and completely than historians. They choose or invent scattered incidents, utterly neglecting all antecedents and consequents (which in their phenomenal forms are really irrelevant); but in neglecting these irrelevant episodes, they revive the chosen theme with as many of its comic lights, false steps, vain hopes, and vainer reflections as they are capable of imagining; and with these they clothe and vivify the chosen episode perhaps more richly and satirically than nature might have done in the real world.

When politicians and political historians have poetic imagination they do this work of tragic and comic poets without meaning to do it, and usually with less success. The memory and speeches of politicians are not good history: in recording the facts they are untrustworthy, except perhaps in minor details, while in comic and tragic insight, in understanding of their own place and careers, they are, with few exceptions, entirely blind. Homer is a pure poet, looks to the end, has no illusions, yet feels the perfection of every great moment. But Virgil, with all his art and taste, is entangled in politics, strains tradition to flatter his country, and while understanding its past and present worthily, if not accurately, he dares not prophesy its future. Perhaps the Sibyl gave him a glimpse of it, and closed his mouth.

Not one political philosopher or prophet that I know of, not one speculative historian, has dared to chart the ocean on which he sails. They can see the universe only in the likeness of a ship, and its history as the log of a voyage. They cannot conceive the wisdom of Aristotle (so little a historian and so much a humanist) when he said that the arts have been lost many times and re-established—although of course differently, which perhaps Aristotle had not realised. Only the solitaries, the stray sages without political illusions seem ever to perceive the obvious about the course of natural events. Perhaps here and there some rough superannuated pilot, unnoticed in his corner, may take secret soundings with an old line and lead; and may mutter a warning that captain and officers are too busy to hear. The very idea of touching bottom would in any case be disdained by their surface navigation. The waves over which navigators sail, they would insist, when navigators are politicians, are waves of opinion. Only conflict of opinion can raise a storm that might wreck them. If they could secure unanimity of opinion they would sail safely for ever. Land does not figure at all in the idealistic minds of these mariners.

The historian who, however genial his intuitions may be, wishes to report the truth of the past must therefore compel himself at every step to descend to the material plane and look there for evidence of events that his dramatic sympathy may proceed to interpret in terms of passion and ideas. Dialectical implications discovered in his own moral problems will only enrich his present self-consciousness, without conveying the least knowledge of the past or of the future. His imagination may have composed a marvellous mosaic of interlaced moral essences, excellent to decorate the walls of his cloister; but if it inspires the rhetoric of demagogues, it only perpetuates profound misunderstandings.

The oxygen in the common air is ready to vitalize impartially all sorts of plants and all sorts of ideas, according as each living organism is capable of profiting by that elixir; but by what right or with what hope can one organism prescribe or proscribe the uses that another shall make of its oxygen? Who shall be rivals and occasional enemies, and who occasional or ideal friends is determined by their respective natures and accidental contacts. Nor need there be any longing for unanimity among them, save as unanimity is a revelation of a perhaps unsuspected natural friendship between soul and soul, joyful in itself and perhaps a pledge of union in action.

There is a vital limit, however, to the licence that one living being can grant to another sincerely to hate what he loves or to love what he hates. This limit is his right to his own opinion and to his own integrity; for if this integrity were lost, charity itself would be impossible. The charity that surveys this polyglot world with a ready sympathy for its needs and aspirations cannot arise except in a heart where nature and aspiration are native; and this determinate Will in the animal psyche, rendering it capable of bias and incapable of radical indifference, when chastened by experience of defeat, enables it to understand and to pity the defeats of other souls even in aspirations contrary to its own. If there could be a spirit not native to a heart (which I do not believe) it would not be able to understand that growth or dissolution had any importance for any body or any idea, as the condensing or dissolving of a cloud has no importance except perhaps to a painter desiring to copy it. It is Will or bias, with the risks which it takes, that leads us to see risk in all mutation, and perhaps charitably, perhaps foolishly, to rejoice or to suffer with it. Did universal sympathies destroy in us all capacity for preference, or produce constant vacillation between one preference and another, we should no longer see any moral qualities or interests in the world, and history and politics would have ceased to exist for us.

## CHAPTER 6

### PROPAGANDA

IDEAS, considered simply, are essences, not pictures in animals; they are therefore not loaded with zeal or capable of self-propagation. What we call the contagious force of an idea is the force of the people who have embraced it; and the perhaps irresistible hold of that idea upon them is not a power or magnetism in the idea itself, but a propensity or fixed habit in them to form that idea or to revert to it in intention as when trying to recall a name. On the other hand the awakened act of intuition when the name comes is a vital process by no means passionless; in framing an idea we successfully perform an act of which we are instinctively proud; we repeat it as we might our own verses. A contrary idea will henceforth irritate or offend us; and if the movement of the psyche culminating in that idea was massive and decided, we may not only cling to our idea tenaciously but undertake to impose it universally, obliterating all contrary ideas that there may be in the world.

Thus there is always something turgid and physical in zeal for an idea; yet this zeal would defeat itself if it appealed frankly to violence and open war. The secular arm might stop people's mouths and exterminate our enemies; yet those hateful enemy

## PROPAGANDA

*ideas* would remain unrefuted and ready to rise again from their graves. Coercion must be accompanied by at least the semblance of a moral victory. Force should seem merely to execute and perpetuate the decrees of reason and conscience. Reason and conscience, however, if left to themselves, might perhaps suggest quite different tenets from those which we have adopted and are going to defend. We must therefore mark beforehand the path that reason and conscience shall be allowed to follow; and in guiding them safely along that path, we shall employ eloquence, personal ascendancy, education of children from the cradle up, and tireless public invective, exalting, impressing, and overawing both young and old. This method is called propaganda and consists in intentionally controlling the movement of ideas by social agencies.

Propagation is something natural, propaganda something artificial. The difference lies in the prior harmony which exists in propagation between the seed and the soil; the seed is scattered generously to the winds, and the soil receives and multiplies the grain most suitable to it; so that the growth is no less native to the land than it is true to its seminal species. Propagation comes as something essentially kindly and clothes each region with its appropriate fruits. Propaganda, on the contrary, begins by raking the ground, and tearing up the native weeds, planting with care a perhaps exotic product, over which it watches with anxiety, fearing a thin crop, or some unorthodox variation in the species. Hence these perpetual calls for manure. And the great fertiliser, for artificial convictions, is the appeal to irrelevant interests. You must maintain religion, because it is good for morality and for commerce; you must keep up sports to avoid dissipation and ill-health; you must raise armies to avoid war. But if really good only for such purposes, you would have only a sham army, sham sports, and a sham religion; whereas if happy circumstances had brought you peace, health, morality, and commerce, very likely, as in the classic world, the broad light of that civilisation would have bred among you true sports, true philosophy, and true friendship.

Propagation, let me repeat, is something natural, propaganda something artificial. Honest moral and political interests propagate and defend themselves by merely existing. Each natural government or social system extends its influence where it can, but admits, beyond those limits, the lawful prevalence of other systems and other governments. Honest science and honest poetry diffuse themselves by virtue of an intrinsic evidence or charm, wherever these can be felt, and neither the pure philosopher nor the pure artist makes any effort to impose his thoughts willynilly upon people too stupid or too differently endowed to understand them. Fanatics, on the contrary, cannot be content to wait, and find their genuine friends where nature has bred them. They cannot afford to let their seed grow and their prophecies fulfill themselves by the moving equilibrium of physical forces. It is the essence of fanaticism to be impatient and to demand that nothing should ever exist anywhere contrary to a utopian regimen adopted in idea, without patent means of realising it either in the world at large, or even in the lives or habitual feelings of the enthusiasts themselves. The fanatic is a tyrant on principle, and often a hypocrite in practice. He cannot exercise the art of government, even over himself, in a frank manly way, with sympathy and understanding for the forces which he must subdue or even annihilate. Such sympathy or understanding would seem to him the deepest treason, a temptation of the devil still troubling his soul; and he will whip himself up to hate and to revile all that side of his own nature which, perhaps wisely, he has decided to sacrifice. He is in hot haste; and he fosters injustice in his heart as a necessary virtue.

There is an evident impurity in this moral condition, a mixture of ideal interests (which, however absorbing, are always disinterested) with a profound physical unrest and insecurity, an urgent need of being victorious, to hide the secret suspicion of having been wrong. This impurity is mirrored in the method by which fanaticism endeavours to maintain and to spread itself. The thoughts to be conveyed are not allowed to recommend themselves only by their own clearness or eloquence, nor the virtues by their intrinsic dignity or sweetness. Loudness and repetition, eulogy, personal influence, affections, self-interest, and vilification of all things else are employed also. It is hoped that social pressure and a sort of hypnotic compulsion may deflect and canalise the spontaneous course of ideas.

The ancient Jews and the Moslems, though we sometimes call them fanatics, were not yet hypocrites, because their enthusiasm was frankly national and warlike; they formed, in their own eyes, an elite predestined to conquer and rule all other peoples, without necessarily assimilating them; so that in their ideas, Moslems at least were not always intolerant or tyrannical, but only a little contemptuous, like Epicureans, towards the delusions of dirtier and more slavish sects. Their fanaticism was only political, and based on a childish simplification of human nature and history, like the fanaticism of modern liberals. They thought that galloping over endless deserts and then, in the cool moonlight, making verses and making love, fulfilled man's highest destiny. This was hardly a faith to impose but rather a model to exhibit, a beautiful poem to exhale once more, before nobleness should vanish from the earth.

In a biological view the agencies that control ideas are always ultimately physical: human nature, race, environment, and the balance of passions and employments in particular men. But in so far as these forces have already gone to form the psyche, and to make man what he is inwardly prompted to become, he adopts these forces for his own. He is the synthesis and voice of those vital currents; and what those forces do or tend to do in him and through him is his own free and only possible work. If all his neighbours share the same endowment as himself, there may be competition in pursuing the same goods which everybody desires but which, unless they are spiritual goods, everybody cannot obtain; but this rivalry in ambition and action will not imply any diversity in ideas. On the contrary, everybody will stimulate everybody else by proposing and perhaps realising the common model. In the tightest tribal dogmatism and morality there need then be nothing forced, or imposed from without. Even the criminal or deserter will inwardly blame his momentary madness, and regard his punishment as just. But such unanimity is precarious; heredity recombines its elements, atavisms, and sports of nature and the beginnings of new types come to the surface, and perhaps vast revolutionary movements, like epidemics, may threaten to set people talking and acting in entirely new ways.

It is then that propaganda is appealed to, and in both camps; in the conservative camp to burnish up the old ideas, and inspire horror for the new; in the revolutionary camp, to discredit everything traditional, and paint some untried alternative in brilliant colours. Yet the difference between the two parties is less profound than it might seem. Propaganda must be speculative: mere cold facts would miss fire. One party, the young party, cries that the kingdom of heaven is at hand. The other, the old party, whispers that the kingdom of heaven is come already, that it is something spiritual, and exists within us. But this makes wretched propaganda, and must be supplemented. "Don't be discouraged," the prophet adds, "the kingdom of heaven is coming again presently with glory; but this time it will be perfectly solid, and will last for ever."

## CHAPTER 7

### VICISSITUDES OF FAITH

LOYALTY to clan or monarch and religious or political faith, however intense or rapturous, have an insecure tenure in the moral nature of man. The doctrinaire who for this reason turns upon human nature and calls it sinful or corrupt may be right metaphysically, but his conviction that he is right should give him no confidence that he can force his particular system upon mankind. He may pile controversial proof or may organise a dogmatic education like the Catholic Church or the Russian State and proclaim inexorable laws, like the Pentateuch, the Koran, or the Medes and Persians. Indomitable aliens will still surround and resist him. His own children will whisper incessant heresies; his very soul will trouble him with doubts or with treacherous extensions of orthodoxy; and nothing he can do will prevent the ground from crumbling under his feet, and the world from moving on to some other unexpected convention.

For the individual on whom all must impinge, in whose soul all must work, is a living animal. He is short-lived and inconstant, having in each generation a fresh admixture of blood, a somehow new private complexion. Even the traditional system imposed upon him, with time, changes its spirit. Every new definition of dogma, every fresh regulation, slightly changes the tone and the living upshot of the whole. Therefore, whoever frames political or religious or aesthetic systems ought not to expect to see them long carried out or widely accepted as their authors conceive them. They must reckon with their host, with the unaccountable, ever young, irresponsible individual. His name is legion; his imagination and his instincts are subject to spontaneous variation, and while he will doubtless always remain subject to panic influences, to social suasion, and to tribal enthusiasm, these subtle contagions will never be quite the same. Society exists by a conspiracy of physiological forces; however rigid you make its machinery, its breath of life must come from the willing connivance of a myriad fleeting, inconstant, half-conscious human souls.

The hold which his own inspirations have upon an individual is even more precarious than that of external influences. It is true that these, to work powerfully, must become personal; they must possess the man, like devils, or impulses which some hypnotising agency has imposed upon him; but since they have an external source they can renew their operation, whereas spontaneous madness, in a healthy man, is a tentative thing losing itself, as a dream does at waking, among the irresponsive and irrelevant influences of the world. Chance impulses are like a hoop which outruns the child that has set it rolling; its very speed condemns it, when left to itself, to meander and to flop. If, on the contrary, the impulse is an adopted one, and needs to be reawakened, it is more likely to be maintained; for its cause recurs. Embody that madness in some institution, book, or sect, and each victim is recalled to it by the example and countenance which the rest give him; and his delirium is canalised, reasoned out, and turned into a little orthodoxy.

Hence that extraordinary assault on innocent nature called propaganda. A missionary sermon is an unprovoked attack; it seeks to entice, to dictate, to browbeat, to disturb, and to terrify; it ends, if it can, by grafting into your heart, and leaving to fructify there, an alien impulse, the grounds of which you do not contain understand, and the consequences of which you never have desired.

That which preaching tries to do openly other hypnotic influences do more efficaciously by indirect suggestion. It is admitted that the flame of faith needs to be kept going artificially; it will die down if for a moment you stop blowing the bellows. Leave the natural man to himself and he would forget or transform your legends, fetch a morality for himself out of his heart and his social experience, and speculate on the basis not of what tales he had heard but of what facts he had encountered. But then his imagination would drift; his inspirations, in their variety and tenuousness, would rise out of him like improvised music; it would be hard (unless the obsession was constitutional) to think them authoritative. To preserve an illusion it must be linked to something in the real world; at least to a phrase, if possible to a place and to a ceremony. Even then the illusion will flicker, because its relation to waking belief will remain vague; but this very uncertainty may lend it passionate interest. Controversy will rage about it until science or theology defines it dogmatically. Then the alien dominance of it, as if it were a fact, will be overt and confessed. It will seem a crime or an absurdity to call it in question, so interwoven will it now be with public opinion, convention, and sentiment; until at length some fine morning the enormity of that hoary usurpation strikes upon the soul. Then the astonished dupe rubs his eyes and touches his own body to make sure that he is awake, that the objects of his consciousness are at last actually its causes; and he marvels how all his life he has been walking in a dream.

## CHAPTER 8

### THE DISAPPEARANCE OF CHIVALRY

IN A healthy society the public instinctively runs to help the police; the criminal is felt to be everybody's enemy; there is an implicit brotherhood amongst peaceful citizens, who if attacked may confidently cry *Help, help,* or *Stop thief.* And the moral principle behind this ready cooperation is that no one ought to be a public enemy; that crime ought to be extirpated; and that the police, save for some involuntary error, is always right. It follows that the police cannot be too strong in respect to possible disorderly elements; it ought to be so obviously irresistible, and so supported by universal sentiment, that disorder should not dare to show its face, and that the very idea and possibility of rebellion to the law should be absent from the public mind.

This is the light in which contemporary sentiment sometimes would look upon war. Nations, like good citizens, ought to keep the peace; and armies should be simply police forces at the disposal of an international tribunal. A war would be a criminal outbreak; and the whole world should cry *Stop thief,* if any nation ventured to run amok.

By a curious irony of fate, at the very moment when this view is being advanced, and a pretentious international tribunal (though

# THE DISAPPEARANCE OF CHIVALRY

without real jurisdiction or armed force) had actually been established in the League of Nations and, when it crumbled, has been reconstructed with even greater elaboration and folly—at this very moment the laws of war have collapsed, and peoples glare at each other in absolute hate and terror, like crouching beasts in the jungle.

Wars were not formerly regarded as crimes; they might indeed be begun unjustly or waged cruelly; and this would be criminal precisely because unnecessary and contrary to the true function of war. What was this function? The maintenance of the rights and liberties of some social organism, a state or city or family or even an individual. These rights and liberties had been established and proclaimed boldly, and you clung to them with the same pride and courage with which you would defend your person from assault. And you recognised, in asserting these rights and liberties, that others might have rights and liberties of their own, which it would be their duty to defend. You had no right to assault them, unless they assaulted you. The aggressor, the trespasser, would be a villain—a man who trampled on the rights of others, having no true idea of right. But if by some unfortunate combination of circumstances, the true rights and liberties of two states or cities or men collided, then both were right in defending themselves by force; and war was the judgment of Heaven between them.

In practice, no doubt, neither side in ancient wars was apt to be blameless; and the definition of rights and liberties, being made by each party for itself, would hardly help being biassed and fantastic; yet the nominal appeal was always to justice, and the enemy rights and liberties were recognised to be valid, in so far as they were justly maintained. War was therefore an appeal to God to give the palm to justice, to purge each of the combatants of inordinate ambition, and to restore both to their true liberties and rights. This was the spirit of chivalry.

A chivalrous war was not incompatible with personal disinterestedness or with Christian charity. A man's rights and liberties were a trust; and in going forth to punish injustice the knight errant not only did his duty and vindicated his honour, but could be merciful to the evildoer, once restored to his true place, where a just and religious life was possible for him. So to vindicate one's rights and liberties was a matter of honour, like defending one's body against a blow. If anyone preferred to let himself be kicked, he was either a saint or a coward; and in both cases the man of honour was bound to step in, repel the aggressor, protect the saint, and kick the coward again for having deserted the cause of justice. Even to the enemy, if the enemy too was a man of honour, consideration was fitting. Chivalrous wars were not wars of extermination or willful ambition but, at least in theory and often in the conviction of both parties, wars to maintain the right; and, justice once restored, your enemy could become your friend not merely because there was now material peace between the two, but because there had always been at bottom between them a certain mutual sympathy and equality in honour. The war had been an incidental duel, fought under accepted rules, within Christian limits, announced with eloquent indictments and counter-charges, and sanctified by sacramental oaths; and the tilt, if decisive, could establish a new recognised right with new duties mutually accepted.

All this chivalrous sentiment could not change the foundations of human nature or of natural necessity, only at best add a touch of imagination and nobleness to men's minds. Wars were not often begun purely for justice's sake, or prosecuted with courtesy: ambition and love of gain, hot anger and stubbornness played as usual the leading parts; and the name of right often covered insatiable lusts which included a lust for war and made war perpetual. Indeed, it was a characteristic of chivalry that the gentry should go about armed, and always fighting with no great ultimate settlement in view.

In contrast with this chivalrous skirmishing, fanatical or materialistic wars appear more rational, in that they look to radical and final issues; by exterminating the enemy they propose to clear the air and to make a harmonious world seem, for the moment, attained or attainable. Perhaps if the Crusades and the wars of the Reformation had not been fought by chivalrous princes, the results might have been more decisive; but the leaders were often distracted by personal and incidental interests from their nominal religious mission; they did not hesitate to ally themselves on occasion with infidels or heretics against men of their own faith. This faith, after all, was not chivalrous; it had absolute pretensions, profoundly hostile to knightly freedom of fancy, of self-will, and of spontaneous allegiance; and very likely these lords in their lordly minds were impatient of priests and legal pedants deafening them with arguments. They believed in the right of the sword

# THE DISAPPEARANCE OF CHIVALRY

more than in any revelation, and felt a chivalrous sympathy with a like lordliness in others. Chivalry was something romantic; the knight had a private adventurous conscience of his own; and his imagination demanded, and was not sorry to create, a picturesque medley of attachments.

In one respect, indeed, the ideal essence of chivalry never was obscured by either religious or worldly influences: the knight always preferred death to dishonour. Death he daily defied; at every turn of a corner, in every retort, in every love affair, his hand went to the hilt of his sword. When death is habitually defied, all the slavery, all the vileness of life is defied also. It belonged almost to the pride and joy of life to hold life cheap, and risk it, and be coolly indifferent to losing it, in defence of the least of one's rights and liberties. A smiling and mystic neighbourliness with death, as with one's own shadow, intensified life enormously in the dramatic direction; it kept religion awake; it gave a stiff lining to wit, to love, to fashionable swagger; and it concentrated the whole gamut of human passion and fancy within each hour. Shakespeare's theatre (not to speak of the Spanish) is a living monument to the mentality of chivalry. In contrast with that freedom and richness we can see to what a shocking degradation modern society has condemned the spirit.

There can be no doubt of it: chivalry is now thoroughly dead. Our one preoccupation is to be safe. We don't know what we love, or if we do we don't dare mention it. We are willing to become anything, to be turned into any sort of worm, by the will of the majority. We are afraid of starving, of standing alone; above all we are afraid of having to fight. And when nevertheless we are forced to fight, we do so without chivalry. We do not talk of justice, but of interests. We have become very numerous, we have established a great many industries, we have encouraged a great many peoples to wish themselves very rich. All this has to be maintained, it has a great momentum, which we cannot resist. And we need our neighbour's land and markets and colonies; at least we need a strip along their borders, so as to be able to expand a little, and to breathe. For as it is, we are dreadfully crowded and insecure and unhappy. If only more people spoke our language and were governed by our government, we somehow believe we might be less crowded, less insecure, and less unhappy; as if it made any essential difference whether 20 million more people read the same newspaper, and thought and said the same thing at the same moment. Is there in this megalomania a remnant of imitation of religious propaganda? Is it for the salvation of foreigners' souls that we wish to annex and to standardise them? Is it to prevent those who are unlike ourselves from being eternally damned that we long to exterminate them?

Meantime our society has lost its own soul. The landscape of Christendom is being covered with lava; a great eruption and inundation of brute humanity threatens to overwhelm all the treasures that artful humanity has created. Brute humanity has the power to destroy polite humanity, because it retains the material equipment of modern industry which has recently grown upon man like fresh hide, horns, and claws. Armed with this prodigious mechanism, any hand at headquarters can spread death and ruin over the earth. But whose shall this hand be? Anybody's: the first man's who jumps at the lever, touches the button, and takes possession of the radio.

Yes, but this is so easy, so alluring, that more than one man may attempt it at once. Then the really great war, in the modern sense of greatness, would begin. The whole mechanism in one hand would clash with the whole mechanism in another hand. Will they simply blow each other up, and perish together? Or at the last moment will they agree to pool their machinery and draw lots as to who shall be boss? Or will one of the explosions miss fire, so that only one party survives, and makes an appeal to chance unnecessary? In any case, it will be a war of extermination establishing an absolute power. There will be no consideration of rights or liberties, no talk of honour, and no nonsensical chivalry.

# CHAPTER 9

## REALPOLITIK

MACHIAVELLI and his recent emulators can never be judged fairly unless we begin by making a distinction which they have neglected to make between the efficacy of means and the choice of ends: an omission which turns their honesty into a scandal. Their insight into the ways of the world is genuine; and it was honourable in them to face the facts, and to face obloquy in reporting them frankly. Yet it was a true scandal, born of their mixed moral education, Christian and pagan, to confuse the natural history of politics with rational government. It is an old trick. Nurses sometimes say: *Little boys never do that*; and the tempter will whisper: *Have a cigarette. All the boys smoke*. Both assertions are falsely generalised; but the subtle poison lies in the suggestion that what is done is right, and what is not done is wrong. This is a double *non sequitur*: and apart from logical scruples it is false morality, since much that is done is certainly wrong for its purpose, and much that is purposed is heartless or foolish in itself.

This scandal has been aggravated in our day by the demoralising influence that optimism and the worship of evolution exerted in the nineteenth century. *Most men are not good*, says Machiavelli;[1] therefore *anyone who wishes to hold his own* must learn not to be good on occasion. This would not be evil counsel, if it were not presumed that every man worth his salt will undoubtedly wish to hold his own among bad men, and not rather perish in the effort to make them better: which would not in that case seem a hopeless effort, since human nature, at least in the martyr, would already have proved capable of heroism; and the virtue native to one man might perhaps be propagated by the force of example, selection, and training. Machiavelli, however, was not thinking of the saints; and like Thrasymachus and Callicles in Plato, he thought it a matter of course, if not a point of honour, that at least a prince should prefer to be occasionally wicked rather than to be worsted or die: and he seemed to assume (what Thrasymachus proclaimed loudly) that it is better to be a wicked prince than not to be a prince at all.

But that first assumption (which is psychological) is hasty, and the subsequent suggestion (which is moral) is false. Now it is just these hasty or false ideas that the worship of evolution introduces into ethics; for it is then taken for granted that to survive is the mark of excellence, and that the will to live and to dominate is the basis of morals. But the will to live could be the basis of morals only for a brute that had not discovered that he was mortal, and must ultimately fail in that blind effort; an effort which is no

[1] *Il Principe*, Chap. 15, p. 1.

doubt the occasion of much bravery and many labours, but also of many crimes. Meantime, the only rational aim he can pursue is to live in the best possible manner while he does live. Survival is something impossible: but it is possible to have lived and died well.

In other words, the good to be attained by good conduct need not be personal or national; and the function of a civilised government need not be only to preserve itself (that is but the by-play of office) nor even to preserve the state (which though it need not die at an assignable time is always changing its essence) but rather to redeem human life from vanity and barbarism, even if the agent in this redemption should itself perish. Such an achivement, or even some part or memory of it surviving afterwards, is glory; and when the ancients said that it was noble to pursue fame, we may hope they meant glory of this sort, for in that case they attained it.

There is a deeper insinuation in *Realpolitik* (perhaps an unconscious one) which is morally sound. Convention is not the standard of true virtue; and if *virtù* stands (as it sometimes seems to do) for what is *naturally* admirable and splendid, though carped at by envy, fanaticism, or timidity—then what we have before us is a genuine moral reform, masquerading as satire or licence or devilry. Probably its promoters have not philosophy enough to perceive that they and not the pharisees or the pedants are the true moralists. But by "naturally admirable" we must not understand prevalent in the animal or vegetable kingdom, or producing some good results (almost anything has *some* good results) at a prodigious expense of cruelty, labour, sorrow, and remorse. By "naturally admirable" we must understand what human nature (we are not legislating for other creatures), when the touchstone of experience has fully tested and developed the quality of it, feels and declares to be admirable. The nature in question must be recognised by the moralist as his own nature, not as he is, but as he would be happy in being; and the value he sets on things must be such as he would set upon them with full knowledge both of them and of himself. Lacking this knowledge, his moral feelings may be warm, but they will be misguided. Misguided, very likely, are the reigning notions of morality; and in so far as this is the case, the satirist or the scoffer, however offensive his tone may be to polite ears, is a prophet of true goodness, and not a reprobate. He is not proposing an occasional crime, or a general moral anarchy; on the contrary, it is the conventional moralists that, in the sad name of a mock virtue, are encouraging evil feelings and evil actions.

What wickedness, precisely, did Thrasymachus or Callicles, Machiavelli or Nietzsche require of their political heroes? Was it what a superstitious rabble calls wickedness? Or was it something that these philosophers themselves in their hearts felt to be wicked, but which they had the effrontery to welcome nevertheless, because they craved a certain romantic excitement? The latter, I think, almost exclusively. They were out for mischief; not seeing clearly nor caring much for what might ensue, but bursting with the desire to smash things generally. They would have ostracised Aristides for being called the Just. They loved above all things the consciousness of their own radicalism and the sense of rising on stilts of insolence above the vulgar crowd. Yet there may have been something more in the background: the smart of some veritable deep injustice, or the light of a better world shining through all this impatience.

That a specious idea should tempt people to wickedness—is that a new thing in morals? Does not any temptation allure under the guise of good? Is there not often something charming about the impossible, something it is a pity and a sorrow to miss? Can it be that these *Realpolitiker* have forgotten the rudiments of morals, or have never heard of them? Are these supermen nothing but ill-bred little boys? If so there is little to fear from their momentary domination: they are only sowing their wild oats. They will have destroyed a great many things that had a good side, all of them transitory by nature and destined in any case to perish. If their domination lasts they will have established a social order on the same old foundations of physical necessities and human accidents; and they will proceed painfully to unravel the rights and wrongs of their new experiment. The fruits of their revolution will presently form a crust of conservatism round their hearts. The oracular Zarathustra, become prime minister, will sit at his desk in goggles, ringing for one secretary after another, and receiving some financier who insidiously offers him a plum. Poor superman! As things get rather thick about him, will he regret the happy irresponsible days when, in the legend of a Borgia, he could publicly invite all his rival supermen to a feast, in order to have them poisoned at his table? Or will he remember how, distracted by the heat and nobly fearless, he drank the poisoned wine himself by mistake, and perished instead most horribly? Ah, those bold romantic crimes were not really more satisfactory than the entanglements of this official slavery. Both are vanity. And in that case, what follows? It follows that these wild ambitions (though some lovely things may be summoned by them before the mind) are themselves evil, at least in part; that to yield to them, in that respect, is foolish as well as wicked; and that the misguided hero, like a Damocles or like a poor ghost-seeing and witch-haunting Macbeth, will lose his soul in gaining a sorry world, and his wishes, once attained, will horrify him. These are trite maxims, and elementary: but I am talking of children, to children: a pack of young simpletons led by some young scoundrel.

# CHAPTER 10

### THE SENTIMENTAL BANDIT

IN WALKING through a Zoological Garden we may admire the dignity of the animals—except the monkeys and the peering spectators. True, those animals are caged; if they were free they might make more manifest the normal condition of living beings where each is radically the enemy of all the rest. Here they are artificially prevented from attacking one another; yet the intense way they have of burrowing or prowling or pecking expresses clearly enough the absoluteness of their will. Their noble indifference lasts only as long as their digestion: if all is well within, all is well or nonexistent without. But at the call of hunger or lust or fear, the brave war of each atom begins against the universe; and the universe itself is so tolerant and so indifferent that it suffers the brave atom, sometimes, to win.

A curious complication arises in the absolute will when it becomes sentimental. Are the lower animals, the vultures or the bisons, ever sentimental? They seem so at times: as if the infinite vacuity of a world that doesn't concern them made them aware of their own pathetic predicament in having to act as if they were important. They *must* act so, on occasion, with an absolute conviction and ferocity; but in the long intervals of sleepy leisure, as they blink at the world, they may dimly feel that the world is as helpless and as innocent as themselves, and they may grow sentimental. For they can't change that state of things; they can only be sorry for their victims, and sorry for themselves at having to victimise them.

Such at least, among men, is the sentiment of the romantic criminal. He has reverted to animal war against society; but he was a social being in childhood; he remains a social being in respect to his comrades, and to his wife and children; it is easy for him therefore to extend an impotent benevolence to the people he robs and murders. Poor things, especially if they are young women, and good-looking. He would much prefer to be nice to them; but his professional duty obliges him to waylay or to gag or perhaps to kill them. It is too bad. His professional duty is far more merciless to him than his heart is to his fellow-creatures.

The sentimental bandit is not always a highwayman or a burglar: sometimes he is a monarch or a general or the founder of a colony, or of a great business enterprise. Sometimes too he is a revolutionary leader, an enthusiastic humanitarian. He is not robbing and murdering for his own benefit; he is doing it for the greatness of his country or for the emancipation of the poor. He is cruel only in order to dry the people's tears, or those of a part of the people, or those which he himself has been shedding all his life long at the sight of human misery. Nothing could be nobler than the language and sentiments of such a romantic bandit. His every word is a eulogy of himself. He talks of his honour: tells you how unjustly fortune has treated him, and how wickedly his enemies have maligned him; how he has been driven unwillingly to defend himself; how he detests and despises the decrepit society of which he was a victim; although he may admit that his own victims personally were sometimes innocent. But invective and apology are not his only themes; he is even more eloquent in prophecy and self-glorification. The pure will of man, he says, is above all: if you have the gift of commanding you have the right, even the duty, to command; for the only duty of a free man is that which he imposes upon himself. But ah, what noble storms often agitate his free bosom! He will confess that in the midst of his hard cruel actions a strange wave of sensibility sometimes overwhelms him; suddenly he will cross himself or say the Lord's prayer or found a hospital or endow a college.

All this, however, will be a passing weakness, unless, like the improbable Don Juan of history, he is sincerely converted and reformed. Absolute Will rejects religion as it rejects chivalry; it is on the make. The bandit, however sentimental, is not a gentleman crossing swords in a specific quarrel with a particular person, whom he recognises as an equal, with rights and liberties of his own to defend. The bandit's greed is indefinite, his enemies are simply obstacles to be kicked out of the way. His avowed art is to take them at a disadvantage. You should never, he says, attack the strong; that would be foolish and dangerous; you would be likely to come off crippled even if victorious. And when you think what great losses and sufferings such an equal war might impose, the mere idea of it will become repulsive, and you will make any sacrifice for the sake of peace. The wise, the efficient, the ultimately kind policy is to attack the weak. Then the struggle will be brief, the victims few, and the settlement decisive.

The sentimental bandit, or the bandit pure and simple, can seem a hero to children or to awestruck peasants; they admire his courage, and sympathise with the absolute will let loose in a play world. Yet this benevolence is itself fanciful; at close quarters and in the long run the sentimental bandit will impose his own absoluteness and lack of chivalry upon his enemies. The lack of chivalry is even more catching than the example of it; it appeals to a deeper and more universal impulse of animal life. Any absolute asserters of themselves, any other sentimental bandits will be suppressed by him without mercy, hunted down by police-dogs, and thoroughly extirpated like so many rats.

Of late we have seen, in art, in war, and in social theory, a rehabilitation of savagery. It is not for me to deny that a great deal of affectation, mere restlessness, and ignorant folly is mixed up in these revivals. They are archaistic and the work of people not savages except by choice. Yet these modish or doctrinaire poses have an instructive side. They remind us that savagery, like every form of animal life, may suddenly be recovered and loved by those in whom it lay latent; and then free impulse may be defended more hotly than life itself; because it is less dreadful to die than to live contrary to one's deepest inclinations.

## CHAPTER 11

### THE RAVAGES OF WAR

WE READ with horror of the distant ravages of earthquakes, floods, and tornadoes. This vicarious terror quickens the pulse and we enjoy it. Even the victims of the disaster, in the midst of distracted efforts to rescue themselves and their possessions, sometimes feel a touch of the same exaltation. The pious regard these evils as the work of God; and reverence for God is as often increased as diminished by such visitations. Nor are unbelievers, who perhaps have set their hearts on prosperity as the only good, really in a different case. They may attribute their calamities to natural causes, yet when the blow falls, their dismay will not be altogether without incidental satisfactions. Is not science gloriously ready to explain these accidents by universal laws? Is not international philanthropy quick to relieve them? Is it not urgent at least to form a committee and discuss the measures that should be first adopted?

Human sentiment in these matters must needs be complex, yet it need not be irresolute or self-contradictory. On the one hand, there is an irrepressible sympathy in every sensitive and clear mind for the natural aspirations of all living creatures and for their perfections, each after its kind. On the other hand there is no less irrepressible insight into natural necessity and the ways of the world. Existence devours itself. Wisdom must expect continual troubles, and in view of them has made ample provision of lightning-rods, lifeboats, firemen, surgeons, hospitals, and cemeteries. The optimist will not fail to add that the existence of vice, crime, and lunacy, so blindly regretted by us, adds several prosperous departments to social administration.

It is only in the individual conscience that this conventional equilibrium proves at times insecure, or is upset by some shock particularly terrible or unforeseen. Misfortune may then produce disbelief in God; yet the notion of a merciless natural order may some day acquire its right of domicile in the mind, becoming axiomatic and even sublime; and something very like the ancient reverence for the gods will re-establish itself in the heart of the atheist. Natural piety has never attempted to moralise the cosmos, but only to recognise in that non-moral natural order the reservoir of force and the field of action proper for man and his morality. He is free to incorporate and to turn to moral uses such natural energies as he may learn to control, having in himself, as he has, a spark of that same energy. To the rest he must bow, eluding every fatal contact, and admiring the starry scene from a distance.

The ravages of war excite the same horror as do other catastrophes, with this added note: that since the immediate authors and agents in war are men or nations, horror turns into reproaches, indignation, and lasting hostility. Yet this hatred too breaks in the end, like a loud wave on the sand, against the broad indifference of nature and history. If rage is fiercer at being disturbed or thwarted by a man than by some inanimate power, dramatic sympathy with the enemy, when it supervenes, is more rational and more complete. This enemy is a hero in his own eyes, and may ultimately become one in ours. Moreover, he was no more than ourselves the free or ultimate cause of our conflict. Blind nature was working irresistibly in us both, at cross purposes with herself. Thus horror at war, intense while Troy burns, sinks in time into the tragic yet courageous emotion with which health always views the evils of life. The ravages of war are immense, and have always been irreparable; yet we still exist, and are rich and hopeful enough to deprecate any fresh havoc. Even actual war, when it breaks out again, has not altogether a horrible aspect: there is life in the air, if there is death before one's eyes, or behind one's back; and the exalted imagination cannot help vaguely disclosing the impartial panorama of history, in which no evil, however horrible, has not causes and conditions that are partly good, and effects that are partly good also.

In almost all horror and invective there is in fact a suppressed major premiss invalidating the conclusion which the hot minor premiss, our present passion, would impose. The present evil is truly evil and great; there is no error in that perception. But perception runs easily into idolatry, when it attributes dramatic and moral qualities to diffused natural agencies innocent of any such emotions. We think we are fighting the devil or some wicked race, or some incarnate injustice; when probably the evils from which we suffer have their roots in the very essence of existence, or in cosmic or biological processes quite beyond human contrivance.

## THE RAVAGES OF WAR

These evils, in their essence, would have overtaken us in any case. Our real enemy is too large to be seen, being the universe; or too near, being within ourselves; and we heap our wrath and hatred on some poor visible agent of destiny, from whom perhaps comes the insult, but not the injury.

This is evidently the case with regard to the most deeply lamented of the ravages of war, namely, the loss of life. Death, for the mere animal, is the greatest of evils; yet it is intimately involved in his structure, since his organism is reproductive, not stable, and animal life renews itself in the race, not in the individual. If he dies in war, or is devoured by some other animal for whom he is the natural prey, what he may attribute to this evil occasion is the date and manner of his death, not his death itself. Certainly the date and manner of death are all-important; constitution, conduct, and fortune determine them more or less nobly. One man dies in youth of his virtues, another in middle life of his vices; some die of hardship, overwork, or starvation, and some kill themselves for sheer boredom and surfeit. The majority are overtaken on the way by some violent or insiduous disease or by some vulgar accident; and a few linger on and die of old age, finding nothing else to die of.

Death in battle, being violent and often premature, calls forth loud lamentations. These war-griefs are nobly tragic, in that they rise above the thoughtless feeling that we should live forever or that death in war is worse than death creeping upon us later, and not voluntarily challenged. The opposite is the truth. Death as it overtakes the unwilling, is ignominious; and it is ignominious even in war for the herded rabble, who are not spontaneously or personally soldiers, but poor conscripts with a blank mind. This makes the unmixed pitifulness of many a casualty. So, among the sick and wounded, as with people dying at home, nature tortures herself in the vain struggle to ward off death to the last gasp, prolonging the proof of her congenital wastefulness and irrationality; and when at last she breaks us and leaves the wreck of us in peace, that mock peace is ghastly, sardonic, and loathsome. Fortunately dissolution soon obliterates almost all traces of that vain resistance, and the broad currents of nature swallow and absorb it in some new formation, in which death and life are not to be distinguished.

Meantime something important has happened. The reproductive organisation, which distinguishes life from motion and thereby makes death possible, has raised existence for a moment to a supermaterial status. Spirit has come to birth. Spirit is existentially the most volatile and evanescent of things, yet it possesses in passing a moral reality which cannot be obliterated in the same manner as the organism itself, because spirit is essentially and in each instance self-centred, and indifferent to whether, from beyond, it be forgotten or remembered. And sometime under the spell of love, religion, or war, this spirit is kindled into a distinterested passion, that fears death so little as almost to court it, being purified in the white heat of a generous self-surrender, and sublimated by the very cruelty of fortune. It is easy, almost pleasant, to give up the world, if we know what the world is; and we never die too soon, if we have found something eternal to live with. The aggressive side of war, which physically is brutal, is ennobled by spirit no less than the sacrificial side, which physically is slavish. There is no need of hating or vilifying the enemy. In himself, at a sufficient distance, he might quite properly bark and bite to his heart's content. But spirit, which is the child of a nature specifically and delicately organised, loves and reveres the order from which it springs. It is consecrated to the defence of that order, and to its perfection; and nothing can be more glorious for it than to clear the jungle of dragons and giants, and to extirpate vileness and treachery at home.

War brings many other evils besides the loss of life, some of which, like the destruction of ancient monuments, may be harder to repair than a diminished population. Numbers, where there is room for them, are soon supplied; but war will be disastrous from a humanistic point of view if the new race is of inferior blood, or if with the race that has succumbed the aptitude for a high organisation has disappeared. If this has happened, even population will be permanently thinned, since a warlike manner of life requires a large hunting-ground, and discourages intensive cultivation of land. On the other hand, if only the peasantry be safe, population may increase to the limits of subsistence, as in China and India, without otherwise benefiting by the liberal culture that may exist in higher circles. Wars will be wars of princes and revolutions in the fine arts or in religion. The masses will continue to plod, while those clouds pass over their heads, and will be decimated only by famine, pestilence, and taxes.

It is often said (and I too have repeated it elsewhere) that war cuts off the flower of each generation, leaving only the baser weeds to inherit the earth. Where are the Achaeans of Homer, the Theban band, or the Romans? Where is the chivalry of Christendom? Where even the great lords of the seventeenth and eighteenth centuries? Evidently they have all disappeared; but the question is whether it is war that has exterminated them, or other causes that have abolished their status and made their descendants indistinguishable from ordinary people. It would require separate and thorough investigation to trace in each case the precise decline of particular physical or social types. War may often have crippled an aristocratic class, for instance, the Spartans after Leuctra; yet the Romans conquered half the world after Cannae. Perhaps worse than the loss of life is the loss of confidence in such a case, and the oppressive sense that the world is too large and too irrational for our chosen ambition. New fashions in virtue will creep in, favoured by this discouragement; or even hostility to virtue, and a positive taste for meaner things. Belated Don Quixotes, if they still arise, will pine in a vacuum, or pass for madmen if they venture out into the world. Wars may have played an important part in producing the social transformation that renders old moral types obsolete; but not principally by killing off the old heroes in battle. If the bravest are the most likely to fall in war (and this is now hardly the case) they probably have put many cowards out of the way first. The fallen, however numerous, usually leave younger brothers or sons of their own mettle; and on the whole courage and intelligence seem calculated to propagate and establish themselves through victory, rather than to exterminate themselves in winning it. The cycle in the rise and fall of nations and civilisations, without attributing any magical force to the tropes discovered, may be ascribed to the natural mutability of existence, each phase and each combination of circumstances issuing inevitably in something different from itself. Only where organisms are living bodies, propagating their kind through seed, may we expect cycles of evolution to be roughly repeated: roughly, because even where seeds are almost exactly similar, circumstances will modify the product, these circumstances changing according to laws and at a rate irrelevant to that of the organism in question. Slowly, these circumstances will even modify the seed; so that the disappearance of types of men or of society, whether warlike or peaceful, is a matter of course, because the field in which they live changes physically and politically around them; and they too change it, not always favourably to their original type of life, merely by living in it.

## CHAPTER 12

### THE SECRET OF TYRANNY

Rhetorically the word tyranny is a term of abuse, denouncing any systematic oppression or injustice; and in that sense there is an element of tyranny in almost all dominations, because it is impossible to govern at all without disregarding the aspirations of some people in some directions. It is therefore simply a question of degree whether a government or a constitution, or even a free people, may be styled tyrannical: they will be tyrants if they trample upon many other people in many unnecessary ways.

In a legal and historical sense, however, tyranny means absolute government established by revolution, and not sanctioned by the previous laws of the State; so that if such a tyranny maintains itself and obtains the sanction of a new set of laws accepted by the public, it ceases to be a tyranny and becomes a normal constitutional government. Power in such a case having been usurped by a *coup d'état*, the dislodged party feels the outrage bitterly, and the whole people is more disturbed, and more conscious of being governed, than in normal times; and for this reason, and not at all because usurping governments are more than ordinarily oppressive, the word tyrant, which only means lord, has become opprobrious. Tyranny is a sort of travesty of monarchy. The tyrant is probably a plebeian, or a leader of the plebs: yet he talks and acts and before long probably lives like a king. A popular wind then blows in high places, and opens them to the public mind, if not also the old royal parks to the Sunday crowd as a new promenade for the people.

Such tyranny is the assault of a new and crude regimen upon a society not in its entirety ready for the change; many privileges are abolished and many persons dispossessed who were formerly in the light, and are not reconciled to extinction. Yet extinction is probably their fate, and would have insidiously overtaken them even if the shifts of power in the official classes had continued their legal course. Behind the visible tyrant stands an invisible one: Neptune the earthshaker, a morose deity much disregarded in the public religion, yet no less powerful than his luminous brother, the eloquent Jove.

The secret of this tyranny does not lie in human nature: for that reason it is a secret. Such transitions and catastrophes are not fruits of political calculation, but are forced upon men by physical fatalities, as if by a change of weather. They dominate the tyrant as much as the slave; they exercise a circumstantial pressure, by which everybody is drawn into courses which no one has freely chosen. The art of an intelligent tyrant, like Lenin, is to read the signs of the times, to jump into the breach, "assume the god, affect to nod, and seem to shake the spheres."

This appears if we consider the degrees of subjection which men suffer in their various functions. Their subjection to convention is greater in words than in thought, and greater in thought than in action. A Christian, for instance, calls himself a sinner, but he seldom regrets his sins, and hardly ever corrects them. This is because he has been indoctrinated but not trained; and he remains freer and wilder in his conduct than in his opinions, and more like the blameless Ethiopian; while his opinions in turn are far less Christian than his language. On the other hand, a soldier or a schoolboy will look quite obedient and smart on parade; but there is make-believe in this alacrity, and a sort of mockery which is pleasant enough for a while; yet presently the schoolboy will be making faces behind his book, and the soldier cursing his sergeant, his uniform, and his rations. Discipline may reassert itself at crucial moments, when gregarious impulses and sporting courage bear most people onward without much thought; especially as there is commonly no alternative. There is some difficulty in thinking what else to do, when one is commanded and evidently expected to obey. The slave grumbles, but works, the child and the conscript are unhappy, but on the whole obedient, and willing to do their bit. They might as well. Round the tedium and desolation of daily life there are walls and closed gates, hard looks, and punishments; and beyond, if we can see beyond, is an even more forbidding barrier—isolation and the fog of the unknown.

The world has caught us in a trap; but it did so when we

were born, and we are used to the feeling. Consecrated phrases wrap our minds up in a cloud; we can no more stop using them than we can stop breathing. These are fatalities to which it is wise to yield gracefully; they are unavoidable and they are sometimes pleasant. Those who break away from convention are usually right in thinking convention arbitrary and in some measure oppressive; but they are probably wrong in thinking their own heresy less arbitrary, and not likely to be oppressive in far more important respects. Impatience and criticism are necessarily founded on some friction of surfaces, which it is indeed a pity not to remove if possible; but this regrettable friction does not enlighten the discontented mind about the grounds for those arrangements, or even about the source of its own dislike of them. The mere fact that a social convention exists is an argument in its favour. At least that convention possesses, or has possessed in the past, some congruity with the circumstances of life; and this cannot be said of any dream, or wish, or utopia. No doubt the latter too have adequate causes; and subjectively a utopia or dream may even be more profoundly rooted, and more important for a penetrating moral philosophy, than all the laws of a city or maxims of a Church; yet even in that most favourable case, the prophetic soul may be wasting its eloquence, if the dream is too beautiful or the utopia out of tune with the movement of the world.

The secret of tyranny, then, is not to be looked for in the tyrant's unusual wickedness or love of power. If a desire to lay down the law could make a despot, surely the enemies of tyranny would have become tyrants. It is not the will to dominate that they lack, but only the capacity or the opportunity. Nor is the explanation to be sought in a sudden apathy or servility in the people: under any system of government, even when they imagine that they rule themselves, the people grumble and acquiesce, with no great illusions regarding the wisdom of their rulers. But there are slow mutations in the sub-soil of politics, felt as sudden shocks upon the surface; and tyranny embodies a part of this transitory tension, where society is blindly changing the balance of its institutions.

So it was in ancient Greece, during the epidemic of tyrannies. The aristocratic age was coming to an end; material growth had made that patriarchal regimen impossible. But the noisy wide-awake democrats in the agora had no competence to take charge; a city was a sacred and military heritage. By the skill and impudence of the tyrant this heritage might be accepted and transmuted into a modern constitution. So perhaps in our day dictators or national leaders may be smoothing the way for socialism, and establishing it in a form less hostile to tradition than a revolution could be without a permanent head; because a single mind, however fanatical, is always more conscious of difficulties and of consequences than is a series of factions, succeeding one another in the government. A tyranny, supervening in the midst of some profound convulsion, marks a temporary equilibrium, coordinates the forces at work, selects consistent objectives, and leaves the ship of state already sailing a steadier course. Such at least was the work of those admirable tyrants Caesar and Napoleon.

This subterranean explanation of tyranny would also apply to that margin of oppressive action inseparable from any social order. This order cannot establish a perfect harmony amongst all the interests concerned; and the interests neglected or sacrificed will murmur. They are not to be blamed for murmuring; yet it is not wickedness or injustice from which they suffer. They suffer from the latent cruelty and blindness of all competitive life; and it is their misfortune that their rivals, and not they, have succeeded in establishing a relative harmony.

## CHAPTER 13

### REVOLUTIONARY LIBERTY

IT MIGHT seem a strange outrage to destroy the order that the past had evolved and had exquisitely refined and to allege that ancient institutions impeded the people's liberty. Whence, then, had those institutions arisen if not from the union of inspiration and inclination with necessity in the life of the people themselves? And after this outrage, it might seem an even stranger tyranny, if ever the people were inclined to re-adopt or to re-create something of the traditional kind, to forbid them that pleasure. But the French Revolution and the whole movement, still not quite spent, which proceeded from it, was not liberal except verbally and by accident.

The world was to be freed from Christianity and feudalism; it was not to be free to become Christian and feudal again. These were not regarded as normal episodes in human history, as forms of civilisation as legitimate as any others; they were regarded as fiendish inventions foisted by tyrants on human helplessness and ignorance. That incubus removed, all mankind was expected to found a heroic, fearless, unchallengeable republic, composed by Catos, Brutuses, and Cincinnatuses. This rigid form of liberty being established, no other form of liberty would be permitted.

The revolutionary leaders themselves were hardly men of that type, but ideologues and romantic orators, not always remarkable for their private virtues; and Roman discipline would surely have seemed a cruel and stupid slavery to the whole tender school of Rousseau. What the Revolution was really making for, though hardly expressed with frankness before Nietzsche, was liberty absolute and forever empty; liberty without foundations in nature or history, but resident in a sort of prophetic commotion. Custom, law, privilege, and religion were not to command allegiance, but to be themes only for criticism and invective. Hence the mortal hatred of any view that recognised realities, or built upon them. A truth, a fact, a past, a future, if definite and knowable, would abolish pure liberty, and it was essential, if this liberty were to be preserved, that nobody should build anything on it. If you settled something or made something, you would have become the slave of your action or of your work. The past was the great enemy, the dreadful ghost. You must challenge it, exorcise it, call it unreal, and see it wither and vanish at the word. As for the future, its own absolute free will would shape it as it came; you need not attempt to make it your product; it will know how to flout you, just as you flout the past. Only the present is ever real. A free soul inhabits the paradise of anarchy. Thus while politically the Revolution led to nationalism, industrialism, and absolute democracy, intellectually it ended in romantic egotism.

The conflicts which might arise between different men would then be solved by force directly, as they are solved now indirectly by the intervention of the armed law. Each would either destroy the others, or so adapt his conduct as to suffer as little as possible from their presence. On this principle evolution seems to have established the economy of the lower animals and of the diplomatic world. The shocks that ensue occasionally are no doubt rude;

but if we asked any wild animal, whether by way of insurance against his perilous ancestral way of living, he would consent to become domesticated and tame, he would doubtless reject the suggestion with scorn. To acknowledge a superior authority, purporting to correct his natural Will and his sense of what is good, would seem to him a surrender of all that makes life worth living—its moral spontaneity, its pleasures, and its pride in achievement. Better, he would say, one hour of passionate freedom and battle than an age of constraint, torpor, and peace.

Governments in their origin have always had to struggle against this pride of absoluteness in the primitive soul. The bold pirate, the reckless gambler, the libertine, and the clever burglar remain popular heroes. A suppressed self in everybody would like to play these parts. The same deep rebellion against control reappears in every willful child, and in every willful idea. Heretics feel it in the presence of orthodoxy, and orthodoxies feel it in the presence of one another. They all prefer martyrdom to reform.

## CHAPTER 14

### ALIEN DOMINATION

PATRIARCHAL monarchy grows up in peace, but it is a splendid instrument of war. Being able to conquer, it does so; and by a curious but easy combination, the father of one race is at the same time the tyrant of another. The two may retain different systems of law, language, and religion, but they have ultimately only one and the same government, that of the King. There is a kingdom within a kingdom, or rather a nation above a nation; the first ruled by a patriarchal monarch, the second by a foreign despot, these two persons being one and the same.

The elements of selfishness and beneficence in the ruler are not mutually exclusive nor merely juxtaposed. It is not necessary that in pandering to his own passions he should simply fleece his subjects, nor that when he serves his subjects he should simply sacrifice himself. That this is not the case is evident in foreign wars; for then in protecting his people he strengthens his throne, and in extending his conquered field of taxation he probably enriches his original subjects. Indeed, it is chimerical to demand that a government should be utterly disinterested, and should exercise the art of governing purely for its own sake and for the good of its subjects only, without also practicing what Plato calls the art of wages; that is, without serving simultaneously his personal aims. A government of philanthropists, guided only by a sense of duty, would prove a detestable government. To be beneficent, one must first live; and if beneficence is to be exercised amidst hostile forces and varied accidents, to be beneficent one must first be strong. One must have an inflexible personal bent and a great volume of life obeying it. Now, vigour absorbs energy; it must be largely fed. In other words, a government to be beneficent and morally representative must be autonomous and full of initiative; it must give direction, and not receive it; the interests it discerns and pictures need not be the private interests of its members, but interests seated in their individual hearts, quickening their imagination, and enlisting their continuous efforts. One such interest, in a very kind public-spirited man, may be the service of other people, even in those matters for which he himself cares nothing; he may play with children merely to amuse them, or give an alms out of pure benevolence; yet even here, to play well with children he must first like children, and like playing; and to make his alms truly charitable and acceptable, he must give it spontaneously and without second thoughts. The most impersonal and disinterested arts are also arts of self-expression.

Alien domination cannot plausibly claim the justification that a paternal government may have for its autocracy, namely, that it understands the true interests and fosters the true vital liberty of its subjects better than they, with little experience or traditional training, can do; yet there is another element in wise management that a foreign government may perceive but that a native one, sharing the limitations of its people, might easily ignore; and that is the radical and the ultimate *conditions* imposed by nature on each race or class, according to its peculiar virtues and vices. The foreign tyrant may at least save us from some of our favourite follies.

If a conqueror has a family or bodyguard of his own he may be a double monarch—with parental authority over his house and lordship over his estates. He may further be a prophet, a medicine man, a poet, imposing rites, legends, and maxims on both sets of his subjects.

Perhaps the difference between Oriental and European monarchy lies in this: that the Oriental had no separate family: his wives were his slaves, and his sons had no rights other than those of any favourite; and woe to them if they seemed to be their father's rivals.

Religion and morals are still imposed by family tyranny rather than by the State; for the State can hardly *inspire* them; it can only expose scandals and suppress rebellions against itself. Most despotisms end by being tolerant in religious matters, that is by leaving every sect to oppress those born within its pale. This saves the monarch from religious arguments, attaches the leading ecclesiastics of each faith to his unholy authority, and favours good order within their respective flocks. If ever a universal government is established in this world, it would do well to act, or rather to abstain from acting, on this prudent principle, leaving each nationality and religion to govern itself according to its lights and traditions, not only in manners but in all liberal arts. It was a mistake of the Romans, when they built roads, bridges, and aqueducts, to build also Roman temples and forums for subject nations; and not only a mistake politically, in that it might cause resentment in the native, but a mistake morally, if their aim was to spread civilisation. Not until the provinces and the city of Rome itself lost their classic aspect, did ecclesiastical, military, and domestic architecture, for instance, become free and picturesque, or did poetry and religion become varied and sincere. But unfortunately the Roman peace and commerce of the Empire were lost at the same time.

## CHAPTER 15

### DOMINANT CRIME

ONE of the inspirations of man is his conscience; but if you give this inspiration free rein, it may end by persuading you that it is murder to boil an egg. For if you say it is wrong to inflict injury on any creature or to deprive it of any good, then all life would presently appear wicked and self-contradictory, since it is a choice between incompatible goods, and a competition between rival persons. Or if, to avoid condemning existence altogether, you say that it is wrong to inflict any *felt* injury, but not to destroy the life of a potential chicken as yet unconscious, it might follow that to put a man to death painlessly in his sleep would be, like boiling an egg, a harmless exercise of your scientific domination.

To a sensitive conscience this lordly prerogative of eating, with the prospect of being eaten (by worms and by time if not by cannibals) is far from harmless; it sanctions the universal dominance of crime. The rigid consequence of condemning such mutual destruction has actually been drawn, and the abolition of all competitive existence has been set up as the aim of virtue. Such virtue, however, draws the ladder up after it as it climbs; and the earth remains altogether abandoned to the less sensitive sort of virtue that begins with the will to live. If you love life, you won't complain of a few bruises; you may even court the greatest dangers; and the very precariousness and dubious justification of living will encourage you to push forward, without a piffling calculation of goods and evils, either for yourself or for others. Your will, you may say, is your only rule of virtue. Adventure and labour, glory and death, are like the four points of the compass for your creative purpose.

Very well: when this romantic language is reduced to its bare import, it bleats or bellows the will to live of irrational animals. But in man, who has long walked in the path of reconsideration, repentance, and the desire for union, such absolute willfulness is archaistic. It is an artificial intoxication, and a desperate apology for crime.

The domination of crime over the individual has always been a favourite theme of tragic poets and novelists. It is hardly necessary to analyse this domination coldly, or to show how it is possible and why it is enthralling. But the domination of crime over society is worth a little study, because the first thing that happens is that such crime calls itself virtue. At bottom this occurs also in the heart of the private criminal. In the first glow of his plottings and anticipations, he feels the fascinating and dashing character of his future act, and he always retains a certain fatherly pride and glory in it. Rakes boast of their debaucheries, burglars boast of their sly tactics, at least to their pals, and murderers congratulate themselves endlessly in private upon their admirable precautions. It is true that a contrary voice usually makes itself heard even in the closet; not only misgivings about that cleverness and those precautions—for events are incalculably complicated in this world—but regret for advantages sacrificed to this fell passion, and disgust at the whole business. Such qualms torment the individual criminal because, after all, his ruling passion does not dominate his whole being; and in his inner dialogue he hears voices praising other things and making uncomfortable prophecies. Collective crime soon dispels these conscientious vapours. The commands of the chief, the public spirit of the band, the strict discipline internal to it, relieve the individual of doubts and scruples. He is no longer a bandit, but a hero.

Nevertheless, the enterprise remains criminal; because at the circumference it continually clashes not only with the interests of others, which might be disagreeable in war, but with the unavowed motives for the rash enterprise itself; so that alleged particular injustices suffered or vengeance nobly exacted or feuds inherited or ulterior peace to be ensured must be appealed to in self-justification. In a word, the authority of the public order is acknowledged, and the crime seeks to shelter and excuse itself, within that order, as the lesser of two evils.

To call a man or a government criminal is accordingly to pay them a relative compliment. They would not be criminal if they were animated, as perhaps they are, by an absolute unqualified Will, like the lion and the eagle: but in reality, they are human, so that they can't help looking before and after, and suffering a little at the reproaches of their victims. A conscience exists in them that needs to be appeased by excuses, or drowned in the clamour of sheer effrontery. And such intentional beastliness is, in one sense, better than beastliness constitutional and eternal. It was in this sense that Socrates proposed his characteristic paradox that to do wrong on purpose is better than not to be capable of doing right; as a man who runs slowly because he chooses is a better runner than one who is equally slow at the top of his speed. Better physically certainly, and even better morally (though naughtier for the moment) because he can be corrected. The wild beast, the madman, the fanatic have integrity but are incorrigible in their harmfulness; and in society any absolute singleness of Will and organisation works havoc in the same way. It has to be exterminated, or caged as a curiosity, or disregarded as a minor nuisance. But fanatical consistency is seldom attained; perhaps only by the first prophets of some new revelation. In the later apostles it soon begins to be mixed with some resisting elements of our common nature; and good sense and good humour destroy integrity in an established theocracy long before scepticism undermines the system intellectually. But there is still a third temper often found in the third generation, or in the innocent pupils of the regimen. They have at first the illusion of integrity, throwing themselves without reserve into the prescribed life, as into a good and holy discipline; and it is only later, on further experience, that they awake to the injury which they are inflicting on others and on themselves; and they are horrified at it, and repent—or at least there is a voice audible within them which, though it may be overpowered, prompts them to repentance.

This is the typical state of the sinner, led into an evil under the aspect of a good and sticking in that evil with regret, and confessing his impotence and division of purpose. Christian moral tales had been wont to represent the sinner as casting off his sin, warmly embracing a purer life, remote from his old passions and ambitions, and seeing heaven open before him as he rose from a baptism of universal renunciation. But there is another way of managing salvation in which the domination of crime is not ended abruptly and crudely, by suppressing crime and putting on a white robe of unnatural innocence; on the contrary, the dominance of crime is accepted, enlarged, systematised, until it seems the dominance of crime no longer, but a sort of rapturous natural destiny, above the petty contrasts of morality.

In Goethe's *Faust*, for instance, the ravished Gretchen dies in her misery; and we are consoled by learning that she is forgiven and goes to heaven. She has served her turn and that is the end of the story. But the guilty Faust does not need to be forgiven: he forgives himself. He has only just begun his career; and strengthened by the experience of that first crime, he is ready to start upon fresh and nobler adventures. He will do more deeds, borne up through any incidental mischances by the consciousness of his own noble character; and always equally vain and equally guilty, but always guilty and vain upon a higher plane of activity.

Here is dominant crime *in excelsis*: for the heavens open before it, too, crimson and blue and silver-studded, with the eternal feminine forever leading the way. I am afraid that on earth, however, the *dénouement* may be rather different, with the roles reversed. The ravishing Faust, so lusty in his galvanised youth, and so brave—in spite of a little surviving pedantry—in his knightly trappings, will grow feeble, vicious, and sad, like other sinners: he will revert to his narcotic draughts and his theosophical hocus-pocus; and whether he go to heaven or to hell will soon make no difference to anybody. It will be his victim, innocent Humanity, plying her spinning-wheel in her village garden, that in time will renew her youth, turn to honest loves, and learn in the four watches of the night to despise her shabby seducer.

## CHAPTER 16

### DISTINCTION BETWEEN CRIME AND MADNESS

IT SEEMS necessary to admit that living beings, like the blind forces of nature, may do harm without doing wrong; for like the blind forces of nature, which never cease to work through them, living beings may be incapable of perceiving or of sharing the interests which they trample upon. And this without any lack of intellectual and moral keenness; because the principle of integrity is one, and that of beneficence is another. Incapacity to sympathise with certain animals, such as vermin, or with certain human interests, such as strange lusts or strange religions, may actually be a mark of integrity in clear-cut souls; and barbarians always regard it as disgraceful for anybody to be more tender than they are themselves. In such cases integrity may be compatible with cruelty, drunkenness, lust, vagabondage, witch-burning, and slave-hunting—but integrity is incompatible with crime. An upright barbarian cannot justly be called criminal, however maleficent he may be; he is virtuous in his own world as the vermin and the vultures may be virtuous.

It would be a nice question for the sentimentalist, whether he ought not to sympathise with barbarians, and wish them a happy hunting-ground for their energy, where they should not seriously annoy anybody, as he would wish a happy hunting-ground for those innocent vermin. It is not reasonable to require all animals to be beneficent like the kind sheep supplying us with wool and mutton, nor is it generously sympathetic to sympathise only with those who sympathise with us. The narrow and fierce soul of the crocodile, too, is living and real.

Nevertheless, in practice, barbarians *are* criminal; for they do not commonly attain integrity, although it may be a part of their voluntary obfuscation to proclaim that they do. Just as often religious madmen (at least when the madness is acquired by precept and sustained by propaganda) are only mad north-north-west, and have to train themselves to make believe consistently, their chief madness being the love of going mad, so in the most systematic and sanctified ruthlessness there is something histrionic. Only a part of the soul adheres to that fanatical system, and it has a hard fight against obvious facts and against contrary instincts.

But as the parts of villains in plays are often the most interesting and display the greatest skill and concentration (because the way of the transgressor is exciting as well as hard) so it is in playing the villain in real life—you have to dominate yourself, and keep all your wits about you, lest you lapse from your self-imposed and exacting character.

For this reason when people undertake the defence of systematic crime they cannot do it consistently: they have not the courage of their principles. Some Greek Sophists in their effrontery, some prophets in their zeal, Machiavelli in his cool acceptance of human wickedness, Nietzsche in his ecstatic egotism, may have tried to walk this ethical tightrope. They have done it with varying art and with an expression of countenance different in each case, but always forced. They are acting out a self-contradiction: defending crime, when crime is actually condemning itself, because to be criminal is to plan an injury when you feel it to be wrong.

Whether a passion be called mad or criminal hangs largely on the temper of the judge. A man will often speak of his own passions, when past, as madness. I lost my head, he will say: I was beside myself. This is his way of assuring you what a sound person he is at heart; had he only been himself, his conduct would have been perfect. But when we call the passions of others madness, we mean to condemn those persons absolutely; had they merely been yielding to some human passion, with which in this instance we were displeased, they would appear as normal competitors in the general scramble—though by chance inconvenient or odious to ourselves. But by calling those passions mad, we imply that they work havoc on their possessors. We ourselves are judging impartially: we are pitying our enemies; we would gladly become their friends; but unfortunately they are mad, and what can one *do* with mad people? Father, forgive them, we say, like the coroner over a suicide: they are temporarily of unsound mind.

## CHAPTER 17

### RULING MADNESS

MADNESS, when recognised as a disease, excites distress and pity, or when merely gaped at, as odd and silly, it may excite laughter; or, in its inward misery, it may seem a divine visitation. We are all mad in our dreams, when outer impressions do not check our galloping ideas; and marginal madness plays about us in our waking thoughts; as a dog will scurry before and behind his pedestrian master and is whistled for sometimes in vain. Great passions and excitements touch madness at their summit: so that madness is not really an inhuman or demonic thing. It is only too domestic, too individually human, too headstrong to keep in step with things; so that if it becomes central and directive, it dashes us against the rocks. Not always, however, so soon or so fatally as a summary view might suggest. A boat may lean over very far in the wind without capsizing, when there is ballast and momentum enough; and a mind can yield to a vast deal of extravagance without coming to grief.

Certainly madness involves some waste of energy: the spirit is not disembodied, and wild ideas imply a hectic disposition. But this waste may be inconsiderable (as in dreams) or compensated for by some indirect advantage as in many taboos and panics. Moreover, taken as a personal experience madness may be domesticated by receiving a moral and symbolic interpretation, perhaps actually relieving the stress out of which it sprang, as in ritual mourning.

Ceremonial is a sort of mad echo of rational conduct, but measured and sober in its own field; and this mad music is healing. The great waves of delusion that sometimes sweep over the world come from a momentary attachment of active impulses (not mad in themselves, but restive and ignorant) to some fantastic prophecy: that a land flowing with milk and honey has been divinely promised, that the end of the world is at hand, that a plague comes from neglect of ritual observances, that ghosts are abroad, or that miracles are being worked round the corner. Unbelievers have a madness of their own: that theirs is the one race or the one philosophy predestined to rule the world, or to explain it. These persuasions soon lapse from the condition of urgent prophecies to that of mysteries and dogmas which nobody need quite understand or be much troubled by. The madness is then neutralised by a convention which corrects its implications and rationalises its deliverance. Yet while the embers of such madness smoulder congenially in the soul, any breath may blow it again into a flame: and the day of psychic epidemics is not yet over.

A most beautiful illustration of dominant yet domesticated madness may be found in the Greek oracles. In the first place they gave out no permanent code of precepts or legislation; and they issued summonses to no wars or revolutions. They spoke only when questioned (and perhaps paid) like modern mediums. People seldom appealed to them except in extremities, when reason was silent, and a man or city could only have appealed to some casual omen, or drawn lots. The embassy to the oracle gave pause and ceremony to the deliberation; the response came in an ambiguous verse in which the mutterings of the prophetess were already somewhat humanised; and the questioner still had to decide for himself what to do, with a curious feeling that divine accomplices were half prompting, half baffling his action, and in any case making the issue their own. In this way a truly religious sentiment was, or might be, produced—faith, humility, courage, conformity. Yet the aboriginal madness of the oracle was of the frankest: and the most intelligent and temperate of nations submitted, in the most crucial matters, to the inspiration of idiots. This might seem a horrible fate; and yet if the wisest man of Greece—Socrates—had been asked to pronounce on the same political or military alternatives, would his advice have been better than that of the Pythoness and her tripos? I am afraid that the decisions of oracles or of philosophers at best divert the course of very slender streams; and that a different gas in the cave at Delphi would not have given Greek history a very different twist. Socrates resisted the Thirty Tyrants with heroic courage; but his example, like that of Phocion, was powerless to arrest the general decay. What brought on the catastrophe was not any incidental error or madness; it was a vast silent change in the constellation of forces in the geographic world, producing a transformation of custom and character in all Hellas. There had been something to defend against Persia; but what was there to defend against Rome? Independence is not an important good when cosmopolites ask for it; and an administrative machine, even if jealously local, will not produce anything but taxpayers. Civilisations grow old and succumb to disease like individuals; they become memories and cannot breed after their kind except in the rarefied air of ideas; and races, when they survive, so modify their manners and mix their blood that it seems irony to call them after the name of their ancestors.

It was not the oracles, then, that destroyed Greece: that prophetic madness may almost have been a benefit, a cathartic, purging people of their insane wills, and enabling them to walk about in their sanity. It is almost normal to be partly mad: not only because sensation is visionary, and grammar arbitrary, but because there is a margin of less articulate wildness beneath these conventional fictions, a residue that will not submit to them. The point is not to be mad on the whole; to keep your madness in leash, and to let it loose only in season. Plato, with an inimitable union of reverence and irony, identified madness with inspiration, and called it divine; it comes from the fountains of nature, it is primordial. Yet it is not central or dominant, because the soul or life of the individual is formed by a harmony in his composition and motion. This harmony, in so far as it is achieved, is health and (on the intellectual side) sanity; so that sanity and not madness is the constitutional principle of the psyche, and of all her organs. But this vital harmony is always imperfect, a sort of crust beneath which mighty chaotic forces are at work, as yet imperfectly unified or transmuted into the life of reason. Each of these parts is breeding an inchoate spirit with an incipient rationality of its own. Each slumbers or flares up with its special imagery and method; and it is from one or another of these subterranean souls that dreams and inspirations break in upon the rational man. It is for him, in his sober equilibrium, to accept, use, interpret, and control these promptings. He is not mad for having them; they are the materials for his rational synthesis. But if he lets any of them become dominant he is lost, and they also; because after all the organ or member cannot endure, if it spreads out and swallows up the rest of the body. To be all hand or belly or head, all will or all lust or all fancy, would make a horrible amputated monster, dying, not being born.

Madness is fatal then if it reigns, but it may be neutralised and the energies beneath it may be turned to good uses if it is tamed and governed. After all, to exist and to wish to exist is itself a sort of madness; yet life and passion are the basis of reason. You must live, if you are to live well; you must assume some shape among shapes, become a phantom among phantoms, if you are to be beautiful. In morals and politics the soundness must be begged from physical realities, else morals and politics would become mad in the fanatical sense—tragically, hideously, cruelly mad. But the primal irrationality of the Will, when reduced to measure, modestly rejoins the gentle and universal inebriation of nature, where madness is only innocent sport, exuberantly fashioning all sorts of temporary harmonies.

## CHAPTER 18

### THE PARADISE OF ANARCHY

A GREAT motive invoked by the modern mind has been the love of liberty; but this love, when we examine it, appears to be three fourths hatred. There is the passionate, secret, accumulated hatred towards religion, wealth, and government; and there is the hatred of all the ills that flesh is heir to, easily attributed to the wickedness and folly of other men. Mankind has always been unhappy, more unhappy perhaps when submissive and pious than when rebellious. The rebel is proud of himself and hopeful; these are

## THE PARADISE OF ANARCHY

inspiriting sentiments, and in protesting against his misery he has half vanquished it. Misery in other cases may lead to self-depreciation and self-reproach, as if the fault must lie rather in oneself than in the ruling powers. These powers may even be idealised, in contrast to our wretchedness, and conceived as splendid heroes and happy gods. But such pious illusions are hateful to a free spirit. It will not only defy all tyrants, divine and human, but will declare all the ways and works of man in the past to have been false to humanity. Sometimes the love of liberty becomes open hatred of every independent thing limiting one's own fancy: hatred of tradition, of greatness, of inequality, of truth, and even of matter. "What ignominy," cries the brave young mind, "to allow myself to be hypnotised by some decrepit charlatan, merely because he speaks in hollow accents, has a white beard, and waves a wand! Haven't I eyes as good as his, or much better eyes? Haven't I hands much more skillful and strong? Haven't I a will far more simple, honest, and clear? To discover the true good I need but look into my own breast. There, written in large capitals I find the whole duty of man, the obvious rule for disseminating a perfect happiness. There nature has deeply engraved the eternal law of liberty: THINK AS YOU LIKE, SAY WHAT YOU THINK, DO WHAT YOU CHOOSE."

There is a possible difficulty here, which I will mention in passing: that if in the free mind there were nothing but this law of freedom, the law would remain inapplicable, because that empty mind would never know what to like or what to think. This happens sometimes to young children. If they are awake, and not crying for food, they begin to cry out of sheer boredom. The rattle or ball must be fetched at once to attract their attention, and suggest an employment for their blank liberty. Theoretically, this difficulty is fatal to libertarianism; there must be given motives, given organs, given objects, before liberty can exist or can begin to move. Liberty is not a source but a confluence and a harmony. In practice, however, the very definite structure of the human body and the very definite solicitations from outside give to the sense of liberty abundant employment; so that the little monarch, playing with his toys, never suspects how completely he depends on his heritage and his circumstances even for his liberty.

I turn, however, to another consideration politically more pressing. Suppose liberty has found a field in which to operate and has chosen something to do. If contrary forces now appeared in that field, preventing the desired action, or destroying the free agent, evidently liberty would be gone. In order to be truly and happily free you must be safe. Liberty requires peace. War would impose the most terrible slavery, and you would never be free if you were always compelled to fight for your freedom.

This circumstance is ominous: by it the whole sky of liberty is at once clouded over. We are drawn away violently from irresponsible play to a painful study of facts and to the endless labour of coping with probable enemies. Yet that is not the worst of it. If liberty demands peace, peace does not merely demand that other people should not meddle with us; it demands equally that we should not meddle with them. It would really be as much a breach of the peace, though not so painful, if we broke their heads as if they broke ours. Besides, it would establish a dangerous precedent, and next time our own heads might be broken. But if we are not free to break any head or any heart or any bounds, what sort of liberty remains to us? Liberty to follow the golden rule: whereby our free hearts are at once sobered and transfixed in their inmost affections. What a surprise, when we had proclaimed our complete freedom, to find ourselves condemned by it to eternal vigilance and to the most drastic discipline and reversal of our natural Will! The superman sees himself committed by his supermanhood to the morality of the slave.

But perhaps all this is a mistake, and I have done injustice to the heroism of free spirit in supposing it anxious for peace or security or length of life. Perhaps its joy is to live dangerously and instead of the golden rule which involves the degradation of respecting the preferences of others, the superman may invoke the lilies of the field that take no thought for the morrow. Such mystic placidity after all can survive in this world and is surely in as great sympathy with nature and with the depths of being as are knowingness and craft; which is not to say that the superman need fail to be ruthless as well as placid. At times he may enact the lion, the true lord of creation. Nor is this impulse to live in the magic present merely lazy or merely immoral; it expresses, perhaps out of season, the ultimate relation of spirit to the miscellany of existence. Spirit is essentially the timeless witness of it all, untouched and incredulous, yet for that very reason omnivorous and fearless.

Here is a first glimpse of a paradise of anarchy, in which peace should reign not as in Eden by dint of organisation and harmony, but by the perfect insulation of each life and its utter irrelevance to all others. This is an idea that might perhaps be realised in the interstellar spaces, if free spirits there could forgo that love of preaching which characterises them on earth. They would probably abandon it, or else it would abandon them; because what bends the spirit to the choice of specific themes and affections is simply its roots in the earth, its dependence on the vicissitudes of material life. Could you cut off this attachment materially you would have dissolved it morally. Not being rooted any longer in an earthly person or station or passion, spirit might have ceased to be social and competitive; it might have ceased to be preoccupied even with the defence or propagation of its own life. It would think anarchically, without so much as the notion of a truth to which it might conform. It would pursue that *gaia scienza* which is not knowledge of anything but pure composition. Yes, it would have become too free to think. It would only sing.

As we shall see presently, this is far from the end of the story; but it indicates the direction of spiritual emancipation.

The notion of pure spirit abstracts from human nature, and does so legitimately, because there is no reason to suppose that spirit is peculiar to man. Biological analogy would suggest that any creature moving organically with obvious reference to the past or the future or to distant objects, is in that measure the home of spirit. In such a case, action and adjustment are virtually self-transcendent; in reacting they enact the movement of the object, dancing as it dances; so that the animal not only possesses its own life but lives in awakened sympathy with outlying things, and partly from their point of view. Raise this behaviour to the level of feeling, and you will have synthetic consciousness or spirit; to which some part of the world is revealed, so to speak on a map, impartially, as in fact the parts are distributed in the plane of causation. The centre of action and speculation—it is the same centre—will remain individual and personal; the action will continue to obey an organic impulse; but by the sensibility of the organism the world will have been surveyed; and the organism itself will figure in that survey as an incident in the world explored: now one of the patches on the map will be labelled *Myself*. The virtual self-transcendence of intelligent action will have become actual in a thought essentially directed upon all time and all existence.

Once thus awakened, spirit has turned the tables on life. It has potentially discounted every vital and moral perspective; it has begun to conceive how things actually grow and work; the organism will no longer dumbly undergo the influence of their presence. Spirit is called spirit because it is breathed in and breathed out into the infinite air; it would not be spirit if a certain disloyalty, a certain love of anarchy, were not native to it.

This essential impartiality of spirit is normally exercised within narrow limits. Language, manners, and practical good sense correct severely the childish spirituality that runs too far afield in this world, or finds too much fault with it. Yet the insidious principle of emancipation is at work even in those social conventions, in so far as they are at all understood or focussed in reflection. The philosophic mind will discover that the order of society is unstable, and in the very act of studying the various forms of order and comparing their fruits, it will absolve itself from blind allegiance to any one of them.

Not that pure spirit would tend anywhere to relax the existing order, to which spirit, in this special instance, owes its existence. The disruptive force in society is not that of understanding, but that of some political passion contrary to the prevalent one. Spirit is already free enough both from the unreformed and from the reformers when it has understood various forms of order in their natural diversity and contrary perfections.

Yet this inalienable liberty with which the possession of spirit endows the individual inverts the order of genesis in human life. The individual criticises society, but society has produced the individual. This contrariety—for it is not a contradiction—causes infinite trouble. Society, or those conventional domineering persons who speak in its name, thinks the individual exists only to serve it. But what a monstrous thing to sacrifice all the living parts, in order that the nominal mechanical whole may continue its blind career! We know that the first-born was once sacrificed superstitiously, in hope that the family might prosper. So the individual and his free powers are still perpetually sacrificed in order that the world may keep up any melancholy routine which it has once adopted. And as one day the voice of reason held back Abraham's hand, when he was about to obey the voice of society, so at any time the spirit, morally autonomous though physically dependent, may reject the domination of those social passions which after all are only imposed upon it and occasional.

To live without let or hindrance would be life indeed, and so the spirit actually lives in its happier moments, in laughter or in quick thought. Yet there is a snare in this vital anarchy. It is like the liberty to sign cheques without possessing a bank account. You may then write them for any amount; but it is only when a precise deposit limits your liberty that you may write them to any purpose. So the spirit, before it can be vital or free, must exist; there must be oil in the lamp, there must be substance and organs and circumstances to call the spirit forth, to lend it fire, to give it direction, to offer it entertainment. At the level of complexity at which thought and laughter are possible, to exist means to be distinctly organised, localised, contrasted with other things, and conditioned by them. It means to have a mock freedom only; freedom to exert oneself spontaneously in one way, but no freedom to exert oneself otherwise or not at all or under different circumstances or with another result. In order to live without control and absolutely ungoverned, as the spirit thinks it lives, it must be controlled by an organism that governs itself. In other words, it cannot be anarchical, but must be inwardly, precisely, and irretrievably governed.

I say advisedly, "in order to live." There is a sense in which spirit is not compelled to persevere in existence, or to develop or complete any thought. It may flash and disappear, to be kindled elsewhere, in some other organism or in different circumstances. It may still be spirit in quality, and in that sense a resurrection of itself; and if it could remember these wild vicissitudes (though this would hardly be possible) it might conceive them as collapses and free growths of its own being. Yet in those scattered instances, spirit would be only being born, suffering, and dying; it would not be *living*. It would not be preserving or defending or developing any kind of labour or affection. Its own anarchy would kill it, because life is an exercise of self-government.

No blunder could therefore be more radical than that of destroying the ruling powers in order to enjoy life. The rebellion of Lucifer was essentially a suicide: reducing himself to free spirit he reduced himself to nothing. Real powers are always definite, or they would not have definite results. Even that passive capacity to arise and suffer and be extinguished which I was just now attributing to pure spirit depends on a prior precise organisation of animal life: spirit comes when the occasion has summoned it. And the very pride and joy of spirit in its supposed anarchy are borrowed from its organ. Passions fatigue, cares annoy, much thinking entangles us in vain suppositions: therefore it is a relief to dismiss all responsibility, and float or bask or sing. Dissolution itself may be pleasant if there was a painful tightness before; and one organ in ceasing to function may allow, for a moment, freer play to another organ. Hence the illusion that liberation in itself is a good, and that complete freedom would be paradise. It is true that we live by metabolism, by subduing old substances to new forms; and the inherited psyche within us suffers variation and cyclical decay. This is only another way of saying that a continual dying is a condition of physical life. Only spiritual life can be wholly vital; but for that very reason actual spirit is altogether volatile and evanescent and dependent for its existence on an endless labour of birth and death in the material sphere.

The paradise of anarchy is accordingly but a momentary sporadic enjoyment of an underlying paradise of order. For every unit in nature, and notably every psyche, maintains its order and expands its influence as far as circumstances permit; but when the surroundings prove too unfavourable, that nucleus will contract, and bide its time, until it is wholly destroyed; while a well-knit and proud psyche in such a case may desperately entrench itself in its own apparent sufficiency, and may boast that it will live better or at least die happier feeding only on its own heart.

# PART TWO

*Enterprise*

# CHAPTER 1

DEGREES OF MILITANCY

ENTERPRISE is a form of militancy without moral provocation and without enemies. Like faction it feels itself to be a virtue, not only for showing courage and initiative, but particularly for doing so peacefully, without any lust for blood or vengeance, and purely at the call of some open chance to attempt untried and glorious things. And yet, although so blameless and admirable in itself, enterprise somehow secures less admiration and honour than do military or revolutionary achievements. The abusive rhetorician and the smashing victorious general get all the ovations, and the man who has proved his mastery over the fruitful world is never entrusted with the government. War and revolution are public and dramatic events in which everyone participates at least in imagination; but the private discoveries and inventions of the adventurous mind work the transformation of society often without being noticed at all. Even the disasters of warlike ambition fill history with tales of heroism and martyrdom, and even more dramatic crimes and punishments; while the failures of enterprise, if remembered, excite only ridicule or contempt.

Enterprise is indeed less social than faction in its inspiration, so that the world is naturally less concerned with it as it arises, although society may be more affected by it in the end. Empires and forms of government disappear completely at frequent intervals; while the arts and fashions that distinguish each civilisation, although they may be lost on the surface, usually leave their mark in the habits of at least a part of mankind.

The nineteenth century began with two extraordinary eruptions of faction, the French Revolution, tamed but spreading, and the Napoleonic wars. The first of these is still at work in several different ideologies and parties, while the second has passed away like a summer thunder storm. The second half of that century, on the contrary, was filled with brilliant enterprise in science and industry, producing a revolution in the equipment of human life and mind, which has continued with acceleration to the present time, and is presumably destined to make a wholly new era in the relation of mankind to the latent energies of matter. Medicine, most beneficently, communications and means of transit most astonishingly by radio and air, have respectively relieved and frivolously complicated human existence. Meantime two general wars on an unprecedented scale, and the Russian Revolution, with its repercussions everywhere, have left the intellectual and political world bewildered. It had thought, until 1914, that dominated as it was by beneficent enterprise, it would continue to grow daily more populous, richer, better instructed, freer, and more secure in its picturesque variety of nations, all united in one web of accelerated motion, time saved, labour lightened, and sports, private but more conspicuously public and professional, filling up the leisure of all classes and nations, with harmless excitement.

Still floating in the haze of this mentality, the prophets of enterprise founded the League of Nations and twenty-five years later the rather too similar Organisation of United Nations. In this, as a Charter member, was included the Soviet Union, an ultra-democratic comrade, who had been allied to the conquering Germans, and had been saved by American aid from their treacherous invasion, a comrade who now took the Germans' place, occupied half their territory, and obtained the right to veto, in the Council of the United Nations, every measure that the other comrades proposed.

It might seem that these prophets of Enterprise in their innocent goodness were not militant at all: what other ministers of foreign affairs ever carried goodwill and cooperation so far? I think, however, that the pure essence of militancy is more dominant in these prophets than in ordinary hunters or warriors. The latter are prompted at bottom by material needs or material lures; renown and praise, which saints and poets may also obtain, would not satisfy lordly natures without the general obedience and the material domination which their feats can procure. Their ambition is to improve their position rather than to transform the world. But the desire to improve the world is militancy *in excelsis*. It involves not only the exercise of power but the miracle of creation: to see mankind adopt one's thoughts, obey one's precepts, and draw forever the line between good and evil exactly where we have drawn it. What enterprise could be more ambitious and show a more extraordinary self-confidence than the assumed mission to judge and to convert all the rest of the world? Can these politicians and socialist professors of philosophy think themselves divinely inspired? Or can they regard their own country or their own party as the one right model and right censor for all mankind?

It is not in such plain words that they proclaim their purposes, but rather in terms of the economic or popular advantages that they enjoy at home and generously wish to diffuse among less fortunate peoples. They hardly conceive that these other peoples may have different aspirations. Sometimes, indeed, they seem to say so, and to advocate the right of self-government for all nations. Yet they establish at the same time a universal authority, to which all would have to bow if it were able to govern.

Perhaps the cause of this contradiction lies in the fact that Enterprise in the economically advanced countries has been chiefly economic. All nations would like to be prosperous; and if it were only as a guide to prosperity that a universal authority was to be established, it might speak and act impartially, in the light of science. But some traces of moral and cultural militancy seem to remain in the proposed universal government; and the attempt to impose such constraints, not imposed already by nature at terrible cost on the unprepared, would be of all enterprises the most deeply egotistical and probably the least successful.

## CHAPTER 2

### THE ROMANCE OF ENTERPRISE

THERE is a romantic side to all militancy, conspicuous in outlawry and war and in the lure of seafaring, so magical for the boyish mind; but there is more homely romance in the merchant's fortunes also, with its foreign perspectives, its memories, and relics of successful ventures and varied contacts. Even without now going far from home, the sharer in great engineering or financial operations brings the whole world, as it were, into a focus there; and the wealth that he may amass need not be merely material and enslaving, but a continual bond with far-reaching revolutions and exotic arts. This atmosphere may well surround a great merchant in his old age, and be the medium in which his children grow up, much more liberal than the air of military or factious households. For the young merchant himself, if he plunged without much backing into perilous enterprises, there was a different quality of liberal excitement in earlier life: there was hazard. The risk incidental to all buiness may become the dominant phase of it for the speculator on the stock exchange; and he may be ruined as easily gambling there as on the turf. But the defiance that makes the manly vanity of a wager, even in a game of pure chance, qualifies trade only by the way: because here the occasion for betting is likely to be expert knowledge, or the illusion of expert knowledge: and this is a factor not in the risk of enterprise but in the art and sure conduct of it. When the merchant holds a trump hand, and can guess the hand of his rivals, he is legitimately playing for results that will count in the world, for the right conduct of public operations, and not merely for the excitement of playing, with a superstitious hope of being suddenly rich.

These spontaneous and liberal elements in enterprise should not be lost sight of if we hope to do justice to its political developments. Utilitarian economists, jealous of public rights against all the private passions of the public, may denounce the profits of trade as they might the rents of landlords, as being a sort of antecedent robbery of what should have belonged to the people. Yet these innocent robbers too form a part of the people, with primary human needs and ambitions; and to satisfy these needs and ambitions forms in turn an integral part of the public good.

So the arts and risks of the merchant have a natural attractiveness of their own, apart from any predatory motives that an envious revolutionary rhetoric may eventually charge them with. The dominance of trade comes about as innocently as the dominance of speech, and is just as much an element in the growth of human society. Every lively animal in his idle moments loves to experiment with his tongue or with his claws, and see what things he can do and what sounds he can make; and these manual or vocal sports may become ingrained in his system, pleasant, inevitable, and by chance useful. So singers and poets, comedians and orators, priests and prophets acquire their special arts and perhaps win general applause and public esteem; and yet their position in society remains at bottom precarious. Essentially their hold is only on the imagination. By accident they may acquire a material use; yet there is nothing to insure their arts against proving utterly vain and perhaps pernicious.

So a school of ancient prophets and poets accused commerce of having destroyed human happiness, and spoke of *sacra pinus*, the accursed keel, that had brought foreign wares and corruption into Arcadia. And not only may the enterprise of adventurers be suspected of having evil consequences in itself, but it may be seen even by us to-day to avail itself of all those dubious auxiliary arts that misguide the unwary by appeals to the imagination. Instead of comparatively innocent cries of vendors or heralds announcing their wares or their news, we now have advertising and propaganda: arts explicitly bent on bending the public mind to party advantage. The process is like that of a lottery, catering to human weakness and popular delusions for the benefit of partial interests themselves probably hollow and deceptive.

## CHAPTER 3

### THE MIDDLEMAN IN TRADE

In primitive barter, even when money begins to intervene, there is no dominance of any party over any other. Each knows his own positive interest and need, and closes the bargain willingly, with open eyes, thinking it on the whole to his own advantage. This advantage will not be equal on both sides. The need to sell may be greater than the wish to buy; resources and foresight may be unequal in the two bargainers; one may be making a clear gain and the other only postponing disaster; yet even the latter acts freely, and is not fleeced anonymously, without his knowledge or consent.

Money, while a great convenience in exchange, introduces a middle term pregnant with terrible dangers. Without attempting to enumerate or to trace these dangers, which would involve a whole treatise on trade, I may here notice one circumstance which politically is the most remarkable. When there is a common currency, a third party, a middleman, may intervene in all exchanges. He may know nothing, except verbally and in terms of money, of the needs and interests of any other class. His own interest and need will be simply to buy his wares cheap and to sell them dear. To get the advantage in bargains at both ends will be his whole art and profession; and that element of inequality in making exchanges, which was an inevitable personal accident in primitive barter, now becomes the sole means of living for the middleman, be he pedlar, shopkeeper, merchant, or banker. Trade has become an art in itself, and has bred a whole set of social classes living on an invisible toll which they levy on all people's affairs; it has become the art of "making money." This abstract form of industry or finance is a by-product of concrete commercial enterprise, and not necessary to it.

The pure essence of a merchant and of his eventual domination over mankind may be seen most clearly when he is an intrepid adventurer, sailing to remote countries, and dealing with alien peoples. Then his joy is to be the first to discover some savage strand where pearls may be had in exchange for glass beads, furs for coloured tissue paper, or an elephant's tusk for a bottle of rum. So long as this sort of barter is possible, merchants are men of enterprise, loving finery and rare knowledge. Blue sea ports prosper and colonies pay. Competition, however, soon exhausts those virgin markets, and trade settles down to a normal prosaic level, as if love had passed into wedlock. The merchant is no longer called a merchant but a dealer or a business man. He makes no perilous voyages; there are few perilous voyages to make. Ships are insured, and merchandise also. The owners are probably unknown shareholders, or maiden ladies living on annuities; while the partners or directors are only officials on fixed salaries. They do not sail the ocean blue but sit in an office, telephone in hand, waiting for the next report from the stock exchange or dictating perfunctory business letters to a frizzled and pouting typist.

The profits of prosaic trade, in normal cases, may then loosely represent services rendered in distributing merchandise and making it accessible to the public. Enterprise now appears rather in the invention of mechanical contrivances, partly to cheapen production, partly to introduce new products. It is evidently not enough to invent a new machine; it must either have a use for existing purposes, or it must, by its novelty or pleasantness, become in itself, like the radio, a new object of passion, to diminish the tedium and multiply the commitments of civic life.

The ultimate, the moral, use of such inventions might be hard to determine; but in practice there is no need of doing so. The inventor has his own vanity and pecuniary interest at heart; and the agents that disseminate his invention also have a pecuniary interest of their own to consider. Advertisement, propaganda, missionary work then introduce the new trick amongst the innocent million and develop a new demand. The point is to capture the public, and then, by force of fashion and custom, to induce the public to perpetuate your business. Society is then dominated by the producer's interests, and trade proper takes a secondary and inglorious place.

Capitalists and bankers are merchants sublimated and reduced to the abstract function of doing nothing but invest their money in order to increase its nominal total. Commerce is encouraged by these gentlemen in all markets at once, as far as their influence extends. They have no ships, unless it be a private yacht; they have no warehouse or shop, but an office furnished like a club; and they deal in no special kind of merchandise. All their business is overhead business and all their profits overhead profits. They are international in mind, like the proletariat. They see in everything merely its value in money. Nothing therefore has any quality in their eyes except its quantity. Their incomes, which are sucked out of all their transactions impartially, tend in turn to be spent impartially and in all climates upon all luxuries. They are probably patrons of the fine arts everywhere, and if they smile upon or even practice any special religion it is precisely that form of it which, like a varnish, has the least smell or colour and gives the most polish.

Even for the subject population, commerce breaks down local barriers. It brings nationalities together, not only physically in the great seaports, but ideally in the public mind. And it does so, not as war does or a religion might, by exaggerating the foreignness of the foreigner or the unbeliever and breeding a desire to abolish him. Commerce, on the contrary, after the first predatory and adventurous phase is past, assimilates trading nations to one another, and creates an economic organism larger than the political and moral one and rooted in all the nations employing their services. Those local organisms, moral and political, come to seem to the commercial mind accidental and perhaps troublesome, where they impede at all the pervasive and equalising prevalence of trade.

A cosmopolitan upper class then grows up, all speaking well or ill the same fashionable languages and cultivating the same fashionable manners. Or a cosmopolitan middle class, like the Jews, already diffused throughout the world and dedicated to commerce, may rise to the top, and may undertake to subordinate all nations and religions to international cooperation and prosperity. In rising to the top, this cosmopolitan middle class takes over the arts and sciences and the literary activities native to the older societies and often manipulates them cleverly, with an air of superior enlightenment; but this is merely the subjective superiority of the incurable foreigner, who has no roots in the society he studies and has cut himself off from his own roots. Indeed, the commercial mind has no apprehension of roots of any kind and moves on a verbal plane of conventional maxims and utopian prophecies. This does not prevent it from inspiring respect in the half-educated public, proud to have outgrown old-fashioned ideas which militant intellect never possessed and cannot understand. Wealth and progress in wealth with all its intellectual luxuries are visible gains, like those of a man winning the big prize in a lottery. Yet even wealth seldom comes to the uprooted in a satisfying measure, while the ethos and dignity of the past seem to them absurd or even pernicious.

Thus the commercial mind imposes itself on the urban and suburban population, living in chance rooms or hired houses, easily migrating, picking up work individually, perhaps without friends or family, and guided intellectually by the newspapers, themselves a commercial enterprise full of information coloured by party bias.

The aims and sentiments expressible publicly before such a population are far more superficial and ignoble than those natural to the individuals composing it; even the leaders, in their speeches and proclamations, feel compelled to repeat empty phrases that at least alienate nobody. All they require is that their tone should encourage hope in the multitude and perhaps in themselves. Those who suspect the fallacy, or feel some cross-inspiration, may learn to put these doubts away as temptations, and be actually ashamed of them. Thus the grossest vanity and cheapest rhetoric are likely to carry the day politically; yet they are not likely to

# THE MIDDLEMAN IN TRADE

carry it socially or permanently. An old civilisation sails with enough hidden ballast to neutralise the follies of a random crew. Four futile Republics, for instance, have not upset the balance of the French nation.

The very superficiality of a commercial stratum (for commerce is not necessary to life) prevents a thorough domination on its part over society. If it dominated, it would dissolve society altogether. Yet there is a moment when a healthy community, rural and military, profits by the influence of commerce, and is enriched by it in culture as well as extended in power. A rural population may have had its religion and its minstrelsy; but philosophical debate and the more critical forms of the fine arts require the concourse of many differing minds and of contrary traditions. The idle rich supported by commercial fortunes travel more and are better informed that is a military caste or a local seminary; they elude the domination of any religious orthodoxy; they may even become connoisseurs and counterfeit aristocrats with a veneer of facile refinement if not of distinction. Meantime beneath them, within and beyond a belt of suburban villas, a large commercial class imitates their culture, and makes a point of distingushing itself from the artisan and wage-earning class by cultivating a certain degree of emancipated mental vivacity. They offer a fertile field for party views and theoretical persuasions of every description; they know nothing and criticise everything. Yet their commercial background still demands a modicum of honesty and steadiness; and as they regard themselves as worthily rich and essentially enlightened, they can hardly be drawn away, as a class, from the political ideals of commerce.

Taken by themselves into an innocent mind these ideals are not unattractive. Unattached circulating wealth, such as commerce accumulates, sheer invisible credit or money in the bank, acts as a sort of lubricant, giving a magic power to the mind. It opens up possibilities, uncramps old prejudices, stimulates the arts by the shock of the exotic, and creates a floating, idle, talkative, rationalistic atmosphere of universal information and easy competence. Information and agility, left to themselves, are morally important, but they never exist unsupported by elementary interests and passions, which may use enlightenment as an aid in their animal career. So buttressed and armed, and so enveloped in polite sophistry, human nature seems to justify itself and its ways. It becomes civilised; but its civilisation runs no deeper than an intellectual draping of moral confusion. The high lights of history, the ages of Pericles, Augustus, Louis XIV, or Queen Victoria, mark the turn of some tide at the flood, when material enterprise has clothed itself in some sort of science or art, and is only beginning to decay inwardly and to withdraw the sap of life from those arts or sciences.

I have seen, after the Victorian era, the commercial deluge which covered the earth rise into the air, and accelerate invention and motion so as completely to envelop mankind. This has been accompanied by a sudden, though unconfessed, collapse of the theoretic and artistic convictions which, in the nineteenth century, kept the polite capitalist world in countenance. Conviction has deserted the civilised mind; and a good conscience exists only at the extreme left, in that crudely deluded mass of plethoric humanity which perhaps forms the substance of another material tide destined to sweep away the remnants of our old vanities, and to breed new vanities of its own. Or perhaps the revolution we are undergoing may turn out to be less profound and cataclysmic than the communists have undertaken to make it. Their loudly heralded revolution may internally "wither away," and leave, certainly not a final Elysium, but some reassertion of national, military, or religious positivism, some specific type or types of human order and virtue, comparable to those that diversified the recorded and the unrecorded past.

# CHAPTER 4

### MORAL EFFECTS OF TRADE

RURAL industry must always subsist beneath commerce and beyond the congested centres of manufacture on a large scale. The moral and intellectual principles proper to non-commercial classes must therefore always remain alive, even in the most commercial State. Sometimes, as in France during the Third Republic, a healthy national tradition subsists only as a precious heirloom committed to a dispossessed aristocracy and a despised peasantry, who live like foreigners in their ancestral land, ignored by a government of commercial and official parasites. The automatic political tendency of such a government has properly nothing to do with the fundamental interests of the governed nor, in the long run, with its own interests; because the parasites could not subsist if the body on which they feed should perish. Yet this radical alienation of the politicians from the nation is disguised by a common language and by a purely literary education. Even the demagogues most alien morally are physically natives; they have inevitably imbibed something of the traditions enshrined in the history and the older literature of their country; whilst on the other hand, since the French Revolution, peasants, soldiers, and aristocrats, and even the clergy, have acquired intellectually, in so far as they live intellectually at all, the rhetoric and ambitions of the new age, and a way of life contrary to their traditional virtues. Thus all parties once in office continue to discharge the traditional functions automatically, with less disorder and contrariety than might be expected from their respective principles. The old order indeed lapses slowly and a new order appears unannounced, in complete defiance of the two sets of ideas frantically advocated in the two camps.

In England, first with Protestantism and then with the fall of the Stuarts, a plutocracy bred by commerce began to recruit the old landed aristocracy, and gradually dropped the feudal, local, military domination that it originally exercised. Its pre-eminence has become merely social, administrative, and professional; and its much less princely way of living might be charged, in the national economy, to overhead expenses, or directors' salaries. Political leaders are all constitutional monarchs on a small scale, following the policy of a responsible or irresponsible ministry imposed upon them by a lumbering heterogeneous mechanism which they never devised and probably do not understand.

English national policy, without losing a certain refinement of form, has thus become essentially commercial; with this dangerous aggravation, that the population has far outgrown the resources of the land, and has become, for half its substance, a parasite on other nations.

It is obvious that in a fertile country, or in a country fed by another which is fertile, the parasites may outnumber the productive labourers; and a democratic government may obey the wishes of the majority while oppressing or flouting the only true productive and necessary class. Such a government may think it considers the interests of the majority in obeying their wishes; yet both this majority and the government that serves it may be cutting their own heads off.

Social and economic fusion softens the outlines of these distinctions. Classes intermingle: one man and one family may belong to several classes; and the moral and intellectual atmosphere breathed by all may be almost the same, in spite of radical divergence in their primary interests. The Church of England, for instance, was meant to be, and in part is, a means of unifying politically the most crying material and religious conflicts. In doctrine and in spirit it is an indescribable chaos; yet it serves its purpose all the better for this intellectual disorder when considered as an emotional eirenicon, or ceremonial means of creating a sense of unison, where no moral unison exists. Nor is this narcotic function merely social. The chaos in the private mind is soothed by the same influences. Nice people thereby reinforce their nice feelings, and a sham front of religious solemnity hides the moral insecurity of a life slowly losing its local roots and ancient loyalties.

Not that commerce does not impose a definite morality, which may become traditional. Puritanism (and Protestantism generally) is a tradesman's religion. On the social and political side it enjoins a morality productive of prosperity and material progress; and on the mystical side it excites the self-consciousness and metaphysical agony of a lost soul alone with the Absolute. But this extreme privacy and personal independence is not so contrary as it might seem to that social positivism. The arbitrary and mediocre character of the latter, with its petty meticulous and joyless duties, throws spiritual ardour, when this exists, all the more violently upon abstract speculation; so that in the Protestant communities, on a background of prosaic commercialism, we find Calvinism and Methodism and Spiritualism and Christian Science and ultimately transcendental idealism crying prophetically from the housetops. These persuasions borrow a good deal from the business world in which they appear. For one thing, they all approve, foster, and sanctify business; and they keep their ideality so thin, so amiably impotent and privately visionary, as not to make any incongruous inroads into business life, but merely to supply a safety valve for the spirit, that might otherwise become explosive. Moreover, rectitude, integrity, fidelity to duty, earnest acceptance of public prejudice, or no less earnest advocacy of some moral hobby not yet publicly dominant, are characteristic of a commercial society; such a society requires these vital forces to cement its mechanism and to keep the private mind and heart docile to the industrial work in hand. This, indeed, is what still makes religion and morality such a solemn matter, about which scurrilous doubts are to be repressed severely.

A similar, and very curious, influence is exercised by commerce on metaphysics. Commerce is favourable to enlightenment. It knows the difference between that which can be found, weighed, and measured, and that which is merely imagined: words, ideas, unrealities. While thoroughly contemptuous of mind, taken on its own account, commerce stoutly professes a kind of rationalism. Mathematics it thinks a true science, at least in its applications; and the same may be said of physics, chemistry, and even astronomy. But the diversity of religions and of systems of government renders all argument about them arbitrary and worthless; we may simply observe the effect which, under different circumstances, these dominant conventions have on prosperity and on a placid order of society favourable to commerce. The economic philosophy of the merchant is international, but not so his religion or morality; for these, while different in each country, are in each bulwarks of peace and order. An established Church should nowhere be disturbed, especially not the probably moderate dignified one which he maintains at home. The less meddlesome it is, the better; its function is to keep people satisfied with themselves and with their social order. Variations may be tolerated, and refugees from other countries may be hospitably received, and may add, if not too numerous, a valuable element to the industry of the country; but only if, at the same time, the orthodox native religion and system of government are defended and transmitted, not indeed unchanged—there is no intrinsic value in any one doctrine or law—but with enough continuity to maintain the distinctive morale and working power of the people.

Commerce is favourable to positivism in philosophy, to that sort of enlightenment which conceives that by overcoming a few needless prejudices all mankind might easily settle down in perpetual peace to exchange the greatest possible number and variety of objects. Also the greatest possible number and variety of ideas; because ideas are cheap luxuries, satisfying and harmless. Liberty, then, in matters of opinion and, save as regards crimes against property, liberty, and personal safety. The protection of business naturally presupposes the protection of life. A man of business must not be interrupted or coerced by threats to his person. For him such foolish practices as duelling or carrying arms are anachronisms; his legal rights are defended by the law, and he laughs at imaginary injuries. In case of libel or unprovoked domestic infidelity he feels honourably indemnified by divorce and damages. Such things may secretly distress him for the moment, but he is too proud to allow them to interrupt his public activities or prevent his deserved happiness. A strong man, he thinks, is all the stronger for not relying too much on other people's virtue. Virtue is its own reward and vice its own punishment. Industrious habits, for instance, hardly need to be inculcated or bred into the rising generation by any harsh discipline. In a commercial society, the idle and thriftless sink out of sight by the natural selection of the competent. No need, therefore, of artificial restraints on the young, or of useless instruction beyond reading, writing, and arithmetic.

Not that the higher culture is excluded in such a society; but it floats ornamentally at the top, like religion, sport, and social amusements. Nor does this render such culture inferior; on the contrary, while a rooted national and moral culture would necessarily be one-sided and narrow, a loosely floating supervening culture may be universal. Universal culture is preserved in books and in museums; there it may be reasorbed by specialists in each generation; and a fresh crop of criticisms, histories, and biographies may continually diffuse the traditional treasure, augmented by the contribution which the latest critics supply. The best part, if not the whole, of criticism will soon be to criticise previous critics. Through this rich prism, as well as through that of its own particular temperament, the public will view with interest an ever-changing perspective of the past, of the present, and of the future.

What may be lacking in such a cultivated plutocracy will be only a native culture. No single inevitable tragedy will inspire poets or artists. Even music, which by its abstraction is able to supply to the careworn mind a luxurious interlude to its cares, without demanding any capacity to frame ideas, falls into the hands of professionals without roots, whose art and life are international. No social prescription imposes on their art any definite tone or any definite limits. The artists, or each sect of artists, form a kind of soviet, sovereign in its own sphere, and far from soliciting any higher patronage, decree that the public shall accept anything and everything at its hands.

Yet art for art's sake suffers from a congenital disease; it professes to create substance out of form, which is physically impossible. It suffers from the freedom of emptiness. Without a traditional subject-matter and a traditonal unquestioned method—both of which may be congruously developed and transformed by individual genius and deeper understanding—the strength of soul is wanting which is requisite for great achievements. The artist, even the historian or the philosopher, then becomes an amateur; he plays with surfaces or falls into extravagance. Originality, which in living things comes unasked, is sought for to the point of cultivating absurdity and letting it pass for genius; spells of archaism intervene; savage art or ignorant opinion is rehabilitated and set up as if its very grotesqueness were a miracle of inspiration. The public is overawed, being told it is too stupid to understand; yet perhaps it is flattered at the same time and encouraged to indulge its crudest passions and emotions, no longer secretly or in an underworld, but with a sort of bacchic enthusiasm, affected or hysterical.

Commerce is not without some influence even on science. What we call science, in the narrower sense, may be said not to have existed before the modern commercial age. Diligent measurement and experiment distinguish science from common knowledge, however certain, and from speculation, however clairvoyant. But diligent measurement and experiment are necessary in commerce. They are involved in navigating the high seas and the air and in inventing all elaborate machinery. If science could be reduced, as it may be reduced by definition, to mere measurement and experiment, all images and hypotheses being regarded as incidental and negligible, science would become simply such knowledge as is useful in industry.

Undoubtedly monumental arts like engineering and architecture also require science; but here the process of construction is itself only a means to the possession of the perfected work, which in itself has amiable uses and values for the imagination; whereas the application of science to trade serves only trade and the interests of the middleman without reference to the spiritual uses of his trade or his inventions. It might rather be said that trade and the selfish interests of the middleman have unintentionally done mankind a service in stimulating enormously the pursuit of physical science, which is a spiritual good in itself; and this even if wireless communication, aeroplanes, and atomic bombs proved in the end a curse to mankind.

When science, essentially a liberal interest, is enormously stimulated by economic pressure and rewards, the pure investigation itself need not be infected by any worldly motive, at least not among genuine inquirers. Sometimes, on the contrary, the joy of discovery may be heightened by the warmth of public interest in it, and of the human benefits that may ensue. And subjectively even the obstacles or perversions that the world may have put in the way of true science may intensify and purify the love of it in the struggling mind; as we may feel in the case of Michelangelo, whose genius was harassed by official demands and taboos, how his love of pure beauty was sublimated the more, the more he saw and depicted the contrariety and vanity of the passions that made the spirit so dreadfully groan and writhe under their weight.

But this tragic shadow cast by the world and the flesh over the summits of free imagination is exceptional; the effect that strong material influences have on the liberal arts is usually more direct and obvious. A prosperous society tends rather to increase the number of artists, intellectuals, and scientific experts, while transforming their quality. They all become more ambitious and less disciplined, none apprenticed and all original masters. A public composed of capitalist patrons will prove individually very critical but without any common taste or criterion. The problems presenting themselves for solution will be miscellaneous and constantly more technical and mysterious. Any subject and any method will do for a fresh professorship; but it will not serve for long. The ground will be constantly quaking, and the edifices will never be consistent or complete. Commerce will have produced loose wealth without a function, and omnivorous taste without a standard; it will have multiplied the materials of the liberal arts, and dissolved their types.

## CHAPTER 5

### RADIATION OF ENTERPRISE

COMMERCE produces nothing and yet enriches the merchant. He is a middleman who levies a tax for arranging to collect and distribute merchandise already existing. Also, by exhibiting or advertising his wares, he may create a market for them where they were not previously required. Manufacture may thus be stimulated in one place and agriculture in another, and a division of labour established on a larger scale than would have been possible without foreign exchanges. The necessaries of life being now more abundant in both places, population will increase and the poor will become more numerous, while the merchant grows richer, since he now levies his tax, though diminished for each consumer, on a larger community. At the same time the variety of articles offered for sale will dazzle the eye, and everybody will be tempted to indulge more and more in superfluities. Thus commerce, without directly producing wealth, indirectly produces luxury.

When the arts have only a home market, farmers and artisans can dominate their industry in its entirety, modifying it according to their personal fancy or the needs of their clients; and then the arts are spontaneously humanised. When on the contrary merchants open up distant markets, they facilitate production on a large scale in standardised forms; and then the useful arts grow cheap and mechanical; while at the same time the whole world is flooded with exotic products which confuse the public taste and incite it to be omnivorous.

Militancy in enterprises here has the opposite effect to that of militancy in faction. Enterprise in trade and in industry tends to diffuse knowledge and taste, and by making culture cosmopolitan undermines in each place or period its specific tradition and inspiration, so that the arts become everywhere anarchical and debased. Faction, on the contrary, in narrowing its aim and excluding everything irrelevant to it, concentrates human virtue on militancy itself, bringing out at all costs the chosen type of order and harmony, so that the works of that forced unanimity are meagre, even when imposing by force of the intensity of Will that animates them; but they probably pay for this special strength by a hopeless monotony, ultimately dwindling into decay; so that it is only as fossils that those inane giants leave their trace in the world. Compare for instance, the futile discipline of Sparta with the fragile spoils and allurements of Venice; or the ruins of Norman England with the rubbish heap that may one day remain of its smoking industrial works. Militancy of both kinds is equally distracted and barren, considered rationally; but each has its passions and incidental compensations for those whom it genuinely enlists and inspires.

Politics at the middle of the twentieth century offer an important illustration of this possibility. Trade, at least foreign and seaborne trade, was always a matter of militant enterprise, provoking competition and sometimes war. But industry, in its beginnings and in its vital impulse, had always been a spontaneous habit, even in some of the lower animals, when they possess bills, fingers, or can weave nets with fibres spun within their bodies, as in the case of birds, monkeys or kangaroos, and spiders. And in man this playful industry found many economic uses and at the same time developed a variety of liberal arts. The products of these arts, like those of nature, when anyone had gathered or cultivated them, became objects of possible barter or profit; but there is nothing intrinsically militant about them; since the most recalcitrant materials aid the artist who respects them, and stimulate his invention more than they delay it. As to the destructive accidents that may crush him and his works together, these are foreign assaults, not to be warded off by free industry itself, but only perhaps by some purely engineering or military art developed independently.

Industry and, as the word indicates, manufacture, were long cultivated by single artisans, like the fine arts, in private, by the fireside, or with a few domestic apprentices. These domestic tasks had nothing to do, in their origin and spirit, with exchange or sale of the product. Objects were fashioned for private use, or by personal caprice, or in imitation and rivalry of other performers, as in sports, dancing, and singing; and ultimately, in the most important traditional works, for dramatic and magical effect, to represent persons or animals, and lend them a monumental sacredness in their immobility and their preternatural size and expression. If anyone excelled in these productions, and his neighbours asked for copies, or the tribe or village engaged him to carve their totem or decorate their arms or their family tombs, he might become a professional artist, and live by the gifts given him in exchange for his works; but it would always be by his science and inspiration that he was guided in his labours, like a minstrel or chieftain. There would always be personal freedom in his art, and as much beauty and caprice as utility in its products.

So, before commerce intervened, industry composed, decorated, and varied the paraphernalia of life according to the needs and tastes of each region and of its artisans. These two properties, of being personal and being local, combined to render primitive industry both variable and, at each place and date, distinctly typical; so much so that by the character of potsherds archaeologists trace the genealogy and migrations of prehistoric man. Ancient and mediaeval cities, when of kindred race or religion, no doubt somewhat influenced one another's industry, but less than we should expect; how little contagion, for instance, in the parallel and often contemporary developments of Byzantine, Romanesque, Gothic, and Saracenic architecture and decoration, though they had the same background in antiquity! Yet in spite of their close analogies each kept its own local character and special evolution of taste. No community seemed to be confused in its work by knowledge of the different work of other communities, and industry in each retained something of the character of liberal art.

Even when during the Renaissance, the patrons and critics of art became intolerantly classical in doctrine, the artists in practice never attempted to copy the ancient monuments but preserved the framework and the spirit of their own traditions. Much less did utensils, furniture, or clothes attempt to reproduce the forms they had had in Rome or Athens. That theatrical masquerade had to wait for the French Revolution.

The effects of commerce and industry have been, on the contrary, unintended, profound, and morally fatal. They have turned industry from a liberal art become, for a few, a means of livelihood, into a militant process of making as much money as possible; the investors by gathering higher and higher profits, the workers by exacting higher and higher wages. The free life of neither class has any moral roots in their working life. If competition obliges them to study the uses and appeals to taste possible in their line, those technical matters are relegated to specially trained salesmen or designers on fixed salaries. As for the industrialists themselves, their spirit awakes, if at all, only after business hours. The workmen therefore are always demanding shorter hours and more holidays; but the directors are either only mock business men, who lounge a few hours in their office thinking of their sports and their vices, to be enjoyed on getting out, or else calculators and investigators, studying every market, and every possible financial operation; so that when they go home, or for a rest at some fashionable resort, they are bored to death, except when the post brings them their business letters, or alone in a corner they can take notebook and fountain-pen from their pocket, and make for the third time some important calculation.

A public effect of such militant commercial industry is the dominance of their producer in universal economy. You invent some new article; you advertise it; you perhaps pay some influential person to use it, talk about it, and make it fashionable, and you have enriched creation with a new requisite, a new convenience, or a new vice. This reversal of the moral order, by turning means into ends, might be classed with the fallacy of the miser who lives like a pauper for the sake of growing rich. A psyche, made illiberal by being trained exclusively in one useful discipline, may feel absolutely pledged to that habit, as by a categorical imperative, even when it is worse than useless. Political theorists and even philosophers are often caught in this trap. They may tell us, for instance, that the individual exists and can exist only for the sake of the tribe or the State; a sentiment that probably rests on two different sophisms vaguely accepted: one, that because everyone owes his birth and nurture in infancy to his elders, he can never become or do anything that is not due to society: and the other, that the traditions and culture which civilised life transmits are not dependent in every particular for their origin and continued acceptance on the individuals who have carried on those traditions, perpetually modifying or corrupting them by their personal initiative.

Commerce is inevitably favourable to the growth of great cities and to the domination of the urban mind. Ancient cities were primarily built for defence, and the market was held at the foot of the citadel, often outside the walls. The number of citizens was limited to the local exigencies of defence and subsistence, and the political organisation was incidental to the military, or superimposed, like religion and eloquence, for the real or supposed benefit of the

## RADIATION OF ENTERPRISE

State. But when military government, by establishing order at home and making conquests abroad, has given commerce a freer hand, the centre of gravity of the State passes from the citadel to the market. There is then no limit to the possible growth of the city: a million, two million, ten million polyglot human beings of different nations and religions may swarm within it. A crowd itself attracts a crowd; and the proletariat—the floating masses of the poor, without roots in the soil or social cohesion—will prefer poverty in a great city where at least something may always turn up, to mechanised agricultural labour in a thinned, homeless, and cheerless countryside.

Intellectually, too, a great city is more stimulating. Opinions, like dress, speech, and manners, are brought by commerce into the melting pot: intellectual fashions arise, rule, and disappear quickly by an irresistible contagion. To-day they may be carried in a moment, by radio, all over the world; whereas in a society without foreign commerce, they would be persistent locally, but not much diffused. What is universal in space may be provincial in time. The airy force of novelty is soon deflated, like spent foam in the trough of the sea. Thus under commercial domination useful arts become mechanical, and fine arts a chaos of whims and fashions.

The Reformation, in contrast with the Renaissance, is instructive in this respect. Both were contemptuous of mediaeval art, science and piety. When Luther pours scorn on the monks in his old monastery, he does not accuse them of being corrupt (as we are usually told that monasteries had become) but of being devout and credulous. Yet he himself, in his disordered zeal, remained blindly credulous in spots, and deeply religious in the midst of riot. Concentration on the Epistles of St. Paul had given him the temporary political advantage of seeming more orthodox than the Pope, and of appealing to heated religious minds like his own, incapable of taking a philosophic view of tradition. Yet the permanent advantage and ultimate reward of the Reformation was to secularise society without emancipating it; by keeping it dutiful in its homely business, while making this business soundly mundane and prosperous.

The Renaissance, on the contrary, had been humanistic, aesthetic, and truly scientific in inspiration, however fanciful science might still have been amongst Platonising or necromantic enthusiasts. These humanists laughed at austerity and orthodoxy, or hated them as trammels to their arts and to the free play of speculation. A political alliance was not impossible at times between the fanatics, the humanists, and the ruling class, feudal or commercial: they could unite in pillaging the Church. In this alliance it was humanism that was most compromised: because the fanatics and the new-rich were both interested in tightening the reins of morality, imposing soberness and fidelity to duty, and suppressing imagination and the free joys of life. Humanism might have been crushed altogether between the upper and the nether millstone, had not the merchants drawn the line at the sacrifice of their private pleasures: so that Lutheran Holland and Germany in the seventeenth century retained much of their jollity. The early Renaissance or late Gothic architecture of the towns was still picturesque and ornate; manners were courtly, food succulent and long draughts out of magnificent tankards frequently repaired the ravages of business toil and care. In England the Restoration issued in a characteristic and happy compromise between tradition and reform, between commercialism and aristocracy. Education for the upper classes remained down to our day entirely classical and humanistic; but the taste and intelligence fed by this schoolboy knowledge were soon applied, not ungracefully, to imperial affairs. The Army and the Church retained their respective mentalities, not utilitarian in tone; nevertheless ultimate control of the Church and the Army, and over the mind of the nation, lay always, as it lies to-day, in the hands of commerce. During the nineteenth century archaistic affectations in art and religion float sentimentally in the upper air, whilst legislation and war pursue commercial advantage with implacable instinct. The traditional parties owe at bottom no other allegiance than allegiance to money, diplomatically called the national interest; the only internal question being in what proportion the money shall be distributed at home between the various classes. It would be an error to suppose that, like certain other nations, they set their heart ultimately on the liberties or glories talked about by their orators; these unrealities are exchangeable, provisional, and only means to the great end, prosperity. Why must the expensive British Navy be kept up? To protect the routes of commerce and, by retaining the colonies, to enable the country to keep up an establishment and a population far exceeding its home resources. And how can the Church be justified? Because its elastic theology and agreeable ritual help to keep up the moral tone of the nation, and according to Eddington and Jeans are not contrary to science, that is, to the technical calculations necessary for industry.

# CHAPTER 6

## INSTABILITY OF COMPOUND UNITS

WHEN people make a tool, like an axe, they are not surprised if after a little, the edge grows dull, or the handle loose. Wood and iron are brought artificially together, and called an axe by virtue of the use they acquire in that conjunction. Yet those materials had a life of their own before, and retain that life fully while called an axe; and they continue it afterwards when, being broken up and released from their incidental function, they form an axe no longer. In such a case the independent nature of the materials is obvious, and the precarious and external way in which they remain effectively an axe is plain to those who must be continually sharpening and repairing old axes and making new ones.

On the other hand, when what possesses a useful function is not artificial but grows up spontaneously, like the eye or the liver, like language or religion or government, people are apt to forget that in these compounds, too, substance has a life of its own, quite independent of the ends it may be expected to serve when called by these names. Chemically and psychologically the underlying life goes on uninterruptedly, as that of the wood and the iron does in the axe. But as a man never makes his eye or his liver, he may easily ignore (until he becomes a physician) the spontaneous properties of these materials. He may even forget that they have a material substance at all. In language he notices the meaning, not the sound nor the complicated inflexions and extraordinary syntax. In religion he recognises divine authority or saving grace, not any human inventions, hypotheses, and confused traditions which, when they seem to exercise that religious function, are called religion. Only when his eyes see double, or his liver refuses to work, only when in language or religion he finds what he calls error, does he observe, with no little astonishment, that these names cover natural facts and processes existing on their own account, with a mechanism and a tendency absolutely independent of the service which they may occasionally have done him; and that it is no more marvellous that they should go their own way to his chagrin and discomfiture than that an axe should grow dull or fall to pieces in his hand.

Unintelligent surprise at the essential automatism and irresponsible life of organs that, to a greedy and self-centred Will, seem created to serve it is never more outspoken than in the case of government. People expect that a government should operate simply for their complete convenience. Not only when it taxes, dragoons, imprisons, enslaves, ruins, or exterminates them, but when in any measure it makes for results which they do not desire, they are full of astonishment and indignation, and look for some diabolical influence to explain the anomaly.

Experience since the world began seems powerless here against the presumptions of egotism and ignorance, and against that rooted belief with which all animals seem to be born, that the world exists for their benefit. Nevertheless government, although it sometimes serves to protect, educate, or inspire a people, is in fact a material formation with an origin, life, and tendency of its own. The secret of its activity is its own impulses and not the eventual agreement of that impulse with the impulses of its individual subjects or of other societies. The mistakes of governments, and the fact that governments are often bad, obey the same causes as their most approved measures. As axes have to be sharpened or replaced, so governments (as liberal ages have discovered) need to be constantly refreshed by criticism, by new elections, by revolts, by assassinations, and by other means of grinding their edge; while in the end the only cure is to throw them away and call to life a wholly new government from out of the midst of the people. New axes, however, for all their newness are not disembodied and perfect instruments, with utility for their essence. Living wood and living iron—men and their private interests—are the inner substance of them; and the external joints and wedges that keep these men and their private interests together are as fragile and mortal, as incapable of remaining for two days in the same posture, as is the flux of matter itself, which being the substance of all things keeps them all continually growing old and being reproduced with odd variations.

The substance of a government is the men in office: but the life of a government—its political operation and tendency—is a distinct addition to the social and even moral life of its members. These men become a government by a partial conjunction of their minds and actions. There is only an abstract relation or occasional union of each of them with the others, such as among members of the same opera troupe. As members of a government they have certain interests, passions, and morality which they would never have had as private men. This new element in each is in its quality common to them all: and the mutual contagion of this common impulse strengthens very much the official soul in all the officials. Let not the reader vaguely imagine that this common element in associated persons is a new and superior person, of a mystical, logical, or hyper-psychological sort, a common mind that possesses interests without having an animal body or an individual consciousness. The common medium in which the associated persons move and which hypnotises them into sharing the same impulses and emotions (in so far as they do so) is a natural medium—namely the phraseology, legal duties, and established mechanism of the government they take up. They acquire the habits, taboos, and accepted maxims of the new society they move in, or of such part of it as touches them.

This material environment, where it contains persons, is of course animate, and these persons have emotions and ideas of their own; but it is only by material channels that these souls are betrayed to one another—or can have any mutual influence; so that the social medium, regarded as a hypnotic power and source of contagion, is thoroughly physical. The governmental mind is simply so much of the mind of each member of the government as is subject to these common material influences, and is therefore very like the simultaneous movement of the other members' minds. I am far from wishing to deny that many minds may entertain identical views, in the sense of employing the same logical terms. But a logical term is not a mind; an object of thought is not a natural object or historic event but an ideal theme like the triangle or the centaur; each of the minds to which such essences are manifest has its own currents and accompaniments, independent in existence and movement from those of the other minds concerned: so that the minds are not in the least *one mind*, though they may be swayed by the same influence, and may coincide in the same dogmas.

This common strain, in times of great excitement and close cooperation, may swell remarkably and submerge for the moment those other strains which are different in quality in each of the minds concerned; and the consequent howling and rushing unanimity of the mob—for governments at certain junctions are like mobs—may be poetically called the movement of a single Will; as the froth of a thousand waves, whipped up by the same wind, might be called the fury of a single tempest.

All, however, is not false idealism in politics; and members of a government acquire another faculty besides imitative imagination and supplementary to the contagious social side of their humanity. They acquire a corporate instinct of self-preservation. Office gives everyone concerned a new set of private interests, passions, and necessities, quite irrelevant to the public good, but most influential over public affairs. Quite apart from obsession with party policy, which after all is something verbally noble, a government is wedded to itself, to its own material inertia and effort at equilibrium. Its own life is its first concern; for if it did not endure, how could it work for its political cause, or serve the country it has been called upon to rule? It must first of all maintain its cohesion, and abound in inward strength; then its relations to other interests can be looked into at leisure. What will not a government do in order not to fall, or in order so to fall as to be able to rise again? Long after the delight of giving direction and the hope of realising cherished ideas have been clouded over with sordid business and anxious expectations, the fear of defeat still keeps them at work. To cease governing involves such painful changes of intellectual speed, of executive scope, of public consideration, of proud phraseology, of income, and of residence! Moreover, it is a defeat in the game; it is as unpleasant, as tenaciously resisted, as checkmate at chess.

Such a government is a parasite. Like any organ in an animal body, it is a sort of knot or carbuncle formed in the flesh: a little organism in the larger one, with its own centre and circulation, its own instincts of recuperation and work, feeding on the common blood, and supplying the body with a new local sensitiveness, a new motor faculty, and a new point open to attack.

This parasite is sometimes convenient, sometimes inconvenient, sometimes fatal. The society which it dominates will therefore judge it differently according as its special interests are affected by it; for some it may be useful, for others oppressive and odious. But the balance of these judgments will not trouble its conscience, as if it were a government professing to coordinate and advance all the interests of its subjects; that would seem to it an impossible task as well as an unworthy one for a true master in the art of constructing and directing governments. To rule, for a master, would be a militant enterprise, free and spontaneous, as for the superman of Nietzsche. Like the liberal arts this enterprise would be autonomous and inspired only by the inward vision of a perfect work to be constructed; but unlike the liberal arts, it would choose living creatures to be trained and shaped after its arbitrary Will and ideal. Like the liberal arts, therefore, it would be capable of fixity in its principles; but like any other order imposed on an aggregate of natural units, its works would be insecure, and its own existence in constant peril.

# CHAPTER 7

## DOMINATION AS AN ART

MACHIAVELLI in his treatise *The Prince* chooses to regard every ruler as animated only by the Will to Rule and to describe the policy that this incarnate abstraction should pursue in order to maintain his position. The result is that nothing appears except a pack of unprincipled princes playing the game of diplomatic war. In the classical repertory of absolute passions the pure Will to Govern may be included; but the militant art of imposing a precise regimen on others is less unnatural and has not only been often preached but sometimes successfully practiced. The best-known instance is Sparta, and some Moslem and some ancient Asiatic despotisms exhibit it also. Here it is not primarily treacherous neighbours that preoccupy the commander but rather the faithful under his authority. He is concerned above all for the Law of which he has made himself the prophet or the guardian. He may be, and usually is in the beginning, the chief of only a small band; and he may not aspire to universal dominion or care anything for the fate of the multitude of the outsiders, the heathen, the barbarians, or the rabble at his own door. He may even, like the Spartans and the ancient Hebrews, be proud and jealous of the singular, the difficult *virtue* of his people, its incommunicable superiority: and this, if circumstances permitted, would easily pass into a dream of universal empire. But for the time being, safety and prestige will be based rather on home discipline than on conquests or numbers.

Such at least was the case of Sparta. Amid chequered fortunes intrepidly borne, there had always been a great aridity of spirit in the Spartans themselves and an occasional marked weakness under personal temptation when abroad; and finally a ghostly survival, under Roman benevolence, of the forms of Lycurgus' republic covering an inglorious impotence.

The military Orders of the Mediaeval West were somewhat similar in ethos, although the militancy here, as among the Moslems, was religious at least in theory and the field not a single Greek city but the whole world to conquer, garrison, and convert, and ever after to be dominated from castles or abbeys on every hilltop. There was far more disorder and licence than in Spartan campaigning, but also a Christian and chivalrous desire to propagate to all mankind the spiritual essence of Christian loyalty, something shown again, in both its aspects, in the Spanish conquests over seas, and in their permanent traces in the conquered populations.

There is another, more amiable phase of enterprise in autocratic governments, exhibited first by the Greek overflow into innumerable colonies, and in the conquests and foundations of Alexander, as well as in Roman works everywhere at a later date: I mean the imposing labours designed to make the earth's surface safer, more fruitful, and more worthy of its human masters. All this was partly, no doubt, a financial speculation; it was always militant enterprise rather than faction; yet the spirit of dignity and beauty in form, and of perennial civilisation in intent, dominated the calculation, and mixed magnanimity with the thirst for tribute.

When the modern world began to take shape after the great migrations, with the rapid conquests of Islam and the gradual hardening of the feudal organisation of Europe, there was no occasion for any political régime to become a militant force on its own account. Governments were accidental growths out of extinct institutions and novel rights assumed, and duties imposed by force. The enterprise of governing the lives of men morally, according to a definite ideal system, not a compromise between private interests, but a model of human virtue and art, passed to the ecclesiastical authorities, that drew it from the piety of the Hebrews and the philosophy of the Greeks. Yet, unlike either of these sources, both the Christian and the Moslem authorities were unflinchingly militant. By disputation, zealous education, and on occasion by war, these religions were to be imposed and preserved in unchallenged domination; or if the temerity of unbelievers or of rebellious sects could not be overcome, they might be allowed to exist, but unarmed and cast into the shade by a resplendent establishment. These great religions were militant, but in a war of imagination.

As the Greeks sometimes invoked friendship as an incentive to courage in war, so the religions with supernatural claims sometimes invoked enterprise or war or science as a provisional support; but it was successful only in introducing the faith to astonished and uncritical masses, as the first followers of Mohammed did in Asia and North Africa, or the Spaniards in parts of America. Where the imagination, at certain levels, is empty but potentially keen, it can be easily filled with any appealing fiction; but no material or social force will bend it when it already has its syntax and prosody well rooted and tried. The greatest force of propaganda for the imagination is example, habituation, and rooted attachment to special types of belief. As circumstances cause the balance of this psychic influence to vary in a given population, or this population to come under fresh influences, the hold of its traditional religion will be variously transformed, as well as the susceptibility of that population to alien religions.

During the last quarter of the nineteenth century and the first half of the twentieth I happen to have had occasion to observe at close quarters the movement of public sentiment, in five different countries—Spain, the United States, England, France, and Italy—in regard to philosophy and religion, especially in regard to the Catholic Church. At first doctrinaire intolerance prevailed (among advocates of political toleration as much or more vigorous than among its opponents). Every creed and party stood defiantly on its principles, boasting of their past prevalence or sure future dominion. In regard to religion and philosophy, though there was much prejudice there was little faith; living faith was concentrated on science, liberalism, and progress. It was only in Germany, and in the vogue in academic circles elsewhere of German philosophy, that any different view prevailed in regard to history and politics; but of that I had only perfunctory knowledge. Only recently, the two German wars and the sudden Russian threat of universal domination have proved that the classic tradition, passing through the German philosophy of history, drawn from the Bible, inspired the Russian Revolution and guides, most unexpectedly, a militant art of government intended to dominate the world.

A patient reader of these pages need not be told that in my opinion the course of events obeys the generative order of nature, and not any militant revolt, following the mirage of a humanistic or moralistic ideology. If the communist conspiracy succeeded it would not establish anything permanent. It does not reckon with its host, which is the human psyche.

Meantime an incidental illustration of this process may be seen in the change that has occurred since the 1870's in public sentiment towards science and religion. While the application of science to mechanical uses has become more and more wonderful, and has disclosed fields of complexity and power unsuspected in the depths of matter, the tone of proud finality in science that its popular leaders had assumed earlier has given place to modesty. But meantime speculation in mathematical terms invaded the principles of physics, with a grand air of undermining them. In physics, however, validity attaches to experiment, not to language.

Language serves the humanities better. History and archaeology in particular have much enlarged their investigations, and acquired a respect for ages, races, and philosophies, as well as arts, that were formerly despised as barbarous. And this moral tolerance has extended to the non-scientific religions and philosophies that come down into our times from antiquity, notably the Indian and Chinese, and the Catholic and Orthodox Churches among us in particular. Scientific men and ultramodern poets can now be Catholics if they choose, without losing at all the respect of the public or of their own professional circle, for science is felt to be merely a language expressing the sides of the universe that human observation, in its present phase, is able to plot and to predict; while the realm of imagination is felt to be omnimodal so that the cultivation of one method or aim by no means condemns the cultivation, at other times or in other circles, of some different method. And this liberality might well be extended to methods of government, if only the adherents of each could be peacefully segregated and had the courage to practice their chosen antics at home, without arming to destroy their neighbours for practicing, *in excelsis,* a different acrobatic art.

## CHAPTER 8

### DISSOLUTION OF THE ARTS

IN THE great ages of art nobody talked of aesthetics. Doubtless there was lively criticism of each new tragedy or temple or cathedral; every innovation was hotly discussed by the craftsmen and by the public, and divided them into those who blamed and those who approved. But there was no break with tradition, no thought of irrelevant new beginnings or creations *ex nihilo.* The arts were only skilled and decorative ways of doing what, for other reasons, had to be done; skilled and decorative ways of making pots, clothes, and houses, of speaking and persuading, of praying and dancing. Things had to be made beautiful for the use of the great, and for the honour of the soul. The great could be themselves beautiful; and so were the grand occasions, the feasts, processions, and games, in which major works of art were displayed and admired. The artist was the servant, the studious contriver, of these public splendours; and in the public enthusiasm he forgot himself and joined in applauding the wonders that Minerva and the Muses had accomplished through his guided hands.

In modern times, even before the French Revolution, nations became too large and unwieldy to inspire the arts or to enjoy them in common. Moreover, tradition was divided between a stern homely Christian manner and the restored elegance of the ancients. Art still had patrons, and therefore still had some consistency; the great in their palaces and country seats demanded a certain semi-private splendour; and they possessed a certain semi-private tradition which they called good taste. They might even be connoisseurs, and collect paintings and statues. This was an omen of the end: for works of art now were prized as curiosities, detachable and detached. Soon the expert reviewed them with a knowing smile, related anecdotes about the alleged artist, compared them with Chinese or African specimens, and meantime in his own house allowed some wholesale establishment to furnish him with all his belongings. The artists, on their side, became superior persons, contemptuous of the stupid public and the traditional styles. They strove to be original, called themselves creative, and kept themselves before the public, which might have gladly ignored them, by praising themselves extravagantly, and outraging good sense in their works and often in their lives.

All the arts—except perhaps architecture—have thus become bohemian, as the wandering musician has always been. Is this a gain in dignity? Is there a deeper inspiration in breaking loose from the world and plumbing the secret sensibility of one's own organism? Perhaps it is incidental to democracy to eschew patronage of any sort, and rely only on what the average loose individual can discover in his insulated self-consciousness. And certainly the democratic public respects the self-advertising artist and gives him free rein, as an ancient city or an aristocratic society would never have done. The artist now belongs to the Intelligentsia, which feels itself to be a sort of aristocracy; whereas formerly he passed for a worthy artisan, perhaps a singular genius, but never for a lord of life.

The true lords of life were, and perhaps always will be, the men of action, the masters of things, the directors of political events. This is as inevitable in a democracy as under a military monarchy. Put a lot of human beings, presumably equal, into a camp; enforce peace; forbid bullying; stimulate intelligence and religion by every possible means; and then see who dominates the community. Will it be the poets? Will it be the painters? Will it be the devout? Will it be the learned? No; it will be the athletes, the riders, the huntsmen, the explorers. These will not only give direction by virtue of greater competence and quickness, but also by virtue of the general admiration and trust which they inspire. They inspire such confidence justly; not because they are at all infallible or even very sagacious, but because in their rough, prejudiced, and empirical way they deal with realities; whereas those other mental people, who think themselves superior, stop at ideas, and remain entangled each in his own subjective world.

Your true aristocrat is not without a play life of his own; he is a sportsman; and incidentally he may like to surround himself with a noble setting, in which it will be natural to live nobly. In this the artists and the priests may serve him, if they are not too extravagant; and he is ready to treat both with a qualified deference, not venturing, perhaps, to quarrel with them on their own ground, but taking their measure smilingly in his own mind, and reserving his manly freedom. As the Sabbath was made for man, so the fine arts, he thinks, were made for the gentleman: a feeling that was charmingly mirrored in English art and literature so long as England remained officially aristocratic. But now that every emancipated prig creates his theology, why shouldn't he also create his art? The aesthete armed with his supercilious sensibility and transcendental freedom, intrudes into the workshop of the arts with his nose in the air; but he remains an amateur in his craft, plays a game of bluff with the public (a game which for a time is often successful), but dwindles and soon vanishes from the scene in consequence of his inherent vacuity. For the arts, after all, draw their life-blood from a well-digested craftsman's tradition. But the aesthete, posing in his studio, despises his masters, if he ever had them, and flits from one experiment to another until perhaps his extravagances bring him round full circle to the most primitive conventions. There, by touching bottom and recovering the rudiments, he may really renovate his art and develop it in harmony with the new necessities of society; but the danger is that instead of serving the public and helping them to recognise and refine their natural feelings, he may attempt to stimulate in himself some unprecedented emotion, and may waste his cleverness in abusing mankind for not appreciating his folly.

Indeed, the public is not blameless in this dissolution of the arts; it too has become aesthetic; it too has taken to gathering collections and building museums. A genuine lover of the beautiful would never enter a museum. There the historian might find the sediment which the stream of intuition in the past had deposited as it flowed; and perhaps during the study of those relics, some intuitions of the beautiful might be awakened in his own mind, delightful but evanescent. The artist, the poet, moves in the opposite direction. It is from the daily unintentional aspects of nature and action that he draws his inspiration. The arts, especially the active practice of the arts, will also awaken in him living intuitions; the scene about him may be full of artificial as well as of natural objects, and both equally make up his native world, he being inevitably merged in the atmosphere of their uses and associations. Antiquity, like autumn, has the poetic quality of lost youth, the charm of patina, of ruins, of unrecoverable titanic passions. Even the connoisseur, surrounded by his *bibelots,* may be a poet; he may occasionally catch a glimpse of the fine modish beauty proper to these trifles in their day, when the sun shone upon them. He might, if he had a living and organic imagination of his own, make an epic or an elegy out of those vistas. But this would be a new, a modern, art crossing, and reflecting upon, the arts that are dead; it would not be an unwholesome and vain attempt to feed on their corpses.

The spontaneous artist, the young poet who runs singing home, full of irrepressible inspiration and planning marvellous works, cares for no art but his own. He works in the vernacular, he ruminates on images he cannot banish, because they are the substance of his life. That which is politely called beautiful leaves him cold: the really beautiful hides from him behind the sad or trivial or horrible visions that existence forces upon him; and his art is to draw out and weave it into a tapestry for the eyes of the spirit. The history of art is nothing to him: his art is a fresh image of inescapable things.

## CHAPTER 9

### THE DECLINE OF THE GREAT POWERS

It is not the little powers or any revival of provincial life that threatens the pride and freedom of the great powers; it is the hideous entanglement and moral vacancy of their own governments. England, for instance, in the eighteenth and early nineteenth centuries, acted the great power with conviction; she was independent, mistress of the sea, and sure of her right to dominion. Difficulties and even defeats, such as the loss of the American Colonies, did not in the least daunt her; her vitality at home and her liberty abroad remained untouched. But gradually, though she suffered no final military defeat, the heart seemed to fail her for so vast an enterprise. It was not the colonies she had lost that maimed her, but those she had retained or annexed. Ireland, South Africa, and India became thorns in her side. The bloated industries which helped her to dominate the world made her incapable of feeding herself; they committed her to forced expansion, in order to secure markets and to secure supplies. But she could no longer be warlike with a good conscience; the virtuous thing was to bow one's way out and say: My mistake. Her kings were half-ashamed to be kings, her liberals were half-ashamed to govern, her Church was half-ashamed to be Protestant. All became a medley of sweet reasonableness, stupidity, and confusion. Being a great power was now a great burden. It was urgent to reduce responsibility, to reduce armaments, to refer everything to conferences, to support the League of Nations, to let everyone have his own way abroad, and to let everyone have his own way at home. Had not England always been a champion of liberty? But wasn't it time now for the champion to retire? And wouldn't liberty be much freer without a champion?

The other great powers, for abdicating more unwillingly, have not avoided the same fate; they are embarrassed by greater inertia or rebellion at home, and by the same tangle abroad. The brave pose of Germany in 1914, in the old manner of great powers, after a military failure and a sham quiescence, had a terrible sequel: and everyone suffered from general paralysis, industrial and moral. There was in various quarters a ferocious propaganda of philosophical nationalism, or philosophical communism; there was industrial unrest; but the great powers were completely impotent before the international stalemate of all their real ambitions.

Patriotism attached to a great power is something artificial; it unites two naturally different passions, the love of home and the pride of empire. The love of home is topographical, climatic, moral; it is intertwined with the myths and poetry of a nation, with personal affections, and with the comfort and assurance of moving in a familiar world, where you are master and where you may shine. This domestic attachment has little to do with government, and nothing to do with war. But when home is a city, and this city is at the head of an independent state, foreign policy and war may become the great affairs of the market-place; they may supply the chief excitements of civic and even of private life. So in ancient and mediaeval city-states; and the modern great power is an enlarged and monstrous version of the same double association. To the love of one's home landscape and home ways—a natural and innocent love—the pride of empire, the gamble of war, the lust and vanity of competition are added; and for a floating city population without roots, without native culture (such as peasants had) and perhaps without religion, the sporting passion for what they call their country—that is, for the prestige of their government—a passion fed by the newspapers, like the passion for football matches, carries all before it. But only for the nonce. A different propaganda in the press, a different appeal to senseless vanity may suddenly turn that government of theirs (as they call it) into the supposed enemy of their class and their persons. The pride of empire, the zeal for victory, which were their ruling passions the day before, may seem the day after most wicked delusions; and since these modern masses have no home, and hardly a nationality, no natural patriotism may subsist to keep them from being blown by a wordy blast like so much bran in the wind.

The pride of empire, in the Romans or in Englishmen of the old school, was an aristocratic passion, almost a bond of duty: and it went beautifully with the home sentiment, also very keen in them. Their national character, deeply saturated with home influences and strictly limited in its virtues, enabled them to explore and govern the most outlandish regions, and even to spend their lives there, without dropping one iota of their native orthodoxy; and their function in governing abroad, though it may unintentionally have spread their language and manners in certain quarters, was really in the nature of paid services rendered to the foreigner, with no desire to assimilate him. He was not worthy or capable of being assimilated, and a fool if he attempted it; but he might be initiated into certain material arts and positive sciences, for him to combine as best he might with his own traditions, or in the case of the uncivilised native, with his own temperament.

Empire building may be conceived as a sort of lay missionary work, under military protection; and the army and the government that undertake it no doubt feel and perhaps ought to feel a great pride in the work. It is a big business; there is great good to be done in it, and great fortunes to be made. But now the big business of being a great power has perhaps outlived its function. That function was entirely distinct from natural home patriotism; the latter is attachment of a mind with roots to the roots which it has, the love of home in those who have a home. But the big business of imperialism had better be relegated to some non-sentimental authority, less sentimental perhaps than the League of Nations, capable of discerning and enforcing a material equilibrium in the world. If this authority were that of one of the great powers, the first requisite for success would be to wash away all local patriotism from the minds of those universal rulers so that in obeying them the world might believe that it was free, and might truly be so, in everything in which freedom is a good.

## CHAPTER 10

### NATURAL AND ARTIFICIAL ALLEGIANCE

IN A city, or near it, free men once had their birthplace, their residence; and so had all their known ancestors, relations, and acquaintance. Its authorities controlled their religion, their civil law, their military fortunes, and their festivals and sports. If it was ever in peril, they were in equal peril too, and they normally prospered in its prosperity. It was familiar to them in its entirety, and they knew all its principal men by sight, and heard their orations. And it was as citizens of that city that, if by chance they ever left it, they were known and judged by the rest of the world.

If we ask ourselves how so close and lasting a political society had arisen, I think we should have to consider various alternatives or perhaps converging or successive causes of growth. A village grows up at the place where paths cross in any inhabited region, and it is there that fairs are held, inns opened, and temples built. That would be growth by virtue of economic convenience or necessity. But when instead of a village we find a defended town, though walls are not in themselves signs of militant enterprise, they may indicate that a band of marauders, after pillaging a particular region, may find it necessary to entrench themselves in their cave or their stronghold against probable reprisals; and then we should see the city as a by-product of militant adventure on a large and permanent scale. A great city would be the nest of a numerous and permanent association of bandits. And this would be confirmed by the relation which the citizens of the city had to the peasants in the surrounding country, even if these, and their chiefs, were also legally citizens.

The elders in the city, probably heirs to parcels of the original city lanes, would be heavily armed, perhaps mounted on war horses or chariots, and altogether irresistible for the shepherds or sailors, woodcutters or miners. There would be also many artisans in the city, whose sons might be regular soldiers, or light-armed auxiliaries. Thus we should be in the presence of a complete military and aristocratic organisation, perhaps with a King or High Priest at its head. This would have been a city built up and existing to serve a militant enterprise, perhaps establishing by force a suzerainty over minor cities akin to it. Beyond this limited and easily cancelled expansion a purely military city-state like Sparta was not likely to go; its ambition was not at all to conquer or convert the world, but like a race of hunters or athletes or Pythagorean philosophers, to lead together a severe, brave, and simple life, in contempt alike of the voluntary slave who drudged and hoarded, or the fool with his absurd passions and unnecessary sorrows. This was an essentially moral, or more specifically, an ascetic enterprise, but having the form of a complete human polity, not a separated private society, like a monastic order; it included marriage, political independence, and domination over slaves and helots and a selected friendship in the surrounding political world, with action in the necessary wars. But it was not a faction either political or religious or moral, because it aspired to live its own disciplined life without attempting to diffuse it. Singularity was its pride and disdain of wealth and knowledge its weakness. It sterilised human nature in the vain conceit of showing that it might in each of them become heroic and godlike, all the more for standing, like a bronze statue in the midst of a swarm of howling and hiding beasts.

Why did Athenians, like Socrates and Plato, immediately after the age of Pericles, as well as the conservatives all over Greece, look with admiration towards this artificial barbarism? No doubt because they felt the corruption and inevitable decline of their own country, and of all its liberal glory. But why this corruption and decadence? Consider the contrast with Rome, never in the least Spartan, and yet at that time, by its military and administrative endurance and genius, beginning to dominate the world. Why had Athens, that had repulsed the immense Persian Empire, failed against corrupt Syracuse and meagre Sparta, when Rome was destined to destroy utterly the formidable military empire of Carthage? Rome, like Carthage and Athens, was an imperial city-state; it was not, like Persia, a conquering tribe or nation, extending the domain of its hereditary monarch, in a series of wars of growth rather than imagination or enthusiasm. But the empires of city-states, except that of Rome, were based on commerce and consequent wealth, which a prevalently naval force extended and protected. Roman enterprise had always been political, not economic, and its conquests were made on land, after which a navy was established to protect the commerce in the Mediterranean, for economic objects, not as a help to extend commercial adventures. Commerce, no doubt, served luxury too, during the Roman decadence, and in the Byzantine empire, but in Rome the wealth that supported its luxury was still landed wealth. This makes all the difference in the stability of empire and in its moral solidity. A Venice may be long prosperous and beautiful, but with a meretricious and theatrical beauty. Such, among the Greeks, had been the character of Corinth and Syracuse; but Athens had an early history of internal growth and political discipline, which gave to its imperial enterprise a nucleus of political and moral hardihood, such as the British Empire has had at home, which British administration preserved even in governing foreign peoples, and its colonists carried with them wherever they migrated.

But the most sudden and fruitful of military enterprises, having such a moral nucleus, have been those of Alexander and of Islam. Alexander's enterprise was not arbitrary. The whole history of Herodotus, dedicated to the nine Muses, gives its traditional grounds. It was a war to secure safety for Greece; and in its victory it never thought of peopling all Asia with Greeks, but was content to turn it into a friendly and enlightened empire. The Greeks succeeded in transforming a part of Asia, until the Moslem or even the Turkish conquest, into a Hellenised world. And the Moslem conquest, especially in Mesopotamia, Persia, and Spain, revived spontaneously, in a novel and delicate form, the elegance of the Hellenic arts and manners, without any hostility to the larger spiritual inspiration proper to Asia itself.

Yet there are always seeds of futility in artifice; a foreign conquest cannot knead two peoples into one until several generations of forgetful heirs of the old world and refractory pupils of the new have generated an unwitting hybrid that feels itself young and original. This occurs rarely. What happened in the Hellenised east was that the Hellenic and Christian elements were submerged by Islam, except in Byzantium itself and the native Greek territories; and that almost nothing of the Arab or Moorish civilisation survived in Spain; while even in the Arab countries it is now helplessly struggling under European and Jewish pressure that prevents it from knowing what it wants. Is a convinced and unadulterated Islam again capable of exercising dominion in economics and in culture? That is somewhat as if we asked whether the Catholicism of the thirteenth or that of the seventeenth century was again capable of dominating Western Europe and modern America.

But the subject of religious enterprises and their fate is a large one and deserves separate treatment.

# CHAPTER 11

### MILITANT RELIGIONS

PAGANISM is aptly described by the Germans as "natural" religion, in the sense that it is not artificial, but grows up unobserved and uncriticised, like language. Like language, however, it is contagious, and the gestures, local cults, and stories of wonders and visions, are seen and heard, as they are enacted or repeated, with a sense that some magic or numinous influence envelops them. But these cults are local and ritualistic; the myths that are suggested by them are freely varied, and essentially poetical and fabulous. The sources of these magic influences are represented sometimes as animals, sometimes as human beings, but always more elusive in their substance and apparition. They are therefore splendid subjects for myths and for oracular admonitions, representing secret fears or hopes of perturbed minds.

When the growth of natural religion of this kind has become complex and precise in any people, critics will not be someday wanting that will criticise that fantastic tradition, either deriding it altogether as moonshine, or denouncing some elements in it as unworthy of others, which are declared sacred.

## MILITANT RELIGIONS

The complete sceptics have little political importance, although they never cease to reappear sporadically, or in little groups of moralists or scientific observers, who think themselves absolutely right, and the contrary errors of mankind disastrous.

Local pagan deities and rites may sincerely respect one another; but when zealous souls, far from abandoning their traditional religion, undertake to reform or transform it, so as to render it true and perfect, then faith in it becomes militant and the practice and advocacy of it a positive social enterprise. The previously innocent pagan practices and doctrines, having now challenged and condemned all others, must take up arms in at least verbal defence of their singular claims. Here we have a Church Militant; but that is only a forced and incidental turn of private zeal, and rather poisons than purifies the positive, poetical, ascetic, and spiritual side of pagan worship. Moreover, it is a dangerous procedure for the fundamental tenets which are assumed by both sides in such a controversy; because the arguments and evidences invoked against the heretics may very easily be applied eventually to the orthodoxy that they retain, and thereby also to the foundations of the conservative position.

The career of religious reform, with its triumphs, self-purifications, sudden new inspirations, and ultimate unforeseen alternative results may be studied to unparalleled advantage in the Book of Genesis and in the whole Bible, including the origin of the Christian Church; to which the history of Islam and of Protestantism can be easily appended. The other great religions in Egypt, Mesopotamia, India, and China seem not to have been militant, although their philosophers sometimes advocate sharply their personal moral sentiments or schemes of salvation, as if no other was possible. However this may be, I think the lesson of these oriental religions may be gathered by philosophy better than by any theological eclecticism; and what is philosophy, as the governance and appreciation of life, except religion liberated from groundless fear or anxiety, that is to say from superstition, and also from rage at honest illusions?

Now, the Hebrews, or Children of Abraham, were not at all Orientals in being given to speculation, but an ordinary nomadic tribe with a tribal patron. It is intelligible that a wandering people should not attach their patron deity to any spot, but rather to the fortunes of his People. Changes in their fortunes would be due to their right or wrong conduct towards their God, who yet would lead the faithful in the end to conquer and possess for ever a land flowing with milk and honey.

For this tribe had never, as far as their traditions reported their past, lived in the depths of Arabia or in the vast wilderness of Central Asia, but rather on the borders of highly civilised and populous nations, like Babylonia and Egypt. They exchanged their pastoral produce for the grain and luxuries of those countries, and in these contacts they would have heard, perhaps with wonder, of their cosmic speculations and cosmic deities. The Hebrews were too tightly bound to the worship of their one celestial patron (for it was there that he sometimes appeared and from there that he spoke to them) to be attracted to those strange gods and their monstrous images; and they had never much regarded the gods of other nations except to admonish themselves not to worship them and to trust in the power and will of Jehovah to protect them always. Yet those stories of the creation of the world and of the universal flood, and the notion of a deity ruling all nature and all nations may well have impressed them; so much so that, attributed to their own God, they could accept them without disloyalty. For how, indeed, could Jehovah control the fortunes of his People unless he was master also of all other nations and all other gods? And in that case it became sacrilege even for these other nations to worship any god but the God of Abraham and of Isaac who had appeared to Jacob and made with him at Bethel that memorable contract. It must be, in fine, the whole universe that was guided and planned for the glory and for the chastisement of Israel. All nations were destined to recognise him, and the special authority of his People and his Law; so that Israel by right of divine grace was the one appointed teacher and master of all mankind; and God would one day send his Anointed to make that right effective.

It is only by a slight and automatic change of locus and names that this formidable doctrine has passed to the two international and interracial religions that, as religions, are derived from Israel: Christianity and Islam, which, in the claim to supernatural universal authority, are continuations of Judaism. Yet these two, by their diversified and much richer contacts with the gentile world, have become social, political, and moral forms of culture no less than of religion. Islam in particular, although initially a religious gospel, at once became a military mission of conquest and domination, with

## MILITANT RELIGIONS

a special legislation, oriental and sub-tropical in character, to be imposed on all believers; and belief itself was to be imposed on pain of death on all conquered peoples, unless being Jews or Christians, they were already "men of the Book" and could be tolerated and protected in their special faiths, though not admitted to military or judicial functions. This system produced a special civilisation which had brilliant moments at Bagdad, Cairo, and Cordova, and later several centuries of wide but sleepy and imperfect domination under the Turks. But a militant religion is an embarrassing heritage for nations compelled to live under the tense, noisy, and restless pressure of the modern world; although if this pressure subsides, oases might remain in the desert where that rare seed might again take root and come to flower.

Israel itself, although so strictly tribal, has found it easy to spread all over the world; but its tribal pride, deepened more than shaken by its sufferings, has prevented it either from merging with the gentiles or from gathering them in large numbers into its own pale. The truth is that their religion, after its two chief treasures, monarchical theism and the Scriptures, have been incorporated in other religions, remains distinctive enough, by its exclusions, to segregate them in the midst of a modern society that they love, but that is not distinctive enough, in its religion, to attract religious minds. And how many of them are orthodox enough in their own hearts, if they got complete possession of Jerusalem, to rebuild the Temple of Solomon or even of Herod and to restore all its ornaments and ceremonies, with all the prescriptions, for private life, of the Book of Leviticus? If you remove the cult in the Temple, the observance of the Sabbath and the Feasts, and the miraculous tales in the Bible, what would remain in Judaism that, say, Protestant Christianity does not contain, greatly expurgated and universalised? Liberal Jews are simply humanitarians and positivists: the *religion* of Israel is for them what Catholicism was to Comte. The free-thinking modern Jew may be an artist, a capitalist, a philanthropist, or a communist: his militant soul has outgrown religion without finding philosophy or peace.

The militant enterprise of the Catholic Church in the modern world is particularly interesting and instructive. Two different fountains, both springing up spontaneously in the human soul, itself a living compound of contraries, unite in inspiring and rationalising this religion. The first fountain is the pure doctrine of the Gospel, that can be practiced only after the manner of John the Baptist and the hermits in the desert or, when they turn towards mankind, in the homeless missionary little band of Jesus and his disciples; which with the growth of numbers cannot avoid special settlements in various cities, or in monasteries in the country, combining the little necessary tilling of the soil with much building and much praying.

But evidently this truly evangelical life can be led only by a few selected communities, where each individual has heard a special call, and all are celibate, merely waiting for the second coming of the Lord, either publicly with trumpets, to judge the world and bring it to an end, or privately to each soul for its sanctification. The laity that is converted to this doctrine cannot be required to reproduce its discipline; but by the distinction between universal commandments and evangelical counsels, they will be encouraged to live *in the spirit* of chastity, poverty, and obedience as far as their station and duties in the world permit; and a great tolerance will be shown to human weakness, intellectual as well as moral, so long as it is admitted to be weakness and not defended as manly and enlightened.

Catholic morality is therefore easily compatible with any form of civil or military government that does not itself impose a different religion or morality, but attends to the things that are Caesar's with a benevolent smile at the tastes of mankind in mystical matters. Even a hostile theocracy, if it recognised the Catholic minority as a separate People, and allowed them their own language, religion, education, and laws of marriage and inheritance, could be passively endured, without any rebellious impulses. But the position of a Catholic party in a modern constitutional democracy, where the majority has socialistic leanings and wants to organise, equalise, and train everybody, making them all unanimous, is a difficult and embarrassing one. Christianity is a revealed and militant religion. It would die out at once if it were not expressly inculcated; and although its followers might be dragooned into a political party as they might into a regiment, they would submit only provisionally, under compulsion, reserving for their religion their only real allegiance.

How genuinely and fruitfully Catholicism can be fused into a rich human civilisation becomes clear when we consider the other fountain of its inspiration, namely, Hellenism. And for Catholics this is not, as for Protestants, an appendage, almost a treason, to their Christianity, but a spontaneous, genial, and poetical way of being Christians. This is, in spirit, more marked in the Eastern Church where Hellenism is native than in the Western, although even here, through the Greek Fathers, Plato and Aristotle, it is no less traditional and even more warmly embraced and popular, as in the case of sacred ikons and statues. Into the Hebrew Scriptures themselves, after the conquests of Alexander had been divided into Hellenistic kingdoms, there appears a mature philosophy, freely speculative in Job and in Ecclesiastes, while in the Alexandrian Wisdom-books a salacious knowledge of the world abounds such as we see opinionated old men, in the plays of Terence, rivalling each other in propounding. Nor did the Fathers and Apologists of the Church in the least hesitate to employ pagan philosophy and eloquence in the service of their cause, nor the Councils and the Popes to outdo the neo-Platonists in the refinements of theological speculation, or the other popular cults in the elaboration of pious legends and feasts. It was not by quitting their special revelation that Christians assimilated their piety to that of other men, but by introducing that same humanity into their own, as indeed was already done for them, radically and in principle, by the cardinal tenet of their faith, namely, the incarnation of God in Man.

Humanism was in fact so deeply interfused with religion in the Catholic mind that it is precisely in the most Catholic ages that it flourished most and that a sort of paralysis fell on both, if either was muted. The ages of the Crusades were those of chivalry; and Don Quixote felt no discord, but a mutual sanction, in being loyal to both at once. And yet a philological critic, spelling out his ideas from the letter of books, would have told him that chivalry, with its magic and giants and unauthorised adventures, was a heathen superstition, fostering conceit, pride, and absurd combativeness in a clown masquerading as a hero. But Don Quixote, who read books with the imagination, would have replied: No; no act could be more Christian than to defend the weak from the unjust aggression of the strong, and to turn the thoughts from carnal desires to an ideal and religious love. Compare with this the extraordinary cult of the Virgin Mary, inspired first by profound meditation on the mystery of the Incarnation, reported in the Gospels and itself the taproot of the Christian faith; but this implication was fed and humanised by ambient religious sentiments regarding virginity and also motherhood, popular myths concerning the Mother of the

Gods and Diana of the Ephesians and perhaps also by atavistic memories of matriarchal authority and government. And the vague mystical intuition of God in Man, latent everywhere, became concrete and at once homely and sacred, when concentrated in the figure of God in Jesus, and consequently hidden but actual, once in the womb and always in the heart of Mary. It was also easier to believe in a divine providence overruling the incidents of daily life, if even small favours could be mediated, as at the marriage in Cana, by a sigh at some domestic worry, or a tender sympathy with childish hearts.

I doubt that, in any age, a mature philosophy can have avoided the conviction that it is such humble human models that the religious imagination has enlarged into propitious or hostile celestial giants, visiting angels, heroic Messiahs, mendicant prophets, and domestic wonderworking saints.

But if Hellenism, in its devotion to the Theotokos, had made Hebraic religion at once speculative and humble, there could no longer be any quarrel between Christianity and interludes of gaiety, poetry, splendour, and refinement. These things can never be made pervasive or constant in human life, which can never radically control the physical world or its own irrational growths. But like religion itself, worldly fortunes can be cultivated at the right season in many various places and ways, of which Catholic civilisation gives brilliant though troubled and tragic examples, in Byzantium, and more variedly in the West, where the thirteenth century perfected ecclesiastical philosophy and architecture and the fifteenth century a pure renaissance which the seventeenth sublimated into majesty, magnificence, and baroque exuberance. There had been no lack of exuberance of other less monumental sorts throughout the middle ages. Heraldry shows it to the eye, spreading into costume, sculpture, romantic fabulous histories, and grotesque popular shows and the unbridled fancy of religious sects and speculations. Heresies were, indeed, often cruelly suppressed; but chiefly when they involved social and political rebellion. Towards the ideal play of thought and language there was a great indulgence, and laughter rang as loud as the clash of arms and the screams and curses of the tortured. It was a rough existence, struggling and playing close to the ground; but even in the persecutions which it authorised, religion was an exalting admonition from powers behind the scenes, in whose presence the passing passions lost their finality; as ritual

# MILITANT RELIGIONS

candles, at a wedding or at a funeral, lighted in the glare of day, carry the crude event into another world where it has another meaning; much as the mention of ancient sorrows and glories by the chorus in a Greek play removes the too great horror of the present tragedy, together with all else that is accidental and transitory, into a realm where everything coexists and has become a perfect monument to itself.

Certainly it is no relief to a man in agony to be told that the sky is sometimes blue and that the stars, though usually hidden, are always shining; and these platitudes are no justification for the torments he suffers or for those who impose them. Existence is irrational and so is the love of it; and while we exist we cannot escape either. Yet a man has also a spirit capable of being speculative and disinterested whenever the pressure of hostile circumstances or vicious passions is relaxed. At such times, all things seem to speak to that spirit in its native language. Tragedies become poems; the hopes and sorrows of the world become arguments for religion. Evils remain as bad as ever for the natural man; but for the spirit in him they are transformed; what was a predicament becomes a vista, what was a puzzle becomes a truth. You have begun to live in a new way just as natural (if you are a thinking man) and much less disturbed. This is what society loses if it discards the liberal arts, or the liberating side of religion and philosophy. On their militant side, however, these speculative gifts and ideal systems only overload the weight of scientific and historical knowledge with arbitrary explanations which multiply unnecessary doubts and quarrels about optional doctrine and about groundless duties and prohibitions in action.

# BOOK THIRD

## THE RATIONAL ORDER OF SOCIETY

# CHAPTER 1

## THE STATUS OF REASON IN NATURE

IN POLITICS reason may seem to play an eminently militant part, since when it can it introduces a moral order into the chaos of conflicting customs and quarrels. Yet a moment's reflection will suffice to remind us that militancy itself is a strand in the generative order of society, an eddy in the stream, when one vital interest becomes vivid and turns against the smothering pressure of the undirected flux of events. Militancy is but the integrity of a part asserting itself and seeking to dominate the blind drift of the rest. Now, such integrity in an insurgent Will is itself a triumph of reason and of vital liberty in the individual or the party girding itself for combat; so that reason enters the political arena as an aggressive demand put forward by an eager agent whose Will, suddenly clarified, feels capable of achieving social domination.

An oriental sage, however, might attain perfect integrity and rationality without growing in the least militant or figuring in politics as a reformer. The itch to make war on a drifting world would have to arise in him irrationally, as a heaven-sent mission or a political passion. Reason by no means requires a man to set about making rational those things which are irrational by nature, as life itself is. Don Quixote was kindly and heroically mad, but he had lost his reason. A rational order of society must be imposed on it by art, by express institutions and laws which presuppose birth, death, love, labour, war, and a perpetual fringe of madness and crime surrounding the fortified oasis of reason. And the needful agent in building and defending this fortress can never be reason itself but some sworn band of militant enthusiasts in whom the idea of a rational society has become an obsession.

The primary force in establishing a rational order of society is therefore a purely vegetative growth in the psyche, that easily spreads by contagion to a group of psyches, and forms a political party or philosophic sect. The germ of this political growth is not itself political but biological and moral: it is the seedling of the life of reason sprouting within the secret self, and spreading as it finds the psychic soil favourable and the surrounding climate clement and sunny. Sympathy is a great help in the early stages of such moral integrations; but when the inner domination has become deep-rooted and firm, contrary blasts harden rather than bend it; and zeal in the cause grows faster than does the good work itself. This occurs, however, only in a few leaders and ardent disciples; for rationality is a secondary habit in the animal psyche, a not indispensable synthesis of functions each capable of asserting itself separately, and apt, in rough weather, to lose all contact with its neighbours.

The political *power* exercised in the alleged service of reason is always exercised by persons, themselves fundamentally irrational, but attached in their studious meditations to some rational utopia, or to phrases become catch-words for special interests, but still suggesting the rational aspirations of some political philosopher. A rationalist party may thus arise and govern in its day, as rationalist sects arise in philosophy, probably in both cases animated by an irrational hatred of tradition in general, and of religion in particular. It is not the work of such parties that I wish to study under the name of the Rational Order of Society. Such an Order would liberate all human interests, especially those that being ideal and harmless do not materially trample on one another, and that even psychologically can often be pursued together, to the delight and enrichment of a rational mind; whereas rationalist sects usually favour only elementary material interests and unimaginative morals, counting bread-rations but not moments of sport or laughter.

The militant aspect of reason in politics is therefore accidental, as are aggression and enmity in the generative order. Fishes, for instance, may have no choice but to devour one another if they are to live at all, vegetable food being absent or insufficient in their medium; and plants in the jungle may be by nature pure parasites on other plants, or may, by merely existing, rob them of their necessary space, moisture, or sunlight. This is not militancy, but only involuntary and inevitable rivalry. So the agents that diffuse the life of reason must remove, not from the world but from their own lives and chosen surroundings, all that would destroy or subvert their rational economy. This would involve a strict and "totalitarian" discipline within the rational circle, as within a monastery or school or army, but without the least ambition to make all nature, all animals, or all societies rational after one's own rule. For even the most uncompromising regimen has a natural and irrational nucleus; and as this nucleus differs in different races, ages, or countries, so the rational development there would differ from an equally rational development on another foundation. As to peace between different rational regimens or civilisations, it would depend on the *physical* possibility of their coexistence. If there was room and sustenance for all, they should rationally agree to differ. If only one could subsist at a time, underlying physical forces or economic developments, perhaps without war but certainly without reason, would automatically decide the issue.

In itself, indeed, reason is something internal to spirit: a faculty of seeing identity, affinity, contrast, or irrelevance between essences present together in direct intuition. Though purely speculative in itself, this faculty sheds continual and revealing light on events and on the whole history and composition of the world; because the images and the calculations that reveal surrounding facts to an animal have essentially dialectical relations to one another; and these relations become patent to intuition, if ever attention is directed upon them instead of distractedly following the lures, the threats, and the shocks of pressing events. Language in making recognisable sounds to mark similar accidents tends to cast a net of grammatical relations over the flux of experience, and superposes in this way a partially intelligible syntax on the natural order of genesis in the world. Mathematical science, which in itself is perfectly hypothetical and ideal, carries this application of reason to nature one step further, with brilliant practical and speculative results. These results prove the partial truth of what language and myth assume too sweepingly: that nature, though fundamentally contingent and irrational, falls readily into repetitions and analogies which render possible a rational description and appreciation of what happens in some spheres and in some directions. There can be shrewd divination even in psychology and politics, in business and in war; but all is at best imaginative presumption, which can be justified only where the objects studied are so simple in structure that the human senses can distinguish and measure their elements and movements. This is notoriously not the case in human history or politics; and when prophets profess to see dialectical necessity in the complex and confused movements of civilisation they indulge in a forced distortion both of facts and of logic and morals. The eloquent composition of historical books must indeed be inspired by a Muse, because it treats dramatically the fortunes of some man or some nation or some art; but the dark background of destiny still remains dominant and dictates the moral, unless the partisan author relies on eloquence to reverse the truth.

It is not therefore in the scientific description of society or of government, or in universal history, that any rational order is to be expected, but only, at best, in the exercise of government when this is virtuously inspired and intelligently pursued. The choice of reason as a guide, instead of Will or of faith or of public approval, is itself a matter of vital endowment or character in the individual. It will mark the type of morality that he advocates or actually exemplifies. Reason is a standard that the barbarian heartily despises and that has actually been seldom dominant even in the theory, much less in the practice, of politics. Intelligence has been admired and sharpened in the pursuit of irrational ends; it has seldom been allowed to criticise or to select the ends actually pursued. And this is no scandal or paradox. Distress and vitality in a man breed and employ reason as a method of concentrating natural powers in himself or discovering them in the world; but an intense cultivation of reason sucks up and reorganises all mental vistas into a speculative habit that transcends those animal and social interests which it was cultivated to serve. The chief field in which such a habit has borne rich political fruit is mechanics, where a mathematical formula posited to govern material processes is verified in them; yet even here the traceable rational order presupposes brute facts and arbitrary variations in them which do not become rational or intelligible simply for being habitual. Motion and change are themselves utterly irrational; and both the fact that they occur and the fact that they seem to obey certain laws are factors in the order of generation, not in any way dictated by reason.

Reason cannot rationally deny or condemn nature, or the life and Will that nature breeds; and this for various reasons. First: Reason itself owes its existence as a chief characteristic of the spirit to the spontaneous fertility of those material and vital powers. Secondly: Even spirit manifests an emotional and poetic sensibility which is not rational. Thirdly: On its rational side spirit transcends all censorious judgments or combative Will, and thereby gives *carte blanche* to all logical possibilities, but without sanctioning the existence of any one of them in particular. In all its sufferings and joys spirit therefore moves in the order of generation and not in that of reason. Consonantly with this, when reason becomes by any chance or any discipline a dominant movement in the psyche it tends to deflate all animal and political interests, and to deflate the passionate or playful impulses of spirit itself. It makes for omniscience, equilibrium, and peace: in a word, for Nirvana. Observing or foreseeing this, the domestic and political man, while obliged incidentally to invoke reason as an instrument in his pursuits, heartily detests reason as an inspiration or a sanctuary.

With this reminder that reason is properly a spiritual virtue, having its standards and rewards in itself, we may be prepared to find the rational arts that flourish in the world to be secluded, like mathematics, or festive, like music; also to find little but confusion and tragic failure where reason attempts to clarify such a concrete and mundane subject as politics or even as philosophy. For the life of reason on earth is inevitably distracted. In the presence of the aesthetic qualities and logical relations between things which actually appear to the spirit, a man harnessed to affairs or intent on his own passions will not see those obvious qualities in their rational logical order, but will see rather their irrational comings and goings or will feel only the active impulses which, as signs, they arouse automatically in his body. In this he obeys, like any other animal, the generative order of nature and of economic arts, in which the conjunction and distribution of images in minds is a vain accident and psychic waste, like after-images or dreams; and nothing counts except a man's physical reaction to the physical presence of particular dynamic objects, such as public events, institutions, and persons; compounds that figure as units on the scale of the human body, and that produce that excitement in the psyche of which images and feelings are echoes or prophecies to the spirit.

What wonder, in such circumstances, that the political man should ignore reason, or be utterly confused if he attempts to be rational? Material complications and headlong events are calling to him or threatening on every side. He must pick his perilous way among realities; yet to conceive, remember, or forecast those realities he has only those "inert ideas" which past contacts have imposed on his uncertain and crowded memory; and on this he must model his probably fatuous expectations. His automatic reactions will carry him forward before he knows what reasons he will assign for them if challenged in debate; and in debate a few trite notions and standard phrases will have to represent his vague motives and, by mere repetition and emphasis, to vent his perhaps genuine emotions. If in a quandary he ever feels his terrible ignorance he can look for enlightenment only in the dead dramas congealed in books or in moral or religious precepts. There is indeed a fund of wisdom buried there, to which mankind may appeal when their living Will falters; but like proverbs such maxims, especially in politics and religion, are contradictory, local, and casual. You must first know your aim, before you can choose a precept by which to justify it.

## CHAPTER 2

### RELATIVITY OF KNOWLEDGE AND OF MORALS

MISTAKES and failure of reason occur continually in the exercise of government, and are sometimes recognised afterwards by those who made them. The mistakes made in the programmes and theories of political parties are often pointed out by their opponents, but seldom acknowledged by the parties themselves, because the sources of their views are fixed and the tests to which those views are subjected in practice are never adequate or final, as may be the effect of a single measure or action. I assume that grounds exist, in the Will of certain men or in their education, for the choice that each party makes of its policy; these grounds cannot be rational fundamentally, but they may be consistent in their chosen aims; and irrationality in argument or in action will then appear only if the circumstances are ignored which, at that time and place, may render the execution of that policy impossible. Then any irrational attempt to carry out that policy would be due to ignorance.

If we agree to this, we shall be confirming the doctrine of Socrates that it is *knowledge*, not accidental desires or opinions, that makes conduct rational and right. What Socrates seems to have forgotten to say is that the knowledge requisite to make action rational in this sense lies entirely beyond the reach of mankind. We might be rational in trifles—in taking a bus marked for the place to which we wish to go—but never rational in choosing our political party and never, if leaders of that party, in choosing the man that our supporters must vote for. These major matters would all have to be decided by habit, accidental impressions, or mysterious intuition.

Modern speculation, on the other hand, being introverted, places virtue in sentiment and intention rather than in art, and seeks to found morals on "the moral sense" or conscience, so that morality, private or public, would be entirely a matter of direct intuition and absolute or "categorical" in its spontaneous precepts. I should think, however, that at least in politics, the first commandment of the conscience in a responsible statesman would be to understand the world in which he was playing a part, and the capacities and genuine needs of the people in whose interest he was acting. So that his moral sense, if it was not a mere prejudice, would bring him back again into the hopeless position of Socrates, demanding before he could act rightly, a knowledge that he could never possess.

Socrates, however, was providentially inspired as a prophet of his time, which was the turning point in the fortunes of ancient Greece. The age of political and plastic arts was over, and that of private moral reflection and conversion had begun. His imagination, if we may trust the Utopia that Plato puts into his mouth, was archaically political; and Plato's own testament in the Laws was like the visions of the Hebrew Prophets, a transformation of a militant national past into an entrenched religious discipline, like that of the monasteries of the future. He meant to immortalise Sparta and Olympia, but he unwittingly legislated for Mount Athos and Monte Cassino. What I have called the forgetfulness of Socrates, in proposing an unattainable criterion for the conduct of life, was precisely what made him the herald of two thousand years of subjectivity and political and scientific disorder; not that there ensued any dark ages or mediaeval barbarism for the spirit; but on the contrary that a long and voluntary flight of the spirit into the wilderness was to develop its dramatic sense of isolation and its *fonction fabulatrice*, not only in theology, but in a poetic and historic rereading of the world in romantic and moralistic terms. Has not the time come for mankind to awake to its actual situation, and to that of the spirit that animates it?

The Sophists, who were in one sense the partners of Socrates, inasmuch as they too represented the dissolution of the classic world, pointed in an opposite direction, in that the corruption of the traditional ethos seemed to them an emancipation instead of a divine summons to repentance and to an inner discipline of the soul. They abounded in miscellaneous information, as do the intellectuals of our own age, and being more bold and free than any modern can be, they doted on the relativity of knowledge and of morals, as they understood this relativity: namely, that morals and science, goodness and truth, could never be anything but the feeling or thought that each man had of them at each moment; these thoughts and feelings were assumed, whenever a Sophist lectured to a company of town wits, to be indefinitely numerous and all different and, as assertions, contradictory; so that the doctrine of relativity might easily be expressed absolutely, by saying that all feelings of right and wrong, and all opinions were false: or in the language of Indian philosophy, were all illusions. But the Indians really meant this, and believed that only Brahman, or Spirit, was ever real. The Sophists, like the British empiricists, who have rediscovered this axiom, are essentially social beings, publicists, orators, teachers, and politicians. To them, the axiom that life is a dream, and all objects illusions, is taboo; you must never mention it, because it would prick the bubble of your analytic reform of philosophy.

Now when I say that morals and knowledge (not the truth, but opinions regarding the truth) and all judgments about right and wrong (not all goods) are relative I mean something entirely different. I mean that opinions and judgments arise in psyches and express the capacity and inevitableness of such opinions and judgments arising at each moment in each psyche; but the degree of their truth depends on the relation that their several deliverances have to the facts that provoke them and that they *mean* to refer to. That they refer to something which, existentially, they do not contain is due to the fact that they are not purely logical or psychological phenomena, but spiritual transcripts of biological processes and tensions which are all self-transcendent, as are all the phases of existence. Spirit arises in animals when they react, as organisms charged with specific reflexes and potentialities of growth, which specific occasions excite and turn into action; and as these reactions are directed upon the real objects that provoke them, so the spiritual transcript of them also is turned, in expectation, description, and appreciation upon the power that has evoked it.

It is in view of this biological status of perception, opinion, and moral judgment that these spiritual events are necessarily relevant to their occasion and relative to the character of the organ that produces them under that stimulus. The degree of truth in ideas and beliefs, and the degree of justness in our judgments corresponds not directly to their respective objects, which we can be aware of only by their effects, but on the character of the impression we receive and the complex reaction and radiation of that impression within the life of the psyche.

Nothing could therefore be more false, and willfully ignorant, than to maintain with the Greek Sophists and the British empiricists (when both are radical and consistent) that knowledge and judgment refer to nothing and are always equally true and valid, in the sense that each is equally real—as a sensation when it is felt. Their relativity, properly understood, far from making opinions and judgments worthless renders them capable of some degree of truth and justness, since they express the sensibility of a living psyche, according to its endowment and development, to the influences that reach it, and determine its fate, in the natural world.

The subjectivity of the Sophists and empiricists survives in German philosophy with an interesting difference. As the Sophists were publicists, and inconsistently posited a social but not physical world, and the empiricists, in England and the United States, a moral society, so the German idealists posited a Philosophy of History or a Phenomenology of Spirit. This they drew from the Bible and from Saint Augustine as to history, and from their own inspiration for the Romance of Spirit. There is more air and light in all this than in the other subjective schools; but I think we may say of all without exception that it is precisely when they are false to their subjective axioms, and feed on common sense, on real history, and on natural science, or even on theology, that they tell us anything worth hearing.

# CHAPTER 3

### MASKS OF VICE AND VIRTUE

SOMETIMES an unexpected awakening quickens a dark corner of our nature and for a moment renders attractive, as in a dream, something that would normally seem repulsive. To bask in such a light might dislocate the balance of the psyche already achieved and might gradually poison all our habits and tastes. We should then acquire the *mask* of that vice in the public eye, and not merely, as perhaps we fancied, a philosophic understanding of that odd interest, really no less legitimate for seeming at first exotic.

In this way the young of wild animals, that look so simple and innocent at birth, acquire the mask of ferocity or watchfulness or greed—a mask that bears witness to habits they have learned to adopt. How or why have they acquired these habits? Because they had organs capable of such employment, with suitable innate reflexes, often guided and stimulated by the example of their parents. Each tentative act so prepared has cast a ray of sunshine on a special image and has withdrawn attention from any others, now become meaningless sensations. The keen eye waits for the chosen signals, the paw gathers itself tightly for the sudden blow. The young animal, that seemed so plastic, has discovered his predestined path, without knowing where it will lead him. Lures and feats have been set for him, under the guise of goods; and whatever evils they may entail, *goods*, supreme *goods*, exclusive *goods* they will now appear to his captivated spirit. Mastery and narrowness will increase in him together. The habits which he has acquired as virtues have stamped upon him what seems to us a horrible mask of vice. Not only is his strength utterly cruel and blind to all alien goods, but the vital liberty which that strength seems to serve is a tragic liberty even for him. He is condemned to turn, enslaved and tormented, in an irrational treadmill.

It is important to perceive, for our instruction, that this mask of vice, which makes us shudder, expresses virtue and concentration of Will upon a recognised good. The animal psyche that as it developed its powers in contact with circumstances unwittingly fashioned that mask was bent upon a predatory life. It saw its victims, as it devoted its attention to its young or to its mate, as objects of immediate categorical value, goods to chase and devour or acts to perform and repeat at all costs. That the first set of these actions were wicked and the second set virtuous does not hold for that psyche; both actions are expressions equally of primal Will and vital liberty; both are equally virtuous within the compass of that life. For life itself, the Will of the psyche and of its operation, is not a good, but only the fountain and organ of both good and evil, and the seat of their contrary character. Good and evil, in a dumb

## MASKS OF VICE AND VIRTUE

unquestioned immediacy, exist for the beasts. They are moral creatures vitally, though not intellectually; and their vital virtue creates a genuine moral criterion for their lives, which we can appreciate in their strength, ingenuity, courage, and beauty.

Yet those virtues, divorced from transcendent reason and justice, seem vices to us. In themselves, however, they remain virtues even in us; only that for us, who are inwardly called to be just, reasonable, and intelligent, those virtues are subordinated or forbidden; and when we see them dominant in the bold mask worn by a beast, that mask seems to us hideous, because it would be morally hideous in a man.

Even in the beast it is sometimes intrinsically and painfully ugly, when the species to which it belongs has not attained a happy harmony in its constitution, but is overloaded and embarrassed by its own organs. Yet usually what repels us in natural monsters is not their own constitutional trouble but only the malice and ferocity that their aspects suggest in preying on other creatures. That death should feed on life and life on the death of other life is a first law of existence as we find it on earth; and we accept and admire such alternation easily enough in the inanimate sphere; yet it saddens us when we read into it an irrational hostility of one living psyche to another. This is a human error. Psyches, or forms of life, bear no hatred or ill-will towards other psyches; they simply have no imagination, until they develop a highly social and cooperative way of living. Even then sympathy is very partial in any living creature; for cooperation cannot safely extend beyond those natural processes with which one's own life is allied; and sympathy without cooperation is merely aesthetic and perfunctory.

All integrated psyches are virtuous and their natural masks are masks of virtue, as we readily feel in regard to the mineral and vegetable kingdoms. Stars and flowers differ from one another in glory, and it is no vice or failure in any one not to show the glory of all. But animals possessing initiative necessarily have an optative or militant side. They have, and feel that they have, a standard of achievement and right behaviour; and whatever falls short of this or contravenes it excites their contempt or hatred. Their possessive ethos makes them blind to the virtue of contrary vocations. This intolerance survives in man in so far as he is more vital than rational. Fine art might seem to be a sphere in which alien gifts or standards would surely be respected; but not at all. The mask of virtue in a classical Greek head seems to your realist or futurist dullness and deadness personified; and the pink and gold sweetness of demure images in the style of Saint Sulpice turns his stomach. For him, both are masks of vice. And not only in taste or in ideologies. His militant spirit detests and wishes to annihilate them. Obviously this happens only because he is insecure in his own virtue and dissatisfied with the social authority he possesses, which is casual and transitory like the vogue of Greek heads or simpering Madonnas. But his animal zest will not bear competition. The vital egotism of the psyche prevents in him any intellectual self-transcendence, and absorption in certain chosen masks of life keeps him from sympathy with its groping universal energy.

I have spoken of masks of virtue; but can the visible aspect and traces of true virtue be called a mask? Evidently not, unless the mobility of life has been arrested and a special dominant character has been imposed on all movement and feeling, as if the possibility of anything different had been uprooted from the psyche, and the occasion of anything different had been banished from the world. Virtue so imposed will wear a mask, as in the Carthusian; not that this is not a genuine virtue in itself, but that by making that virtue so inhumanly dominant a militant faith has closed eyes, ears, and mouth in order to listen undisturbed to an inner music.

In a man of the world, on the contrary, various virtues and vices may exist, but he will wear the mask of none of them. Some of these virtues and vices may be known to his neighbours, others unknown; but discretion will keep any of them from appearing out of season in his talk or in his demeanour. For it is only occasionally that those virtues or vices will be congruous with the matter in hand or with the company in which he finds himself. Then, for a while and without losing his self-control, he may indulge them without offence. But once the occasion is past or the company changed, he must not show any displeasing traces of those episodes and must lend himself as far as possible to the dominant mood of the world.

A radical potentiality for sympathy with all virtues and all vices belongs to primal Will in every creature, but the direction and the degree in which such sympathy shall become actual is a question of contingent endowment and opportunity. Reason demands integrity; but integrity may be thin, when there is little in the psyche to integrate, or it may hold in suspense and harmony a great wealth of motives. The perfect actor can play all kinds of parts. God can forgive all sinners and provide distinct mansions, discreetly spaced, for all sorts of saints. Yet as for God all finitude is impossible in his own person, so for a good actor there is no danger of such immersion in any of his dramatic parts that the passion in it should storm the citadel of his inner commonwealth. His genius keeps always present in the background the partiality of each virtue and the disaster of each vice. He therefore acquires the mask of none of his stage characters. His own figure shows only the plasticity, the precision, and the discretion of the artist.


## CHAPTER 4

### RELATIVITY OF REASON IN POLITICS

By the term "reason" I understand not a new force in the physical world but a new harmony in vital forces. It signifies a conjunction and mutual modification of impulses or impressions in a man or in a society: a life led in the light or the shadow of the past and the possible.

Such lights and shadows may reach the spirit in the form of images or emotions; but even the most explicit deliberation or reasoning can never do justice to the elements that render a decision rational. That would require not only superhuman penetration but a superhuman freedom from distraction by irrelevant accidents. The net of true reason, however thin its web or wide its meshes, must be cast over the whole psyche and the whole world. Even the great moments of intuition (which often come at the crises of action) are mere flashes over sudden and partial perspectives. They are wonderful visions; but events shape themselves afterwards, as before, in obedience to a thousand other currents. So when Caesar said: "The die is cast," there was an unusually just realisation of the past and future destinies of mankind. Ordinary rational decisions make only short, clear runs amid the turbid rapids of existence.

However unified the world may be mechanically, it would be

an utter chaos historically if certain coordinations were not often reproduced by being ingrained in self-repeating tropes or by seminal involution in hereditary psyches. Such material rhythms introduce permanent forms into the flux of events, but they are not in themselves rational since the dynamic rhythms do not vary at each reproduction *pari passu* with the variations in circumstances. So too the instruments and methods adopted in the arts, without reproducing themselves biologically, become habitual. Even if adopted consciously and by concentration of attention on things, these tricks of the trade are not embraced or preserved rationally, but by a sort of confluent affinity or amorous attraction of the artist towards his subject-matter and its life. The image so clarified and the twist so given to the hand become fixed in the delighted craftsman. He feels that he has been inspired and has become a master; and his sense of mastery blinds him to the generative instability of nature, both in himself and in the world. He clings, and his apprentices cling, to their primitive images and primitive tools. The world outgrows them, and seems to forsake the element of rationality which they, in their momentary mastery, had thought they had found and acquired for ever. But their knowledge and skill have come to them by an inspired empiricism, without any clear understanding of nature or of themselves; and their discomfiture is inescapable, since so long as they cling to their special style they must exaggerate more stubbornly the claims of their art as it falls more and more short of its rational function in the eyes of the rising generation.

In politics, however, as in trade, the element of rationality is explicit, and the whole is carried on in conventional terms of interests, claims, and wrongs, the nature and grounds of which seem self-evident. As in a market nobody questions the value of money, so in a political debate or election nobody questions the value of victory for his own party or his own opinions. Prosperity in the country and influence in the world make success in government, as gaining or retaining votes marks success in debate. Yet the character of that prosperity or influence, and its consequences, and the character of the opinions and passions displayed in that debate would alone determine truly whether that debate and that government had been rational.

The real but relative place of reason in politics was better understood in the absolute monarchies of the seventeenth and eighteenth centuries than it has been afterwards under liberal parliamentary governments. Proprietary dynasties and their ministers knew, as any landlord and his agents and solicitors know, what the object of their policy really was. It was copious rents peacefully collected, which would secure splendour at home and glory abroad. Personally, the King might be weak or licentious; but in so far as he was intelligent he could not help seeing his own or his servants' folly in neglecting his interest and duty as the head of a royal house. The very precision of these interests and duties, however, would make evident their conflict with the similar but rival interests of other monarchs and their estates; so that politics could have the precise but futile rationality of a game of chess, or a perfectly written tragedy. Politics was the art of winning a worthless or fatal prize, which custom and emulation prompted you to play for. There was excitement in the game and perhaps glory.

The leaders and orators in parliamentary countries have inherited something of this proprietary sentiment of princes; but the nominal as well as the real objects of their zeal have become confused. Their nominal enemies are contrary opinions at home; and the real interests which those rival opinions defend are supposed to be rival interests of the home population. But what could be more irrational than a soicety where the *real* interests of each class are opposed to those of all other classes? If, then, rival opinions represent rival interests, they represent false imaginary interests; and then politics would be not an art designed to secure real benefits to society but a scramble for office among sophistical rhetoricians. Rhetoricians may be sincere, and must be so at least momentarily if they are eloquent; and the same may be said of sophists, whose sophistry may become a faith. The defence of any faith may be rationalised in everything except its foundations, which remain out of sight. Modern politics have inherited the traditions of religious propaganda and apologetics; so that the natural interests of society, which would be the inspiration of a rational government, may be deliberately subordinated to the supernatural interests of the soul, as defined by revolutionary prophets. Modern politics thus have an emotional mainspring, so that opinions are advocated apart from political considerations; and this prophetic and fanatical spirit may be merged, incongruously, with the advocacy of grossly material interests and private passions. So liberalism has preached religious toleration and a lay scientific education for the people, while the real interests that it furthered were free trade and the concentrated wealth that this facilitated. A paternal government that imposed a particular religion and social order on its subjects inevitably stifled trade and stabilised social classes; it was therefore odious to merchants, and also to eccentric sects and individuals, who therefore became political allies of the enterprising capitalists and monopolists. The banners of humanitarianism and equality, which the rich liberals carried aloft without any sense of hypocrisy, have now been snatched from their hands by a return wave of communism and dogmatic unanimity. But can unanimity and communism coexist with vital liberty? Liberalism secured vital liberty for the rich and for the geniuses, if the latter could make themselves known; for the liberty fostered by prosperity is intellectual as well as personal. It is on the varied fruits of this moral and intellectual liberty that the spirits of unanimous mankind might feed at first; but what fruits would a unified human society bear, if it must remain unified? The animal material needs of the human race might be unified by a severe medical and economic regimen universally imposed; but primal Will and vital liberty are centrifugal and divergent, so that the goods they pursue are incompatible existentially and complementary only for pure spirit seeing them ideally under the form of eternity.

# CHAPTER 5

## RATIONAL AUTHORITY

UNIFORMITIES in nature are neither perfect nor pervasive; it would be superstitious to regard them as obligatory. Where elements are similar and conditions similar, effects are similar too: perhaps that is the deepest uniformity, itself possibly not absolute, which might seem to explain the others. Yet in animal life and in human society, the truly efficacious elements are so complex and obscure, and the conditions so miscellaneous, that uniformities often seem to establish themselves miraculously, at a distance, by a mysterious contagion or mimesis, as in gesture, sentiment, and speech. Being

# RATIONAL AUTHORITY

spontaneous, yet involuntary, and at the same time socially approved, conformity to usage in the tongue seems to everyone correctness, and in the heart virtue. Society thus breeds superstition to defend it, and the mechanical domination of usage passes for authority.

Yet the more a custom or opinion flourishes by contagion the less rational authority it has. Diffusion in such matters does not even prove that the epidemic usage is either useful or congenial to those who have adopted it. It may be, for almost everybody, only a vested automatism. So swearing, smoking, tattooing, and other barbarous fashions or mutilations are not originally congenial to most people. A defiant puerile conceit in doing something odd and a little painful may have started them; foolish provocation or mere involuntary contagion may have spread them; and tradition may keep them alive, like contagious diseases, against the organic health and simple happiness of all. They are parasitic vices which the body can endure and is equipped neither to resist nor to expel.

Is there *any* personal or social habit that might not conceivably be in this case? I can think of but two proofs which custom and public opinion may put forth in defence of such habits as being suited to human nature. One proof is that the habit or opinion in question has not, as yet, proved fatal to all who adopted it. So sexual inversion, which must tend to die out in each case, nevertheless reappears occasionally. The other proof is less cogent but more suggestive: namely, that the person who initiated the given usage may have felt an unsuspected advantage attaching to it, or perhaps only a symbolic appropriateness, which in the absence of all utility might nevertheless heighten the pleasantness of life, like good manners. This sort of apparently empty yet beneficent artifice appears clearly in rhetoric and in music: optional but cherished complications in the exercise of human faculty, which add new dimensions to the moral world by giving free rein, without disaster, to vital liberty.

Casual practices of this kind may become automatisms, irresistible as idle impulses, like biting one's nails, even if detested in their effects; or, when fashionable, they may even be defended, on specious grounds, such as that the ugly results are not essential to them, but due to other causes; and cynics may always advocate old follies because worse follies would probably take their place. There is really one virtue that custom and public opinion possess even when most irrational: that they give a popular form to action and thought by which these are rendered distinguishable and open to criticism and improvement. Facts and logic may well be outraged by tradition, but at least tradition articulates manners, defines the arts, and renders social types clear and dramatic. With the cards distinctively marked and the rules fixed, the game of politics can be played to a finish, even if only to prove its own vanity. A round of errors may sometimes be more tolerable and interesting than a life-long tete-à-tete with the obvious: is it not actually so in philosophy? Freedom is legitimate when it does not usurp authority; and a radical critic of current follies is likely to betray his own, and to prove odious rather than persuasive. His own rational conscience, if he had it, might falter and accuse him of becoming inhuman by his insistence on being quite right.

When, then, has a political movement or institution rational authority? When is it "right"? Let us first set aside certain absolute standards which, even if they were admissible philosophically, could have no foothold in politics, such as the divine origin of particular precepts or the truth of the dogmas involved in them. For the believer such precepts and dogmas are evidently above criticism; yet interpretations of them may vary, and there is politically a prior question to be solved. Are the motives and sanctions supporting a given theocratic faith themselves humanly and socially good? The Covenant, for instance, of Jacob with the Lord [1] established a worship and an oracle that should henceforth be preserved absolutely; but Jacob's conditions in proposing this covenant are rational politically: they exact the Lord's help in war and in tribal economy. Even, then, if Jacob's dream be dismissed as a normal illusion, the psychic disposition that prompted it is thoroughly, even crudely, rational; and the covenant based upon it imposes no alien domination on Israel. Human policy, mythically sanctioned, remains autonomous. So long as events justify the policy pursued under such religious auspices, they go to prove that myth, when positivistically inspired and positivistically sanctioned, is harmless in politics, and may be psychologically useful, or even a true premonition of destiny.

In Jacob's vision there is much more than this opportunity to secure a sure invisible ally in the perilous government of a maraud-

[1] Genesis, XXVIII, 10–22, quoted, Book First, Part III, Chapter 6, pp. 149–150.

ing tribe. There is the religious imagination; but this, though it may eventually supplant the business of politics, has no authority to direct or to limit it.

What, then, apart from the celestial assistance that may have been secured by contract, can determine the rightness or wrongness of a ruler's policy? It cannot be primal Will alone, either in himself or in his people. This primal Will supplies the vital force at hand and determines its blind endeavours; but it has no inner light to distinguish its possible from its impossible future achievements. Primal Will justifies naturally, in that it loves them, all its errors and vices. We are not concerned now with this self-judged rightness of all actions, but only with the *rational* justification of some against the folly of others. And the first answer suggested by primal Will itself to this question, when faced by some immovable obstacle or by some horrible unintended result, is this: that which makes an action rational is the material possibility of carrying it out successfully. In a word, *Circumstances* render one action rational and another irrational.

This first answer at once suggests but corrects a maxim decried by moralists but for ever reasserted by natural Will: namely, that Might is Right. In identifying authority with the favour of Circumstances, we deny all *intrinsic* rightness or wrongness to any form of Will or action. The difference lies only in the suitability of that impulse to the world in which it arises. You have a right to be what you are and to become what you can become. To deny this is literally superstitious: it stands aside from the vital fact itself, and seems to feel the presence of another impulse spying on it and loathing it. Then, infected with this alien Will, the native Will is perturbed and hesitates. But the alien impulse is a form of primal Will just as absolute and groundless morally as the native Will that it detests. And it is mere confusion and cowardice to fear to like what you like because another person dislikes it. So far, the willful man who says that Might is Right is a true man, and rational; yet he would be mindless in the highest degree if he meant that all initiatives are equally fortunate. He may always do as he likes, but he will seldom get what he wants. He will prove himself a fool, in little things and in great, if he persistently pursues what Circumstances deny him. Circumstances are indeed changeable and may be rendered more favourable by a man's own action; but to that extent his action was well adapted to Circumstances, and rational. In order, however, to render the whole government of a soul or of a nation rational, it would be necessary to select, from all the natural impulses that presented themselves, such only as at each moment conspired with Circumstances; and this would require perfect knowledge or magic sympathy reporting, at each step, the whole complexity and momentum of the universe.

Rightness, then, in action or opinion, in so far as it depends on sagacious conformity with Circumstances, can never be complete in any case, nor can it be summed up adequately in any maxim, since Circumstances are variable. But rules of thumb can be accepted as rational in spirit, when they indicate the prevalent conditions in the immediate sphere of the action or opinion concerned; as for instance the maxim, "Do to others as you would be done by," is rational in spirit, although in the concrete not all men like to be treated in the same way, nor do any class of men wish to be treated in the exact way that would actually be best for them, or best for their neighbours; and this last is probably the motive behind the maxim adopted; for if you treat people as they like to be treated they will become more friendly and useful *to you*. Other people figure in such a rational policy as an element in Circumstances not, at least rationally or calculably, as centres of imagined life on their own account.

This last observation applies unexpectedly to the rationality of conduct for one's own good. To transcendental spirit, speaking for the posture of living Will at any moment, a man's character, his past attachments and future needs, form part of that imposed world which confronts it so irrationally. All other movements, rooted in the same psyche as the spirit, but latent for the moment, seem alien Circumstances, to be discovered, explored, and transcended if possible. They fill an inner circle of Circumstances with which reason must reckon, if it hopes to direct action. And this inner ring of neighbours is more limited and familiar than the great ring called the world, but impossible to escape and hard to modify: whereas a competent man, sure of himself, can often escape from the social and topographical world that he first drops into. But to change the character of one's own psyche is, in the direction of origins and memory, impossible, and in the direction of conduct and belief, terribly difficult.

Thus, unless Circumstances are adequately known, action and

opinion cannot be rationally justified in the world; and unless the elements of the inner man are harmonised, action and sentiment cannot be rationalised in the Will and the conscience. Failing in either direction, no principle of action or judgment has any rational authority. For in the first case, you are contradicted and defeated by the facts; and in the second case, you are contradicted and defeated by the outraged cries of your own bosom.

## CHAPTER 6

### RATIONAL REFORMS

A FIRST condition for the rationality of a reform is that the pressure of extant interests should demand it. That the new habit should seem valuable to the imagination, when imagination is merely visionary, does not render that proposed habit politically desirable. For instance to have web feet and hands, with longer fingers and toes, might be better for swimming: but swimming is a rare and usually optional occupation for a human being, and greater proficiency in it would be a curse if it handicapped us in other directions. So with all fantastic reforms proposed by eccentric interests, and perhaps enforced by them.

This first prerequisite shows that all sound reforms must be massive generative movements and not thinly militant strains. I think that many animals and many human societies are burdened with distracting organs and distracting gifts. They have undertaken too many incompatible things at once and they are condemned to be for ever ugly and unhappy.

A reform, then, to be rational, should be *needed*.

But many reforms, in education for instance, are notoriously needed, because people are given tasks, like political votes, for which they are woefully unprepared; and yet to give them the necessary education is impossible, and to withdraw the vote from them, now that they have it, might not even if feasible produce a better order of society. Perhaps the incompetencies and delusions of ignorant voters may balance one another, while the mere possession of a vote tends to secure a general acquiescence and peace in the body politic. For a proposed reform to be rational, then, the state of society should be such that the alien branch grafted upon it may take root, and may prove self-consolidating and innocent. It must be a reform not only demanded by the present, but organically *acceptable for the future*.

This second condition for rationality in reforms is often insisted on by enthusiasts to the exclusion of the first. The reform will work, they say, because the whole world will be reformed so as to like it; no need, therefore, that the world should demand or should like it now. It *ought* to demand and to like it, and we must change and reform it until it does. But reformers of this mind are not reformers; they are revolutionaries. They don't wish to improve the existing order, or bring it to its natural perfection. They wish to destroy it, and to establish another order, after their own particular plan. No doubt their plan will be the reproduction of something once actual or suggested by something once actual to their fancy, which is itself a part of the current world; an element congruous with the generative order of nature will therefore be found in their endeavours. But it may be an insignificant, eccentric, short-lived caprice, contrary to the general and fundamental movement of history; and their reform, if they can carry it out at all, will be a false step, a waste of effort, an impediment to the easy attainment of greater and more fruitful developments.

In modern times the use of the words "reform" and "revolution" has often been misleading. The French Revolution was a real revolution; but the English "Revolution" of 1688 and the American Revolution were essentially reforms: they respected and liberated the previous generative order of life and of institutions in those countries. The movement called *par excellence* the Reformation, however, was not a reform but an insurrection, a fundamental revolution and break with a still vital past. It aimed at reversing the first principles of traditional authority. Logically and politically nothing could have been more militant, since a direct appeal was allowed to primal Will, in each individual, nation, or government, to decide every issue. Historically and emotionally, however, an appeal was made from one authority to another, from the Pope to the Prince, from the Church to the Bible, and ultimately from the Bible to science, to the conscience, or to the heart. Only in extremities, or after centuries of dilapidation, did the free spirit perceive that it was denying all authority.[1]

Yet in spite of historical criticism and subjective philosophy, the shell of Christian Orthodoxy still holds, at least nominally; for there is more conservative force in institutions than in sentiment. More than half of Europe had resisted the religious revolution, while in the Protestant countries a halt had been made at different points in different places, the quarrel seldom reaching any radical position, but always taking some accidental interest or tenet for an axiom. Even philosophy in Germany or opulence in England never conceived itself to be anti-Christian, or really began a reconstruction on solid ground.

In this so-called Reformation both the attack and the resistance were strengthened and confused by a great normal genuine reform that was going on at the same time, called the Renaissance; but I think it more truly designated by the term afterwards given in Germany to one of the later phases of it, namely, the Enlightenment. It was neither a rebirth of classic Antiquity (something impossible) nor a stupid doctrinaire attempt to revive it; something that occurred only in the age of the French Revolution. The Italian enlightenment was an enthusiastic rediscovery of the human greatness and wisdom of Greece and Rome; not a foreign civilisation but a legitimate parent of Greek and Latin Christendom. Tradition is necessarily syncretic and fails to distinguish the heteroclite elements, originally incompatible, which it has transmuted in merging them into its own constitution; so that as now represented, or held in solution, these elements no longer possess their native quality

---

[1] This view is boldly maintained by a Scottish Member of Parliament who cannot be suspected of Catholic breeding. "The Renaissance," he writes, "was achieved at the expense of the old rigid ascetic monotheistic dogma, with the cognizance of Rome; and we look back to it to-day as one of the great creative periods in the cycle of history. The Reformation was characterised by a revival of the 'neat' semitic doctrine at the expense of culture and civilisation, and was a bloody retrogression, not incomparable with that which has occurred during the past two decades. . . . The new Protestant Churches ranged themselves uncompromisingly behind the rising tide of virulent nationalism. . . . [Abuses in the old Church] could and should have been eradicated, or at least mitigated, by patient reform from within and not by secession, insensate destruction, slaughter, hatred. . . . By the end of the Thirty Years War the condition of Europe was no less desperate than it is to-day." Robert Boothby, *I Fight to Live*, Victor Gollancz, Ltd., London, 1947, p. 412.

and force. The moral rediscovery of the ancients was greatly aided, both materially and ideally, by the commercial expansion of the Italian maritime cities, and their close contact with Byzantium and the Levant; and it was politically and scientifically buttressed later by the discovery of America, and the communication opened with India, China, and Japan. An inkling of the true character of the cosmos dawned upon the Christian mind; and more slowly, more stealthily, an inkling of the true character of human history and of Christianity itself was bound to permeate philosophy.

This development, by enlarged contacts, critical study, and experimental investigations, was, or was capable of becoming, a true enlightenment. It was guided by no hatred or prejudice or local willfulness; it was lively, but not militant; and in disclosing the relativity of traditional knowledge, it would, if fairly pursued, disclose also the relative rightness and human justification of traditional institutions when Circumstances have imposed them and not some overweening conceit in defiance of Circumstances.

Enlightenment does not tend to destroy institutions or philosophies before they dissolve themselves. It may destroy some illusions in society as it does in the philosophers: but, in both, the illusions of vanity are only too tenacious. Cynical positivists are supposed to advocate the teaching of old myths to the people in order to comfort them; but I think the people, if left free, will invent or embrace comforting new myths enough of their own accord. It is never the enlightened who break images, abolish monasteries, or turn churches into cinemas; it is only some rival victim of illusion or of ambition or of avarice. The mere existence of enlightenment softens the fury of contending sects. If enlightenment extended to politics, it would soften the fury of parties, without abolishing them, since there are natural interests that parties are thought to serve. Enlightenment is more dangerous to fanatics of all sorts, and more hated by them, than are other fanatics. So during the Reformation the various wild spirits let loose could not rest unless they were absolutely sure (and radically mistaken) about something precious, beginning with the Bible.

In modern times rational reform has been the express ideal of liberal circles: abuses were to be abated, ignorance was to be dispelled, comfort and leisure were to be largely diffused, and national feuds were to be abolished by the arbitration of all claims. All opinions, especially in religion, were to be freely expressed. Ventilation of itself would disinfect them, and produce a practical unanimity in spite of unimportant differences in cult or in dogma. So in politics, discussion would explain and conciliate all differences, and compromise would render all actions complementary and compatible, each in its own measure and sphere. In a word, all human quarrels turned upon *vain objects*. All real interests were harmonious.

What interests could these be that liberal opinion regarded as harmonious? I think they may be reduced to two: the interest in material comfort, and the interest in moral liberty. Equality and, later, democracy have been nominal battle-cries of liberalism; but liberals have never really desired such things. Real equality is incompatible with that private wealth and that moral liberty which were at bottom the aspiration of this school. Moral liberty invites diversity, and presupposes it. Why should we be incited to differ if we all in fact and by nature agreed? And we do agree in fact and by nature in wishing to be comfortable and free; while we profoundly differ by nature and in fact as to what we are able to do, or would wish to do, with our comfort and freedom. We are different from one another; we wish to grow more different; and for that reason, to be truly ourselves, we passionately demand freedom.

The age of liberalism, the second half of the nineteenth century, succeeded in describing this natural diversity of life, zoological, historical, and moral; but it failed sadly in universalising comfort, and spreading through all nations an individual moral liberty. It had reckoned without its host. It had enabled mankind to grow far more numerous and more exacting in its standard of living; it had multiplied instruments for saving time and labour; but paradoxically had rendered life more hurried than ever before and labour more monotonous and in itself less rewarding. The people had been freed politically and nominally by being given the vote, and enslaved economically in being herded in droves under anonymous employers and self-imposing labour leaders. Meantime the liberal rich, who had expected to grow richer and did so when individually enterprising, became poorer and idler as a class, and more obviously withdrawn from the aristocratic leisure, sports, and benevolent social and intellectual leadership which they had supposed themselves fitted for. Nothing was rationalised by the liberal regime except the mechanism of production. Society meantime had been unhinged, and rendered desperate, and governments had been either incapacitated by intellectual impotence or turned into party tyrannies.

The same nominal humanitarianism, inwardly contradicted by a militant hatred towards almost all human institutions and affections, has descended from the wealth-loving liberals to the poverty-hating communists. The moral inspiration of communism is brotherly, pacifist, ascetic, and saintly. Christianity was originally communistic, and all the religious Orders continue to be so in their internal economy and discipline. It is built on tenderness, on indifference to fortune and to the world, on readiness for sacrifice, on life in the spirit. It cannot be militant. But what is now called communism is more than militant, more than a doctrine and a party bent on universal domination; it is a conspiracy. It is ferociously egotistical, and claims absolute authority for the primal Will of a particular class, or rather of a group of conspirators professing to be the leaders of that class. This class, far from embracing all mankind, does not include all the poor, nor the fundamental rural population that traditonally till the soil and live on its products, but enlists only the uprooted and disinherited proletariat crowded into modern industrial towns, with the politically inspired unions of sailors, miners, and railwaymen. Thus the authority of the "Communist Party" usurped without previous delegation, like the authority of conquerors and bandits, proclaims itself to be absolute and to extend prophetically over all mankind. And whose interests meantime does it serve? At bottom only the imaginary interests of a future society, unanimous and (like the Prussians of Hegel) perfectly free because perfectly disciplined to will nothing but what the State wills for them.

Meantime, in order to clear the ground for that ideal plenty in peace, war must devour millions of the faithful communists themselves, as well as millions of their surprised and unconverted fellow creatures; there must be slaughter of enemies, forced migrations of whole peoples, disappearance of institutions, civic and religious; destruction of all traditions. Such purgations in theory express the zeal of heaven-sent leaders for the redemption of the people. The methods may seem harsh; but they are the more merciful for being rapid and radical. How should strife and hatred and discontent ever cease until all mankind are unanimous in deciding which of them shall be allowed to live and which of them shall be exterminated?

In such a conspiracy there is the same intrepid consistency or internal rationality as in any theocracy. Paradise when it comes may perhaps cause the blessed to forget the price that many a previous generation has paid for their happiness; those generations after all were not capable of happiness, and by abolishing them, root and branch, a rational and unanimous society has been made possible for ever. Let us therefore make haste to obey the prophets and to exterminate the heathen. By dialectical necessity only the unanimously happy will have survived.

Both reform and reason would thus be banished from the scene, and eclipsed by faith and by prescribed action. That the undertaking is not only horrible in its methods but vain in its promise would become evident if the order of genesis in nature and the function of reason in human life were considered soberly, and not misread to feed the fires of gregarious passion.

# CHAPTER 7

## RIVAL SEATS OF AUTHORITY

AUTHORITY in classic antiquity was attributed to the natural institutions of the family and the tribe. Inheritance gave to the head of each household the right to his home lands, his cattle, and his slaves, a right sanctioned by the cult of traditonal deities, agricultural, civic, and domestic. These landlords and their sons were the free citizens of the fortified market-town in the midst of their estates. The whole formed a compact territory, closely bounded by other States, or extending more vaguely, with more questionable rights of possession, over the inland mountains and moors, or the islands visible beyond the little port. The fundamental political duty and pride in such a domestic society was to perfect and defend it, that it might last for ever.

Yet though the number of estates and of citizen proprietors might be limited by law, it was inevitable in prosperous times that the number of younger sons and their children should overflow the prescribed bounds, and threaten to merge, materially and morally, with the floating population of merchants, artisans, and foreign immigrants that crowded the market-place. In Rome a certain largeness of vision and impulse to venture on complex and boundless undertakings led to the doubling of the patrician citizenship with another unlimited class of plebeians, citizens also and soldiers, eventually electing their own tribunes, to match the traditonal consuls; and at last it became impossible not to admit conquered nations and cities to the privileges of citizenship; not to mention the multitudes of foreign slaves and adventurers that ultimately formed the proletariat of Rome, which, together with the barbarians introduced into the armies, drowned ancient society in their flood and became the staple of Christian nations.

Greek cities for the most part had less elbow-room geographically and were less inclined or able to conquer one another, in spite of their continual neighbourly feuds. There was a religious, fabulous, and festive kinship among them, enveloping their political independence and rivalries, somewhat like the unity of quarrelling Christendom when Christendom was morally one. But the Greeks could not live loyally under a common government; the Athenian empire never took shape, and that of Alexander was parcelled out at his death. When the population of a Greek city outgrew its narrow limits, a colony was sent out beyond the sea, to form an exactly similar city; until the pressure of larger units on their borders, Macedon and Rome, at last overshadowed them all, putting an end at once to their quarrels, their expansion, and their liberty.

The ancients had tried to live as if the universe were a farm and man the farmer. But the universe is inhuman; even mankind is too numerous, too various, and too unteachable to suffer anything reasonable, in politics, in manners, or in speculation, to subsist in peace. The classical city-state could not long practice only human arts or nurse only human convictions. Man needs to remember that he is also a beast and to discover that he is also a spirit.

Since those days exploration has disclosed the extent and variety of the political and economic forces with which rational policy anywhere would have to count; and a better equipped natural science has disclosed the nature of the cosmos and of its natural history quite sufficiently to dispel ancient illusions about the status there of mankind and of the human mind. Nevertheless these illusions

# RIVAL SEATS OF AUTHORITY

have not wholly disappeared, and a rational policy has nowhere taken root. The authority of facts has been verbally admitted by some philosophers, who often jeopardise their own authority by their blindness to the vital and imaginative nature of man; but this vital and imaginative human nature, which was itself initially blind, has continued to rule society. The verbal acknowledgment of an immeasurable universe, both in space and time, engulfing mankind in its fertile indifference, far from inspiring modesty and homely wisdom, has filled the industrial and political world with self-complacency at its dangerous ability to control and exploit matter and even to remodel human nature; this because remarkable new arts, in mechanics and medicine, could now be practiced with dazzling immediate success. What other ruins and other plagues these developments may bring does not concern the vital Will. Nor does pictorial knowledge of the variety of civilisations that have flourished or now flourish in the world, with their mutually incomprehensible sentiments and tastes, give any pause at all to political dogmatism and conceit, but the fact that something hostile to one's own policy may be embraced by other nations or religions only serves to kindle the more fiercely in each camp the *ignis fatuus* of its rightness and universal authority. Even professional philosophy often stimulates this folly by building an ideal mirage of the universe, and substituting it for the material one in which all these developments are found to take place and to carry with them the fate of nations and of their boasts.

The result is that to-day, after the general war of 1939–1945, we see nations with Western equipment, material and political, driving one another from their lands, imprisoning multitudes in camps, mines, and workshops, forcing them to serve foreign interests and indoctrinating them in foreign principles; for only by extirpating all other ways of thinking and living does each party propose to secure universal peace and unanimity under its own domination.

The migrations of the barbarians were carried on with the same justification in need or in ambition. To-day, the earth being pre-empted, we see instead an insurrection from below of parties or classes that feel, or are persuaded by their leaders to believe, that fate has been unjust to them.

Such local or partisan rebellion possesses, at least momentarily, the initial authority of primal Will. Were this wanting, no knowledge of Circumstances could have any moral force, since nothing that could happen would be relevant to any need or desire. But primal Will is utterly ignorant. Its normal adaptation to possible achievement, which might seem prophetic wisdom, hangs on the fact that animal organisms are reproductions of organisms previously existing. The reproduction cannot help showing the dispositions which had enabled the parents to live. Yet as reproduction is never perfect, and the environment may be modified too, there remains a broad margin in which the Will may display its primordial blindness. Its initial vital authority therefore continues to be entirely subjective and irrational.

When reason dawns it does not destroy the initial power of this irrational Will, which indeed reason comes to serve, but to serve it when enlightened by a gradually extended knowledge of Circumstances and of the radical contingency and endless contradictions of primal Will itself. At first this enlightenment touches only the means and methods that Circumstances impose for giving that Will satisfaction. The Will might seem, therefore, not to be modified in itself, but only in its policy. Attention to conditions and to dangers, however, imposes constant checks and discerns by-paths for the Will to follow; so that without meaning to repent, it learns to withstand its inopportune impulses, and to acquire a certain plasticity; for by-paths may have their charm, and in any case teach new lessons which unwittingly deflect the course of Will from within. Enlightenment sinks in this way into the psyche. Often attention given to Circumstances becomes pure curiosity (which children and idlers show) or dramatic appreciation of the objective order of events. Reason then begins to live freely, for its own sake; but it can hardly remain pure reason, being the keenest faculty of an impassioned psyche. The alien realities observed begin to be loved, and the subjective native authority of Will begins to be challenged by sympathy, by self-depreciation, perhaps by shame. Ultimately a vivid realisation of Circumstances and of Destiny may even rebuke Will altogether, little suspecting that this impulse to rebuke nature is itself a product of nature; and passion may be condemned for being irrational, as if the *love* of reason were not, in its pugnacity and its exclusiveness, an instance of unreason. The contradictions of Will in its vital and social manifestations may be further condemned as criminal, because they strive to destroy one another. All Will ends by thus seeming both vain and wicked; as if the conscience that so judges were not a militant passion, explicable biologically, but rationally groundless and self-annulling.

Fact or Power, taken absolutely, contain no authority. Authority is a relation; and it accrues to a fact, a power, or an idea when any one of these is found to confront, or inwardly to control, the satisfaction of primal Will. The rationality of such an acknowledgment of authority depends on the reality of this alleged confronting power or mysterious control; and in the absence of genuine science and sharp criticism, imagination, custom, and superstition naturally play a leading part in the attribution of authority. Yet the errors involved are intellectual rather than moral. The great moral error is not to admit authority at all. In so far as Circumstances are truly conceived, in their relation to the life of the psyche, and the real demands and possibilities of that psyche are fairly recognised, authority is rationally placed. And this respect due to authority is well expressed by attributing it simply to the will of God; for God is normally conceived to be the power governing the universe of Circumstances, and at the same time is felt to be the secret fountain of all true virtue and joy within the soul. To place honour or conscience in the seat of authority, however, is merely a moralised echo of the blind Will. The question would then be whether this blind *feeling* of authority in some rule or duty is justified by Circumstances and by the total ultimate capacities of the psyche concerned. It is the actual environing facts, by that which Kant called heteronomy, that exercise authority; but they exercise it only because a particular psyche loves a good which they alone render attainable. Allegiance can be rationally imposed only on a heart that is vitally autonomous.

# CHAPTER 8

## UTILITY OF GOVERNMENT

It is more natural to say that a horse is useful to his rider than that the rider is useful to his horse; yet with a strange egotism, peoples ridden by governments talk of the uses the government may have for them rather than of the uses they have for their government. We have just seen how governments may indeed be useful even when moved only by the crudest self-interest; as horse-breeders and trainers are useful to horses, which they breed scientifically and keep fit and well-fed. Some romantic person might here suggest that to be tamed is to be degraded, that the wild ass is infinitely superior to the market donkey, and that the mustang leads a happier life than the hunter or the war-horse. If any polite admirer of barbarism sincerely holds this view, he may not be easy to refute; but he may be invited to retire unmolested into the wilderness he loves. He will probably not be happy there for long, because shelter and society under a government are a relief, and become a necessity, to anyone whose vital liberty tends to grow rational.

The simile of horses and riders may seem inapplicable to politics since in this case both horse and rider belong to the same species, and there is no such diversity of endowment between the governed and the governing as between the strength and speed of horses, and the agility of man, with his ingenuity in making halters, bits, whips, and spurs. No: there is not among men any such physical diversity; but it is within this human sphere that human capacity branches into endless moral diversity, and the inventions, virtues, and thoughts of some become the guide, the defence, the prison, or the death of others.

Perhaps if all men had been born similar in capacity, as they are born similar in helplessness, government would never have arisen among them. They might have remained like other mammals partly gregarious, and partly segregated at the breeding season. The development of mankind, however, has been diversified; and when obviously different tribes and races, speaking radically distinct languages, became rivals for ranging over the same good territory, it was inevitable that the stronger, better disciplined, and more militant should press hard upon the more peaceful and more thinly scattered. If these could not develop an adequate defence nothing remained for them except servitude or extinction. Migration, as appeared in the colonising of North America, was only a source of greater weakness in the natives who withdrew and of greater strength in the strangers who took possession.

From the point of view of a subject people the chief benefit hoped for, if not found, in possessing a strong government was a modicum of protection. A leader or a band that had become master over them might prove victorious over their other enemies, and might secure a temporary peace both from raiding strangers and from violence at home. For this boon the people must be content to pay tribute, in supplies and in labour, and on occasion, however, clumsily and unwillingly, to serve in the government's army.

Meantime there is something else secured by a settled and authoritative government: a moral peace unknown both to the wild man and to the emancipated soul. Even in the jungle, where savage life seems to the traveller so poor and monotonous, the insecure spirit, in its solitude and incoherence, suffers from waking dreams, notions, and fixations, which make existence an incubus, when it is not a mad hunt or a digestive torpor. A recognised public authority, a chieftain, or a tradition vested in priests or elders, diffuses in society a moral peace, a refuge from vain sorrows and vain doubts and vain family quarrels. This authority is religious rather than political, but religion would only be another problem, another enemy, if it were not established by custom and not sanctioned by superstitious awe and a sense of invisible but unavoidable perils. Where such an established authority fails, moral society is dissolved; so that the autocratic voice of religion, echoing from the night of time, and supported by the daily suasion of a living society, is needed to save that society from moral anarchy and from political sedition.

It is not, I think, against political governments that the free soul protests with the greatest force and conviction. There were worse and less explicable constraints imposed by animal instincts and passions that had to be heeded in order that mankind should exist at all. What dangers, what battles, what obligations had to be faced and accepted by the wild solitary soul in obeying the summons of sexual, parental, and gregarious impulses! When those seasons of mad adventure have passed, with what a mingling of epic wonder and sage horror would not an aged eagle or an aged bull remember his past! It is the contrary native compulsions and revenges of life at this first stage that form the substance of Greek tragedy: crimes of wild will against the bonds of custom and blood, which provoked counter-crimes against those very bonds, and brought madness and death to the individual heroes, while providentially establishing political order in the world. Rebellions against this order when established can never be so radical or so tragic. Nature has gradually compelled the Will to organise and limit its impulses. The anarchic hero is exterminated; the plodding citizen survives.

The pressure that government exerts on an individual who is tolerably tame, though it is more pervasive, is less felt and seems less brutal than that which nature and other wild men exerted on him in the jungle. Here lies the first utility of governments. It solves quietly the problems that beset primitive life without ever being solved. Precarious hunting yields to much less precarious agriculture; and the quarrels that would have ended in murder and hereditary feuds are solved by relieving both sides of a constant fear of violence. In so far as people love to be quiet or to practice liberal arts, this relief seems to them a clear blessing.

Yet peace, though it is a prerequisite for the birth and the pure growth of life, is not the initial object pursued by it. On the contrary, the first sign of life is initiative, or primal Will: a sudden spasmodic effort to exercise power, and see what happens. The act if unimpeded and its product if satisfying become the fixed objects, so far, of that Will; and it becomes thereby the mortal enemy of everything that might stop such exploits in the future. Budding life is weak, and it needs peace and a favourable soil to strengthen it; but when strong and well-knit, life becomes brave and even truculent. It declares war on all its enemies, without knowing who they may be: and if its immediate neighbours at first are by nature friendly to it, it flourishes confident and self-satisfied. If a pure vegetative soul of this kind could think, it would say that it loved only the good, and had nothing to fear; which morally is true enough; since death overtakes it before it understands anything.

Primal Will or blind initiative of this kind remains fundamental for the organism in all its animal phases; so that a man, beneath his intelligent perceptions and arts, retains a pervasive blind courage and absolute willfulness. This private economy of the organic psyche is deeper than all that it has been bent to concede to circumstances; and it exercises a pervasive pull over the moral incrustations that in arming the Will for action oppress its primal liberty. Thus, like the hidden fires of a volcano, ignorant energy, convinced of its own rightness, will burst spasmodically into civil and rational life. In modern philosophy it has been largely dominant, and is called Egotism.

This is the radical source of hostility to all alien forces and

## UTILITY OF GOVERNMENT

authorities, and especially in politics to the government, of whatever kind or party it may be. It is also the source of crime against individuals by other individuals whom the government arrests and imprisons; and sometimes it causes the most ardent haters of government to appeal to government against the agents of the government itself. This theme fills the pages of legend and history, where we find passionate appeals against official decrees or unjust sentences of some local judge that brought indignant vassals and weeping women to the foot of the throne; and the chief function of monarchs, when they were good and beloved by the people, seemed to be to redress the wrongs done by their own governments. It is true that these subordinate officers were often closer to the people, with more ancient and indispensable functions to perform in society than had the suzerain himself; and we might almost liken a government to a Tower of Babel, in which every platform is raised in the hope of correcting the mischief done by the structure on which it rests. So all modern parties and ideologies savour of protestation, hatred, and rebellion against government as it exists. And as each reforming party pushes its way, by denunciation, to power and by denunciation is presently destroyed, a prodigiously complex legislation and organisation, every part inspired by a grievance, imprisons vital liberty and condemns it to perpetual forced labour.

This perpetuity of civil war, crime, conspiracy, and latent insurrection does not contradict the initial need of government and its continued utility. It was needed in the first nest or hut in which prehistoric man reared his family and it remains natural and indispensable at every stage of social and industrial complication. So, as life has grown more diversified, it has brought more difficulties and predicaments, or rather it has multiplied and varied the occasions on which the eternal difficulty and predicament of existence confronts the living individual. The arts are simply the methods by which the psyche meets these challenges and, if it survives, accepts them. Acceptance is much easier for the blind Will-to-live than it would be to an enlightened will that knew the past and the future. To a philosopher watching the storm the waves may seem mountain-high, and endless; for although this storm will pass, no end of others will follow. But to the labouring ship or life-boat or shipwrecked passenger with his life-belt, only one wave at a time, one blast, or one ducking threatens to be fatal. The crisis at each moment is unavoidable; it may be surmounted; in any case, it will solve itself. What is beyond, to the Will, is out of sight; so is what went before. Action first casts the die or cuts the knot. Then reason writes the commentary.

In a world of miscellaneous interests, control by a government and absence of such control may be equally useful in different directions. Absence of control remains the ideal of enterprise in its active phase; but control becomes useful in preserving the fruits of enterprise. Free trade may be useful for commerce and protection for industry. An aristocratic domination, in its austere phase, may exalt the arts by demanding strict styles and grand monuments, and in its luxurious phase it may patronise decorative ingenuity and variety. But it is not in anticipation of such incidental and contrary fruits that any form of government arises or endures; the demands of society must take shape spontaneously, as do the primary needs of life; and government or traditional order, which is one of these primary needs, will then prove useful or thwarting to each of the other interests alive in its world, without having taken them for its object or drawing from them its proper authority and power. Government is only one force among many social and historical forces. They interact, affecting and transforming one another; and it is idle to expect government to be favourable to arbitrary interests that have not been among the social habits and material conditions that gave it birth. These, indeed, meant it to be useful and will become its enemies if, on the contrary, they suffer from its interference; but the effects of government, like the "created interests" that buttress any abuse or delusion, will not prove that it was useful if by creating those morbid interests it ruins its normal adherents and destroys itself.

## CHAPTER 9

### THE IRONY OF GOVERNMENT

NATURE, in fashioning and animating any specific animal, prepares it for a special round of actions, such as, at once or by stages, its organs and impulses will tend to perform. Nature thus supplies that creature with an innate program of life, abstract and unconscious,

## THE IRONY OF GOVERNMENT

but apt to become decidedly concrete whenever a suitable opportunity offers. And such an opportunity, in general, must be generously provided: for nobody would have eyes if light did not often flood the earth and were not usefully reflected from objects according to their position and physical texture; nor would sexual aptitudes and passion persist in us if our ancestors, for endless generations, had not possessed them to good purpose. Nevertheless, rain does not always fall when the grass thirsts for it; and Nature has not prearranged an exact distribution of opportunities to meet the ripe moments of the Will, or of succor to prevent its extinction.

In other words, the exuberant radiation of matter into every possible trope, species, and novelty prevents any exact harmony from ever being established among its endeavours. Every form of Will realised insists on maintaining its ascendency and of extending it if possible; it cannot succeed in this perfectly, but it clings to what it can achieve without any mercy for the defeats which it may be inflicting on its competitors.

A fable may perhaps exhibit this predicament better than an argument.

Imagine a model game-keeper guarding the partridges in a park. The barbed wire round their special preserves will always be in good order; live wires and traps will intercept all poachers, stray dogs, and foxes in their wicked incursions, nor will there be any overcrowding or too numerous bereavements in the partridge family itself. Yet all these undoubted benefits begin to seem ambiguous when the shooting season approaches. Three parties are formed among the partridges; the Conservative Party, composed chiefly of parents and old residents, who aver that shooting has always prevailed in this world, and that before there were barbed wires and keepers it was far worse and went on all the year round. The radicals or the Republican Party, on the contrary, cried sharply that they were all victims of tyranny, game fattened for the slaughter, and that they were preparing to peck the keeper's eyes out, and fly for freedom into the woods. A third or Liberal Party pointed out that a distinction should be made. The keeper was a good man; the real tyrant, who kept them only to shoot and eat them, was the landlord. They must wait until the keeper and his friends had made a revolution and expelled the landlord, so that henceforth partridges and good men would possess the land together in perfect friendship.

Rumours of these dissensions reached the landlord at the Manse, and one fresh dewy morning after a hearty breakfast he came down, in gaiters and a sporting jacket and broad-brimmed hat, but with only a heavy stick in his hand, to have a word with those silly birds.

"What is this," he said gruffly, but with a humorous undertone, as if he brought something good for them hidden in his pocket, "what is this that I hear you are cawing and croaking and crowing among yourselves about politics? Do you say that the keeper is a friend of yours, because he keeps off the poachers, but that I, who give you board and lodging gratis all the year round, am your enemy, because I only do it in order to shoot you and eat you up at the end? What a mistake! You talk about the end, when none of us can know what it will be, and do not consider the beginning, which is the source of everything and perfectly well known. How can I be your enemy, when but for me, and my love of partridges, you never would have existed? Had I not bought this land, which was an unfenced waste moor, enclosed it, cleared away all that could be a nuisance to partridges and planted these lovely thickets and delicious coverts and bought two or three pairs of prize birds, your ancestors, and let them multiply here and feed for years unmolested on the fat of the land, where would you all be to-day? Nowhere! And when you were becoming too numerous, and quarrelled among yourselves, was it not for your good that a few, not all, of you should meet a sudden and painless death, and that just at the season when perhaps old age and certainly the desolate winter was upon you? And were you not always especially protected and fed at the breeding season, about which you rightly care so much? Indeed, that is a point in which you seem to approach the just feelings of a Christian and an Englishman. Whom should you love and honour more than one who has been the cause of your existence, and has heaped on you all the blessings of this life, which for all of us at best must be short and somewhat chequered? If having considered all these things, you still call me a tyrant, I must say, I am *sorry for you!* Before long you will be caught blaspheming against your Creator."

Without venturing to approve or condemn the order of nature on moral grounds (which I think would be impertinent) I seem to see a logical flaw in the sportsman's apology. Nobody can ask for existence before he has it; he therefore need not regard it

# THE IRONY OF GOVERNMENT

*a priori* as a favour. No doubt, existence compels him to wish to keep it, because it is essentially a propulsive movement, but this wish in itself is so far from a good that the most venerable of philosophies, the Indian, regards it as the source of all evil. The landlord breeds his partridges for his own use and pleasure; in respect to them he is a foreign militant power exercising a domination partly protective and partly fatal, as do many civilised governments over their possessions. The hearty sportsman's interest in this affair illustrates the intrinsic value that management may have as an art, in both breeding and shooting and then in eating the birds. The primitive impulse to hunt for food has, in the country gentleman, been almost lost in the sport of shooting and the vanity of supplying a good morsel for his table or for his friends.

Advantages of this kind, which an autocrat may secure by the exercise of his power, are not to be counted among the strictly political merits of a government; they are only its sweets. The public could hardly be expected to consider them benefits conferred on themselves. Yet sports are surely a benefit to mankind, that needs to play and to be entertained by spectacles; and even partridges are an asset to the community, not only to be shot and eaten by the few, but to introduce a little festive variety for those who pluck, cook, and serve hem. How far the partridges, if they knew how useful they are in these ways, would be reconciled to their fate, or would die happy thinking how superior their life in a private preserve had been to that of uncivilised birds, and how much nobler is a dish of partridges than a boiled fowl from a barnyard, I cannot tell. But there is an unintended heroism woven into the texture of life which sometimes breaks out in morals, to the surprise of rationalists. For this vital heroism is not militant, like rationalistic politics, but obedient to spontaneous impulse, as in the other animals; only that man has outdone the sagacity of the others in finding rational means to irrational ends.

But this eager use of reason in incidental tasks sharpens and strengthens reason in its own methods and insights, until some day it becomes aware that, by thus rationalising and complicating the irrational, reason increases distraction for the spirit, and swells the intermittent burdens of life into a petrifying tyranny; so that in the end what reason can best do is to disinfect existence as far as possible of illusion, pride, and wanton militancy, and for the rest to accept the natural diversity and inconstancy of Will, only moderating its fury; as can be done by fostering, in due separation or harmony, all possible contrasting virtues, which never would hate one another morally if they never conflicted materially.

## CHAPTER 10

### CONFUSIONS ABOUT PROGRESS

VERY great evils are self-destructive: at last they destroy the beings that suffer them, and restore a relative peace. But why should something better always follow upon a moderately satisfactory state of affairs? In fact, something better does not always follow, but often something worse; and yet, in spite of history and experience, many believe in a Law of Progress. The future, they say, must always be better than the past because it has outgrown the past; and it will leap forward to a still better future. I think the secret of this strange belief is well expressed by Hegel in his doctrine that reduces the universe to Spirit in quest of freedom. In this view nothing is admitted to exist except this Absolute Spirit, which is human at one stage of its self-expression, but is essentially divine and unconditioned. Circumstances are here supposed to be simply the husks which Spirit has sloughed off in its progress. They litter the ground, but are of no importance, except as occasions for further advance; and every later stage of the world is necessarily better than the previous one, since the Spirit will find in it a more adequate embodiment and a wider freedom. It therefore matters very little how bad any state of the world may seem, or how good it may seem; for the only real value of it, in any case, will be to lead to a better state: better not because happier or less horrible—for tragedy is a noble thing—but simply because it is a stepping stone to something "higher." The eternal feminine is always beckoning us, and I suppose beckoning itself, towards a greater freedom.

What we shall do preesntly with this greater freedom we do not know. How should we, seeing it is a vacant freedom? Our whole heart and soul on this hypothesis are addressed to the future, and the future, in our minds, is necessarily empty. Singular doctrine of progress, that the present, so magnetic when it was the future, should always prove merely an incentive to escape into something else, and to turn itself into a portion of that dreadful past, from which, forever, we must flee.

But let me turn back from the outburst of militant Will that devised this philosophy, and that deceived the nineteenth century and blasted the twentieth, to the purer phases of Will on which it fed. Fundamental and most influential was Biblical prophecy: Jehovah guiding history for the salvation, chastisement, and ultimate glory of his Chosen People. This glory, though miraculously bestowed, was to be thoroughly earthly, temporal, and public. The godly man would be rich and long-lived and the People and their Law universally dominant.

The chastisement included in this providential plan proved severe; but far from discouraging the faithful, it led them, in the Prophets, to revise the notion of what allegiance to Jehovah implied: not merely ritual and legal obedience but righteousness, loving kindness, and spiritual exaltation. When this insight became dominant and dropped altogether the political and earthly reign of Jehovah, and on the contrary foretold a speedy destruction of this world and the beginning of a celestial, purely religious, life, Judaism became Christianity. Progress, according to this bi-mundane cosmology (for the goal was still to be a temporal and social existence of the elect with their risen bodies), meant conversion of mankind to militancy in the Church here and mystical ecstasy in the other world.

This ideal, however, was very imperfectly realised even in the most Christian nations. Besides the recalcitrancy of the natural man to an ascetic and militant regimen, Christendom was the heir of pagan civilisation; this tradition was revived in contact with the Saracens; and when paganism seemed to have invaded the ecclesiastical sphere as well as the arts, another tradition, the original Biblical one, was revived in its turn, in the name of Christianity itself. There was now to be progress, not only in luxury and learning but in individual moral liberty and in private direct inspiration from God. This was an equivocal demand, because individual sentiment and free criticism of authority would easily undermine not only the Christian transformation of Judaism but the original Biblical promises also.

So far the idea of progress in all its variations remains a strictly moral, humanistic idea. The question is to determine the means of reducing the evils and increasing the goods of human life, in each man, in a given society, or in all mankind. And this progress has a goal, an ideal condition to be approached even if it cannot be perfectly attained. So marked is this moral essence of progress as orthodoxy conceived it in the West that the goal of it was a wholly spiritual life in another world. But within and around this esoteric tradition there was always another conception, not moral but historical and political, the conception of genesis, of growth, of evolution; and for many minds the great vista, the great insight for the sage, was not a path of progress but a process of metamorphosis. And a purely scientific or theoretical mind might even come to despise moral aspiration, as simply instances of animal Will, and to see the only possible escape from evil in identifying the process of metamorphosis with the nature and the truth of things, in recognition of which the intellect triumphs, no matter how rudely all human wishes are brushed aside.

A poetic rendering of this tragic naturalism appears in Greek mythology. Here was a gifted race, in a happily parcelled territory open almost everywhere to an inland sea in a clement climate; the sympathy of nature with man could balance here the sympathy of man with nature, and allow him to leave remote and inhuman depths of reality decently veiled. Veiled, but neither denied nor misrepresented.

The early Greek philosophers, some of them still poets, could imagine the vast process of nature producing and dissolving all forms of life, without giving man any special privilege or any special blame, nor seeing in the transitory bloom of his arts any reason for despising their ingenuity and beauty or for not counting on their reappearance. This was the philosophy of the true philosophers; but those whom the folly or disaster of their cities had embittered—for the Greeks were nothing if not rhetorical politicians—became tragedians, emphasising the personal and local catastrophe in each career, as if that cancelled the charm of youth and the sweetness of life, so justly celebrated by the first great poets, whose epic or lyric sense for tragedy was no less sincere but more discreet.

Socrates had been stunned by the same tragedy of his country—very much as Europe is stunned to-day—and the refuge he took in the inner man gave the signal for the current of Greek philosophy to turn away from its honest naturalism and merge in the turbid but impetuous flood of supernatural revelations. But this was not to be at the flood for another four or five hundred years; and meantime the philosophers scattered into sects politically either archaistic, with Plato, or indifferent with the Cynics, Sceptics, and Epicureans, or with the Stoics and Neo-Pythagoreans intellectual or mystical worshippers of the rational order of the cosmos.

There is only one philosopher, Aristotle, who seems to me to have placed progress where it is at once morally real and physically possible. He did not call it progress, because he was not thinking of evils to be escaped, but of perfections to be achieved. Existence was perpetually addressed to exemplifying in time and through motion certain ideal models always present in the mind of God, and exerting a profound attraction on matter, where and when matter was prepared to respond to it. The ethereal substance of the heavenly bodies obeyed its model perfectly: their "progress" was a perpetual triumphal procession. Sublunary matter, on the contrary, tended to obey its various natural forms or models, but did so amid many conflicts and impediments. Mankind, in particular, had many times developed its appropriate arts and then lost them, through physical cataclysms or internecine conflicts. But human virtues and human forms of society had various natural models, according to differences of nature or of circumstances. Virtue, like health, has different shades according to race, sex, age, and personal endowment. In each phase of life and art a different perfection may be approached. None can be maintained unchanged, but like the different generations of one family, they may revert in different accidental ways to the same congenital virtues.

I recast this doctrine in my own words because it is my own conviction; and the moral terms in which Aristotle describes biological growth, while they reverse the natural order of genesis, must be restored if we are to regard that order as a progress. The flux of existence, taken absolutely, would be pure metamorphosis, no phase implying or promising any other and no beginning or end or continuation being assured. Evolution could appear within such a flux only if tropes, repeated cycles, and reproduction of similar runs (as in the generations of a family) would be observed in it. Then, if we personify the first phase of each repetition and think of it as a Will or demand, the rest becomes a fulfillment or realisation of that Will, and the movement involved in each case becomes a moral growth or progress. But where alterations in that process arise, no matter for what cause or by pure chance, the process ceases, to that extent, to fulfill any Will or demand latent in the first phase of it. The process has reverted to pure metamorphosis, as in the successive patterns in a kaleidoscope.

There is an internal contrariety, if not contradiction, in thinking of the whole process of cosmic existence as a progress. Aristotle himself and the Neo-Platonists did not think of it so. There were degrees of fullness or perfection in the attainment, by each kind of existent being, of its participation in divine glory; and when a soul passed from one of these stages to another it progressed or declined in its virtue. But these climbings or backslidings on Jacob's ladder were incidents only when seen temporally, from the relative and reversible point of view of other phases. For in the comprehensive glance of God, which all souls approached according to their enlightenment, all those incidents became fragments in one eternal mosaic, there all lights shone in harmony, each with its own colour and brightness.

Modern philosophers of history, like Hegel and Bergson, are not clear about the relations of time with eternity. As controversialists and critics they are advocates of the metaphysical reality of change and time. The terminal points or moments of a process are false abstractions from that process, which is real in so far only as it is on the wing. This is good literary psychology or introspection; we cannot fix a term without coming to it and placing it on a background which lends it its function. Progress would be the transit of life itself. But if so, what moral gain can there be between one phase of life and the next? Both are equally transitions between untenable stations.

In this quandary, the saving tradition of Biblical prophecy helps the sinking metaphysician. Time and change are intrinsic to this world; but this world is finite. All time is embosomed in eternity. Morally we are, in Saint Augustine, in the world of Aristotle and the Neo-Platonists; but physically, as a matter of experienced fact, God is only an abstraction from our living selves. The moral world has a goal, not temporal but ideal, attainable at moments by the Saints, but never attainable by the living universe, which must go on rolling for ever. There is infinite occasion—*la carrière ouverte aux talents*—for everyone in it, and the goal is not far off from any one of us. Our moral destiny (never finally rested in, but occasionally touched) is definite; defined for each of us by his own genius. It is, after all, as the ancients said, perfections after our own kind in our own time and place.

I think this was really the belief of Hegel, not that there was any progress *beyond* his own Germany and his own philosophy, but that an analogous success was always open to the strong in their special circumstances. The living world of perpetual mutation involved perpetual imperfection and conflict; of making many such worlds there was no end; and yet to become itself was the goal of each of them.

It appears, then, that flux or pure metamorphosis becomes evolution only where it falls into self-repeating tropes or cycles, where, as in a word, the first syllable or letter appears only when all the rest are already actively potential, so that any interruption defeats a propensity. And such an evolution becomes a moral progress when this propensity ceases to be purely automatic like the sprouting of a beard on a schoolboy's chin, but engages the general life of the psyche in its movement, as would winning a race or writing a prize essay. These performances, which may have involved a good deal of effort and anxiety, would have been accompanied by an intense consciousness of the object to be attained, not only during the process but long before and after. The purpose fixed and the permanent satisfaction felt in having realised it turn the steps in it into steps in a progress.

The same moral conditions determine progress in social and political enterprises, but the material conditions are different. Societies and nations are aggregates, not living organisms; and the moral fruits of any development there are not inherent in the social or political result itself but in the sentiments and effects produced by it in all the individuals affected. But the effects in such a case are dispersed and various. Victory in a war, for instance, the most indubitable of political successes in itself, may bring many troubles on the victors, not to speak of the vanquished; and parties losing office, grumbling or disabled soldiers, and disappointed or criticised officers, may see no progress, but only the seeds of ruin in the event. Nor can it be a census of opinions, contemporary or subsequent, that can determine whether any historical revolution is a progress or not. The standard and the information by which contemporaries judge are alike repudiated by historians who in turn are repudiated by the politicians of a later epoch. It is by their own party policy that politicians judge opponents, foreigners, the ancients, and all the possibilities of the future; and academic professors would not represent the mind of their age and country if they did not learnedly justify the principles of their governments and the opinions of their public. Nor are the voices of prophets crying in the wilderness better inspired or more unanimous.

Is there then no ascertained progress in history? Are we no better off than savages or gorillas? Not all other animals might envy us: but there are certain demands common to all living beings which it would be a progress for them to satisfy more fully. A greater satisfaction in finding food, for instance, would modify all the impulses of any creature; if these modifications in turn secured new satisfactions, that race, if not the original individual, might be said to have progressed. They would certainly think themselves better than their predecessors, if they were stronger; if they were weaker, they would also think themselves superior morally, and those others monstrous. We do not think ourselves worse than the elephant for being smaller and shorter lived.

I think it is not possible, impartially or rationally, to establish any moral progress in the forms of being. There are measurable degrees of complexity and of influence, which in animals may become positive control of the environment. And when such control becomes hereditary, it establishes for that race a common and cumulative progress in the same art.

It is perhaps only in transmissible arts that human progress can be maintained or recognised. But in developing themselves and developing human nature these arts shift their ground; and in proportion as the ground is shifted, and human nature itself is transformed, the criterion of progress ceases to be moral to become only physical, a question of increased complexity or bulk or power. We all feel at this time the moral ambiguity of mechanical progress. It seems to multiply opportunity, but it destroys the possibility of simple, rural, or independent life. It lavishes information, but it abolishes mastery except in trivial or mechanical proficiency. We learn many languages, but degrade our own. Our philosophy is highly critical and thinks itself enlightened, but it is a Babel of mutually unintelligible artificial tongues.

Institutions that men can retain (not everywhere the same) and that circumstances can allow to endure are the sole vehicle of possible progress. Since it is relative to temporary needs progress cannot last without losing gradually its moral identity; but the very impossibility of an absolute moral standard justifies the relative moral authority of vital Will, in its own sphere, wherever it arises. The contrary values that the same events may have for contrary interests does not obscure the exact value that each event may have for each of those interests. It is these interests, by their endless radiations, each from its own centre, that flood the universe with their tragic and comic lights, and turn it from a physical process into a variegated moral drama.

## CHAPTER 11

### PUBLIC OPINION

A SCRUPULOUS logician might insist that the phrase "public opinion" makes nonsense, since the public is not a person, has no brain, no consecutive memory, and cannot opine. It can only assemble and shout, and many shouts make a public demonstration; but many ballots do not make a public idea. And yet a public act may ensue which a possible idea might justify; and if the act excited a public interest which did not exist before, the possible idea might well become actual in the persons who had acquired that interest. A crowd or an electorate may vote for war, and thereby create a thousand commercial and moral interests in portions of the public; parties who will tend to embrace ideas that justify the interests so suddenly thrust upon them. Then each variety of interest will favour a different type of opinion: first, for instance, a common enthusiasm for war and confidence in victory (though none of the persons concerned may have originally desired that war or dreamt of its possibility). Later, perhaps, a common desire for peace may follow in order that one man may escape taxes, another bombs, another military service, and another the ignorant tumult of public passions.

Public opinion is therefore a most real thing, and often a dominant power; many individuals habitually and all individuals occasionally embrace opinions together, under a common provocation and expressed in the same words. This public opinion is a distinct psychological event in each person, with a different intensity, duration, and field of suggestion; and this seems public opinion to each only in the measure in which its special character in himself is not distinguished. Nothing is heeded except some public action, sentiment, or words in the midst of which that personal opinion arose, with a powerful sense of being backed or borne forward by an irresistible persuasion, at least momentarily unanimous. The force of such public opinion in the private mind comes in no way through argument or evidence; for even if some eloquent phrase or the report of some crucial fact has occasioned it in each person, its *public* force lies entirely in the social blast that carried it, with magic conviction, into many minds at once. If the argument or evidence that rationally justifies this conviction is considered separately, coolly, and reflectively, the opinion so revised becomes a purely private opinion, independent of the character and number of the people that may happen to agree with it. Only if the prevalence of that opinion is expressly made the ground for accepting it, as in the maxim *quod semper, quod ubique, quod ab omnibus,* does public opinion still govern the private mind; and we shall probably find on examination that the society so clothed with authority is strictly limited and congenial to the man who adheres to it, and contrary to the prevalent opinion of mankind at large and in most ages. Under criticism, such a trust in unanimity becomes a private preference; the man respects a public authority because that particular public authority teaches what he likes to believe.

The spell of unanimity can therefore be exercised by a small assembly, with all the emotional magic of profound, blessed, invincible agreement. Indeed, two persons are enough, when they agree, to defy emotionally all the edicts of earth and of heaven. It is finding the *alter ego* who thinks as I do that is the satisfying, the reassuring support for the misgivings of solitude. These misgivings are animal, not logical; and the logician can overcome them by repeatedly agreeing with himself.

Public opinion and "the public" itself are conceptual fictions; yet nature is full of compound bodies that count as units in physics as well as in politics. A constellation in the sky may be a mythical entity; but a bear and a crab on earth are concrete and vital agents. Even a snowball is a dynamic unit when it flies, well aimed, and hits the passer-by. Each snowflake was light and fragile, and floated through the air without apparent aim or momentum; but when a mischievous urchin has compressed it, together with a thousand others, they have become as hard and as tight as ice. So the vague notions and animosities of an irresolute individual may become compact fury in a crowd; and the words that some demagogue selects to fix that notion or to whet that animosity may turn, for a moment, into a sudden passion in a thousand minds. Is this passion then a public passion? Yes, politically, for the moment, that concourse is dominated by it, and asserts and perhaps enacts it with an intense outflow of free will. Nevertheless not one, except the orator, might ever have found those words to represent or to transform his feelings nor, without those imposed words, might any one of them have ever felt that irresistible and glorious passion.

All feelings, then, in their living actuality, are private feelings, and all passions private passions; but by animal sympathy and contagion, the *sense* of each single feeling or passion sweeping through a crowd may possess each member of that crowd. And such an experience, even if no overt action comes to turn it into a commitment, warms the whole heart and leaves a durable nucleus in the psyche for all further enthusiasms and opinions. Public opinion, for a politician or a journalist, may ultimately become the whole furniture of the private mind; that which everybody thinks, or that which the majority are likely to think before long, becomes his standard of solidity; solidity rather than truth, because public opinion having become the test of private opinion, there is no truth to be considered except the political trustworthiness of such opinions as the public entertains and esteems.

The individual, however, has a memory as the public has not; and civilisation implies records and institutions which, for the reflective, enlarge private memory into some knowledge of other times, and of other forms of public opinion. Current public opinion may therefore sink, for the critic, into a passing phenomenon, necssarily partial and possibly pathological. Private judgment here has its innings again; not through ignorant egotism but on the contrary through respect for a wider view and a better understanding of the causes of public opinion. Public opinion is inevitably vaguer, more variable, more impulsive than the opinion of such members of the public as are particularly well informed; and it is morally less responsible, less prudent, more animal than are the actions of any sane individual. For the reversion to reason and conscience from the intoxication of tribal passions is not confined to learned or exceptional minds. The most helpless of the shouting mob in the circus is capable of it on the way home. Suppose as the crowd thins, that a man finds himself alone with his mate, who has shouted hurrah as loudly as himself and nudged him to express how great a man the leading speaker was. The two, after stopping to light their pipes, might begin to question this or that phrase of the orator's, saying that they were not sure that they liked that. Perhaps he hadn't quite got their own idea. In this way the unanimous enthusiasm of that public at its height might conceivably not represent the sober opinion of a single one of those present, except that of the orator himself. And I am perhaps not doing justice to his eloquence. For the more extraordinary his eloquence was, the more likely it is that what he said had never been his real and final opinion before, but came to him from the depths in the heat of improvisation; and though probably, in that case, he would adopt and repeat it perpetually henceforth in his propaganda, it is not inconceivable that, in his waking meditations in the silence of night, he might say to himself that it was nonsense.

If this ever happened, public opinion would not, in that instance, represent the private opinion or sober judgment of a single one of those who had contributed to form, to swell, or to diffuse that public opinion.

## CHAPTER 12

### SPONTANEOUS DEMOCRACY

Democracy may arise in various ways. It may come to exist, unintended and unopposed, in the generative order of society, by a brotherly identity of impulse and interest, like that of crawling cubs in a litter, a concord which rivalry has not yet disturbed. So "leaves of grass," that sprout side by side without too much crowding, bend and sway like a unanimous people. What, indeed, can blades of grass do but grow all more or less in the same direction under the same influences? But animals also, though they have the power of locomotion and are intrinsically independent scouts, will sometimes compose a natural democracy, not dominated merely by the herd instinct, but having a common object in view. Shipwrecked sailors, for instance, in a boat, though there is likely to be some boatswain or some temperamental leader to seize the tiller and shout unauthorised orders, yet will not resign their private intention each to save his own life in his own way; and it is in this boat that each sees his best chance. Therefore any usurped authority over it will be instantly challenged, unless it coincides with the judgment of all. A democratic distribution of supplies will thus be enforced under the sharp and knowing eye of all those involuntary comrades; no unruly conduct will be allowed, and no course taken without the tacit consent of a clear majority.

Brotherly democracy also makes its appearance at certain moments in the lives of pioneers. There may be some semblance to blades of grass in their individual independence and apparent freedom from all ties, possessions, or prejudices. And there may be some semblance in their lot and in their meeting to a boatful of wrecked sailors. Yet nothing brotherly, no common memories of affections, appear in their respective ambitions; they are not met to help one another, but each is there to help himself and to help himself to the largest possible portion. This mate, who to-day may be an independent ally, tomorrow will be your rival. You will be good neighbours so long as it pays; but you make no vows of eternal friendship with any casual neighbour. You may find yourself shooting him the day after tomorrow.

There is a curious mixture, among adventurers, of good fellowship and bitter rivalry. The talk round a campfire must not be thought to reveal fundamental motives. A rough tramp may be sentimental; under fire he may be heroic; but he is out on business. He is on the make.

Such a vigilant, casual society, to become a political democracy, requires the absence or suppression of willful, ignorant, or frantic individuals who cannot feel the grave need of order and equality in a common plight. At close quarters in a ticklish predicament unanimity is imperative in action, no matter how absent it may be in thought. Tyranny, the tyranny of events that must be forestalled or if possible circumvented by human intelligence, will then be felt hanging over this company of political equals; and the moment land is reached or a sail sighted, the bottled wrath of all these mute captives will burst out in invective against one another and against heaven. I say against heaven, although some god may be verbally thanked for having saved them; for when the secret forces that govern events are felt close at hand but not closely distinguished, the sense of helplessness, of injustice, and resentment pierces them through all the veils of convention, and the radical nature of things is frankly blamed by those rebel wills for its cruelty.

Brotherly democracies of the spontaneous kind, idyllic or recovered in the extremities of fortune, exclude almost all the passions of passionate man; yet by their simplicity they please him in idea. Any moral or political utopia may be advocated in opposition to the special vices of one's own society; the difficulty lies in catching such a moral meteor and caging it in an earthly system of government. Yet this sometimes seems to occur. The more rural Swiss cantons, for instance, present the classic picture of democratic simplicity, comfort, and peace. Yet from that paradise the more adventurous spirits do not cease to escape to the towns and cities in the lower valleys, where the society is much like that of the rest of distracted Europe. There remains, to those who prosper in business or in the professions, the satisfaction of breathing the free air of their mountains and of escaping service in the foolish wars of the Great Powers.

Hence the contrast, notorious in the middle of the twentieth century, between a democracy formed by a concourse of adventurers migrating separately into a new and relatively empty world and a democracy of crowds, accustomed to troop in armies or in gangs of workingmen, like flocks of sheep scientifically guided by expert shepherds and their well-trained sheep-dogs.

Originally the American colonists breathed independence and individuality, religious and political, at the same time feeling confident of their vocation and ability to grow rich and to save their souls with none but divine guidance. Their zeal for democracy had a political root also in their Protestantism. They remembered the revolt of their kinsfolk in the old country against ecclesiastical and royal despotism, and against landlords; and this sense of ancient grievances was kept alive by daily defiance of all barriers that might block a man's way in his private enterprise, especially so long as experience proved that the more successful each man's enterprise was the more favourable paths it opened to the enterprise of others.

## SPONTANEOUS DEMOCRACY

The Russian democracy on the other hand has been dominated by conspirators, themselves perhaps dominated by ideologies. Personal ambition and apostolic zeal were inextricably blended in the leaders; and while they were not without a certain congenital or mystical sympathy with "the people," they remained essentially politicians, counting not so much on the loose lost orphans of society as on the organised working classes, that could be indoctrinated, trained, and mobilised into a political army.

In spite of this diversity of origin, I think that the two kinds of democracy may generate similar regimens. Both aspire to be universal; and under either of them, if absolutely dominant, mankind might become safe, law-abiding, sporting, and uniform. America has the radical advantage of being a democracy by nature and habit, at least in respect to the dominant types in the population, all having been adventurers, voluntary colonists, thirsting for independence combined with readiness to work hard, to surmount difficulties, and to prosper. The presence of hereditary wealth and of alien races or religions have been only marginal dangers, ignored officially, and not felt to contaminate hopelessly the political and personal equality of all regions and classes. The demand for unanimity, latent in democracy, was felt only in matters of industrial and social morality; and the deepest or wildest contradictions in opinion and sentiment were passed over as unimportant; and in fact they have been largely concealed and neutralised by the diffused cordiality and good humour of American intercourse, which can skim the surface of business and pleasure without concern and without time to consider any hidden dangers. And to preserve a decent equality without imposing any constraint, the guiding policy has been not to suppress originality or wealth at the top but to diffuse a complete education and a substantial comfort from the bottom upwards.

If these and other measures succeed in preserving (what existed originally only in separate local communities) a general moral and social unity in the United States, now explicit in the policy and legislation of the whole nation, the very object would be attained here that the Soviet Government is striving to establish by force throughout its possessions. The end there would have been attained by harsh means, whereas in America it had been achieved by social contagion and attraction, and this would no doubt leave its mark, in each case, in a different quality and degree of political union.

But this is not the Russians' fault. They are heirs to autocracy and religious dogmatism, to both of which their people are accustomed and probably have no objection, rather perhaps an instinctive attachment as to a just and worthy authority. And since their future autocracy would have freed them from their past regimen, economic, military, and ecclesiastical, the new form of all-pervasive authority under which they would now live might seem to them perfect freedom for so much in human nature as is just and good.

And would this not be exactly what the Americans of the future would say of their competitive society of perfectly educated and legally disciplined equals?

# CHAPTER 13

### ABSOLUTE DEMOCRACY

Spontaneous democracy, as we have pictured it, is far from absolute. Pioneers are common men or men estranged from their native background, and they are individualists, ready to face danger and hard work, who claim no privileges but insist on independence. They are ambitious persons and reject socialism as a nursing home for invalids. Revolutionary democracy, on the contrary, instinctively accepts the leadership of other persons or of a single dictator, but looks to equality and unanimity in the status and minds of all members of the community. The dictator is thought of as the impartial protector and father of all the people. There is therefore equality in this kind of democracy but no liberty.

If we ask which of these actual democracies is more truly democratic we are driven to attempt a definition of democracy in its logical essence. If we bend the original meaning of the word to its present use we may say that democracy is power exercised by the proletariat for its own benefit. "Proletariat" is an ugly modern word for an ugly thing: what the Greek *demos* or the Roman *populus* may have become when it lost its birthright in a well organised City, lost its trades, lost its foreign slaves, lost its ancestral gods, and all its local feasts, traditions, and privileges. The proletariat is the vast crowd of exiles in their own country whom the lure of industrial wages and town amusements have uprooted from their villages. They have nothing in common save the physical and vital powers of mere man; whatever traces of civilisation each individual may have brought with him will die out in that nondescript and unsettled society; but those who find employment in some particular industry will be drawn into a trade union; not a guild of the old sort, local, hereditary, and proud of its special art and its festive and civic function. Trade unions serve in the first place to secure shorter hours of work and higher wages, and ultimately, by alliance with revolutionary politics, to make themselves masters of the works that employ them: although this ambition threatens to be intercepted by the socialist governments which they support, when all industries, at one fell swoop, pass into the unseen hand of some national or foreign official.

The other democratic trait of proletarian government, that it aims at the good of proletarians only, characterises the system in name rather than in fact; as indeed happens in every system of government; for all obey the influences to which the rulers are personally subject, seldom pursuing any clear object beyond escaping from the most pressing immediate trouble. In the case of Russia at the present time (1950) does the proletariat exercise any power at all? Or do the vested interests at work regard the special interests of the proletariat or of their own prestige or chosen ambition? Here is a revolution entangled in the complexities of its own success and carried by its organised instruments into enterprises of which it cannot plan the course or see the end.

Meantime, what may we expect the spiritual condition of the people and the character of the liberal arts to become in this future realm of equality and unanimity? The temper of the communist masses and that of the young middle classes to-day may give us some hint of it.

In all "advanced" countries, intellectual perspectives, temporal, cosmic, political, and personal, are extremely short. Everything not now going on, and going on here, is disregarded; and the flying present is occupied with flying excitement, for the sensation of it, with no concern but to pass as rapidly as possible to the excitement of the next moment. The past with all its works and passions may indeed be exhibited, when it is absorbing as a spectacle, at the theatre or in a museum. It may cause a moral shudder and warn the young not to take anything that appears there as if it could still live as a power or a conviction or an affection. Nothing but his own passing warm animal existence can ever be real for the momentary man. All else is nonsense for him. The undifferentiated proletariat would glorify undifferentiated existence. Such may be the ultimate voice of revolutionary democracy.

Constitutional democracy, on the contrary, is only a means to an end; it has no occasion to frame a moral philosophy, either sublime or absurd. It recommends and practices frequent appeals to public opinion, to control the easily deranged mechanism of administration and lawgiving. It counts on this method to secure public acquiescence and to diminish the friction involved in maintaining order in a society which should be highly differentiated, since it means to be vitally free and traditionally continuous.

A clear test of the distinction between democracy as a means to liberty and democracy as a means to equality may be seen in the demand for unanimity. This is a militant demand intolerant of the generative order of nature, which radiates centrifugally into as many incomparable perfections as the crowded jungle of existence will allow. But in each indiivdual, and in each species or institution, egotism inevitably reigns, until it is corrected or rather transcended by the disinterested imagination of the poet in man. To him nature and logic are dear, not because useful in feeding and indoctrinating mankind but because they liberate him, when he loves them, from subjection to his own animal interests or to those of that universal animal commonwealth in which all that is not common will have been stamped out.

Instrumental democracy, when it falls in love with itself, as all absorbing instrumentalities are apt to do, also tends to demand and to produce unanimity. Compromise is accepted reasonably, when it touches only a choice of means towards a common end: but in deeply democratic hearts it is accepted religiously, as the saintly sacrifice of a random personal passion or tradition. This is justified in view of a glorious unanimity to ensue in the world, by the sacrifice of all individual preference.

The tolerant liberal may be at heart an aristocrat, a nationalist, a profoundly sceptical scholar and lover of tradition, as some of the old Whigs were; nothing may be further from him than the desire that his heart should beat as one with that of the majority; but he may smilingly conform to foolish old hobbies and even put up with the suicidal measures carried out by the demagogues. Things have to change and disappear at last, and a good-natured acquiescence with human folly, avoiding it privately as much as possible in one's own person and society, will only help to preserve the spirit of the liberal arts, and transmit it to the next civilisation.

The passion for absolute democracy is the refuge of those who, being unable or unwilling to live in harmony with the hierarchy of nature and of the arts, and being at the same time conscious of the folly of subjective cosmologies, find at last an always contemporary absolute in an always different unanimity of mankind, to be secured by the continual suppression of minorities. And these minorities would in fact be easily stifled at birth; for if all other men were unanimous it would be almost impossible for any callow individual to escape that contagion. Nor would such unanimity preclude changes of will and opinion consequent upon changes in circumstances or in psychic growth; for every fresh perception springing up from such a soil of moral and intellectual agreement would seem to all an orthodox corollary from orthodoxy.

This ideal of a perfect ultimate democracy rests on two assumptions: that human nature in all men is essentially similar, and that consequently mankind could not fully develop its vital liberty without coming to a unanimous vision of the world and a cooperative exercise of the same virtues. I think this is a biological error, and that what is identical in all life is only its germ, from which all plants and animals have developed centrifugally, as circumstances have allowed them to develop. Human society offers but a special instance of such a plastic reaction of living matter to whatever extent circumstances permit it to reach any of its perhaps endless potentialities, all different in their direction, and capable of realising incomparable forms of virtue and beauty. But, even on this naturalistic hypothesis, we should admit that the ideal of human unanimity makes absolute a demand for agreement and cooperation which belongs legitimately only to special human societies and arts, and in each case is limited to special ages and special groups of men. The ideal of a family, or an army, or a philosophic sect, or religious community cannot help being unanimity and orderly life amid natural differences of rank and function.

Absolute democracy is one of these ideally possible forms of social harmony. And like all exclusive recognition of one sort of virtue or art, it ignores its own extreme relativity; and with a child-like innocence that can become militant folly, it denies the intrinsic value of all other possible perfections. This persuasion that human morality, and human morality of one particular type, has an absolute authority, and measures the value, even to themselves, of all possible beings, is the cosmic assumption beneath the democratic demand for unanimity. It is politically less important than the assumption of a single good for all men in one society at one time; but speculatively it is even less judicious, because it swells the demand for moral identity not only beyond the limits of a sect or a nation, but beyond the limits of the human species, and of the whole world open to human inspection. The moral dogmatism which, for momentary local cooperation, might be thought a happy blindness, then becomes a sort of cosmic madness and blasphemy.

## CHAPTER 14

### MORAL UNANIMITY IMPOSSIBLE

SINCE absolute liberty is the primary claim of life, cooperation can never be pervasive. We must presuppose pure spontaneity in the persons that cooperate; otherwise there would be no genuine interests to reconcile, no sacrifices to impose, and no possible happiness to secure. On the other hand, beyond the range of cooperation we must leave a margin, if only as a safety valve, for the waywardness of individuals. It is one of the anomalies of the English mind that while in moral sentiment it makes this margin very narrow, especially among strict liberals, in political theory it leaves it immense; for in the doctrine of liberalism, which is an English product, only the province of the police (that is, safety of person and property) stands subject to control and imposes a duty to collaborate; while in everything intellectual or ideal each man should bravely paddle his own canoe.

But nature does not allow this sort of division of labour, because in the actual order of things what is ideal and intellectual is but the free life and expression of what is material. If you organise the state and industry (say, on the immutable basis of universal competition, free trade, and the right of inheritance) with compulsory state education, monogamy, severe laws against libel and slander, and a science in which all men share, accepting one another's discoveries, then it would be perfectly idle for you to leave thought and love and religion free; a bird in a cage is free in the same way to flap its wings. If you establish monogamy you impose a special ideal of normal love. If you set up an official education you create an official mentality and morality. If you sanctify private property, you impose a corresponding set of virtues, distinctions, ambitions, and rancours. It is a material social bondage that enslaves the mind, which cannot be otherwise enslaved; and freedom of mind depends on freedom to rearrange material conditions so that, living under them, the mind may flourish effectually. It is only in reference to this basis in matter and its arrangement that moral diversities become social conflicts, and engage the passions; it is by impinging on matter that thoughts meet. In the realm of pure conception they are all idle and all compatible. Nothing could be more sapless than an idea that does not express a particular physical order, and does not demand one. It would be like a language that nobody had spoken or was expected to speak. Liberty to frame such a language in the closet is not the liberty which a poet or a saint demands; he demands a world in which the language of his heart shall always be spoken.

The political order that a radical liberalism would establish is therefore a Domination and not a rational order. Any perfect social order would be excluded by it; for it demands acquiescence in the Will of the majority and in the ways of the average man. The liberty that it would leave to the private mind would be a derisive liberty. For we should be invited to make our own way through the uncharted spaces of vacant possibility; yet in reality, unless we participate in some specific human enterprise, we shall be simply drinking the winds. To drink alone and to talk when nobody listens is a doubtful privilege. Liberal society is therefore compelled to form all manner of voluntary private societies to replenish the human vacuity of its political life; but these private societies, being without power or material roots, remain ghostly and artificial. Private busybodies cannot fill the void in the heart of the political animal, hungry for friendship, for action, for distinction, for perilous adventures, and for rare accomplishments to be achieved in common.

It may be urged on the rational side that all society ought to be voluntary and simply a concourse of such private associations as individuals enter into of their own accord and for their own benefit. But this is an illusion, a myth bred in political discussion on the false analogy of commercial agreements where each man pursues his own advantage, measured in terms of a common denominator, money frankly valued by all. But no natural or liberal society is of this kind, neither the family, nor the State, nor the Church, nor any company of friends, sportsmen, soldiers, or bandits. And the justification of any society exercising coercion on persons born and bred in its territory, as does the government of any nation or country, rests precisely on the *necessity* of such government, which softens and controls the fatal pressure that in any case nature and savage man would have exercised on the individual. Society arises by natural instinct, occasion, and habit; it may be in turn a saving aid and a cruel domination; and the rational criticism and reform of it undertaken by liberals may correct some of its evils, but cannot replace its efficient causes and foundations. In so far as any such criticism exercises a physical suasion and modifies society, it is in itself a source of good and evil in probably unexpected directions; but expectation of these effects, if it existed, would be a fresh political insight and judgment, not a part of the truth or error of the criticism itself.

A man cannot serve two masters. If at bottom we respect only the organised core of society and of the mind, we shall despise the idle play of individual fancy around it, and call it a waste of energy, dissipation, and fireworks. We shall also regard as selfish and demoralising any disposition to live one's own life, absorbed in interests which the public cannot share. If on the contrary we truly love only play of mind and the liberal arts, we shall regard as a necessary evil this hard nucleus of material being and human convention round which we are condemned to gyrate; and we shall constantly ask ourselves whether so much matter, so much labour, so much organisation, interference, morality, and monstrous official dullness are really necessary. In lighter armour and in a fresher air we might be more alive while we lived, and perhaps even live longer.

The various combinations of these rival virtues that arise amongst living creatures may trouble the vanity or the conscience of each, if each conceives that his own aspirations should be those of all other men, and that nature should be favourable to no other demands. But nature is equally the source of all demands and of all aspirations; and it is only the blind exuberance of nature that renders living beings quarrelsome, and all in some measure unfortunate. Yet in this irritating way nature does bring to light a great variety of beauties, many of them lasting or perpetually renewed for long stretches of time. There is room, there is peace, there is opportunity, here for one type of life and there for another type. And so political ideals have their innings, none of them perfectly realised. For when perfection is too quickly and absolutely demanded, there can only be a brilliant flare and a quick collapse. If anywhere a deliberate choice is seriously intended to be permanent, that choice should not be arbitrary. It should express an innate moral character in the people, and a dispassionate perception of the circumstances. Nations as well as individuals must be satisfied with their special virtues, or they will never have any. It is enough honour to be a good thing of one kind in a living but inconstant world where no good thing can flourish out of place or out of season.

In practical "politics" a momentary unanimity can be secured on particular points at a mass-meeting or in a well-disciplined party; but there will be no unanimity in the execution of the measure adopted or in judgments passed on it afterwards; and there will be little rational continuity in any series of measures secured by such means. Morally, therefore, there is as great and as chaotic a flightiness in a life newly single-minded at each moment as in a mind always divided against itself: for those mutually irrelevant unanimous moments will neither share nor realise one another's Will.

## CHAPTER 15

### RESTRICTED DEMOCRACY

A THOROUGH scientific psychology of the workings of universal suffrage in populous nations would be instructive. It is being attempted in the United States, not so much, apparently, for the sake of science as in the service of business organisation and of democracy itself, assumed to be a sacred principle. But between the lines of these statistical investigations, there looms the spectre of universal hygienic hypnotisation; for when the statistical psychologists find out what strings and wires move the human psyche, they will have all those strings and wires in their hands and, being legally commissioned to pull them, will have to do so. And then the truly political question will arise for them: *To what end* should the race be scientifically caused to act, to think, and to vote? Have they all a similar primal Will? Are they all capable of the same ultimate virtues?

The white population of the United States is composed entirely of races that in the Old World had possessed distinct and sometimes, as in the case of the Jews, very ancient, exclusive, and tenacious traditions. Had these races arrived in America simultaneously, in the proportions in which their blood now flows in the veins of United States citizens, perhaps the striking homogeneity of language, spirit, and manners that now appears in them all would not have arisen. But chronologically, during the seventeenth century, apart from a few Dutch, all the colonists were British, and it was not until the nineteenth century that floods of Irish, Germans, Jews, Italians, Scandinavians, and Poles added themselves to the British stream which still continued to flow in. Those late-comers were plunged into a social and political *milieu* already highly characteristic. It had institutions, manners, and ways of thinking, and often a religion altogether new to the immigrants, yet so self-complacent and insistent that it made it difficult for the strangers, unless received by groups of their own countrymen already separately settled and organised, to preserve their old ways. Especially in the larger cities the pressure of the American method of working and planning for quick returns imposed itself on everyone who wished to keep his head above water. Nobody could afford to sulk or had time to think, except about business; and the trade-winds of prosperity, ruffling over small personal failures, were so impetuous, hearty, and kindly that the passion for sailing before them was irresistible.

This uniformity of American manners and sentiment is a product of contagion; it works from outside, from popular schools, sports, newspapers, films, and political cries: a daily round so continuous and monotonous as to become automatic and seem to those who undergo it the only natural thing. It might well be expected to cancel all racial and traditional diversity in the people, if the source of it were not external even in the old American stock and sustained even in them only by mechanical compulsion and social pressure. Everyone is caught in the same vortex and, in so far as the soul is vocal, in a vocal vortex also.

But the human psyche is not altogether vocal or mechanically moved. It has a seminal bent, a spontaneous inner proclivity, often an individual originality and turn for invention. This was clearly proclaimed by the New England sages of the age before the Civil War. But they were few and idealistic. They were overwhelmed by the major current, into which they themselves wished to pass; and they were increasingly subdued to the colour of what they worked in, and hailed as prophets of the brave new world that was taking shape in complete disregard of their private spirits.

The uniformity in American principles, as proclaimed publicly and as genuinely felt by most people, is no index to a natural unity in the vital forces at work among them. The proof appears if we consider a notorious fact: the Constitution of the United States, since the Civil War, establishes the equality of all citizens, irrespective "of race, colour, or previous condition of servitude." And this is not merely a constitutional sham, like so many of the provisions in paper constitutions in other countries. It expresses an earnest conviction, dearly defended, by a great part of the people. Nevertheless whenever a difference of race, colour, religion, or breeding is not so overcome in the rush of common work or duty as to pass unnoticed or even unknown, if an attempt is made to ignore it in comradeship, society, marriage, or place of residence, the real difference in the soul is instantly recognised, and an irresistible impulse causes the groups to segregate.

This is set down by democratic doctrinaires to prejudice or snobbery. They do not perceive that contrasts of character and taste can be ignored when people are engaged in some *instrumental* action, to which their moral diversity is irrelevant; but that as soon as the labour is over, and the *liberal life* of play, art, affection, and worship begins, both sides equally require moral comprehension and are equally chilled, bored, and rendered sterile when comprehension is absent.

That a white man *ought* to hobnob with a Negro because otherwise he would not be Christian or unselfish involves a flagrant assumption of superiority. The Negro, if he is not a fool, loves his own inspiration, and expands in the society of his own people. Vital liberty differentiates. Only vacant freedom leaves all in the same anonymous crowd.

The contrast of sentiment on this point between North and South America is instructive. In both there is confident optimism regarding the future of their societies; but I have read an enthusiastic prophecy made by a young Brazilian who looks forward to the mixture of European, American Indian, Chinese, and African blood to form the most beautiful and gifted race that the world has ever seen. The question is one for anthropologists to discuss and for experiment to solve. European nations, especially the more westerly and southern, are extraordinarily hybrid, within the Caucasian family; and they have produced a rich and varied civilisation, though one singularly unstable and factious. It was in the city-states of antiquity and of the later middle ages that the arts and sciences, and the pride of life, appeared at their purest. In contrast to eastern culture, which is more traditional and exquisite, but less ambitious, ours shares the fortunes of our militant nations, who have never learned how to live. Perhaps only a thorough levelling and kneading of all human protoplasm in a universal trough could eliminate from it all the too vigorous seeds of gratuitous violence and madness that now infect it. But then, from that blameless and level lawn that would cover the planet, somewhere one blade of grass would have to grow into a fern and another into a tree, if that varied and tragic flora that we call civilisation were ever to arise again.

I should like to believe with a distinguished follower of Darwin,[1] that the secret of moral progress is inbreeding, which allows the special potentialities in one incipient variety of human beings to develop. If the mating organisms are inwardly diseased or unfit to prosper in their environment, that breed will quickly disappear; but when their special predisposition is opportune, they will initiate a special line of progress in human nature and human arts. The cultivation of *different* characters and arts, when such characters or arts are opportune, is therefore requisite for the emergence of any eminent beauty, culture, genius, or virtue.

It is therefore a healthy and fruitful sentiment that prompts Anglo-Americans to preserve as far as possible their special tradi-

[1] Sir Arthur Keith: *A New Theory of Human Evolution*, 1948.

tions in manners and morals, language and religion. They may fraternise as cordially as the national spirit demands with all their fellow-citizens, when they all find themselves essentially equal in ability, on the common stamping ground of business and politics. Equality and a ready interchange of leadership work well where the equality is real; and there is a natural hierarchy in every profession, wherever the *authority of things* backs and sanctions the expert; but the mutual attraction of persons and minds, of kindred tastes and manners, needs no criterion beyond the absolute liberty of the psyche to invent the inspired style of its growth, passionate, speculative, or satirical.

## CHAPTER 16

### THE AMERICAN "MELTING-POT"

THE early history of government in the United States exhibits different types of democracy, both locally and morally commingled.

Natural democracy appears among independent pioneers, joining forces casually or in small emigrant groups. These casual comrades were not foreigners to one another: they were chiefly British, chiefly Protestants, all were enterprising, all bent on gaining great wealth while preserving a radical independence. Yet there was likely to be, from the beginning, a profound distrust of one another latent among them. In spite of belonging to the same rising flood of revolution in Christendom, they represented various currents within that flood, taking different turns and sliding into various pools of a relative tranquillity. Some emigrants represented factions in British political life that already demanded a revolutionary democracy; others felt themselves to be potential landlords, more absolute and on a larger scale than the Old World, already preempted and riddled with privileges and mortgages, allowed to its hereditary nobility. A few were actually cavaliers, younger sons of great families, bound to outdo, in El Dorado, the unfair advantages of their elder brothers at home.

We may say that in this democratic concourse of social atoms there lay types of oligarchy in the germ which would assert themselves when they got a chance. Even in public and political life, oligarchical instincts and intuitions reassert themselves when planning or where executive capacity is needed. The few whom education and private fortune had accustomed to understand and manage complex affairs put their heads together, took the lead in framing resolutions and proposing measures; and if they did so in conventional language, without any air of superiority, the vaguely puzzled and vaguely trustful crowd accepted their suggestions, so that a private minority actually dominated the popular majority that nominally dominated the active members.

The American passion for organisation is no doubt fostered by the competition in efficiency and commercial economy; but I suspect that it is secretly stimulated also by thirst for distinction. For this passion appears where no material advantage is expected: in amateur sports, for instance, and in the innumerable Societies and Associations and Clubs and Greek Letter Fraternities that segregate their members, not because initially distinguished, but because they thirst to become in some way segregated and distinguishable. Sometimes—I think exceptionally—real affinities produce special clubs; but often a club is founded for no reason except the hope of creating special affinities. Two fraternities or two houses will be founded in a college instead of one only, so that emulation may supply an interest in belonging to them at all and a flattering belief in each that it is better than the other.

Such feeble echoes of tribal feuds and tribal taboos may seem ridiculous amidst the swarming, rumbling, and smoking flats of modern industry with their tragic revolutions and wars; and certainly those manifestations of homesickness seem impotent bubbles in the flood of democracy sweeping over the world. Yet in the midst of this deluge, in the family and social life of those most identified with the new order, there are more serious symptoms of a radical aversion from it, an aversion that may well survive the inundation, and reappear, like the submerged crests of the ancient mountains when the waters recede.

The most obvious of these latent but ineradicable diversities in the American people is that of race, which in the case of the Negroes can hardly be made to disappear by fusion. An exceptional strain of Negro blood, diluted in each generation, may remain in a few white families; but the mass of mulattoes will remain attached, even if

# THE AMERICAN "MELTING-POT"

in the capacity of leaders, to the black population, which will know how to develop its own institutions in the places where it congregates and where it might govern itself to advantage. Some European groups, preserving their language and religion, might also form local societies. It happens that the Catholics, who have the strongest religious organisation, with a complete Catholic education possible for their young people, are socially segregated, even when they belong to the professional classes; but the fact that many of them, being of Irish extraction, speak only English, has made this social segregation less profound and less general than it would otherwise have become. I think, however, that they are already socially, happier and more complete in themselves, with perfect friendliness to the surrounding Protestant community, in which religion is less distinguishable from the lay spirit of the times and of the political ethos of the country.

The most distinguished, most equivocal, but I think the most profound of these special societies is that of the Jews. Besides their traditional financial activity and influence, they play a leading part among the intellectuals and the artists, so much so that at times it seems as if they were simply, in those spheres, the true leading Americans. But this is a false appearance produced by publicity, which is an omnipotent but superficial force. It is superficial even in the Jews who most engage in it, and both they and their public really need something better, and will recognise it when it appears. How uncomfortable the Jews are in their expertness, how dissatisfied in their success, cannot escape a careful observer; and their philosophies too are insecure, serving two masters, and not knowing whether they wish to be submerged in the Gentile world, provided they may lead it, or to conquer that world expressly for Zion; but in that case would not Zion itself have lost its sacred and specific character? Where language and culture are no longer distinct for the Gentile and for the Jew, something else still separates them. The true virtue and the supreme pleasure of the Jew were always a closed book for the Gentile; and the true virtue and supreme pleasure of the Gentile are a closed door for the Jew.

If these observations are just, the American "Melting-Pot" is not destined to fuse all the ingredients thrown into it into an indiscriminate mass. It may prove rather like the caldron of boiling oil into which Saint John, the Beloved Disciple, was cast, according to the received tradition, near the Porta Latina in Rome. He thereby earned the palm of martyrdom, which he had come to challenge; but he now knew the spirit he was of, and was miraculously rescued, to live to an extreme old age and compose his immortal works. But perhaps from this Modern Melting-Pot, two different Johns will arise, the one Jewish, to compose a militant political Apocalypse, and the other Gentile, to write a disillusioned spiritual Gospel.

## CHAPTER 17

### NO FIXED IDEAL OF SOCIETY

THE ideal of absolute political stability would be rational if it were practicable, but nature interposes a double veto. In the first place, it is impossible that in this world a complex system, such as human society, should be predetermined to fulfill the primal Will of all its diverse members, so that no class and no individual should lack a vocation for the mode of life that is allotted to each of them. And in the second place, even if such a miraculous harmony could be reached for a moment in any society, and were capable of becoming hereditary there, all the rest of the environing world would continue to evolve independently; and the changing circumstances would require changes in the disposition of the citizens and in the spirit and action of the government. The less elastic and adaptable the established polity was, the more sudden and total would be its approaching ruin.

The marvel is, in view of this general fatality, that any ideal is ever seriously set up by utopians, and that at times such ideals seem to have been approximately realised. But not, I think, if all classes and all individuals be honestly considered. For instance, Sparta seems to have preserved its constitution for several centuries in spite of severe trials and reverses. But there was never any complete harmony in that society. Its longevity was like that of the monastic orders. No attempt was made by Lycurgus to conciliate and discipline all mankind. On the contrary, a limited number of citizens, a militant order, was established expressly to face and defy

## NO FIXED IDEAL OF SOCIETY

helots and foreigners and any rebels or deserters from its own serried ranks. Such an artificial discipline, within a special circle, could be contagious. It appealed to elementary animal and spiritual potentialities undeveloped in most men, but latent in all; it was well devised to excite a narrow but intense unity of feeling and action among the elect. Club spirit when thus systematically fostered has a self-preserving effect. In narrowing and specialising the ethos of the group, it redoubles the intensity as well as the uniformity of the authorised passions. At the same time these passions become ideals and standards of virtue, protected by local opinion and by ignorance or scorn of anything different. Just because a fashion is cruel you may be heroic in following it. You learn to detest all alien vices and to be proud of your own.

The defect of such moral horticulture is that of all militancy. Nature prompts the ideal that rebels against vulgar nature; and the nature that rebels is moral and courageous, while the nature that is contravened is only automatic. Yet the harmonies established by automatism are broadly based and capable of subsisting so long as the circumstances that bred them endure; tradition therefore enlists the rational allegiance of a wider circle than a militant order is likely to do. An artificial morality strains the heart and rends the world, and the majority always hates it. At bottom all moralities, and life itself, which any morality somehow represents in a measure, carry on a utopian war against ultimate fate; so that popular hatred of each militant ideal, be it Spartan, monastic, or puritan, does not itself escape partisanship, and in that sense forms a kind of counter-militancy. But this is the militancy of the many against the few, of the normal against the exceptional, of the inwardly simple and obvious against the violence of theory, passion, and fanaticism. Horticulture aims at the wonderfully beautiful, perhaps monstrous, while nature covers the fields with little daisies, never out of fashion, and breeds orchids and birds of paradise also, for an occasional surprise.

On the other hand a forced growth of flowers, and the grafting of one species upon another, discover wasted possibilities of beauty, which spontaneous nature might never have brought to light; and there is no reason to expect that these modified types should necessarily prove sickly or barren. Man is a part of nature and his militant intervention does not in the least disturb the broad order of generation in the universe. All the products of art and industry, and all experiments in politics and morals, take their chance, like the humblest fungus, in the lottery of life. Everything artificial will indeed be short-lived, if the artisans of it themselves are inconstant or disappear. Gothic architecture, for instance, had a short, local, eager development, arrested suddenly in part for overleaping its possibilities, in part by a change of public taste; yet it created exquisite and inspiring works, which, however, are perhaps less beautiful when finished according to the original plan than when interrupted, half ruinous, or invaded and enriched by features in another style. A romantic suggestion of frailty or of early betrayal, by a world that seemed to smile, makes doubly tragic the valour and intelligence lavished on such devout labours. But political structures do not normally survive the struggling Will that established them. This Will was probably turbid and estranged from itself by a thousand compromises; and the statesman's ideal had perished before his work was done. In the prophet or speculative moralist, on the contrary, allegiance to a pure ideal is apt to precede and survive any semblance of realisation of it that he may force on the world; and it is only in himself and in his doctrine that his militancy comes to a head and can leave its mark upon history. The Spartan regimen does not survive anywhere, but the ideal of austere militancy in a band of comrades survives in Plato's philosophy and in religious Orders, usually monastic but sometimes military. And this survival merely in a mind or in a sect is all that could be reasonably expected. For what is the motive power in militancy? The Will of an individual or a group diverging from the wider automatic course of nature, and attempting to transform it to suit that group or that individual. This can be accomplished by the manual arts, and also by politics in so far as its effects may be inserted, like mechanical instruments, into the native automatism of nature; but in that vast tangle each particular thread is soon lost to sight in the grotesque tapestry. There may still live for ever, in the microscopic but profound visions of the psyche, the chosen colours and the ideal patterns of whatever might be its own life in a congenial world; and these will always be important so long as psyches of that temper endure. Yet in time all ideals like all costumes become archaic and all languages die; so that it is wiser to transfer at once one's treasure to the realm of spirit, where if they were glorious once they are glorious for ever.

## CHAPTER 18

### EQUALITY NOT CONDUCIVE TO PEACE

UNIFORMITY between classes or between nations is not favourable to peace, except as it destroys units capable of action. There must be organic units at some level or there would be no potential moral agents or combatants; but similarity in these units, if they live in the same habitat, renders them rivals and therefore, in spite of their brotherly likeness to one another, involves them in war. The traveller passing from Northern France or Belgium into Germany, or from there into industrial England, sees absolutely the same type of animal, the same state of civilisation. Those frontiers are accidental and arbitrary; those recent and terrible battles seem unintelligible. If one of these industrial towns can be at peace with its next neighbour, within the political frontier, why should it go to war with an exactly similar town, only a little beyond? Ah, beyond, perhaps, these indistinguishable creatures speak a different language: which signifies that they are affiliated to a different government, and enlisted in different armies. Therefore they *can* go to war. Each town would go to war with its next neighbour also, upon occasion, if a common government did not suck up the fighting energies of both towns and enforce peace between them. And just as the similarity of those governments and of those nations, making them rivals, makes them enemies at heart, so the similarity of those twin towns would do, if each were an organic whole, capable of action and war. But the old independent boroughs have become administrative centres, ruled by prefects named by the government, and by laws passed by a parliament sitting at the capital; they must endure the tides of enterprise and population passively, without a thought of resistance, since they have no organ with which to resist. Remove those industrial regions from the domination of their respective governments, and place them under the irresistible police of some single power, and they would all prosper or wither together, like spears of wheat in the same field.

Similarity is therefore a danger to peace, and peace can be secured only by organisation. But the collateral completeness of similar units excludes organisation; and then war becomes inevitable at the first shock of competition, unless some higher power, itself organised, stifles that conflict.

The class war now preached by the official communists illustrates this. When there is no real diversity among classes, but only a difference of income in cash, envy and hatred between these classes becomes more intense; ill will is sharpened, as never before, by a sovereign contempt. There might have been some dignity and good humour in the humblest station, when this carried with it a special costume and speech and licence and knowledge; but there is no dignity or humour in merely having less money to spend than another chap who goes to the same cinema, only that, being a capitalist, he goes oftener and sits in a better place.

On the other hand, diversity may be a source of positive sympathy, inasmuch as it enlarges vicariously the interests of each class and makes their common world more beautiful. This advantage, of course, is only moral, and presupposes an accepted order of society. It vanishes, and turns to utter hostility, when the organs of these diverse classes collide in the realm of matter, and interfere there with one another's development. For instance, in universities, the natural sciences and the humanities happily complete and enlighten one another in the pure ether of ideas; yet they are sometimes impelled to quarrel lustily over their local or national elections and mutely to compete for public recognition, student favour, and professorial chairs. Luckily none of these prizes is so dazzling as to provoke mortal combats.

CHAPTER 19

MYSTICAL EQUALITY

A RELIGION may be founded on charity; an earthly society must rest on friendship.

Charity does not imply *liking* your neighbour; but there is a transcendental element of sympathy, even of respect, in acknowledging in every atom a centre of existence and force, in every living cell a centre of life and a potentiality of spirit. The more odious, infected, deformed, and beastly a creature is, the purer will be the charity that can take his point of view and minister to his necessities. But with odious, infected, deformed, and beastly creatures no man can wish to live or to act. They must be eliminated; and if charity forbids you to destroy them directly good government requires you to render them impossible in your society. They are political vermin; and social duty does not counsel you to favour their reproduction or to smile on their vices.

The motive that prompts charity to love all human beings is not that they are all beautiful, perfect, or good in the sense of beneficent. From the human point of view, which is that of sane politics, many of them are notoriously loathsome or wicked, and government, in their case, should hasten that extinction which nature decrees in the end for everything. Such is the morality of man as a fighting animal and a social architect. Yet speculative reason in him cannot help perceiving that each living being or society is animated by this same vital morality, in each case with its special purposes and hatreds. Wherever spirit is incarnate it becomes the lover of some perfection and the accomplice of some partiality. It cannot blame its other incarnations for limitations to which it is itself condemned; yet by this very justice and charity it transcends them. Love cannot love without loving a special good.

It follows, however, from this equal vital franchise of all creatures, that in being loved impartially, they must all be impartially pitied. For how precarious is the special life stirring in each of them, how buffeted at every turn, how diseased, and how tormented! And it also follows that no creature, in loving the rest, need take them for its model. In the first place, they are variously endowed, capable of living only in incompatible ways, and continually at war with one another. Moreover, it would be madness in us to abandon our own aspirations, which we are capable of satisfying, in order to adopt the aspirations of alien creatures which exclude our possible virtues.

Nothing here suggests that an equal love and pity are due by each creature to every other. Most animals are incapable of rational love or pity at all; and even their instinctive sympathy is limited to their own young and their own tribe. What reason opens up to us is only the truth that even hostile animals are admirable and tormented, their very insensibility to the good of others proves their integrity; a primary virtue which they exercise in a narrow field. We too could not live without this virtue; only that in us the life to be integrated includes participation in social and technical interests, and perhaps even aspires to transcend in its sympathies the animal passions of man.

We may then really love and pity the cruel and intense integrity of the brutes, without any temptation to imitate them. We may show the same charity towards our own kind, without exception, but in each case for different reasons and with a different degree and quality of feeling. Our sympathy would not in any case be ready-made and applied indiscriminately, but plastic to the special virtue and fate of the person or society considered. This adaptation of sympathy would simply flow from knowledge of the facts. It would show how far our imagination could reproduce the dramas actually enacted in the world.

The real equality between men is thus entirely spiritual. It is an equality in misery, but is also an equality in spiritual autonomy and pride; since if the spirit suffers allurements and denials that enslave it or exasperate it, this is possible only because the spirit has a life of its own, which those allurements or denials interrupt. Essentially and inwardly, each man is autonomous, the only seat and absolute final judge of all judgments; and this transcendental centrality of spirit is the same in every man, and its authority, in each case, equal and inalienable. And this every man acknowledges when he speaks to any other creature and posits that other mind.

On the sympathetic moral side this insight bears the name of charity and appears in Christianity, as also in Buddhism and in the sporadic wisdom of many a sage and poet; and we need not wonder that it comes forward in politics, when national, or commercial, or intellectual ambitions have lapsed, and attention falls instead on the amorphous masses of mankind, on the proletariat. They multiply like wild animals, but find the wilderness occupied, every field fenced, and themselves without attachments in any organic society, with no art, no religion, no friends, and no prospects. Work for them is a sheer evil, picked up by chance, and paid for by wages, to be spent in forgetting their work and enjoying, for as many hours a day as possible, comforts and amusements that shall have nothing to do with it. Their chief effort or ideal aim will then be to diminish the work and to increase the wages. Yet the absence of work is a still greater evil than work itself: it means starvation,

## MYSTICAL EQUALITY

loneliness, emptiness physical and moral; and it has a tendency to become chronic, to sever the casual connections by which work might present itself, and to break the habit that may sometimes render hard labour automatic and uncomplaining.

Proletarians thus tend to become equal in the only thing in which equality is possible—in their misery. And this is a great bond; especially when the proletarians are intellectual, conscious of their misery, and endowed by tradition with a vocabulary that can express that misery eloquently. Such was the case amongst the early Christians, as it is still among the Jews. Rousseau was intellectually a proletarian. Human society seemed to him a prison, and the prisoners pure equal spirits capable of the most exalted happiness, if only they were left free to wander in couples through a new Garden of Eden as through a landscape of Watteau.

Such is the origin of the notion that all men are equal by nature. It is perfectly true that a spirit is awake in them that at every moment is a centre of intelligence, will, and affection, no less central and absolute in one person than in another, and at one moment than at another in the life of each. Yet the intensity and scope of this inward life change from day to night, and from one season to another; various and often contrary impulses meet in the same breast or contradict one another in the same career.

The equality of all moments in all souls is therefore abstract only and transcendental in that all are truly conscious. The quality, scope, and significance of this consciousness will differ indefinitely and boundlessly, passing from joy to agony, from hatred to love, from stupor to intelligence; and this in respect to worlds of the imagination often practically irrelevant and ideally incommensurable. Such diversity does not in the least nullify the equal appeal of spirit everywhere to brotherly recognition and charity from the spirit; but this appeal is only to that mystical insight and disinterestedness of which pure spirit is capable, when liberated from all special private or earthly attachments. There is no equality thereby established between persons, no unanimity or harmony amongst animal wills. There can be harmony only in so far as all are willing to renounce their wills, in order to secure harmony; and there can be equality only in so far as each renunciation reduces each person to the pure spirit within him, similar in all, and capable of understanding without adopting all the passions by which incarnate spirit may be distracted.

Thus a true equality or moral identity between souls is a purely spiritual equality or identity involving the most ungrudging recognition of inequality and even mutual hostility between the same souls, in so far as they are personal. Incarnation involves this dispersion of spirit amongst many persons and societies, each with a different earthly vocation and individual virtue, intently directed upon a particular natural good.

## CHAPTER 20

### REPRESENTATIVE GOVERNMENT I
### ONLY GENERATED ORGANISMS CAN LIVE OR THINK

IF HUMAN society were a generated organism it would not require a government. Its limbs and organs would then have arisen by gradual segregation and distinction within a self-developing and self-reproducing body. So a seed possesses from the beginning a specific power of growth, in so far as circumstances provoke and permit it. All those eventual limbs and organs must then remain rooted in a single body and can live only by inclusion in its collective life. If ever one of them was maimed or hindered in its action, all the others would more or less remotely feel the shock, and if possible, by transfusion of their vital energy, would help to repair the damage. Thus all natural organisms, even if injured only in part, in some measure suffer and recover as units; notoriously they awake, move, fight, and die as units.

No inorganic aggregate, such as human society, has this vital unity. It forms a colony of units, many perhaps derived from one another and collaborating, while others may have attached themselves ready-made to the group or may hang on to its fringes as parasites or rebels. The life of the society as a whole will be a mere resultant; feeling, intention, and vital initiative can spring up only in one or another of its members. Yet this actual life in particular psyches is itself organic, even if separately only vegetative and unconscious. The successive phases and epidemic passions of a society have therefore a marked analogy to the animal and moral life of an individual, and phrases like the "spirit" of an age or a nation, of the "will" of a people, though metaphors, are apt and convenient.

Much nonsense, however, passes for insight when the essential difference between myth and fact in this field is ignored. The dynamic unity in a society is material only, and its moral unity mythical or verbal; while the moral character of a psyche, in passion and in thought, is actual; and its dynamic physical unity thereby becomes personal. Nothing, however, condemns poets, philosophers, or even historians for being more interested in ideal harmonies than in psychological facts. That is merely a matter of individual character. Are you more deeply stirred by astronomy or by the misery of mongrel and stray dogs?

If society does not actually feel or think, actual feeling or thinking, in its turn, is not a society of self-existing "ideas" or "perceptions," as British empiricism would have it. Actual sensibility is a function of the total psyche in its total balance and momentum at any time. Particular ideas or feelings are only momentary focal points or features in this total apparition. All the instruments in the psychic orchestra are playing or have played or are ready to play; and their latent rhythms or strains fill the vague background of somatic feeling. We are alive with changing needs, and there is a world to supply or deny them, or to break in upon us with arbitrary assaults. These assaults, and the sharp reaction they cause, for a moment absorb attention, and for a bystander seem, like a cry, the first and separate evidence of life in the other creature; but for this creature himself, his cries, reactions, and sudden perceptions are transient variations, in a continuous broad stream of existence, without clear boundaries; and in this continuum particular perceptions arise, vary, and lapse, like so many waves. Caricature and artifice could not go further than to reduce this awareness of restless existence to a few pictorial features or cries that receive names as if they were separate unconnected events, which though absolutely self-existent and groundless, could pop up again more faintly in memory and could produce a new perception of their past relations of succession and difference!

This potential revival of past perceptions really occurs, and they may perhaps recur very much as they came; but now they will be always framed in a new perspective, drawn from the whole life of the psyche since they first appeared. Such recurrence is naturally explicable only because the same living organism endures, with its always total, though always differently focussed and selective consciousness. So the feelings that were once new and central recur marginally or merely suggest themselves, whenever the original process that caused them is reawakened in the organism; yet those feelings now reappear in a perspective that lends them a removed station in time together with a dramatic and legendary quality: for they now seem ghostly in contrast with the foreground of crude sensation due to present surroundings and to the moral climate of the psyche to-day.

This protest of actual apprehension against a verbal reduction of conscious life to detached and definable sensations may be confirmed by a logical analysis of the spectacle of the world as we constantly find it. It is a world all depth, motion, and variation in space and time. Yet evidently it is only within the compass of a synthetic glance that related terms, contrasts, and temporal perspectives can appear at all. The whole wealth of imagination or knowledge ever actually possessed by the spirit must be crowded into a single picture filling and constantly overflowing the scope of apprehension. Not all can be named or distinguished at any one moment; yet the recent and the coming revelations are neither lost nor unexpected, but are posited and felt to complete the passing procession, in a manifold order that the eye may never exhaust; so that it is, for us, by the very partiality and transitoriness of each apprehension that the greatness of the object and its eternal order are divined. For those past or future reactions have all been planted or become seminal in a single living organism to whose apprehension they never appear wholly separate and absolute, but always as interruptions and incidents in a fundamentally continuous and equable life, where each is seen, from its birth, in its temporal and logical relations.

Mind has this comprehensive outlook because it is the sensibility proper to an animal psyche, full of specific potentialities responsive to specific impressions: vital reactions naturalised in the psyche and revived on occasion as memories and habits. Mind can therefore arise only in individual living beings. Occasional aggregates like governments and societies cannot be rationally guided except by the mind of some individual; and the vicarious wisdom that may be found in intuitions and laws, once devised by some sage, loses its value in proportion to the degree of change in the world to which it is applied, until some new sage arises to adapt that wisdom to the later tensions between men and things. Politicians may seem to be pitted only against one another; but except in the measure in which they speak for natural forces or control them, their hopes and their hatreds are entirely groundless. Spirit could never fear or oppose spirit save for animating and serving some material engine.

## CHAPTER 21

### REPRESENTATIVE GOVERNMENT II
### MORAL REPRESENTATION IN NATURE

A LITERARY philosopher may imagine that moral harmonies presuppose reason; yet in the generative order of nature the opposite is the case. Many a harmony must be established in the cosmos and in some animal psyche before reason dawns on any living mind. The political result of this is that moral harmonies may exist in society without reason having ever puzzled any of its members or society ever having a mind of its own. Reason is a species of insight, by which essential relations are seen to obtain between ideal terms. It therefore cannot arise before animal sensibility has offered such terms to actual attention, and until the stress of anxious life has given the mind time to pause and notice the peculiar character of one given term contrasted with the peculiar character of another: as for instance the difference, when a cloud suddenly hides the sun, between sunshine and shade. Before reason exists there must be, therefore, not only a varied sensibility in the psyche but comprehensive and synthetic power to perceive the essential contrasts and similarities between given ideas, and eventually to designate these contrasts and similarities by appropriate words.

The moral quality which concerns us in politics accrues to reason when the contrasted or implicated terms designate actions or the fruits of action. Now, the human psyche being exceptionally complex and plastic, its passions are too simultaneous and conflicting to allow a simple round of distinct and unequivocal actions, such as blesses most animals; so that the more a man's interests ripen and multiply, the harder it will be for him either to pursue each of them in turn wholeheartedly or always to feel and judge each with a just and steady regard for them all. Yet it is precisely this joint awareness of the passions, with the need, but hardly the power, of reducing them to harmony that renders human life *de jure* rational and *de facto* tragic. Hence the paradox that the one animal who calls himself rational is the most inconsistent in his Will and most distracted in his thoughts, and is alone capable of despair and suicide; while the heavenly bodies, that have no mind, and the brutes that have very little, seem to the philosopher to preserve a wonderful order, irrational indeed in its existence and lack of an ultimate *raison d'être*, but normal and regular in its method. Had the conflicting impulses that madden a man been distributed among separate creatures, they might have formed links in a perfect economy of nature, where discords all presuppose vital harmony in the parts and continually induce some dynamic balance in the whole.

The miracle of essential vital offices performed regularly by one organism for another occurs in Nature by chance, yet once occurring maintains itself by virtue of its utility; an *imperative* harmony, since if it failed the species to which these uncovenanted graces had become essential would disappear. Typical of such unwitting cooperation between diverse organisms is the function of insects carrying fertilising dust from the stamens of one flower to the heart of another. The bee, minding only its own business, cannot visit too many flowers for a drop more honey; and then innumerable seeds fall where they will be duly fertilised which otherwise would have been blown about on the slight chance of finding a nourishing soil.

Among fishes, no liaison parasites being provided to mediate between the sexes, an immense profusion of seed spilt in the water has to waylay the female with a diffused assault; while in land animals male weapons automatically unsheathed at propitious moments have to be developed, and graces and arts of courtship, to secure a direct and violent union of the sexes. *Sic vos no vobis*, nature seems to decree satirically; and the deepest irony of all appears in the prolonged, apparently irrelevant, emotions of both parties in human love affairs.

This is what Hegel called the *List der Natur*, the guile of nature, and what Schopenhauer made metaphysically farcical by saying that the force that drew lovers together was the Will to Live of the child that they might, or might never, have. How accidentally, and how imperfectly, these moral harmonies take root may be seen in maternal love, so powerful and self-sacrificing at first and in tragic crises; yet love amid the drudgery and worries of indigence soon becomes irritable and even cruel. If mothers were allowed habitually to neglect their young children, the race would die out; though we shall survive continual beatings and howlings, and a terrible average infant mortality, if only there are love-affairs and births enough. Families and tribes do constantly die out, and the vacancy sooner or later is filled by others whose balance of propensities fitted better to the balance of their circumstances. Barren experiments and reversed successes fill the whole course of history.

Myths about the "wiles of nature" or the magic influence of alien or future interests describe moral harmonies more firmly rooted in the world than any artificial cooperation can be. Not that cooperation, unselfishness, and sacrifice of any kind are difficult or rare in the complex equilibrium of nature; but that the spontaneous fertility of matter must run into them when circumstances open the way, and render them fruitful and lasting. And indeed it is only the awakening of this potentiality in the psyche, together with the perception of the possible happy results, that prompts the imagination to dwell on that possible action and the Will to embark upon it and to call it rational. But were the judgment of reason merely logical, without a prior vital impulse to carry it out, it would have no moral authority even in prospect, and all esteem for the action it adumbrated would vanish with the hollow words that recommended it.

Such an ingrained bent in one person to bring about the existence, welfare, or safety of another, I call *morally representative.* Autonomously at bottom, but eventually with feelings of positive love or sympathy, nature knits life in one place or of one sort with life in another place or of another sort. The most different gifts and labours may become secretly cooperative; and unintended beneficence may attach to the least sophisticated or obsequious lives. When this natural harmony is observed, different classes and unlike individuals may form a society in mutual respect without mutual assimilation or envy.

## CHAPTER 22

### REPRESENTATIVE GOVERNMENT III
### MORAL REPRESENTATION IN SOCIETY

THERE is no social system more admirably rational in its working than is the spontaneous cooperation of irrational impulses in diverse individuals, under the influence of sexual and parental passion. Each person freely obeys his bent and sacrifices selfish interests to ideal interests which have become organically dominant in the psyche. The mechanism of such virtue is the same as the mechanism of vice, when selfish interests are sacrificed incorrigibly to bad habits; but where the dominant passion serves to enhance the existence of a race, a family, or a civilisation, the end secured, assumed to be a supreme good, turns the irrational impulse of the agents into a generous virtue.

A worthy suitor, prevailing over hesitations in the lady, and a parent teaching and correcting a stubborn child are judged to represent morally the true interest of a woman or a child. Eventually, when they look back upon the result of the social influences under which they acted they may possibly blame those influences; but this private judgment does not destroy the average value of such influences and of the pliability of those who ordinarily yield to them. Society judges that society should be served, and in any case nature has contrived its survival. Whatever machinery secures this end is therefore justified biologically. The cost to individuals and their selfish or capricious grievances may be regretted by the humanitarian; but a rationalist may observe that ships that are not seaworthy had better not put out to sea.

If the social harmonies achieved by nature have this painful side, social harmonies achieved by governments and civilisations cannot be expected to be perfect. When they arise in the order of genesis, like patriarchal monarchy, they do not last long; and where a militant party, foreign or native, has imposed them, they bear the birth-marks of ruin and violence, and can never meet the inner complexity and continual transformation of natural demands. Let me consider, for instance, the form of government best known to my probable readers, government by elected magistrates and legislators. How far is the society that elects them represented by them morally as well as officially?

In the first place we may observe that the parliaments and the administrative councils such as ministries, which these deputies now compose, were not, in their origin, deputations at all, but spontaneous groups of notables representing only their personal interests, rights, and powers. They came forward of their own initiative to exert pressure on one another, on the leaders, and on the people, in favour of such measures as they thought urgent and just, or to give their judgment on the conduct of offenders, or on the justice of current law and morals. In other words they were free men speaking their own minds and defending their own interests, which they felt to be also those of the country. They met to negotiate and to avoid conflict if possible, as diplomats do now; and behind their demands or concessions there always stood the threat of secession, rebellion, and war. There was no tacit promise of accepting the policy of the majority. A man might be temporally cowed into acquiescence by superior numbers or superior force; but he would bide his time, and never represent anything but his rights and his conscience.

Such a man, if firm and eloquent, might well become the leader of a party; or the common people, if they felt that he took their side, might shout for him, and actually invent for him the office of tribune. The tribune would then be deputed to speak for them; but he would be elected to represent them legally only because, in his heart, he represented them morally.

The Gracchi, the first tribunes, lost their lives for being representatives of this kind; perhaps they overestimated the possible virtue of both plebeians and patricians, and represented ideally more than there was to represent; while various abstracted enthusiasts lost their heads during the French Revolution for morally representing too little, and underestimating the good sense of their fellow citizens.

In contrast to such militant heroes, why are the selected, elected, and paid representatives of the people in modern parliaments so safe? Because they are seldom original or important enough to be dangerous. They are rather docile followers of a party, or of its leaders, who may represent a subversive policy, but who prefer docile adherents and easily find them among men with average, half-educated, confident minds and fluent language, glad to adopt a plain party orthodoxy and to earn a decent living by defending it. Only a revolution, such as is not expected by parliaments, sweeping all other parties out of existence, would threaten private disaster to an active politician. A hundred other social jobs are open to him if out of office.

To be an average man, and in that sense a fair social representative of the people, is not to be a "moral representative" of them. Only an exceptional person could be this, as he would have to appreciate justly all the people's interests and to know, at the same time, which interests and how far each of those interests could be successfully served at the moment. This task, evidently too great for a single unaided individual, is therefore assumed by the various parties, each with its first principles, supposed to be the only right ones, and its tradition of gifted leaders, who have had ample occasion, each in his own direction, to apply those principles to all human affairs. It is therefore the party, rather than its elected members, that professes to be morally representative of the people, and might really be so, if the people were all animated by the same spirit, and had only the interests which one of the extant political parties was conscious of and ready to serve. This is assumed to be the case when only one party is permitted to figure in the government.

This result is sometimes approached without being secured by force, as when only two parties are rivals for power without diverging seriously in fundamentals, so that they can alternate without destroying each other's work, as has been the case normally in England and in the United States. Hitherto, in these countries, the two parties have represented but a slightly different balance between vested interests and social reform, so that a continuous evolution of commerce and industry was possible, to the conscious satisfaction of the public at large; but whether this evolution was in the ultimate interest of the nation (not to speak of the world) was left for future historians to consider. A unanimous people governed by a single legal party would be in the same case; but all parties inherently tend to become sects and to develop an "ideology" in which the only right method of life and government is set down for all future time. Such a speculative sect breeds a militant faction and in the changing world is almost certainly based on illusion.

Now, in the middle of the twentieth century, it might seem that one, at least, of the principal parties had a solid backing in the real interests of its members, namely, any labour party that represented the trade unions, since these are devoted to securing for the working people higher wages, and ultimate control of industry, thus doing away with the illegitimate tax which the idle owners or shareholders levy upon it. That shareholders, who may not so much as know where their income comes from, should live on it in idleness for ever is surely an anomaly. The legal right to this property hangs on traditional claims based on conquest, grants, or inheritance proper to social conditions now obsolete. Here too we see the danger of reducing property to the abstract common denominator called money. Suppose for a moment the natural identity re-established between those who possess the property and those who render it profitable and enjoy that profit. The hands and the managers would then divide the proceeds of their industry between them. There might be at first some doubt as to the proportions due to each; but if the industry was well established, experience would have proved how much should be assigned to apprentices, how much to ordinary workmen, how much to experts, and how much to business directors: since a modern industry involves buying materials and machinery and selling the product in a suitable market. The maximum prosperity of the undertaking would be the common interest of all alike, each receiving the share proportionate to the tested importance of his service.

This is an ideal. It suggests cooperation without jealousy, as if all could find work suited to their capacity, and might turn it, morally, into a liberal art. But the complexity of modern industry has rendered many of the humbler tasks trivial and monotonous; so that the workman's life is divided into empty work and empty pastimes. His free life, when his wages arrive, is like that of the idle capitalist, a parasite without a function or a vocation, and probably not without several vices. And his fate is probably worse, apart from any deceitful preference for the rich man's pleasures; he is as desperate a slave to his holiday stupor as to his forced labour.

The effort of social reformers to supply intellectual as well as material luxuries to the poor fails for want of roots in primary human nature. Reform, if it meant scope for popular genius, would let progress come from within, in harmony with economic arts and traditional morals and myths. To dump into the poor man's mind the products of a decadent aristocratic culture will perhaps accelerate their decomposition, but it will not sow the seed of anything better. While the pagan gods survived nominally it was in vain to multiply them; but when quite fallen and forgotten, they left an inner vacuum that the saints came to fill.

The claim of manual labour to control its own practice and even to inspire all society with its zeal and constancy would be both just and feasible if the reward of that labour were found in its immediate products, as in domestic agriculture or in the work of artists. But unskilled labourers, whose work makes them masters of nothing except the day's or the week's wages, are like slaves without a master, with freedom to wander but without any foothold anywhere or any assurance of finding work. And even when they find it, as its product for them is only money, the benefit of it is perpetually evanescent; and that benefit is itself ambiguous, since the occasional possession of money, without thrift, is a perpetual temptation. For labour really to become a school for political competence and also for personal virtue, it must be spontaneous, on a human scale in the object and in the strain of it, and capable of becoming in part a liberal art; for as an art, it trains the workman to respect the nature of things and to prosper by cooperation with it. And what better lesson would there be for the practice of government?

When the nation or the territory to be governed has never had moral unity or has lost it, the government cannot be rational; it can never be an art; for the country supplies no guiding purpose to its rulers. They must live from hand to mouth in the midst of traditional and revolutionary currents; and unless a political prophet can impose a faith of his own, government must be by politicians. That has been happening in Europe under our eyes; for it is materially impossible that the proletariat should govern itself systematically: it can only flow like a swollen river wherever the suction of the water takes it, with a dumb exultancy in its mass, its motion, and its irresistible advance; but the demagogues who seem to direct it are themselves caught in the current, and can neither represent the real interests of the people nor foresee their own fate. They might, indeed, become moral representatives of their people if they defended their spontaneous diversity, harmonised, not for universal dominion, but for diverse arts and free associations and special moral disciplines, in which the original genius of each might be developed. But that could be attempted, if not fulfilled, only by some wise leader who came not to destroy the natural order of society in the past but to purify it.

That an elected assembly, though it might initiate a revolution and control, especially by holding the purse strings, the rash impulses of the ruling powers, would be incapable of itself governing was clear to the earliest philosophical students of representative government, especially Montesquieu and the framers of the American Constitution. The executive, though controlled by the legislature, should be autonomous. It also should be traditional and consecutive, so long as the nation is in a vital stage of development or activity. It should be embodied in an institution, if not a hereditary monarchy, a self-perpetuating body like the Roman Senate, naturally representative of the historic and moral vocation of that nation. The American President and Senate were originally conceived to perform the function of the King and the House of Lords in England, but in England those functions soon became little more than symbolic and ceremonial, and in the United States until recently little exercised. Now, however, the autonomous function of a great government has been made inevitable in the United States by its international hegemony; and international affairs will be the most important and exciting issue in the public mind; and since both President and Senate are now elected by a direct vote of the people, there is not likely to be any prolonged divergence between them and the House of Representatives. The real question, perhaps, will be whether the President and Senate shall control the Administration or the Administration, with its learning and its enterprise, shall dominate the President and Senate.

In the semi-public world of affairs also there is everywhere a marked tendency for initiative to pass from legislative bodies to the managers of trade unions; for moral representation lies in furthering the interests, not in catching the votes, of the people represented. But the interest of the labourer is to be well paid, not overworked, and to be supplied gratis with schools and meals for his children and all sorts of "social services" for himself and his wife; and that is precisely what his leaders, while they lead an attack on the proprietors of lands or mines or factories agitate for and gradually secure. But it is obvious that this process must end very soon in the disappearance of landlords and other private owners, the State having rendered their property profitless, and taken their place. But how, if all profit on land and equipment is abolished, is the State to continue paying always higher wages for shorter hours of work, and supplying a more complete system of free social services?

Evidently when a government has assumed possession of all means of production and controls all business, it cannot distribute in wages and public services more than industry, so organised, will produce; and it will probably, and perhaps beneficently, produce rather less than was at first produced by rival capitalists and private enterprise, since there will be less ardour both in running risks and in earning higher wages. Society will be perhaps happier, but more slack and more resignedly traditional. The fever of the nineteenth century for sudden wealth and of the twentieth for mechanical marvels will have yielded to a classic wisdom, at a new industrial level of life.

I think that such a government, if rationally guided by science and history, might prove more truly a guardian of all natural interests, and therefore morally more representative than either tribal and patriarchal or elective governments are able to be. The rulers and managers would be selected, not by popular elections, but by co-option among the members of each branch of the service, as promotion normally ensues in armies, banking-houses, universities, or ecclesiastical hierarchies. Rational government is an art, requiring the widest knowledge and the most perfect disinterestedness. It should be steady and traditional, yet open to continual readjustments with the natural shifts of customs, passions, and aspirations in the world. Reason cannot define or codify human nature: that is the error of militant sects and factions. But it can exercise a modicum of control over local and temporal impulses and keep at least an ideal of spiritual liberty and social justice before the public eye.

## CHAPTER 23

### REPRESENTATIVE GOVERNMENT IV
### SHOULD IT OBEY PUBLIC FEELING OR PUBLIC INTEREST?

A MORAL dilemma, which custom obscures, besets a representative officer. If he is merely an instrument or blind vehicle, like a messenger bearing a sealed despatch, he is not *an officer of government* at all, but only a servant of the government. Anyone who wished to maintain literally the claim of the people to govern themselves would need to reduce all legislators and administrators to executants of exact instructions issued by the persons who had elected them. Yet obviously such instruction could never anticipate the terms of all measures that would have to be voted on or executed. A certain initiative must therefore be left to a representative agent to decide particular questions, on the understanding that he will be faithful to the general intentions and sentiments of his supporters.

A more delicate point, however, is this. Elected representatives are elected by a majority of votes; even if all voters were unanimous they would themselves be virtual representatives of other members of the community, who did not vote, such as minors or travellers, whose interest the elected person is expected to keep in mind, no less than if they voted. And almost always, at his election, besides the numerous absentees, there will have been a large minority who would have given him contrary instructions. These the conventional sentiment of democracies allows, or even commands, him to oppose or to ignore altogether. But this is a congenital defect of government by election, mitigated only when, in crucial matters, the whole elective body is unanimous, and their party quarrels touch only incidental, personal, or irrelevant matters. A party is not the whole people, and if a representative is bound to express only the will of his party he is not a fair representative of a truly self-governing people.

Yet if a people by mistake ever appointed a philosopher to govern them, the case would become much worse. For the philosopher would not fail to see the impossibility of satisfying the wishes of his electors if these wishes ran counter to the laws of nature, or to the conditions imposed by neighbouring powers; and he would go even further and ask himself if the interests of all other living creatures should not be considered in adjusting our wishes to our circumstances. Supposing the most favourable possible case, that all physical and military obstacles could be easily removed and the purposes of the philosopher's people could be wholly realised: would it follow that only the express neglect of all foreign arts and the extermination of all our passive enemies would really secure the vital liberty of our people?

The matter depends on the moral composition of each psyche and the degree of its organic unity. There are loose psyches, which at different seasons or on different occasions feel and judge in different ways, being now mastered by rage, now by sympathy, here by an idea, there by a vice. And there are close well-knit psyches that utter always the same note, cultivate the same fixed group of virtues, but are blind to all other interests and eager to extirpate all alien customs or opinions. When a State is morally homogeneous as, with negligible exceptions, is each primitive tribe or religious community, any elected representative will have an easy conscience in his politics, because he will feel no temptation to deviate from the beaten path of his supporters, nor, while he walks in it himself, any fear of their disapproval. But in a mixed society or a decadent age, where rival conditions clash and every sort of morality and immorality finds publicly respected advocates, it might conceivably happen that a pet virtue of his electors should seem criminal to him, who for some special service or distinction had been chosen to represent them. If a war or a persecution, for instance, were enthusiastically favoured by the people he might, on resigning his post, scarcely escape with his life. Or if the government were in the hands of a traditonal ruler who felt that he was the appointed guardian of the people's highest interests, as did Charles I of England, he might find himself in this dilemma: either to die as a traitor for resisting the apparent will of his people, or to lead that people to their moral ruin. This instance may seem to show the futility of obstructing the spirit of one's time; yet King Charles' sacrifice did represent the deep roots that the Church and the monarchy had in England, such that although restored unsatisfactorily and transformed clumsily, they have ever since preserved a refinement in English life and feeling which might have been missed if England had developed entirely like Holland and Germany.

## CHAPTER 24

### REPRESENTATIVE GOVERNMENT V
### ACTUAL FUNCTIONS OF PARLIAMENTS

IF THE moral authority of government rests ultimately on the judgments of individuals, how shall these judgments, in a numerous people, be so unified or collated as to be rendered effective?

By a parliament? By an assembly of elected representatives, who in turn elect a government?

It is often assumed that modern democracies are too populous to elect rulers or pass measures directly. This is hardly the case historically, and it is not at all the case in practice. Historically, members were first summoned to European Parliaments to voice their personal rights and interests, afterwards those of their class or corporation, and finally those of their party. In societies naturally and really democratic, like free settlements, the men chosen for representatives were naturally representative men, because almost any one would have been representative; they were not expected to report the expressed mind of their fellow pioneers, but to feel and to find it in themselves, and to give it original expression. They might almost have been chosen by lot, as jurors are; they might have been trusted to be true to the local type, and to know, like all their comrades, what was economically good for their camp.

If only one man or a few are now entrusted with the legislative function, rather than all, it is not because a means of consulting the public directly could not be devised; there was always the town meeting, and the referendum was not an unheard of or impracticable thing. Rather the legislative body, at first all the citizens in the agora, was reduced in number so as to render discussion possible. Politics were a practical matter of mutual consultation and compromise that had to be entrusted to the delegates—even to those that in the United States were to elect a President. Far from being sent to enact the previous will of their constituents, these delegates were sent to make, in face of rival interests, the needful and prudent concessions and, by persuasion, to secure concessions in return. They went as ambassadors, to investigate, negotiate, and speechify; their very existence betrays the jealousy and local independence of newly federated communities, where not merely each State was sovereign, but every village was self-directing. Congress, and especially the Senate, was a diplomatic conference; the affairs there dealt with were to the scattered rural population foreign affairs.

If Parliaments were judged by the theory of morally representative government—that they represent the Will of the People, which in turn expresses their true interests—there is no condemnation of their modern form that would be too sweeping; for everything about them, the character of the deputies, the reasons why they are chosen, the reasons why they have (or are supposed to have) their party opinions, and the causes of their voting this way or that—all have little to do with the Will of their constituents (probably never expressed on those issues); and this Will, if it could be discovered, would itself have little to do with their true interests in the play of international forces. A shrewd man of business will judge well what is for his private interests, and even what is for a like interest in others; but the more saturated he is with reality in that sphere the more casual or blank or contemptuous will be his sense of all other interests.

A parliament seems to relieve tyranny because it *ventilates grievances*. The little knot of persons who sit in the cabinet and in the ministers' offices are sensitive to censure and to suggestion. They are ordinary, quite ordinary men; and they are more slaves to routine, to lobbying, and "the forty thousand things" of Lao Tse than to any settled purpose or design. When they hear themselves criticised, they look at what they have been doing; or they even look at it before they do it, thinking of what those irresponsible carpers will say of it in the press. And however little their policy or sympathies may be affected by such prospective or actual censure, their conduct is affected by it; because they consider and look about them and formulate their own intentions as otherwise, were they safe from public invective, they might never do.

Moreover, a parliament serves the useful purpose of *cumiliuting the governed* who vote for its members; and just as we are all pleased to be asked for advice, even if it is not followed, so people are pleased to be asked to vote even if their vote has no real influence. For this reason universal and woman's suffrage are less disastrous than they might be expected to be; for what takes place is almost the same as if instead of an election there were a lottery; but the appearance of being considered, and of being a source of decisions which shake the world, if it is more diffused, seems more massive; and the wider suffrage wins the wider acquiescence. Besides, the very illusion of power, when it brings no harm to others, may have a sobering and deepening effect on the self; and good women who never cared for anything beyond their street may go seriously to vote with an enlightening sense that they are living in a vast, foreign and portentous world.

In the good old days of rotten boroughs the House of Commons was filled with younger sons, local magnates, and young men distinguished at the Universities for the gift of the gab; these persons, like the Lords, had acquired by tradition or experience a certain sympathy with the ruling forces of the State; ambiguous forces, as the sharp division into parties testified, but still living elements in that historical entity called the Country; they had a real stake in it, and might say: The Country? 'Tis ourselves. For they, their relations, their school friends, their ancestors, and their descendants had figured and would figure in the annals of the Navy, the Army, the Government, and the County Families, which were the essential annals of the Country as a political entity. The landscape of the country, with its fields and towns, customs and varied inhabitants, formed a much loved theatre for the drama of this political society, whose vocation was not to conquer or rule any other country, except occasionally by accident, but only to defend, preserve, and enjoy its own distinction and virtues.

Democracy, as we know, has changed all this. Everyone votes, but it is not yet clear whether he is expected to vote in the interest of his "country" or only of his own person or trade, or of the working class in general; or whether this moral providence should be limited by national frontiers, or, if extending beyond himself at all, should not be exercised equally over all living creatures. Meantime it remains necessary for the sovereign individual, swamped in his own universalised function, to decide everything by deputy; or rather to decide nothing, but only take part in the election of one or another deputy selected by rival party machines; who when elected shall decide everything for him, or leave everything undecided, according to the instincts and interests of that party machine.

In some parts these deputies are now a class by themselves, living on the salaries, allowances, and more or less legitimate profits of politicians; they are sometimes idle gentlemen and sometimes idle workmen; but more often small lawyers and busybodies looking for a job. In their humble beginnings they frequent public houses and operate by cajolery and the repetition of catchwords and anecdotes calculated to create animosity against the rival caucus; although these functions are now better fulfilled by the party newspapers than by the party candidates. But, once an accepted and active member of the machine, the politician never thinks of his constituents save when, on occasion of some election, he repeats to them from many a platform with much fatigue and perspiration what his party newspapers or party leader have already said. And if he becomes a party leader himself, or editor of a party newspaper, his object is clear: to obtain or to stay in office.

Unless a certain genuine humanity, shrewdness, and good humour adorn the politician, he will soon fail in his profession; because the public has instincts and perceptions even if it has little knowledge and no means of action. Even a party leader or a party newspaper may be discarded in time. What kills them is not responsibility for disaster or the advocacy of impossible measures, or the misrepresentation of facts; on these things they often prosper, since their readers have no independent lights; it is rather public feeling and the course of events taking a different direction; for these professors of demagogy are not prophets—though they use confident prediction as a means of silencing reason and self-defence on the part of their opponents. The course of opinion and of history is guided by forces far beyond their apprehension, and even more beyond their control.

The domination of politicians—which is what representative government means in practice—although the most ignoble of governments, is not necessarily the worst; for such a bevy of vivacious adventurers is dominated by no secret political passion or sacred unity; they merely wish to live and thrive in their profession and to have the pleasure of seeing the views they have adopted (probably by chance) triumph in the world. They are not cut off from the people round them in spite of their party machine, but can change their catchwords when these begin to fall flat and turn to the service of any new movement which seems to offer them room for prosperous activity and advancement. They are really too much in the same plight as the people they profess to represent; they are keyed intellectually by what they first happen to have at heart, perhaps in childhood. But they are capable of revolting in the end; they can come to recognise folly and ineptitude in particular matters; they will abandon an old master for a new one on occasion, with the probability of at least temporary advantage; for a domination just arising can hardly be without some justification—the life of the victor must be at least for a while vigorous, and not without a certain value in itself—whereas domination by inertia may endure when it brings nothing but suffering both to the government and to the governed.

The ceremonial of casting a ballot, with the rival party campaigns that precede it and the rival speeches in Parliament that ensue, may thus become means to the diffusion of that directive imagination which I have described above; for this diffusion is not limited to any form of government but grows with all dramatic participation in affairs of state. A tyrant, a prime minister, or a commanding general, who may be personally responsible for crucial events, may be absorbed in claiming the credit or disclaiming the blame for them: while the crowds watching a procession, or philosophers deducing a moral from remoter effects, may feel to the full the glory or the shame of their national destiny. Political conscience and political wisdom are not bred by political life; they are rather prejudiced and cheapened by it. Only exceptionally noble minds, an Alexander or an Edmund Burke, can preserve their freedom in the midst of faction.

The maxim that power corrupts, like other maxims, is a half-truth. There are cases of it; but what corrupts is not power itself, in those born or fitted to exercise it; rather what corrupts is the new atmosphere that envelops a mediocre nature seduced and lost in the great world, when it had been accustomed to thrifty morals, starved dumb passions, and provincial habits. The *parvenu* is intoxicated by the chance to do big or clever things never open to him before, and he blunders in doing them. But for a rider to find himself in the saddle when he knows how to ride quickens his faculties and exalts his purposes; because no true artist lives except in the life of his work.

Democracy in choosing its agents is therefore faced by this dilemma: shall representatives be expected to voice the opinions or advance the schemes of their electors; or shall they be trusted, in view of their acknowledged gifts, to serve their electors by serving the best interests of all who are affected, and thereby to secure the greatest spiritual satisfaction for ourselves and our people, even at some sacrifice of what we clamour for at the moment? In a word, is a parliament a central exchange for current demands or is it an *élite* commissioned to govern justly?

To govern was not originally the function of parliaments. Their business was to talk, to argue, to impress, as in a lawsuit; and to this day the majority of the members of parliaments are lawyers. Moreover the power they came to impress or persuade was not composed of any of their own members, but existed and governed for the most part independently, by its own right and resources. Where this ceased to be the case, parliaments sometimes as in Prussia acquired a stranglehold on government without any direct responsibility or participation in its action, since they now controlled its supplies. At the same time a further transformation followed in many cases: that the political efficacy of speeches in parliaments no longer turned on their eloquence or competence, but solely on the number of members already pledged by their party leaders to support or oppose the proposals to be made. Speeches by members of the minority are wasted, except as they may serve, if reproduced with large headlines in the press, for party propaganda; and all speeches by ordinary members of the majority are wasted in the same way, since only those made by members of the cabinet will forecast legislation and policy, to be officially proclaimed to be the Will of the People.

A curious transformation in the industrial world is tending now, in the middle of the twentieth century, really to make the voice of the people control governments, not through their legally elected parliaments but through organised labour unions and proletarian mass-meetings in the streets. I said at the beginning of this chapter that the members of popular assemblies originally represented only their own personal or class interests. This genuine value of collective demands made by an economic power already active was obscured after the French Revolution by philosophic sects, forming political parties on the basis, not of real interests, but of speculative opinions or "ideologies"; and the expectation of liberal democracies was that the people's interests should be identical for all, while bloodless and always "creative" conflicts should enliven their ideas. In politics they should be, on each occasion, practically unanimous, but in philosophy originality and variety should flourish for ever. This has rendered not only parliaments but wars gratuitous and useless, since they no longer arise by the inevitable rivalries and alternatives proper to the generative order of nature, but according to the accidents and confusions proper to imaginative passion when detached from material issues. Trade unions therefore threaten to replace parties verbally political in seizing the reins of government. They may do it by force and with the idiotic conviction that they are guided by an infallible theory; but they might actually confiscate private capital and construct by natural pressure of circumstances a new industrial and political order.

## CHAPTER 25

### ON THE SUBJECTS AND OBJECTS OF GOVERNMENT

AMONG nomads the chiefs command a movable company of kinsmen and servants with their flocks and herds and their portable possessions. Here government will not extend over a definite territory, but primarily over a definite People, and only incidentally over the territories they may occupy from time to time. In such territories there may have been previous inhabitants, some of whom may still remain, and strangers may intrude later; but these aliens, even if tolerated or friendly, will form no part of the People ruled by these chiefs according to their special customs and religion. The aliens will be regarded either as collateral Peoples with whom there is a tacit truce or alliance, or else as guests, prisoners, or slaves, subject indeed to the government but only as strangers, not having the rights or the duties proper to the dominant People itself.

Such is not, however, the fundamental concern of government in definitely bounded, settled, and civilised States. Here the chief function of government is the administration of its dominions. It rules primarily over its possessions, which are traditional, complicated, and precious; and its subjects are all the native inhabitants of the territories it controls. Some of these territories, or even all, may have been acquired by conquest or by cession from a previous government; and there may be any degree of diversity among the inhabitants in regard to race, customs, language, and religion. A fairly efficient proprietary government of this kind, such as most of the European monarchies in the sixteenth, seventeenth, and eighteenth centuries, tended to create a political nationality common to their heteroclite populations; but there always remained a cleft and a maladaptation between the interests of the government and those of the various Peoples caught, by geographical and historical accidents, under its net. Revolutions, secessions, ambiguous and reversible alliances were thus made possible and frequent under these landlord governments, who did not represent the spontaneous generative order of society in all or perhaps in any of their provinces, but rather the domination of some military or doctrinal sect, or of some class of landlords or merchants dominating the government itself.

This autocratic idealism in politics is a late militant philosophy, contrary to traditional religious and humane morals: not that humane morals and traditional religions, if pressed, do not also turn out to be idealistic and sacrificial at bottom, but that they borrow this self-transcendence from nature uncritically, and in sympathy with the procreative and poetic essence of animal and sensuous life; whereas Plato and Hegel were critics respectively of the Sophists and of the French Revolution, and preached a conceptual idealism with a militant philosophic and political zeal. The ideal to which they wished to sacrifice natural freedom was not the many-sided ideal radiation of spontaneous life, but a particular type of society or a particular method of change which they chose to impose on mankind or to attribute mythically to the universe. Their idealisms are therefore heretical from the point of view of traditional religions and of humane morals.

In the Old Testament, for instance, the primary object of divine government is the People, an essentially nomadic people, without a native land and its native deities, but relying only on a single God of Heaven, who came down sometimes to Ararat or to Sinai, and afterwards to his new Temple in Jerusalem, but who was worshipped distinctively as the God of Abraham, Isaac, and Jacob, who led his People Israel out of Egypt, and promised them a land which was in no sense their native soil. God's Covenant was with his People, on condition, not of their residence anywhere but of their spiritual fidelity and legal righteousness; and although the People were conceived collectively as a social and historical unit, the tendency of the Prophets, and later of the derivative religions, Christian and Moslem, was to conceive the bond of faith to be personal, and God rather the God of the heart, the conscience, or the intellect, than the God of any nation. The social bond of orthodoxy might be as tight as you please, but it had nothing to do with a particular territory or a particular lay government.

So too in the case of the British colonists in America, who often liked to identify themselves spiritually with ancient Israel, authority was rooted in persons, not in land, and society was cemented rather by community of manners and interests than by having converged by chance on the same place. House and home were easily transferred; one set of neighbours, being also settlers, would do as well as another; there was land enough for everybody, a whole continent sparsely occupied by natives that could easily be driven away; and the colonists being at first tolerably homogeneous, and all able and determined to look out for themselves, government was a simple matter of personal discussion and agreement; especially as a common law, for grave quarrels, was familiar to all. There was no prior territorial authority; nobody any longer belonged anywhere in particular; every interest and every criterion was fresh and private; yet there luckily was, in the crucial places, a similar background, religious and political, behind them all in the Old World, from which they also brought their applicable notions of history and the arts; so that they could spontaneously establish a government ruling the People according to the sentiment of fairness and prudence in the People themselves.

This absence of local attachments and possessions, combined with a common moral temper and practical competence, has set a special standard and method of procedure for American political action. There is a great confidence in discussion, great expectation of possible agreement, and a great simplicity in nominal purposes, in spite of the fact that the interests to be served and those to be confronted are now grown complex and heterogeneous. Everything seems to Americans to turn on a new organisation of enterprise and of education, not on a division of old real estate.

But a government that really dominates its territories can gradually, and sometimes suddenly, transform the inhabitants in language, manners, religion, or even in race. It will not govern the country, as Americans expect, by governing the people, but will govern the people by governing the country. It is true that this kind of government is often disastrous, and the rulers are themselves destroyed first; but fate overwhelms everything in the end, and territorial domination has secured, for instance, the long prevalence in large areas of Hellenism, of Islam, and of Protestantism. The study of these epidemic systems in their different modes of diffusion and prevalence would be instructive. Hellenism was spread by the conquests of Alexander in the East, where its influence was lasting as that of a fashion in manners and the liberal arts, but transitory and only marginal in morals and speculation; whereas, through the Roman conquest, Hellenism became the foundation of culture in the West down to our own day. The spread of Islam was essentially militant and aristocratic, establishing government, public works, and civic manners for the conquering race, but leaving the natives if also "men of the Book" largely free to live in their own way with their own languages and religions. It was what the British conquest of India might have been if the British monarch and all his people had migrated to India and established themselves there with a mixture of contempt and goodwill towards the Indians. Very different was the imposition of Protestantism in England, Scandinavia, and many parts of Germany, where the princes changed the religion of the people by availing themselves of a religious rebellion in some reformers and at the same time of great greed and pliability in their own courtiers, in the interests of national pride and royal absoluteness. Here, as in the first establishment of Christianity by Constantine, governments could not so swiftly have changed the people's religion, had not a strong wind of religious change already prevailed; but they revised the new system, which might have developed or evaporated otherwise if left to itself, by establishing some official church, pledged to defend a special orthodoxy.

Government is an art and like other arts it may be practiced for its own sake, as well as for other objects. Absolute despots are supposed to govern for their own pleasure; but they are often proud of their works, and of the prosperity of their dominions. They might also, like Augustus, pride themselves on the literature of their reign. Nor is it necessary that these achievements should be due, or attributed, to a single monarch. They may be more long lived than any one man; and a general order and glory in the world may well become the criterion by which both government and people judge the value of their own characters and actions. It was so normally in classic antiquity. The dominant concern of the government was not the private welfare of the inhabitants, however numerous they might become or whatever habits they might develop. Their number, their education, their privileges were to be made comfortable to the needs of the State for the time being. So too the privileges and functions of each class or profession. The priests were not to upset this world for the sake of the other, politicians and sophists were not to demoralise the public for the sake of popularity, nor generals to lead unnecessary expeditions for the sake of fame. The order and glory of the city, for generation after generation, was to be the common object, both of glory and of sacrifice, for all the citizens.

The People, the Country, or the State may thus be in turn the direct concern of a government. But only a perpetually migrating people could fail to acquire roots and possessions in a particular region which would become their country, and be a subject of interest to them in itself, for its development, monuments, and physical character. Even an ideal concern for a national State and its history could soon grow up, as in the cases otherwise so different, of Sparta and of the Jews; nor could any government ignore the material and domestic welfare of the people, or avoid all attachment to the places where they lived and the possessions they might have acquired there. Yet the subordination of one of these objects to another is always possible and sometimes optional, and the critic of governments needs to understand them all.

CHAPTER 26

"GOVERNMENT OF THE PEOPLE"

If we suppose various families together with stray individuals to be wrecked on a desert island, we can understand how, finding themselves in a common predicament, they will sometimes cooperate and sometimes quarrel; and then leaders will spontaneously appear who by the force of their words and actions will secure the obedience or acquiescence of their companions. A government will thus have arisen. Its function will not be to defend the territory, which is not being attacked, nor to build houses or occupy lands, since everyone will be quick to do so for himself in his own fashion. No one will have had prior possession of the soil, or will put forth ideal prerogatives as a prophet. The function of this government will be only to control such voluntary cooperation as there may spring up among the people and to settle their contentions by natural equity or common law. Individuals and families will look after themselves, and government will interfere with them only when they interfere with one another. It will have nothing to govern except the People.

It is not, however, in this purely social function that most governments are interested. Their concern is chiefly with the resources and political greatness of their dominions; and the constant stream of anonymous inhabitants that are born and die there preoccupy them only as tenants of the land, labourers in the mines, soldiers and sailors, taxpayers, and persons who otherwise the rulers wish to see flourishing in the State committed to their care.

Had Abraham Lincoln this broad contrast in mind when in his Gettysburg speech he defined the ideal character of American democracy? If he had he was giving to the first phrase in that definition "a government of the people" a more realistic historical and descriptive meaning than it carries to-day when it is perfunctorily repeated. I remember what violent emphasis, in the 1870's and 1880's, boys declaiming at the Boston Latin School, and other orators generally, would lay on the three prepositions in that formula, shouting almost angrily that a government *of* the people, *by* the people, and *for* the people should not perish from the earth. Nobody (except me) felt that the phrase "of the people" might have been originally a calm objective genitive implying, if anything, that the people required a government. And the language of the Gettysburg speech is so noble, so sober, and so carefully studied, that even now I doubt that Lincoln, in composing it, could have meant that first phrase to be a vaguer anticipation of what the second and third phrase announce explicitly. But in the popular mind, with frequent repetition, rhythm and enthusiasm have merged the whole into a ritual symbol; and that legal objective genitive has become decidedly possessive. It means that the government to be preserved shall be not only democratic in form and beneficent in operation, but precious and dear in itself, popular and homely: the People's Own Government. To be drawn from one's very vitals is indeed the radical sense of the genitive case; so that grammatically as well as emotionally this reading of the clause "a government of the people" is legitimate; but what does it signify politically?

This expression, "the people," though now often used to designate all the inhabitants of a region or of the globe, retains a rhetorical and political quality that limits it rather to one class of the total population. The official title of he Roman Republic, *Senatus Populusque Romanus*, explicitly distinguishes the people from the patricians or original landed families; and it ignores the slaves and aliens altogether who may sometimes have outnumbered the plebeian citizens. And there was another People to whom at least the Puritans in America felt themselves akin, the chosen People of Israel, even more sharply opposed to mankind in general or to the mixed population of great cities or recognised States. Even apart from that religious and moral idiosyncrasy felt by those who called themselves the people, there were in almost all American colonists bitter memories of proprietary monarchy and landlord tyranny; if a government was necessary at all, let it at least be composed of persons of their own class, knowing their needs and sharing their thoughts. No government, then, of aristocrats: no king, no priests, no landlords, no generals, no bureaucrats, and (they might have added prophetically) no professional politicians. Let all officials be plain men, drawn for a short time of service, by the general voice of their comrades, from the plough, the mine, the workshop, or the counting-house; and let them—since power corrupts—return soon to their old occupations, to drink in again the healthful atmosphere of labour and the rude but sound wisdom of unlettered men. Such is, as the people understand it, the true burden of the phrase "a government of the people."

It is obvious, however, and soon confirmed by experience, that as the business of government becomes complex—and it is complex beyond imagination—specialists may be employed to prepare its plans and to execute them. The common people must trust in most things the judgment of others; and how shall they decide whose judgment to trust? Waves of contagious feeling sweep through the public; and on these waves men of eloquence and tact rise in turn to power. How far can the government of the people, in these circumstances, remain the people's own government?

## CHAPTER 27

### WHO ARE "THE PEOPLE"?

WHEN moral philosophy passes from an oracular phase into one that, at least in theory, is exclusively humanitarian, the object and criterion of good government will be said to be "the good of the people." This way of expressing it does not exclude from the functions of government all concern for country, glory, monuments, science, letters, or religion. The cultivation of these interests might well form a part of the good proper to the people, or to a part of them. Yet humanitarian morality excludes ideal aims except as they may be psychological demands in living persons; that they may have been occasionally the goods chiefly prized by mankind, or may be such in the future, would not make them the good of the people now. Leaving for consideration later what the good of the people may be, I will first consider more carefully the scope of this term "the People."

At first blush it may seem obvious that "the People" means all the inhabitants and that the people whose good a good government must serve comprise all the population subject to its jurisdiction. But these words are scarcely uttered when questions come trooping into the mind. Are resident foreigners, or tourists momentarily in the country, a part of "the People" that the government should serve? It certainly affects the strangers' comfort or welfare; should it provide for them gratis out of universal goodwill, or only in view of reciprocal favours to be expected by its own citizens when travelling or trading abroad? May not a good government conduct its foreign policy in such a way as to support kindred nations even at the cost of some sacrifice of material interests at home? And here subtler questions begin to appear. Are the purposes pursued by a nation in the past to be counted among its true interests apart from the degree of attention that the public may be giving them at the present moment? Should not a good government direct the people to a recognition of their *true* good? Should it not, for instance, leave them free, if their true good is liberty, even if they clamour for protection, prohibition, compulsory education of all grades, and guaranteed work, lodgings, pensions, and social services? Or, if the clamour is against these alleged benefits, should not a good government make itself the representative of the people's higher selves, show them what they would be missing without its guidance, and for their own good compel them to be healthy, educated, virtuous, and happy?

Whatever course the government takes it would seem to be condemned to secure the good as recognised by only *some* people. And this theoretical difficulty becomes a burning political problem in fixing the limits actually set to "The People" at various times and places.

## WHO ARE "THE PEOPLE"?

Thus the ancient Jews frankly called themselves the *chosen* people, limited in race to the children of Abraham and in moral identity to faithful adherents to the Law of Moses and the spirit of the Hebrew Prophets. The same principle of selection for merbership in the one rightly dominant people on earth and triumphant society in heaven appears in Islam and in the various forms of Christianity, modified by historical circumstances; and it reappears now, disguised in secular terms, in the two rival "ideologies," communist and liberal, ready to exterminate each other. The "People" in the one case include only the Communist Party, faithful to its providentially self-imposed leaders; and in the other it includes all men in so far as they agree to differ in thought, but in action always follow the majority. The People, for the communists, must be unanimous. For the liberals all parties are admitted, except the "criminals" who attempt to impose their special opinions by force or by guile. Even here, therefore, the police must impose respect for what one party esteems most, namely, for liberty.

These attempts to be rational are really militant; and we must look to the generative order of society to see what "the People" in fact may signify. In tribal societies it naturally means the tribe; and when agriculture has domesticated and rooted them it means the *local* population in contrast to strangers and the *common* people in contrast to their natural leaders. The classical case, from which the word "people" is derived, is that of the *Senatus Populusque Romanus*. Verbally, the contrast here is between patricians—the landowners with their children and dependents—and the artisan free population of the City. But there was another class (or classes) excluded from the People politically: namely resident foreigners, chiefly merchants, and slaves who served the patrician and plebeian landlords or householders. It was only the natives that formed the *Senatus Populusque*; and those together formed, not the population, but the government.

This articulation of the contrast between the government and the governed was transformed by the barbarian conquest, the feudal system, and the Christian types of peasant serfdom and domestic service. Peasants and servants then joined the artisans in the towns in composing "the People"; and distinct, though often derived, from them were the clergy and men-at-arms, commanded by a nobility composed of military chiefs turned into local proprietors and potentates. A complicated hierarchy of lieges and vassals of different ranks arose both in Church and State, with Popes, Emperors, and Kings, by divine right, occupying exalted places, often rather dignities than powers. Yet, especially in the commercial or industrial cities, vestiges of the *Populusque Romanus* re-appeared in picturesque Christian guise. The trades became institutions, with legal privileges and rights, such as the plebeians had extorted in Rome from the patricians. These townspeople could well resist the exactions of their feudal overlords. Merchants, artists, doctors, and clergy began to form a bourgeois class, distinct from artisans and shopkeepers, and began to feel that they were not essentially part of the People. They became the upper middle class. Yet it has been they, backed by militant eruptions from the working class beneath and the aristocracy above, that have constituted the liberal and democratic parties of recent times, invoking and professing to serve the People, without being a part of them.

In modern England social and political custom has never sharply distinguished the "People" from the nation or from the government; and it can hardly be said that universal suffrage, for instance, has brought the government nearer to the heart of the people than it was under Queen Elizabeth. Nevertheless the social hierarchy has nowhere been more clearly defined or respected than in England until the twentieth century. Snobbery, of which satirists accused the nation, was a peculiar sentiment of duty, deference, and sympathy in the humbler persons, at each stage, towards those above them; and emotionally the Court and the government felt themselves to be as much a part of the people as the shopkeepers, servants, or sailors.

The same continuity of political consciousness runs in the United States through all degrees of wealth and forms of labour; and the same good-natured pleasure at the greater wealth of others is seen in the common people as in England at their higher station, which is not long distinguishable from hereditary wealth.

Perhaps the most genuine line of cleavage in human society, in all ages and countries, is that between the rich and the poor. The poor we have always with us, and in some form the rich and the privileged also; but while wealth, at least great wealth, is not visible in a man or woman, but only in their houses or other belongings, poverty can be recognised at sight, and is distress made visible. It also has the property, proper to the generative order of things, of being in flux and removable, at least in its casual forms and distribution. In the East, where extreme poverty is often patent and widespread, it seems too human and exchangeable a condition to form a particular people, especially where traditional wisdom and refinement of feeling may often be present in the poor more than in the rich.

It is precisely in the East that the naturally distinctive properties of a people become obvious, crossing all boundaries of States and established jurisdictions. A people is properly speaking a civilised tribe, united by blood, language, and religion. In its origins a people may be as hybrid as you please, but in so far as it is morally and politically one people it will tend to become, by inbreeding, a pure race. If a mixed population in a given territory tends to segregate rather than to merge (as whites and blacks seem to tend in the United States) they will become two peoples: which would not necessarily prevent them from living side by side in the same country under the same government, if this government were not totalitarian, but respected the moral and civic individuality of each people.

Contemporary support for this analysis of the political essence of a people may be found in the language of communist governments. They demand that all political parties and influences be inspired by the people: but this "People" is not the whole population, nor the majority of it, nor the part that preserves and transmits ancient tradition. It means often a small minority of the inhabitants who have recently embraced (even in Russia) a foreign theory of government. Yet these few converts compose a people, and even the People, precisely because they are the proletariat, that is to say, the outcasts, without possessions or allegiance of any sort, and are therefore called to gather from all nations, like the early Christians, and form together a new universal People, unanimous in faith and obedient to a rule of life which the whole world ought to adopt and must adopt if it is to establish peace on earth and to enjoy it for ever.

Government is an art, serving economic and moral interests. The limits of the people who inspire and obey it are properly vital and moral limits, not geographical or racial except by accident. A people may migrate, and in proportion to the strength of its vital unity it will tend to fuse its blood and its moral heritage into a single race and language. Tribal bonds are usually local; the local cohabitation may be the occasion of vital fusion among peoples originally strangers and rivals. On the other hand a purely moral bond, like religion, may sometimes suffice to cement and distinguish a scattered people. The Jews are the palmary example of a great and long-lived people closely united without a government or a territory; and Islam, while essentially militant and haughty, can unite many different regions and races into one people by attachment to a common way of life and sentiment. And it seems to me not impossible that in a similar way the Catholic Church, without anywhere retaining political domination, might subsist throughout the world as a distinct people, in larger or smaller groups of different races and speech, everywhere faithful to the same religious customs, philosophy, and arts.

Such a diversity of civilised peoples, each with its vital inspiration and traditional regimen, flourishing perhaps on the same universal basis of a rational economic order, would seem to me highly desirable. Mankind walks on one material planet under one material firmament; these conditions it is to their common advantage to respect. But, that toll once paid to necessity, why should not vital liberty in each heart devise the private or social or ideal order by which it would live?

## CHAPTER 28

### "GOVERNMENT BY THE PEOPLE" I
### HOW POSSIBLE

WHEN the People are the *object* on which government is exercised, there might seem to be a paradox in saying that the same People was the *agent* in that government. Government is needed only where, if left to themselves, a part of the people would make life and property insecure for the rest. In a small, homogeneous, and highly civilised group, such as once were the travellers in a first-class carriage, a policeman was not required. The individuals could be relied upon to respect and if necessary to assist one another. And the same thing happens, in spots among exiles and refugees, when the destitute practice charity among themselves. Ordinarily, however, it becomes necessary to entrust charity as well as repression to a special body of professionals, probably under a chief appointed to keep those agents themselves in order. Thus government is never long exercised by all or sundry members of society, but by a single specially instituted government.

Unless this governing body is foreign, the people may nevertheless be said to govern themselves in the sense that the members of their government form a part of that people, and govern in its name and with its acquiescence. A successful popular rebellion would either destroy that government altogether or secede and form an independent people.

Nor are the operations of a government separable from the people on which they are performed. They are necessarily a part of its life and history. They had causes and leave incalculable effects in its institutions and habits. But the cause of these effects can never flow from every member of that community equally. The measure most unanimously approved at one date will have different roots in different minds, and will assume different meanings at later times; and the verbal and public objects approved in debate may bring, when attained, no comfort to any heart. Government is an organ superposed politically upon a society each member of which is a complete organism in itself; and even when the political machine unites the living machines into one efficient engine, the moral function of the whole is altogether of a different order from the moral function of each constituent. Benefits and scourges of many kinds may come to individuals from government, but they are properly not parts of its own aims. They are like the wounds and the promotions incidental to an officer in war; they may partly exasperate and partly reconcile him; they were no part of the government's objective.

When occasional enthusiasm at public achievements warms the cheering crowd, it is for no ulterior benefit expected by each of those individuals. It is by a self-transcending flight of imagination, as if the spirit in each had become for a moment the mythical Spirit of his whole nation in all its wars, and he saw the glory of it like one of the constellations in the firmament. This is indeed, when it occurs, a truly human satisfaction; but it belongs to pure intelligence and abstracts altogether from economic attachments to one nation or epoch rather than to another. It therefore cancels all properly political interests, to which the man who has fallen or risen into that trance must revert in his accidental life and duties. This essential contrast, yet possible concomitance, of earthly life with spiritual peace is beautifully expounded in the Bhavagad-Gita; and in various forms it has been recognised by all free sages of whatever epoch or nation.

Emotional participation in the fortunes of a government is disinterested, like emotional participation in any drama, real or imaginary. It involves a certain moral identification with the Will of the victorious or tragic heroes concerned; spiritually the public makes itself a moral accomplice in these perilous deeds; but the most frenzied enthusiasm of that public cannot render it in any measure the agent in that action. The people may be carried by storm; they may identify themselves momentarily with their rulers; but it is not they that are governing.

A sympathetic fusion of another kind occurs in practical politics between the governed and the government. Except where the rulers are foreigners, they are members of the society which they control; if they are virtuous they obey the decrees which they issue. In this measure they actually govern themselves. Now this double movement of the Will, by which they at once frame and carry out a plan, may be repeated sympathetically by various classes of their fellow-countrymen. Their very professional thoughts and interests as a government will be understood and shared at least by members of their party: for the exercise of government is not only a passion for the statesman but a matter of moral concern to the intelligent citizen, and a moving drama for the patriotic historian. Thus, no matter how autocratic a government may be, the whole nation over which it presides lives its life and its vicissitudes with a more or less lively interest. As an excited spectator, as a moralising chorus, or as a conscious victim, the individual finds in the conduct of the government a daily portion of his joys or sorrows. If he belongs to the party in power in a democracy, he may fancy that by his vote he actually contributed to carry out its policy; yet this diffusion of political responsibility is not less felt by ardent natures where it does not exist on paper. Political keenness and eloquence become even more passionate when people feel that they are being governed by others gloriously or disastrously. In a Greek tragedy it is pure politics or the momentous governing of human life that is exhibited in its first commitments and ultimate fruits; and there the chorus, which represents the people, is neither the agent nor the object in the action but only the spectator and moral judge of its course; yet the whole soul of that chorus is suspended on those tragic events which lift it to the greatest heights of poetry and philosophy. In this same way, a nation that feels the life of its government invading and animating it may even outdo its government in precipitating the action which both are meditating together. Driving, then, rather than driven, the people may be prophetically ruling their rulers and themselves. Such moments, however, are few and brief, and the natural dichotomy between the government and the governed returns with its moral friction and mutual discontent.

## CHAPTER 29

### "GOVERNMENT BY THE PEOPLE" II
### PSYCHOLOGY OF AGREEMENT

THAT it is permissible to say that a man may govern himself must be accepted as an axiom in morals; otherwise precepts, or even private decisions, would be entirely vain. Yet on reflection the axiom appears self-contradictory, or at least equivocal. If one part of a man can govern another, neither part could be said to be the whole man, and the attribution of dominion to himself cannot be strictly correct. Theology has wrestled with this difficulty, sometimes pronouncing boldly that it is only God, or the total automatism of nature, that can govern any event, and sometimes deciding that only the part that freely governs the material part of the man is truly the man himself, the "flesh" being only an alien burden or recalcitrant instrument with which he has to struggle.

But it is not when a man is divided against himself or hard pressed by a hostile world that he enjoys the glorious sentiment of self-mastery. This arises spontaneously when as yet there is perfect health and harmony in the psyche, and the man is swimming with the stream, finding in things only the resistance that is needed to develop his powers and to offer him materials plastic to his hand.

Or else, rarely and through heroic discipline, perfect integrity may be attained when the body and its passions have been thoroughly trained and coordinated, so that they have become docile vehicles for the rational will. Self-government, between these rival forms of perfect harmony, can only grope and stumble along through conflict, compromise, disappointment, and renunciation, to sad conformity with a destiny that one would never have chosen for oneself.

This analysis of self-government in the soul can be transferred instructively to self-government in the people. Fundamentally, in a simple uncorrupted society in simple unmistakable circumstances, such a thing is spontaneous. Then, to vital health in the soul, corresponds unanimity in the community. When a common danger threatens or a work in common must be undertaken, the whole people, or at least the heads of all the families, can meet; the same preoccupation, the same readiness, animates them all; someone, no matter who, will speak for the rest; either he will meet with instantaneous general approval, or someone else, aware of dissent in the faces of the crowd, will make a different proposal; and it will be this that everyone will acclaim, even the man who at first suggested another course, which he now acknowledges not to be the right one. The people will then begin to carry out systematically the measures which they have approved. They will be governed, they will be dutifully obeying an appointed order and an appointed leader; yet they will be governed only by their common free and deliberate will.

This is an idealised picture; yet it was often almost realised in many a primitive American settlement, and it still swims before the public mind, not only in the politics of English-speaking peoples, but in the thousand semi-public meetings in which groups of them discuss their business. It survives best—and this is a circumstance worth noticing—where some special purpose or special bond brings these persons together only occasionally. They now have more various and probably more vital interests than those which they gather to discuss; and in each club or each political or charitable gathering there is probably a small committee or merely a chairman who does almost all the work and has almost all the enthusiasm. The others sleepily listen and assent willingly; for they share the fundamental views of their associates (else they would not have joined that voluntary and unnecessary society) but the matter is not central or urgent in their minds. Even if they do not altogether like what is being done, they let it pass; and the consensus of opinion in such gatherings comes largely from laziness of thought and indifference to the consequences.

There is a normal psychological transformation of private sentiment in public or even in the presence of a single fellow-being. Each becomes cognizant not of what he is, but of what he seems or of what the other man may say; contagion and dissimulation operate together. Both persons begin to think and feel histrionically, not according to their own reason; and the points on which the two agree are the real convictions of neither.

Here we see how imperfect the analogy is between self-government in a soul and self-government in a people. In both these agents there is an original multitude of vital elements or living cells, sensitive to one another's proximity and force, that are attracted into a dynamic unity. But in the case of a person this dynamic unity is a biological unit. As a drop of water, composed of many molecules, is bound together by surface tension into a physical unit, and runs down the window-pane with a single combined impulse and cumulative speed, so the many passions and interests in a living man are caught and held together by the network of his brain and of its living cortex. We may say that two souls are wedded irreparably by the surface tension, so to speak, of his skin and of his single heart. They may cause that heart to beat alternately, but they cannot breed a heart or a skin or a pair of eyes and hands, each their own, to live in apart. The vital elements or living cells that compose a people, on the contrary, are themselves natural units, incapable of living except as wholes, or of forming together a larger whole that shall be truly living. Society is psysically a concourse, not an organism; and it lives only by virtue of a modification that such a concourse produces, for the time being, in those organisms which are naturally separable and separately alive. The unity which a soul may establish among its passions will be a vital unity, in which those passions will lose their separable being, and leave only a heritage of memory and experience to instruct and strengthen that single surviving soul; but the unity of a people, though it may be a dynamic and emotional unity at certain moments, like the unity of a hurricane, dies away at once into silence in its members. They have each a separate and compulsory life of their own, full of private needs and cares, against which their public enthusiasms are likely to seem, in the end, verbal, artificial, and tragic.

Something may nevertheless arise in a society that corresponds in part to the integration of principles and virtues in an individual. As there are traditions and customs in primitive peoples, so in civilised peoples there are laws and institutions. These form the mind of each generation on a common pattern and become in each man, if he is loyal, a force in the formation of personal character. A people so trained and rendered unanimous may then govern itself in so far as it is already governed by what is called the "spirit" of those laws and institutions. We are here, however, in the realm of metaphor and rhetorical illusion. Each man remains a fresh centre of life. The traditions he inherits and the institutions he finds, if in part they mould and inspire him, must in part be a drag and a burden to his vital freedom. Few may perceive their plight intellectually; but practically and emotionally all youth will be restive under the imposed common life; and the escape from the tyranny of society entrenched may drive the majority rather into the arms of society dissipated and factious than into the wilderness, where the soul, stripped naked, might think to recover its liberty.

Government by the people, except in small, simple, and previously disciplined communities, is therefore something elusive and ambiguous. The people is a unit only for apprehension, covering a variable and diffused concourse of separate lives and interests. That which enables a people to exercise the function of government is the prior existence and tacit acceptance of traditions, laws, and institutions which already govern them and which supply models, subject to opportune variations, for the action proposed and for the selection of officers who may carry that action out. For it is not ordinarily the whole people that are being charged with executive functions, but only certain persons appointed for the purpose. It is by deputy only that the people can steadily govern. But deputies are men placed in privileged and dangerous positions, which vitiate the transmission of commands supposed to be originally given by the people to their elected representatives. This is a delicate subject to which I shall return. For the moment it will suffice to suggest two possibilities: that a man selected for his eminence to represent the people may care more for the general interest, and may understand it better, than does the average citizen who is supposed to direct him; and secondly that either by this superiority of insight or else by the growth of special party interests or private ambition and vanity in the governing class, government may cease to be even indirectly government by the people and may become an oligarchy or a bureaucracy.

From these sundry considerations we may pass to a general remark about self-government: that it can never be fully realised except where, in the soul or in the community, there is absolute unanimity. Where any superficial diversity of thought or will cannot be reduced to agreement by a moment's reflection, a dualism is established between that part of the soul or of the people whose will is done, and that part whose will is defeated and ignored. Then to say that the soul or the people governs itself can mean only that the power that dominates it is native to it, and one strain in its own life. It cannot mean that all govern and all obey, but that the stronger part, in ability, material force, wealth, or numbers, rules the weaker part. There will be a domination, not self-government, in such a psyche or such a people.

Sometimes, however, such domination by party loses half its venom when, as often happens in Anglo-Saxon countries, the rival parties are only two, each officially unanimous in itself, although not really so, and the two so little at variance that they can courteously take turns at the bat, causing no inconvenience and much entertainment to the political public. There is evidently at such happy times, a genuine fundamental unanimity as to how they wish to be governed and to play their part in the international game; and they can identify themselves as heartily with the action of their government in time of peace as with that of their army and navy in war.

There is always something satisfying, even inebriating, in the shouts of a vast crowd or in an epidemic revolution. These shouts promise Unanimity. Far back and deep down in animal life *mimesis* determines the growth of structure and aspect, not coercively as material pressure might, but vitally, by precipitating one out of many potentialities in a plastic psyche; for the less elaborate and tightly organised are the tropes which matter has adopted, the readier it is to adopt new ones. Yet the indeterminate cannot choose of itself how it shall be determined, but waits in permanent suspense for some accident to determine it; and the rhythm of a neighbouring movement, etherially transmitted, may easily be caught and perpetuated by an innocent being. Such mimesis, I suppose, occurs by dynamic contagion far beneath the surface of things, as it does in heredity. It is not by dint of gazing at his father's beard that a son grows a beard like it. At the due age it would present itself on his cheeks and chin even if his father were dead and had been clean shaven. As Pasteur discovered that contagious diseases never jump through vacancy, so a thorough zoology, I believe, would discover dynamic bonds in mimesis. Where a type had become rigid neighbouring types will not induce imitation, rather if anything mockery or hostility; but where structure is still plastic and mind vacant every suggestion is catching. As in a forest fire sparks break out in various places until the flames meet in one conflagration, so impulses spread in an ignorant crowd, long sullen and inactive, but full of suppressed grievances. A single unforeseen action will then let loose a thousand imitative Wills.

Such occasional unanimity, with the ruthless action which it often prompts, though actual psychologically, is socially and politically an illusion. No two living creatures are ever in their hearts unanimous. The momentary unanimity they may feel is an effect of possession in each by an alien power, not an expression of true self-knowledge or vital liberty. Nevertheless the ideal of unanimity has an invincible hold on the human imagination, like other mystical ideals in which a primary simplicity and an unclouded faith, proper to budding Will, rise again like a flood from the depths and drown all the distinctions, troubles, and doubts that anxious life has involved.

## CHAPTER 30

### "GOVERNMENT BY THE PEOPLE" III
### ETHICS OF COMPROMISE

IN THE human race Unanimity, which is essential to a just democracy, may have arisen spontaneously or, more often, it may be obtained for a time, in a special society, by force or by propaganda, as we find it in the history of Islam and of Christianity or in the

# "GOVERNMENT BY THE PEOPLE" III

Communism of to-day. If these militant systems could be pursued thoroughly and continuously they might even bend the hereditary constitution of the psyche in those peoples, so that their children should be born unanimously ready to be Moslems or Christians or Communists, as ants and bees are born unanimous in their social tasks. But this would be exceptional, for nature hardly allows artificial virtues to flourish for more than a season; and when they are lost, the lovers of moral unanimity are perhaps tempted to appeal from nature and the arts, which are historical growths, to reason, which is a moral ideal. Reason never rules the world, but it sometimes beckons in the conscience and seems to shine in a specious harmony of chosen words or ideas. Now, amid the quarrels and disputes of social life, reason, aided by convenience, sees a particularly simple, practicable, and easy path to unanimity. This path is Compromise.

Compromise appears, without being noticed, in the economic arts. There it imposes itself at all the difficult cross-roads in the execution of a work. For when an obstacle presents itself, and the momentum of happy invention or labour is arrested, what can the workman do but circumvent the difficulty by surrendering a part of his original impulse and satisfying the rest in conformity with unforeseen circumstances which he cannot escape? And this is a tacit compromise of Will and Fate.

Materially and in detached cases the surrender to Fate touches only the method or the amount of labour concerned, not at all the end pursued. If the highway be blocked on a journey, a by-path is taken and the intended inn is reached a little later, with somewhat more fatigue. But suppose a sculptor finds a flaw in his material which compels him to modify his design; it may happen that the variation by chance imposed proves to be better in his own eyes than was his original idea. Then the apparent hindrance brings a new inspiration. In this case his art has coalesced with the generative order of nature, and has advanced one step in the discovery and manifestation of a form satisfying the heart and sanctioned by confluence with necessity. It was indeed by such adaptation to the possible that the psyche in every species consolidated its form.

In politics, however, it is with other Wills, not with physical circumstances, that conflict arises and solutions, painful or fortunate, have to be found. Yet even here it is rather in trade than in government that compromise begins to seem the best path to agreement. At a country fair, which is a festive occasion, everyone arrives with high hopes of buying cheap and selling dear. But not everyone else is a fool, and many are old acquaintances; bargaining begins; the wares are respectively praised and criticised, and after the buyer has repeatedly offered a little more and the seller demanded a little less, both agree on a middle price, by which each makes a tidy profit without cheating the other fellow; and the two go and have a drink.

This pleasant method of letting different intentions disappear in a social haze is eminently sensible in regard to things in themselves indifferent, and proposed only as means for obtaining other things valued on their own account. Partly for this reason Compromise holds a high place in the eyes of American politicians; for "lobbying" in the legislatures, national or local, seems to be chiefly concerned with the minor matters of patronage and private interest, often not those of the Representatives themselves but of their importunate supporters at home. No wonder if they care more about dispatching these multitudinous affairs than about the issue in each case. Is not everybody in America agreed on fundamentals? No need, then, to think of them. What is of present importance is to satisfy one's constituents, to please the leaders of one's party, and to secure one's own re-election. When the two disputants meet in some committee, or in private conversation with the agents of a rival interest, the flat contradictions at first shouted across the table may eventually be shown, with goodwill, not to involve insurmountable difficulties. Each may consent to drop a part of his demands; he may bravely abandon some exaggeration in his statements or some illusion in his hopes and be content with what it is possible to obtain amicably. And the advantage gained will not be merely to have settled a troublesome affair with some material compensation. The moral atmosphere will have cleared. Both sides will justly feel proud of having been so reasonable, a generous glow will replace their initial acrimony, and will confirm their faith in the providential virtue of Compromise.

The psychology of the country fair will then recur in the Senate. The late antagonists will instinctively drift into the bar. They will shake hands warmly on their happy agreement. When they separate, "Jack" will say to himself, "Did I really care so much for that bill to increase Old Soldiers' pensions?" And "Jim" will say to himself, "Did it really make much difference whether that canal crossed my father-in-law's farm or not?" And both will inwardly answer: "No! What I really needed was this cocktail and this friend."

Such might be the surface glow of universal social unanimity secured by compromise. There is joy in jettisoning useless troublesome commitments that burden our lives. How genial public life becomes when reduced entirely to cordiality and platitudes! The leaders in such a society need not be superior to the crowd in knowledge or virtue; they must be simply quicker. They must be first to name, and loudest to demand, something that, for the moment, will appeal to the average man. This is not machination on the leaders' part; those will succeed best who are sincere and have divined the people's instinct by passionately trusting their own. In choosing a government a truly homogeneous and unanimous people would best proceed not by ballot but by lot. A ballot occasions jealousies and disappointments, and opens the way to intrigue, intimidation, bribery, and propaganda. The custom of drawing lots, on the contrary, assumes a genuine belief in equality, at least for the business in hand.

In trial by jury, where property, reputation, and life are at stake, the jurors are chosen by lot, and unanimity is required to secure a verdict. Here democracy appears unalloyed, and gives general satisfaction. It is true, however, among Anglo-Saxons, that the judge supplies an important element of authority, tradition, legality, and political wisdom in conducting the case and pronouncing a sentence. To the jury only those points are submitted in which common sense is the best judge: the credibility of witnesses, and the character and probable motives of the litigants. Human nature may understand itself at home. But human nature only marginally and in exceptional persons approaches any understanding of the physical world, of the past, and less of the variety and relativity of its own assumptions. Yet these unknown or misjudged realities have to be actively faced in government: which explains why a good government has never existed and perhaps can never exist in this world.

Compromise in general extends to morals the rational procedure of the economic arts when they modify their action to meet the character of different materials and the different occasions on which their works are required. This is legitimate in economics because action here has an ulterior object and is not its own end. But in the liberal arts and virtues existence reaches its perfect function and ultimate end; so that compromise here, though often necessary, is never welcome. It is an amputation.

Rational compromise is thus only a manoeuvre executed in the service of primal Will. Primal Will is unconscious of everything except the present lure. For the most part it sleeps with all its eventual demands still only potential; not all will ever come to the surface, and many alternative developments are equally possible to it. A willing cooperation with circumstances is therefore no ultimate sacrifice, but only an occasion for realising the opportune part of one's vocation. And we may distinguish two stages in this rational cooperation with circumstances: one stage political, when we change only the method or the instrument by which we meant to achieve our end; the other a deeper stage, when we suspend a given aim, substituting another no less truly compatible with our primal Will and vital liberty.

Being a trope in matter, the psyche possesses a genuine though limited plasticity. Up to a certain point it can vary its action and adopt such habits as circumstances make tempting and fruitful. Who can tell what accidental compulsions launched our race, at each turn, on the course it has taken? A new accident or a new compulsion may at any time launch us again on a happier or a more arduous voyage. Events in this world are determined by a confluence of accidents, not by a disembodied Fate.

Such supervening habits may be superficially imposed, like fashions or slang in a casual *milieu,* and easily abandoned or exchanged; and no predisposition to reproduce them would then be communicated to the hereditary psyche. Changes of climate, vices, and diseases may indeed affect the seed of a species in a random way, by feeding it differently or even fatally; but its positive potentialities and tendencies will not have changed. Beyond a certain point, however, mutations imposed by *force majeure* will not modify the psyche but kill it. The primal Will of that lineage will have vanished. The matter which it had animated may perhaps continue to live dispersed in more elementary organisms; and this transformation may dazzle the poet, who sees eyes become pearls and bones coral: a magic kaleidoscope cosmically fruitful but morally deadly. Such metamorphosis transcends the sphere of politics which, being a moral art, sets human, not cosmic, standards.

Whether compromise is advisable or not thus appears to turn

entirely on how radical the particular compromise is. It will be reasonable when it involves a change only in the *methods or instruments* of action, by which your ultimate aim can be secured in spite of difficulties which otherwise would have defeated it; but when the compromise surrenders the ultimate *object* that you pursued, it indicates mere weakness or vagueness in your moral nature.

Allied to this is that irrational kind of moral plasticity which suffers Will and action to change fundamentally, as if they did not arise in any prior specific body or soul or people, but suddenly burst unaccountably, miscellaneous and disconnected, as rockets might seem to an innocent child to burst uncaused in an empty sky. There is a philosophy that cultivates this kind of innocence, in its profound hatred of institutions, compulsions, and predictable issues to familiar actions. Compromise with circumstances then turns into absolute abandonment to chance. Existence becomes a perpetual surrender to the drift of casual passion. There could be no accumulated knowledge or progress in virtue. Reality would be a series of phenomena, to enjoy if you can and endure if you must, or to cut off altogether, if it wearies you, and you can really turn off the light. But this is a pose rather than a philosophy, and possible only in periods of moral dissolution, when society is the prey to violence, to sophistry, to frivolity, and to despair. The delirium cannot last. The dead doubters in time will be forgotten, and the survivors will grow up under some new moral and political regimen imposed by foreign compulsion or formed spontaneously among them with a new dawn of the serious arts.

CHAPTER 31

"GOVERNMENT BY THE PEOPLE" IV
ACQUIESCENCE

GOVERNMENT as a philosopher or a saintly king might conceive it would be a comparatively simple matter; so simple that philosophers and saintly kings are apt to fail in this complicated business. They have already amply considered the place of man in nature, his possible destiny, his highest good; and they probably see some circumstance at the moment that seems to permit that highest good to be approached in some direction. All that remains for them to do is to have precise measures framed to this end, and to find faithful persons capable of carrying them out. It would seem that an honest government, with all expert information and advice at its disposal, ought not to find great difficulties in accomplishing this task.

But there is something else to be considered, something which in fact absorbs almost the whole attention of governments, and constitutes what we currently call politics. Wise decrees and good administration are nothing to the purpose if you do not secure acquiescence in the public at large. You are governing living beings; you will never do anything for them or with them unless you enlist their labour and goodwill, or at least secure their passive submission.

Simple minds might suppose that if you adopted the best measures, in the interests of the people, the acquiescence and even the enthusiasm of the people would follow as a matter of course. And no doubt if your measures were allowed to bear fruit, the people would prize the advantages so secured; but even then they might not attribute their well-being to your action, but to other circumstances or to the intrinsic nature of things; since what is welcome soon seems normal. Moreover, the good fruits may never ripen, because ill-will, obstruction, contrary unforeseen accidents may intervene, tempting you into many a blind path of the labyrinth, in spite of your thread.

Nor is acquiescence requisite (and precarious) only in the people at large; you must obtain it from your agents also. In a civilised State, such for instance as France under the Third Republic, the more or less grumbling acquiescence of the people can be counted upon for almost any measure adopted by the government, even for measures that demand the greatest sacrifices, like war, or that most uselessly outrage the feelings of pious people, like persecution of the Church. After all, even war or irreligion leaves the structure of society standing; lives are lost, property destroyed, prices disturbed, old pieties abandoned; but all this might very well have happened sooner or later even without government action. The people will probably endure it. Government, with such security from insurrection, would seem to be at liberty to govern intelligently, like the poor, incapable, saintly kings or legislating philosophers; but not a bit of it. Never perhaps was a government more absorbed in politics, more tremblingly solicitous of acquiescence here and compromise there, than the third French republic:[1] not acquiescence from the people—that is taken for granted—but acquiescence from the other politicians, from the groups, parties, ex-ministers, syndicates, lodges, and trusts. All is a perpetual search for combinations, expedients, formulas, readjustments, by which the same set of politicians may come recurrently into office. If there is a slide to the Left, or a reaction towards the Right, that too is a search for acquiescence. It is felt that the people, or a small shifting minority sufficient to turn doubtful elections, is out of humour with one or another measure, or with one or another phrase; and in order to secure acquiescence there, it becomes necessary to shift, for a moment, the centre of intrigue and rival ambitions amongst the politicians. Whether any of the measures offered like patent medicines to the public really makes for health, or what the health of the State really is, or would be, is not a practical question. Ideologies reduced to catchwords may be invoked, again to secure acquiescence; but the only living issue for any government is to keep its majority in the Chamber of Deputies: that is, to obtain the acquiescence, for the moment, of other politicians.

Acquiescence being thus, as it were, the silent partner in all government, and indispensable, we may well enquire how it is obtained. A young child is not cooperative, except in sucking; he is not to be controlled by what others wish; yet he is plastic and imitative and may be guided by gentle force, suggesting what he might like to do. He will soon learn the game, if it is suited to his powers. He may also be easily quieted, at least for the moment, by concessions, by sugar-plums; but concessions encourage willfulness without always developing natural powers; so that control by this means may only introduce lasting rebellion and indulgence in caprice, without forming permanent tastes or habits.

Custom is the greatest source of acquiescence, when the custom is congenial to the native temperament; by invoking custom, a government seems to make a concession to the popular mind, while in fact reinforcing compulsion—since custom is contagious and intolerant. Custom is the soul of law, law being useless unless customarily obeyed; and only custom with the temperament expressed in cus-

[1] Written in Paris during the 1920's.

tom can reassure a government about the future, as every government needs to be reassured. Yet customs themselves grow stale; and a break with custom, when bold and timely, may sometimes popularise a government; but that popularity will bring ruin unless the custom abandoned was unnecessary in itself (as are particular religions and laws of property) and had already become irksome or ridiculous at least to a part of the people. Otherwise, the break with custom will tend to dissolve society, and kill happiness in society. It will also render good government impossible in the end, because no great, permanent, recognised interests will survive for government to further.

Brute force does not secure acquiescence, so long as in active exercise; the child being beaten does not acquiesce while screaming, kicking, and biting. But he may acquire a "conditioned reflex"; and if his mind is dark, or if the habit imposed proves in the end congenial, he may come to do freely what at first he rebelled against; and in that case the use of brute force will have been justified as an instrument of government. Yet the question remains whether gentler force could not have secured the same result more decently. In one sense, all action and all influence is an exercise of force; and all pressure is useless, so far as acquiescence is concerned, if the psyche to be disciplined is not thereby recast, so that acquiescence may become spontaneous. If this transformation is impossible, the oppressed people will run wild again as soon as let out of prison. Even when this is not altogether the case, and forced discipline leaves some relevant traces, there will be a mixture of sullenness and hatred in the acquiescence secured; and the government would have done better, for its own good as well as for that of its subjects, to have been more conciliating, and to have modified its aims so that they might have become the sincere aims of its people.

I should not be tempted to say anything more about acquiescence, but for the curious turn that modern politics have taken in the matter. Acquiescence has ceased to be regarded as a minimum ulterior requirement for the exercise of government. Under the name of "the consent of the governed," it has been turned into the positive source of authority. In a government by politicians, kept in office through popular elections frequently renewed, public acquiescence in what is being done or proposed is really the foundation of power and the test of success for those politicians. The people, however, whatever their disease, may soon wish to change their doctor, and the doctor must do his best to retain his patients. It is as if the politician said to himself: "No need of inquiring what may be for the people's interest. It is *their* business to discover that. My duty is only to do as they say." The people, however, may need a little prompting, because, unless very unhappy or very fanatical, the people are apt to be dumb. They might forget to call in the doctor. The politician had better come forward with some idea which, at the moment, will be likely to appeal to their imagination, reminding them of their grievances, and promising them better times. The more abstract the idea is, the better, so that it may attach them for a longer time to his party, and enable him to remain in office perhaps for his whole life. There will be no difficulty in finding something suitable to advocate, even if elections and the need of arousing popular enthusiasm come round rather often. The people are never free from genuine anxiety; they always have desires which they find impossible to realise; they are always suffering from distress which it would be a mercy to relieve. This is true of the rich also. Both rich and poor, if they considered the matter more closely, would also wish to be less unhappy in their families and in their friends, to see and do and possess all sorts of great things, which fortune denies them; and if prosperity, on trial, only proved a new burden, they would perhaps wish not to have been born, since having been born is after all the source of every possible evil, even of death.

Government, however, is hardly to blame for these things or able to correct them. Government is itself a natural fatality. It grows up; its excuse is that it may be a lesser evil than anarchy. A party that rules by promising to satisfy all the people's wishes therefore rules under false pretences; and such in its essence is a government by politicians. What more cruel mockery could there be of human unhappiness than to keep suggesting measures likely to please the public simply in idea? This is the art of the dishonest advertiser, the quack, and the swindler. The art of government begins at the other end, by studying the nature of things, and of man in the midst of them, so as to devise an equilibrium in which man may attain, as far as possible, to his natural perfection. In the process he will have to surrender a great many fond wishes, a great many fine plans; but he will be happier, and more humanly happy, in the end for that discipline. The process will be perpetual, because nature and human nature are always varying, and any harmony between them must be plastic and ever renewed; yet even in the process, acquiescence may be easily obtained with a little prudence; because the sacrifices imposed by good government are balanced by many immediate benefits, which the people, or large portions of them, will not fail to appreciate.

For there is another side to political, as well as to natural life. All is not difficulty and defeat; all is not suffering, and grumbling, and revolt. There are pure pleasures, satisfactions not based on illusion, actions and arts congenial and perfect in themselves. Now the genius that finds expression in such arts or actions is positive and self-sufficing; it neither springs from consultation, nor asks for acquiescence. It moves in the sphere of freedom; whereas acquiescence is rooted in the sphere of necessary servitude, where natural freedom is limited by a physical collision, actual or imminent, with the natural freedom of other powers.

For this reason a customary acquiescence, and not a more explicit consent, is requisite for good government. Acquiescence expresses an adjustment already made, or in the making, to normal conditions, not in themselves favourable, yet impossible to disregard if action is to be successful, since it is precisely these imposed conditions, and the requisite adjustments to them, that good government embodies. So a good motorist acquiesces in all the curves of the road, and readily adjusts his gear or his brake to the ups and downs of it; he would seem drunk if he made unnecessary meanderings, or changed his speed without reason. The ideal for the government, as well as for the governed, would be to turn such acquiescence into a second nature, into a habit of adaptation to circumstances so immediate as to seem spontaneous. Yet if it were really spontaneous, and expressive of a positive inner Will, no government at all, no trained eye or expert hand, would be required; because a ruler who imposes unnecessary restrictions or sacrifices would be a meddlesome and fantastic tyrant, and would forfeit that claim to obedience which government borrows exclusively from the obduracy of the facts facing the interests of the people.

If now, in order to avoid the appearance of tyranny—since nothing seems more tyrannical to an innocent mind than does the nature of things—the government asked for more than acquiescence, and sought to base its measures on a previous assent obtained from the people, or even waited for the people to suggest the measures to be adopted, then government would be nothing but pensioned go-betweens and officious parasites, as politicians actually are. If the people could initiate policy and direct the execution of it, no governing body, no laws, traditions, or hierarchy of officers would be required. Popular initiative, popular assent, and popular direction are not impossible in certain matters at certain moments; there is lynch law and mob-rule and acclamation of some hero, carried shoulder-high, to be Caesar; but as this last instance shows, such positive sovereignty of a common Will can only be instantaneous; it dissolves upon being exercised; and either primitive anarchy returns, or some governing body survives, takes the reins in its hands, and requires only popular acquiescence to do its work properly.

## CHAPTER 32

### "GOVERNMENT FOR THE PEOPLE" I
### FIRST AIMS PROPER TO GOVERNMENT

ALL moralists might perhaps agree that a good government is one that secures the good of the governed; and if we agree that in a particular case a government is charged with the care not of a country or a State but of a people, we may say confidently that the moral function of that government is to secure the true good of that people. Success in exercising this moral function will then depend on two things: whether the government sees, or instinctively pursues, what is truly the good of the people, and whether it is intelligent and courageous enough to secure, in the circumstances of the time, as much of that good as possible.

I say advisedly "the *true* good" of the people, because I am considering a moral question of *ultimate* aims, not the means of satisfying some accidental passion such as ambition to become and to remain the government in power. Now, the criterion by which to judge what is the *true* good of a people or of an individual lies within that individual or that people. If it were sought outside, in the Will of the monarch, or of God, or of the universe as a whole, or in the conscience of some foreign people or individual, the power exercised by that government would be an instance of militant domination. It must be therefore in the Will of the people, not of the government, that the criterion must be found for determining the true good of that people.

Here I must hasten to remind the reader that by Will, written with a capital, I do not mean incidental wishes surging in a man or in society, and expressed in eloquence, in party policies, and in popular elections. There is a great difference, as Plato shows in the *Gorgias*, between doing as you like and getting what you want. And there is a greater difference still between getting what you wanted and finding what you needed. Now, by the Will that determines the good proper to any creature I understand the demands and potentialities of his nature, not of his consciousness. Plastic as his nature may be, it is always pregnant with capacities and secret needs which have not come to the surface, although they may betray their presence by his superficial incoherence and irritation, and beneath these by his profound dissatisfaction. Will, then, with a capital letter, here serves as a name for fundamental needs and capacities, not for casual desires or conventional judgments.

Now, we may see in the new-born child, as soon as the rhythm of his organism becomes normal, that the first and perpetual need of the primal Will is food. Therefore, the first duty of a good government is to see that the people have enough to eat. As food, however, is something that man, like other animals, has always known how to find for himself (else he would have perished) governments are apt to overlook this requirement, and rather to levy a good percentage of the food that the land produces; seeing that rulers in their parks and palaces, with the mercenaries that defend them there, have no time, except occasionally in the chase, to procure food for themselves. And evidently it will not be their fault, but that of the weather or of the farmers, shepherds, and herdsmen, if there is not enough to go round.

That there should not always be enough to go round, even before there were governments or mercenaries to levy any taxes, follows in fact from the nature of things, and is hardly anybody's fault. Besides occasional bad seasons, a cause of periodic scarcity lies in a second fundamental demand in the animal Will that must be satisfied on pain of extinction, and this is the universal, unavoidable, and immoderate impulse to reproduce the species. Only the dangers and hardships of life keep all kinds of living creatures from multiplying prodigiously; and if the oppression and waste of governments did not contribute to keep population down, half-starved hordes would still be driving one another all over the earth into the sea or the desert.

This second duty of a good government, to regulate population so that it may not outrun the means of subsistence, has been as little recognised by most governments as the first duty to forestall famine; and yet indirectly, without knowing it, civilisation has in many ways reduced the birth rate and generally so lowered the vitality and thrift of the old primitive society as to leave fertile regions sometimes almost waste, and ready to receive new barbarous people.

Here we come upon the function that governments most readily exercise and make the basis of their permanent domination: the function of defence. Any settled population, if unprotected, is exposed to invasion: if prosperous, its lands and possessions tempt ruder neighbours; if poor and sparse, richer neighbours will insensibly oust it or reduce its remnants to subjection. In either case the conqueror will become a government, and pose as protector of the conquered. A home government, even if originally founded on conquest or revolution, might have proved or at least seemed a lighter burden. The need of defence will then justify any actual government and make it seem, in so far, to operate in the interests of the people.

The people, however, will soon have occasion to ask: Who shall defend us against our defenders? And it will probably find in its own customs, or in those of its masters, a tribunal to which it can appeal; because the office of judge is paternal and was sanctioned religiously long before there were political governments. The abuses of one agent of government may thus be controlled by appealing to another agent, morally independent and prior, although perhaps later absorbed and corrupted by the political authorities.

Unfortunately the greatest abuse of governments, by which they act most radically against the good of the people, is one which no judiciary can control even if its own authority be traditionally higher than that of the actual power. Defence, the palmary use of government, requires an instrument able to cope with the aggressor: it requires a police and an army. And who, in the end, can compose these forces except the sons of the people? The greatest tax levied by government will therefore be a blood-tax. It will sacrifice the cream of the people to defend its skimmed milk. Moreover, this defence will often be preventive defence, that is to say, timely aggression. And timely aggression will not always prevent an attack on the people's interests; when most successful it may rather enlarge the scope of the government by new conquests and alliances, leaving the people who helped to obtain those advantages for its rulers neglected and absorbed into a large State where their traditions are despised and their freedom lost.

A final and comprehensive public good which it is a function of government to facilitate is prosperity. I say to facilitate, not to procure, because economic arts and the wealth they produce are proper to individuals, to families, and to other private societies; and in a simple phase they can develop beautifully without the aid or the existence of political government. But the military and provident functions of government depend on the prosperity of the people for their success; roads and bridges, for instance, are crucial in war, as are stores of provisions; and it is evident that the richer the people the more the government can reasonably draw from them for its undertakings. And although arts arise and develop best under free competition, competition may become wasteful and end in monopoly; and when a monopoly is important it can hardly remain justly in private hands. The government therefore has to take it over. But I think there is a natural limit to the advantage that government direction can confer upon industry, or upon education, which is another function that it now often assumes. The limit coincides with the distinction between economic and liberal arts.

I have just indicated how economic arts may require political control in advanced states of civilisation, although their vitality and progress always remain dependent on private zeal and inspiration. Imagination is something personal and labour becomes a burden when it does not excite the imagination. Education, for instance, may be regarded as a means to economic work; reading, writing, and arithmetic are necessary for tradesmen. But when they are taught and learned only for that purpose, they are diverted from their natural use, which is to merge into liberal arts and be intrinsically liberal, since they employ and liberate the spirit. They should be taught, even in their elements, as arts, as games, as occasions for delight; and then their utility in the business world will not prevent them from remaining essentially liberal. Even if not pursued beyond their material occasions, they will retain an intellectual vitality and be play for the mind while they serve the world.

Or consider the case of religion. Governments, especially when the people have a single traditional religion, do well to respect that religion, knit as it is into the moral and imaginative texture of their nation. But they must never touch or reform religion for its own sake. Individually, and even ceremonially, all the members of a government may bow to that religion; but they should never base their policy on religious motives. Churches on the other hand should be considered by them, in their government, only as factors in politics. To act as missionaries would be an impertinence to the public and probably a heresy in the Church itself; while to persecute or disestablish or denounce that religion, in their capacity as statesmen, would be to stimulate sedition and destroy culture. Things of the spirit are not their business; but it is their business, as guardians of the people's interests, to keep the doors open to vital liberty for all men in the spirit, and to preserve the works of spirit in the past as their greatest treasure.

## CHAPTER 33

### "GOVERNMENT FOR THE PEOPLE" II
### GOVERNMENTS CANNOT SERVE ALL INTERESTS

IN DEMANDING a government "for the people" Lincoln gave no indication of what might be, in various cases, for the benefit of each people. He was thinking of the United States as a signal exception among nations, as by the occupation of a vast and almost empty continent, it certainly was; and he was contrasting the vacant freedom of such an opportunity with the notorious domination of many other countries by governments that served the fancy of extravagant monarchs or ministers, often in contempt of the public good.

I think that the prudent Machiavelli, even when serving only the interest of his "Prince" (that is, the stability of any given government) would have directed that Prince's attention to the need of maintaining the economic and intellectual vigour of his subjects. Such vigour, with peace or with few, short, and successful wars, would strengthen the Prince's authority at home and his reputation and influence abroad much better than could the best planned intrigues and assassinations. Similarly an ecclesiastic who governed the Church with a spiritual and charitable zeal would establish the ascendancy of his faith more securely than by persecution and nepotism. Machiavelli, himself, in his *Discourses,* where he philosophised more freely than in *The Prince,* dreamt of greatness for Italy rather than for its petty tyrants. It is the absence of solid intelligence that renders governments cruel to their subjects and fatal to themselves. The happy operation of a government, on the contrary, silences grievances and interweaves its action with the rooted habits of the people, no matter how casual the forgotten origin of that government or irrational its traditional form.

The people that counted in Lincoln's world, and especially in his party, were self-made men like himself, and it was natural to assume that they knew their own interests and if left alone would spontaneously secure them. There were, indeed, political storms, even tornadoes; but these were abnormal and unnecessary, born of ignorance and ancient usurpations. The natural success of each enterprising honest individual would open fresh opportunities to the enterprise of others; and the freedom of each would make the happiness of all.

Such was the ideal prospect; but soon the complication of industries and of civilised life bred private societies, educational, religious, and commercial, to cultivate the liberal interests of like-minded groups better than each individual could have done for himself. As those private institutions grew powerful and semi-public, national and local governments also became complex far beyond the intellectual range of any one man. Ministries and departments of State acquired an inevitable internal autonomy, with technical methods and indispensable permanent officials, ready to advise and to check the ignorant ardour of reforming ministers, dupes of their own eloquence. A traditional, practicable but cumbrous way of doing everything imposed itself on each newly elected government; and the vested prejudices of each department even became, in many cases, the fountain of orthodox public sentiment and policy.

May we assume, in traditional governments of this kind, a clear sense of who the People are whom they exist to serve, and what are the interests of that People? I think that this sense in governments is often clear but seldom just. The Judges, Kings, and Prophets of

Israel, for instance, knew that the People were simply the Jews, in so far as they obeyed and enforced the Law of Moses. And similarly most of the communist governments of our time know that the People are simply the communists of all nations, in so far as they obey the central inspiration of Moscow. These are militant sectarian or party governments, that may be perfectly just within their fold; but neither creed is ideally content with that limitation and both propose for their ultimate goal the unanimity of the remnant of mankind, when all recalcitrants have been exterminated. For the point of view of mankind at large, and even of human nature in professed communists or orthodox Jews, this is a cruel injustice to the natural centrifugal development of vital liberty in man, in which the ancient Jewish and the modern communist regimens are only local, temporary, and arbitrary formations.

These are extreme cases of militancy. Ordinarily the question of whose good and what good a government should pursue solves itself without discussion. The people to be served by a government are all those within its jurisdiction, whom it can actually control, tax, imprison, execute, or forcibly enroll for military service. Less clear is the question what good the people, or special classes among them, will derive from being thus governed; but this question for the government is not urgent. The government has its traditional well-known daily duties to perform. It is the people's business to get as much good out of their government as they can. They too have current commitments, chiefly financial but also domestic, moral, and imaginative; commitments that, like family responsibilities, it is for each of them too late to elude; and the original grounds for these vested interests are too complex and perhaps remote for practical minds to trouble about or try to understand. What a man lives for is hardly better known to a man, or less often falsely described in orations, than what the government works for. There are, for both, incidental successes and failures clearly distinguishable, but ultimate aims are not discerned, for the excellent reason that they do not exist. The generative order of society proceeds not towards an ultimate good but by a concourse of tentative actions, each more or less expressing a particular need, passion, or purpose; and the total issue is a compound of clashing endeavours and chequered fortunes.

In the individual, however, there exists at least potentially a natural living witness of these psychic dramas; that synthetic glance which Kant called the transcendental unity of apperception, and which I call spirit. Spirit, arising in a man, can feel those diverse inclinations surging within him; it can see them evoking images and precipitating worlds that anticipate their possible satisfaction: it can perceive one or another of them dragging in and absorbing the whole momentum of his life for a moment, as if only that master impulse were real and were right. If the moment is propitious, probably action follows, and the intoxication of it slowly yields to the perception of the material consequences, making success or failure, or a troubled mixture of both; and later the other inclinations, obscured for a while, come trooping back disgusted at having been neglected and still clamouring. Each passion initially claims a right to its vital liberty; but when in the tight arena of the psyche and of the world it finds itself thwarted or stifled by rival passions, it egotistically detests the others, and would prompt the spirit to call them sinful and wrong. Thus the poor spirit, in its unarmed intelligence and justice, is torn between natural sympathy with each of those passions and the hatred felt for it by all the others.

This war in the psyche, so dimly and sadly lighted by reason, is reproduced on a larger scale in society and in the rivalry of nations. But there is a radical difference between the status of reason and justice within an individual and their status in any political conflict; for in any concourse of individuals there is no living seat for observation or judgment except those individuals themselves; and it is sheer conceit in a contemporary neutral or in a later historian to pose as a superior and impartial spirit; for his spark of spirit is kindled in a human psyche no less subject to passions and accidental interests than those that, from a cold and distorting distance, he presumes to understand and to criticise. He is indeed free and even obliged to judge from his particular point of view; but his judgment will represent the scope of his own knowledge and sympathies, not any valid criterion present in the facts themselves. Moral distinctions express the bias of primal Will, grown clearer by differentiation into more and more particular and complicated psyches. You cannot recede from distinction into impartiality; you can only enlarge your imagination into charity (not connivance) towards all life, and prize all harmonies attainable, whether simple or complex. Reason is itself a particular standard proper to spirit, which glows and sings in the measure in which it escapes distraction and beholds the ideal of every effort without undergoing its strain or sharing its cruelty.

Thus a psyche (the unified movement of a natural organic body) when it is well-knit and capable of self-knowledge may possibly establish liberty and justice in its internal economy and in its action. But the life of families and nations is many-centred; and the social impulses that sway such an aggregate take root more or less deeply and more or less casually in each individual. Therefore in the state of nature there can be often wild rebellion, when the individual asserting liberty and justice after his own heart becomes indistinguishably a hero and a criminal; or else there may be only mindless submission to the domination of custom, of a magnetic leader, or of a superstitious spell. A social order approaching rationality can be secured only by institutions; that is to say, by artificial organisms, robber bands, secret societies, religious fraternities, or political governments, that can sanction verbal laws by force.

In civilised States the strings that secure concerted action are more complicated and bear official names, but they are essentially the same strings. Sometimes a quasi-religious movement of public feeling is fused with semi-rational political aims. When Gladstone, for instance, launched an oratorical crusade against "Turkish atrocities" in Bulgaria, it was not because the British Government had undertaken to stop atrocities all over the world. It was rather by the coincidence of two motives, one moral and sectarian, the other commercial and patriotic. Humanitarian liberal feelings in Gladstone and his supporters suffered at the thought not only that there should be atrocities at all, but that they should be going on in a region where energetic use of British influence might arrest them. Moreover in this case the victims were Orthodox Christians, sound enemies of the Pope; and the tyrant was the Porte, a power in whose crumbling empire Great Britain had a comprehensible and almost legitimate interest. Intervention, if it became necessary, would be justified both as morally urgent and as politically far-seeing.

The objects intimately important to each human being are inevitably various, and the active pursuit of them is let loose by the opportunity that circumstances seem to offer for this or that satisfaction. To secure such satisfaction for everybody cannot be the express aim of any government or of any social institution, since such an aim would be infinitely complex and variable. Neither good government, therefore, nor high morality but the play of vital liberty is the immediate multiform source of human happiness; and the best government and the best society, from this point of view, would be those whose pressure never makes itself felt. This does not mean that a man, to be free, must revert to the jungle; for in the jungle he would suffer the unmitigated pressure of all the untamed forces of nature and of wild animals and men. A good government, by economic arts, turns the forces of nature, as far as possible, from enemies into servants and the pressure of society into friendly cooperation and an opportune stimulus to each man's latent powers. It is in these ways that government can be government "for the people" and society a benefit to its members.

A radical liberalism in social philosophy would limit the function of government to the defence of liberty in each person. Economic and liberal arts would be left entirely to the initiative of individuals or of voluntary groups; and private and public morals would also be free, so long as they involved no physical aggression against others. This might seem to invite moral and aesthetic anarchy, and a tendency to such anarchy has actually come to the surface in the twentieth century; yet the liberal leaders of the nineteenth century had, and expected to foster, a strictly uniform humanitarian morality and social decorum. They were Protestant pedants in frock coats with virtues protected by wealth; and they hoped soon, by education, to raise mankind to their own level. Theirs was a kind of vital liberty, strictly limited, but limited by choice; and they did not perceive that what they offered mankind was vacant freedom only, with no direction assigned to it.

In other words, they left human nature free because they assumed that human nature was predetermined to develop a particular, unchangeable type of virtue and happiness, the type which they loved and assigned to themselves. They thought it pure benevolence and unselfishness on their part to teach every child and every foreigner the way he should go and the way he should think; for it was only backwardness in the world not to have discovered it. The belief that we know what is good for others better than they do may be foolish or wise: foolish when it rests on the presumption that life is everywhere radically addressed to what we address it; wise when we see the difficulties and the failures that external and persistent circumstances prepare for the unwary.

Liberals are not the only dogmatists who when in power think they are ruling for the good of mankind. Kings and nationalist dictators often repeat that they are the servants of their people; and the Pope styles himself *Servus servorum Dei*. They are often sincere; but it is not the miscellaneous vital freedom of actual human psyches that they are serving but a speculative vision of their own: their country or the Kingdom of God. It is only canalised liberty, like that of water flowing through a lock, that excites their zeal or gives them satisfaction.

That the people need such locks in order to flow to advantage must be assumed by any government that undertakes to train and to manage them. Silent acquiescence on the people's part or protests from a noisy party among them prove nothing one way or the other. The Pope and the nationalist dictators have at heart for the world a higher good than it knows of. The service required may be sophistically called perfect freedom, if the people will only train themselves to love nothing else; yet in reality it presupposes a terrible sacrifice of almost all that their nature craved; and this sacrifice becomes more tragic and annihilating as it becomes more enthusiastic and more complete. Let us grant that it may be the ideal of a saint or of a soldier; it remains, even so, the fruit of a most special passion. Glorious as it may be thought by those who seek to attain it, even for them it is a martyrdom; and if imposed by a government on a whole people, it condemns them to a collective suicide.


CHAPTER 34

"GOVERNMENT FOR THE PEOPLE" III
RATIONAL LIMITS OF GOVERNMENT

THE control exercised by society over its members has two forms: one, the control exercised by government, with explicit laws sanctioned by military force; the other, the social control by natural contagion, cooperation, or suasion. In civilised countries non-official societies are not allowed to use force in dominating either their own members or outsiders whom they may wish to annex or to destroy; but originally parental and tribal authority extended over everything equally, and punished cruelly any contradiction of its traditional, vague, but ferocious principles.

Yet secretly these principles had rational sources in two different quarters. On the one hand there was really a kindred direction and vocation of vital liberty in all men which, in so far as it existed, inwardly prompted them to live together, join in the same labours, share the same pleasures and dangers, and emulate one another in the same liberal arts. But this friendly side of social cohesion and control was crossed and almost obliterated by the most terrible punishments and prohibitions; often superstitious, and yet often symbolising the inexorable nature of things, conditioning the direction of vital liberty in men no less than good fortune in asserting that liberty.

Now the indignation caused by the cruelty of governments falls often on the person or office of the ruler, when his intentions and the political principle of his action are blameless. If it was the prevalent false notions about causes and effects in nature that imposed the measures the ruler adopted he would have acted against his will. So when Agamemnon in the story sacrificed his daughter, he did not prove himself an unnatural father or a bad king; on the contrary, it was his duty to the allies whom he was leading against Troy that overcame with difficulty his horror at his own crime. If the irresponsible dreams of the prophet or priestess of some oracle could truly discover the causes of winds and calms, the self-sacrifice of Iphigenia and the tragic act of her father would both have been heroic and even rational. Not rational absolutely, but politically: for absolutely neither the expedition to Troy nor any other human undertaking could be anything but an irrational and unnecessary commitment. Yet granted a living nation armed for a crusade, the general chosen to lead it is politically committed to that duty and to all arts requisite to carrying it out.

A relative rationality hides also in other parts of this fable. That the winds should blow at the arbitrary fancy of the gods is simply a poetic way of expressing at once our ignorance of any cause or law for the winds, and our dire need, if we are sailors, of their favour and their mercy. And if there are gods that govern the winds, primitive man, imitating his habitual practices in his cults as in a dream, will beg and bribe those gods for their assistance. It was a savage but intelligible notion that the supreme bribe should be a victim's life. That the virgin goddess of moonlight and of the chase, being the patroness of Aulis, should command the winds there, and should require a virgin as an offering, are poetic accidents or refinements. So the goddess is sometimes said to have substituted at the last moment a young doe for the king's daughter. Myth, where science is absent, has to take its place; and the philosopher is satisfied if the myth inspires a kindred sentiment and an analogous behaviour to that which the true facts, if known, would have inspired. A wise priesthood will insensibly remould its fables and its maxims so as to keep both humility and courage alive in the people, taught to bow to the conditions of human life on earth without ever surrendering their own vital demands.

These are indeed the two authorities that by their interplay determine the forms and the rational variations of morals: the *authority of things,* that permit, prevent, reward, or punish our actions; and *the authority of primal Will* within us, that chooses our path and discriminates between success and disaster in our careers.

Other men or other interests than those that a government serves form, from its point of view, a part of the world of things; for alien minds or intelligible movements are simply, for government, natural conditions with which it has to count in achieving its designs. Governments, however, are composed of men whose whole soul is probably not absorbed in statecraft, so that individually and even collectively they may bend the purely economic art of government to serving other than political purposes. Princes have sometimes been ecclesiastics and sometimes saints; and in both cases they are apt to employ their whole temporal power to serve cultural or religious aspirations; and if their people have the same mixed interests, they may applaud that policy. Nevertheless it is an abandonment of rational politics, and involves confusion and probably deterioration, if not ruin, in the liberal arts or sciences thus taken under government wing and rendered official, if not actually compulsory.

This is not to say that if the people, or some part of them, spontaneously develop some form of fine art, philosophy, or religion, the government is not rationally bound to defend and encourage that expression of vital freedom. As a form of life and action the practice of any art enters into the vortex of material social currents that aid or impede one another in the world; and these a government, if it would serve the vital liberty of all, must seek to harmonise. It will impose restrictions, and appoint places and occasions to which the special activities of each private society or liberal art must be confined so as not to encroach on its neighbours. In doing this the government only announces beforehand, to each private enterprise, the material circumstances in which it will have to be carried on; it will anchor buoys in the shallows and build lighthouses on the dangerous reefs; it will circumvent the defeats or hardships that nature imposes on ignorant or rash action by using or pointing out timely material means of defence or escape or safe advance.

Government in this way becomes the rational art of minimising the inevitable conflicts of primal irrational Wills against one another and against the forces of nature at large. If government attemps to go further and to approve one set of irrational Wills and forbid another, it becomes itself the agent of a particular irrational Will; and instead of speaking for all Wills that move in its domains, and showing each the best terms it can make with Circumstances, it becomes itself a particular net of Circumstances hostile to all other Wills, instead of wise friend to them all.

In other words, a rational government is one that speaks to its people in the name of the nature of things, and acts by that authority. Its criterion and method must be a scientific criterion and a scientific method. Therefore the members of a rational government would never be prophets, reformers, agitators, politicians, or demagogues, never persons elected by majority votes, but educated and trained in the science and art of government: persons able to discern the possibility or impossibility of human ambitions. Such persons might have to be, like the Roman ruling class, all soldiers; but besides the requisite military capacity they should be experts in economics. Yet in modern times, rather perhaps than soldiers, they should be anthropologists, medical men, and scientific psychologists; for it is the psyche that is the agent in politics. Such a government would hear sympathetically and understand perfectly the grievances and the claims of all social and private interests; but it should never follow blindly the policy of any party or sect, possessed, as such a government would be, of distinct institutes and experienced masters of all economic affairs and, as it were, psychiatrists of nations; and the traditions and experience of that government, up to any given date, would sufficiently suggest to it what reforms and what new institutions would be worth trying at each new juncture in public affairs.

Such a scientific regimen, if established anywhere, would doubtless be only local and peculiar to an exceptionally gifted and moralised community; yet the very nature of rational economy could perfectly well extend its authority to other nations or even over the whole world. And this political possibility, which is also a rational ideal, brings us back to the first principle of rationality in government: that it should protect and encourage vital liberty, in whatever quarter or form circumstances render its expression possible in action.

The authority of this government would be autocratic but not totalitarian; for it would speak for the material conditions imposed by nature on the realisation of any ideal without dictating to any person or society what its ideal should be. Its own aim would be only to prevent conflicting desires from becoming material conflicts, fatal to both sides; while by being temporarily content with what could be obtained peaceably, nothing alien would have to be hated and crushed, but order could be preserved, and a quiet hibernation secured for the seed of every native aspiration. This is the discipline that reason, when alive enough, imposes on the individual psyche that breeds it, and might eventually impose on the world, if the world could develop a political organ of reason, an enlightened and distinterested government.

The difficulty is that intelligence, though often keen enough, instead of establishing order among the irrational passions, vital or frivolous, that distract the psyche, hastens as soon as born to devise ingenious ways of satisfying one or another of those passions, regardless of the others in the man himself or in his neighbours; and this rape of intelligence is no less violent in those liberal arts that possess an internal rationality, such as logic, mathematics, music, and poetry. It would be ridiculous for a serious scientific direction of society to meddle with these things. It would only protect them from actual assault by possible fanatics of a different school.

A rational government of this kind would entirely cease to cause enthusiasm or hatred in the public. We should hardly recognise it as touching politics; and that would be one of its advantages. The hot bloods and the ambitious talents would turn to the separate irrational rival forms of culture, and preach and work for some reform in some one of them; but they would be prevented by the police in the service of that uninteresting government from smashing one another's idols or breaking one another's heads. The tempests would all be cerebral, and would not hurt anyone but the militant hotheads who raised them.

## CHAPTER 35

### LIBERALISM IN A THANKLESS WORLD

THE virtue of liberalism is a sort of intellectual kindness or courtesy to all possible wills. Yet what a melancholy kindness is this, to leave the inoffensive liberal helpless before unkindness! Government needs to be based on the principle that men are by nature fundamentally helpless and automatic. They are not wicked expressly or prevailingly, but only when it happens; and they have benevolent impulses too, as the existence of society and of liberalism sufficiently proves. But all living creatures become wicked under pressure. Absolute singleness of purpose cannot but be ruthless; it is ruthless initially, because it has no eye for any contrary interest; and it becomes ruthless again deliberately in the end, because all contrary interests seem odious and sinful to its fanaticism.

In such a world, beneficence cannot be all-comprehensive. The Church was right, as usual, in maintaining the doctrine of eternal damnation. Love, even infinite love, cannot save or applaud everybody; and any definite beneficence—giving soup to beggars while burning heretics—is condemned to be heartless beyond the circumference of its charity.

Moreover, as if aware of this latent doom, tolerated people are never conciliated. They live on, but the aroma of their life is lost. When, as in England, institutions are at once conservative and progressive, they seem to reconcile loyalty with convenience; but if we look beneath the surface, and beneath the sham acquiescence of all parties, we see that such a society is continually transforming what it inherits. The old house, just because it is still inhabited, must be continually patched and modernised, until little remains of it but the name and the invisible foundations. The true past, if some accident now suddenly calls it up like a ghost, appears strangely foreign, disquieting, and disagreeable; and the shreds of antiquity which may survive in legal nomenclature, in education, or in religion take on a modern aspect, half humorous like a jolly judge in his dusty wig, and half stiffly false, like a High Church bishop in his fresh cope and mitre. There is at best a superficial continuity; but the present fills that masquerade with its crude business, speaks those archaic words in an affected voice that publishes their archaism, and allows no implication of their old force to disturb their modernness and freedom. It is a triumph of progress under the mask of conservatism. Decorum takes the place of discipline; the latest view and the nearest interest dominate as if by divine right.

The historian who is not a bookworm, but studies the past in order to enlighten the present with a sense of direction in its ambitions and of the possible range of its rational hopes, will shudder at the folly of this political myopia. The brutes indeed survive by following the call of the moment, and it would be felt by them as an indignity worse than any free struggle to be compelled to suspend their impulses and to abandon their simple and free life. But they survive only because they keep to their special hunting grounds and breeding seasons; and their independence turns and turns in a narrow circuit where it has some chance, though no certainty, of being able to turn a number of times. Liberalism revives in civilised man this instinctive self-trust and this preference for struggle over subjection; but civil life is highly conditioned and its sphere of action is wide and variable. Before the plain man could judge wisely any political policy he would have to dominate that public field of action intellectually, comparing and balancing all the interests and dangers involved in public affairs; and what is even harder, he would have to dominate his own strongest inclinations, and perpetually postpone or dismiss the satisfaction of his passions. And if, by a heroic self-discipline he became reconciled to a decent poverty and a special form of economic drudgery, would he not at least expect all his fellow citizens to accept the same fate? For if he allowed some of them to be guides to the others and to cultivate the more speculative or artistic possibilities of their nature, would he not have saved civilisation by abandoning liberalism?

This paradox may seem absurd, when liberals are the most civilised and culture-loving of beings; the ripe, in fact the over-ripe, fruit of a civilisation of which they relish all the intellectual and artistic achievements; but coming when that civilisation has spent its force and is rapidly declining, they are full of scorn for its conventions now become empty and its principles proved false. Their love of civilisation is highly critical, and they wish to reform it. But, alas! this wish to *reform* a decaying civilisation is itself singularly naive; it is fundamentally ignorant, under all the plumes and furbelows of a superficial omniscience. They do not see that the peace they demand was secured by the discipline and the sacrifices that they deplore, that the wealth they possess was amassed by appropriating lands and conducting enterprises in the high-handed manner which they denounce, and that the fine arts and refined luxuries they revel in arise in the service of superstitions that they deride and despotisms that they abhor.

They were no doubt right in the nineteenth century to be confident that the world was moving towards the destruction of traditional institutions, privileges, and beliefs; but the first half of the twentieth century has already made evident that their own wealth, taste, and intellectual liberty will dissolve also in some strange barbarism that will think them a good riddance.

The concupiscence of the flesh, the concupiscence of the eyes, and the pride of life exhaust and kill the sweets they feed upon; and a lava-wave of primitive blindness and violence must perhaps rise from below to lay the foundations for something differently human and similarly transient.

## CHAPTER 36

### WAR *VS.* ORDER

War in its sheer malice is the worst disorder possible; nevertheless, being declared and continuous, the disruptive action of the enemy becomes a great lesson in the rational ordering of one's own conduct. The enemy is in that respect like any dangerous natural force—floods, pests, or storms at sea—against which the arts of government and defence were originally devised; and war therefore very much strengthens and tightens order within the lines of each belligerent. Yet to destroy this order in the enemy, to disperse his forces and annihilate his power, is precisely the purpose of war; so that there is a kind of formal contradiction or irony in it, heightening and concentrating order here, in order to produce anarchy there. For civilised war is a struggle between governments, not between peoples. On submission, the enemy population is to be spared, assisted, and perhaps annexed, which is the greatest but most unwelcome compliment that one people can pay to another. At any rate a very strict order is at once to be established among the vanquished and prolonged afterwards under a treaty of peace. So that the systematic effort to create disorder in the enemy ranks is only incidental and provisional; what is to be disorganised is merely the power of the enemy to interfere with one's own organisation.

Yet the dust, the thunder, the carnage, and the ruin of war seem to make visible some deeper disorder, some suicidal madness in the human race. And it often is so. There may be rational wars, as there are rational surgical operations; not only preventive wars, such as only a very exorbitant power or very Machiavellian government is like to undertake, but wars arising by the accidental outbreak of latent antagonisms. The war will be rational, on one side or on both, if the true interests of the nation would suffer more by avoiding it than by waging it. This is a dubious calculation, and seldom made in cold blood; almost always a wind of excitement and ambition, at the very thought of war, fans the embers into flame; and the conflagration, as we saw in 1914–1918, is likely to prove a disaster all round. There is a sort of subterranean chaos, sometimes bursting through the crust of civilisation; and something in the individual heart rejoices at that eruption, feels that at last the moment has come to break through its own crust, and build itself, as well as the world, on some different plan. Not a better plan, since there is no deeper organism to pronounce on the matter or to have any stake in it; but simply a relief from this plan, from this routine and this morality, from these surroundings, and these prospects. It is what Descartes called the infinity of the will, contrasted with the finitude of reason; but perhaps we might more accurately say that it is the indetermination of matter, or of protoplasm, contrasted with the definite organisation of powers and habits in man. A sort of self-hatred and self-contempt: a wild throw for something different, and a deep, dark impulse to challenge and to destroy everything that has the impertinence to exist.

## CHAPTER 37

### SUPPRESSION OF WAR

It is said: "Wars have always existed, therefore they will always exist." Such empirical prophecies are, in form, utterly fallacious. Their substantial truth, if they are true, hangs on the assumption, which may be true or false, that the same nature, cosmic and human, is at work in all ages. We may safely say: "All former men have died, therefore all future men will die too": because all future men will be animals bred out of a seed and endowed organically for reproduction, not for immortality. Any other sort of being would not be a man. Our inference is justified, not empirically, but by the nature that we find proper to mankind. If, on the other hand, anyone had said in antiquity: "Parents have always sacrificed their firstborn; therefore they will always do so," that prophet would have been mistaken. That which caused parents to sacrifice their firstborn was not an integral part of the mechanism of reproduction; it was not involved in fatherhood as death is involved in animal life. Mankind could accordingly survive, and survive better, without that sacrifice.

Empirical science is valid only when it is a method of observing and testing the constitution of nature; it is utterly worthless, or positively superstitious, when it connects surface appearances directly; because appearances do not depend on one another, and their sequences are never, in fact, exactly repeated.

The question therefore is: Has there always been war in the world because war is involved in the nature of men, and in their inevitable relations? Or is war due to some adventitious circumstance, to some falsely stimulated passion, similar to the superstitious fear that led primitive man to imagine that by sacrificing the firstborn the whole tribe might be saved?

## SUPPRESSION OF WAR 441

I reply: Endless conflict arrested at some temporary equilibrium is essential to all forces meeting in the same field: either the forces are not distinguished, and there are no units of which we can trace the history, or the equilibrium (which always exists in nature) is only a pause between two blows or between two battles. In this sense Heraclitus said the last and the first word: War is the parent of all things. It is also the destroyer of all things; because physical things are unstable by nature, and ironically sustained by a balance of power essentially hostile to their specific being. But there are endless eddies and backwaters and meanderings in this treacherous flux. Often the alternative forces are unconscious and the issue placid: there is no regret for what is excluded, because it was never desired or conceived; and all life seems to flow for a while unanimously in the victorious direction. The old historians were right, and history is a tale of wars: but the modern historians are right too, because in the midst of those wars, and behind the firing-line, the arts of peace are able to flourish.

Spiritual things, too, in which the moralist is ultimately interested, escape in their own sphere the curse of competition and of living by one another's death. It is only in respect to their material organs that they are rivals; and the more the mind is emancipated from concern for the body, the less it suffers and the less it fears the encroachment of foreign things, because to pure intellect nothing is foreign.

But this escape from war is upward, in an intellectual dimension, into an impalpable world. The question for politics is rather this: Need the forces that decide the course of history take the form of armies advancing to capture or to destroy one another?

And to this question the answer is surely No: because the decision can be made more directly, antecedently and perhaps insensibly, by the very forces that would secure victory in war, if war broke out. Why fight if the issue of the conflict can be foreseen, and the conditions of peace can be imposed and accepted beforehand, without the convulsed attempt at mutual destruction? The wisdom and the fatigue that accept peace at the end might, with a little more reasonableness, accept peace at the beginning. What prevents is only ignorance, rage, and frivolity; and these passions may be, and are, modified in governments and even in peoples, on certain occasions. When numbers, wealth, energy, and discipline are all on one side, resistance would seem unreasonable; and yet it is often in such desperate cases that war is waged most stubbornly and heroically; because beneath and beyond all rational considerations there is the instinct of the hunted animal to flee, and if possible to turn, and to die fighting. Reason can never persuade anybody to change his nature; and the mere prospect of death, however certain, never prevents life from going on automatically to the last gasp. There are irreconcilables; and even if the more organised groups of them are exterminated by the ruling powers, a sprinkling or margin of irreconcilables will always spring up like weeds in the garden; they will be called criminals or heretics, and they will continue to carry on a desperate private war against society. Nevertheless, since these domestic rebels are outlaws, and in theory are to be eliminated, the force engaged in suppressing them is the police rather than the army; and the perennial conflict of society with them is not called war.

One way in which war might be abolished would be this: that all armies should exercise only the function of police; a universal government having established, for all nations, laws which it would be able to enforce.

Wars fought in the dark, between governments both hoping for victory, are gambles; and they enlist the same passions as gambling for money. There is not only avarice, or more probably debt and destitution, but even more prominently there is love of excitement, faith in one's luck, and eagerness to try a system said to work miracles. Such war is barbarous, not only for being cruel and wrathful, but for being hysterical. The herd instinct at work produces frenzy in individuals otherwise sane. There is a rush of a thousand hearts in a vague cause, simply because it has become the common cause.

Here is an occasion for the wise ruler to prove his skill. Nature has given him a pliant instrument; all are ready to fight and die for the common cause, and nobody knows what the common cause is. He can define that cause as he pleases. He can decide what shall be the common purpose for which his unanimous people will take the field. If he does not decide, or does so foolishly, very probably his unanimous people will take the field for nothing. In divining some notable advantage that might result from this blind conflict, and setting up that possibility as the object to attain, he not only rationalises an irrational movement, but trains the people to set their hearts on a public good; because nothing endears itself so much to us as that for which we are making unreasonable sacrifices. In this way the eloquence of leaders, grafted on practical commitments and automatic emotions in the people, can fix ideals like national independence or glory, for which nations may be ready to wage enthusiastic wars so long as the nations exist. And very often they exist as nations only by virtue of those superimposed unnecessary interests. Did official eloquence and military discipline leave modern nations alone for a moment they might break up into local units, or be merged in larger empires, without any material inconvenience, and perhaps with advantage to the intensity and fruitfulness of their domestic cultures.

The blind wars waged between nations out of national rivalry are therefore easily preventable, in so far as the nations themselves are artificial units. If the organisation which makes them units, and enables them to fight one another, were destroyed, wars of that character and on that scale would be rendered impossible.

In the end, however, we come to the natural units, economic or moral. Moral units are groups of similar minds speaking the same language, having the same religion and arts, and stimulating by social sympathy and applause the genius native to their members. Economic units, on the contrary, are formed by the interdependence of dissimilar arts; they extend as far as do economic exchanges; they are unconscious systems of cooperation, like that which makes insects contribute to the reproduction of flowers.

Moral units, if they could be purely moral, would not be bellicose, because no injury and no real diminution of dignity is caused to one spiritual good by the mere existence of other spiritual goods. But in this world nothing is merely moral. Moral realities must have a physical basis; and, through their physical basis, they may become competitive. The existence of a different language or religion, just beyond the frontier, or even in the bosom of one's own household, then becomes a danger and an offence. Moral units appeal to the secular arm; and we have wars perhaps begun in self-defence, but often carried on by fanaticism. It is the most legitimate self-defence to resist interference with one's moral traditions; but it is fanaticism to desire that there should nowhere exist any moral traditions but one's own. Between this self-defence or love of vital liberty and this fanaticism the hearts of heroes and apostles are divided. There is in almost all, I think, some admixture of both elements.

Economic units also wage frequent wars, sometimes intelligently, but more often and more largely with a suicidal blindness. When economic units are simple and closed, as in some agricultural island with only home manufactures and no foreign commerce, there is no occasion for war, since there are no enemies; and to break up the world again into such isolated units would be a means of securing peace between them. Even when commercial relations are more complicated, economic systems may exist side by side without conflicting, if they cover separate fields. But fields in this world are not easily separable; there will be rivalry for colonies and ports and raw materials and markets; and there will be occasional piracy and pillage turning that rivalry into aggression. But the ensuing war will probably not very much enrich the victor in ruining the vanquished; because the threads of industrial interconnection are many and largely invisible, and any important local breakage will derange the whole world of commerce.

In so complex a matter no one is sure of his diagnosis; and it will rather be some non-economic motive that will inspire even one's economic policy. Often the units called economic, like Labour or the Proletariat, are not really economic but moral units. They are composed of similar persons, not of interdependent activities. A war of one social class against all others may be successful in destroying the enemy classes, the social types detested by the fanatic who will have only his own social type in the world; but that moral victory will not enrich the surviving class economically. On the contrary, unless variety of moral types and of ways of living is somehow re-introduced, the qualitative riches of the community will be terribly diminished and reduced to the lowest common denominator; the principle being that no one shall enjoy anything that everybody may not enjoy with him.

I think that clear intelligence, if armed with sufficient authority, could easily avoid wars for economic motives. Population could be controlled by indirect methods, financial and educational; and production could be organised internationally so that all nations would be interested in keeping the peace. But probably this economic interest would be insufficient to curb other ambitions: and war could not be effectively repressed save by a central universal government, self-inspired and autocratic, always ready to wage it with overwhelming force.

## CHAPTER 38

### FALSE ESCAPES FROM DOMINATION

THE distinction between Dominations and Powers being moral, we may expect to find it present in the heart of the individual; indeed its source and seat cannot be other than the heart. If vital impulse had not become conscious in the passions (and conscious especially by feeling them thwarted) the models for a Domination and for a Power would never have appeared. We might have been moving mechanically under pressure from our fellows, like grains in a quicksand or snow-flakes in an avalanche; and we should never have minded it, unless some vital impulse within the single flake or the single grain had resisted that pressure or strained to push even harder and move even faster. So children and rustics endure political revolutions without knowing what the word means, or caring to know, if their daily routine is not disturbed; so many things of no consequence are talked about by the bigwigs! Yet children and rustics feel intensely the difference between Powers and Dominations in their private lives. They live surrounded and smothered by unintelligible fatalities; and they feel themselves brimful of suppressed powers for which they have no name. Their ignorance is in one sense wise; it anticipates the ultimate decrees of fortune in this world.

Sophisticated classes and governments, on the contrary, see too many possibilities to resign themselves to their troubles by repeating a few old tragic proverbs. They, with their superior intelligence and knowledge of the world, can easily see at each step how to clear the path before them. As to the result, when it appears, they will decide what to try next. Life for them shall be no wretched routine, pulling the same heavy ferry across the same dull stream from birth to death. It shall be a perpetually fresh adventure. Why be dominated by the past or the future, when both are now only imagined? Yet when they deride imagination as attention wasted on absent things, they are abandoning the function of imagination in directing the present. They have indeed become incapable of directing themselves, and are dominated by futilities, never being interested in anything but the morning's news and the day's accidents.

If they had time to reflect, they might feel as helpless and as ignorant as do the rustics and the children.

This predicament sets the problem for rational politics and I believe involves the solution. Human beings are subjected, from birth up, to a Domination contrary to their caprices: to leave a newborn child entirely free and alone would be infanticide. For their own good (if existence is a good) children must pass years under an imposed regimen, dark to them in its motives and origin, but sometimes welcome, and hardly to be defied without disaster. When they are well nursed it is not so much the things that are done to them that annoy them, as the moments when those things are forced upon them or snatched away: for initially in any automatic life innovation appears formless and inconsistent. Children want to repeat what they have once succeeded in doing; and only the tempo of their routine is different from that of their parents or of change in the social weather. For this reason they are driven to play, and to like impossible stories: the real world is too hard to live in, and it is a relief to imagine another where everything happens more as it should. Only in the holidays, in the pauses of compulsory life, can they be free and happy.

This is a first solution, that suggests itself when the pressure of circumstances is not too crushing and continuous, and there is plenty of time and energy for play. But it is not a true solution: only a false escape from the problem. False I call it and not merely partial: because even in play and in the holidays the problem recurs. The material of fancy wears thin; or the rules of the game spoil your freedom; or your opponents, who ought to have been there only to serve your sport, become real enemies and bullies. Later if your play-life becomes a passion, at cards, in racing, in politics, in love, in religion, you may find yourself more deeply involved, more harassed, more utterly defeated than you need have been in the working world.

Yet there is a simpler way, avoiding those moral vicissitudes, that leads the young mind back from play to reality. The pride of knowing may drive away the pleasure of making believe. Real things reward the respect that we show them, and imagination is as much excited by them as in any dream; moreover, our direct sketches from nature, if less inventive and dispersed, are more consecutive. A mind capable of discipline can therefore transpose itself ideally to the side of surrounding objects, and learn to live their life rather than only that of the human body, in its animal absolutism. To that extent domination is abolished by taking the tyrant's part. Yet this solution also is false: because if a man really took the part of things against his humanity, he would have attempted to kill himself while still living. He cannot have it both ways. Either the daemon of things actually takes the place of his human soul; or this soul smoulders in him, dishonoured and sadly starved by that inhuman gaoler. Your perfect pragmatist therefore would not have eluded domination by things, but would have cheerfully died of it.

The ignominy of the childish life, when domination is most galling, lies in being subject to casual commands and vindictive punishments, mitigated by forbidden sweets. Compulsion and prohibition then seem to cover everything, and leave no room for unclouded freedom. Freedom then must be rebellious, as if Powers were essentially tyrants; whereas we know that they become such only through a reversible relation which they bear to often reversible wills in their enemies. The true problem is therefore not how to abolish any natural Powers, but how to establish a sufficient harmony between them, so that they may support one another, or at least avoid contact, where harmony is impossible. The human soul may then develop its ideal life, as far as possible, in dynamic union with the world; and since such union involves difference, no soul need ever attempt to impose its language or habits upon other parts of nature, nor to renounce or deny the originality of its own ideas and pleasures.

## CHAPTER 39

### THE PRICE OF PEACE

LIBERTY habitually exercised presupposes peace; but the price of peace, as men are actually constituted, is the suppression of almost all their liberties. The history of liberalism, now virtually closed, illustrates this paradox. The individual expected to be morally emancipated; he panted to live in the paradise of anarchy. But this paradise is metaphysical only; to enter it you must love war and peril and change and irresponsibility and the mystic joys of mere being. A sober, thrifty, kindly liberal would shudder at such a prospect; his promised land must be peaceful, cooperative, and safe. He counts on progress, and is intent on building up a future that shall be always freer and freer, but also richer and better ordered.

Order, for a liberal, means only peace; and the hope of a profound peace was one of the chief motives in the liberal movement. The traditional order, which was pregnant with all sorts of wars, civil, foreign, religious, and domestic, was to be relaxed precisely for the sake of peace. The people, the sects, the young, and the intellectuals were everywhere restive and ripe for revolt; the threatened conflicts in Church and State, in industry and morals would be odious, and in any case fatal to the old order. Better, then, relax that order in time, and yield gracefully and peaceably to the inevitable. When we have conceded everything that anybody clamours for, everyone will be satisfied; and then if any picturesque remnant of the traditional order is left standing, we shall at last be able to enjoy it safely and with a good conscience. Swimming in the holiday pond of a universal tolerance, we may confidently call our souls our own. Impossible that such harmless liberty should arouse hostility in any quarter. Originality will no longer need to be shy, and offer excuses; heresy will be protected forever against social obloquy. What more justification could there be for anything than that somebody likes it, and why should anybody else wish to object to it for him? So, all grievances being righted and everyone quite free, we hoped in the nineteenth century to remain for ever in unchallengeable enjoyment of our private property, our private religions, and our private morals.

But there was a canker in this rose. The dearest friend and ally of the liberal was the reformer; perhaps even his own inmost self was a prepotent Will, not by any means content with being let alone, but aspiring to dominate everything. Why were all those traditional constraints so irksome? Why were all those old ideas so ridiculous? Because I had a Will of my own to satisfy and an opinion of my own to proclaim. Relaxing the order of society, so as to allow me to live, is by no means enough, if the old absurdities and the old institutions continue to flourish. They offend me by existing; they are odious and intolerable. No pond is large enough for this celestial swan, my divine animus; no backing out and self-effacement, no scurry into backwaters will save the ducks and geese from annihilation. How should I live safe or happy in the midst of such creatures? And to call our cohabitation peace, when they so trouble my soul, would be a mockery.

Merely to relax order and to be more and more tolerant will not therefore secure peace, unless this liberal peace works as a magic sedative, and gently destroys the possibility of discontent. Such was perhaps the secret expectation of liberal statesmen. Open every door, let in the light and air, smile upon the Red Indian in his feathers and the Chinaman in his pigtail, and the diffused and placid twilight of goodwill would bathe the moral universe for ever. Everybody would be happy at home, like the Englishman having his solitary tea in his garden; and all wars would be at an end because, at heart, there would be nothing left to fight for. Good will and mutual acquaintance would gradually rub off those remaining differences. The Chinaman would voluntarily cut off his pigtail; the Red Indian would desire not the white man's scalp but a cloth cap for his own head; and the Englishman would find it more convenient to take his tea in a teashop, no longer knowing any solitude or any garden. Toleration would have proved the euthanasia of differences. Everybody would be free to be what he liked, and no one would care to be anything but what pleased everybody.

Concessions and tolerance and equality would thus have really led to peace, and to peace of the most radical kind, the peace of moral extinction. Between two nothings there is eternal peace; but between two somethings if they come within range of each other, there is always danger of war.

## CHAPTER 40

### MANY NATIONS IN ONE EMPIRE [1]

A FATAL difficulty for the law-giver wishing to establish a perfect society lies in the teacherous character of his material, which is a nondescript mass of human beings inhabiting a given territory.

[1] This chapter and the next appeared in September, 1934, in an ephemeral review called *The New Frontier*, published at Exeter, New Hampshire. After fifteen years, rather than rewrite them in view of the important events that have intervened, I think it may be worth while to reproduce them, with only insignificant corrections or omissions, and add, by way of contrast, an account of the prospects now apparently open for the establishment of a universal government.

Not all these beings can possibly be of one mind; not all can possibly sincerely aspire to the same virtues, or recognise the same hierarchy of excellences. There will not only be sluggishness or error in doing one's part, there will not only be ineradicable vices; there will also be ineradicable virtues and aspirations contrary to the prevalent public ways. The legislator will therefore be assuming the character of an odious tyrant, in respect to these natural heretics and virtuous rebels; and unless he can thoroughly suppress them or banish them for ever (which is difficult in this crowded world) he will find his work always spoilt and poisoned at its roots, by the existence of that contrary drift in the souls of his people; while they, the discontented minority, will regard his exemplary discipline as sheer oppression, and themselves as martyrs.

So insidious is this native treachery in human nature that even if a few chosen saints were conveyed to some uninhabited island, and there established a sacred city, in which all heartily rejoiced, yet in the next generation trouble would begin. Some of those children, so strictly nurtured, would be atavistic; they would put their thumbs to their noses at those holy things; and the very need of correcting, or at least insulating, such wickedness would corrupt the original regimen, which had come to fulfill human nature and not to suppress it.

A solution to this difficulty suggests itself at once: Why not divorce moral societies from territorial or tribal units, so that membership in these moral societies, as in a free Church, should be voluntary, adopted only by adults with a full sense of their vocation for that special life, and relinquished, without any physical hindrance, as soon as that vocation flagged, or gave place to some other honest resolution?

The case of free Protestant Churches shows how such voluntary association is possible, and may foster an inner life not without sweetness and depth, and not without notable influence on the community at large. At the same time we see that in becoming free, in abandoning theocratic ambitions, these bodies have become marginal and secondary even for their most zealous members; for they supply only a nook for quietness and a Sabbath refuge, feeble in thought, null in organisation, animated by little more than traditional or censorious sentiment to be applied to current opinion and to the conduct of lay life. This yields us, then, a moralising society, but not a moral one: the world is to be served and if possible purified; but it is the world, and not the free conventicle, that remains the home and training ground for the spirit, and the real moral society to which the free Christian belongs.

This illustration suggests the difficulty, but does not exhibit it in its nakedness, because in a Protestant household there may be as strict a discipline and as stifling an incubus of authority as in an ancient Roman family or in a convent school. A Baptist minister will not christen his children until they are grown up and have experienced a personal conversion; but he will have brought them up in the way they should go, and the shadow of those withering parental disapprovals and precise expectations may remain all their lives long a cause of secret constraint and unhappiness. So that in reality the influence for good or evil exercised by a free Church is due to the absence of freedom within it. That influence is strong only because a definite austere tradition has been imposed by Authority. Had there been simply spiritual liberty and a rational concurrence of adult minds, all that impressive social power, all that moralising force, would have vanished.

Even Royal Academies and Masonic Lodges, if they are more than convenient clubs, exist to dominate the mind and not to express it. We know beforehand in what direction all those sheep will be shepherded. A liberal regimen requires many such voluntary associations to perform the social functions not assumed by a liberal government. These associations arise and disappear easily; they fill many an afternoon with meetings. Meetings of Societies having ancestral traditions and substantial backing may keep alive a certain moral and social rigidity; but in general they are entertainments rather than powers. The waters that the conduits of official authority rejected waste themselves in these sands.

Spirit has and can have no other consistency than that of its organ: if the organ is fluid or ephemeral, the thought and feeling that belong to it will drift like a cloud. When, on the contrary, the organ finds a firm lodgment in the body politic, when the free association takes root in society, the government may disregard the thing officially, but the private body will become in fact a second government, a part of that officious social order which really dominates mankind. If the free organism is harmless, and can cohabit with the legal establishment, the latter need not take alarm, although its importance and authority will be diminished. So with the many colleges privately founded in the United States; so too, everywhere, with sports in the last half century: they have become the chief free and spontaneous interest of the young and have even enlisted a sort of mock patriotism, very like that required for waging wars. If on the contrary, the free organism seems a rival or enemy of the ruling system, like the Catholic Church in France during the Third Republic, the ruling system may feel obliged to forget its principles in order to maintain its existence, and may proceed to stamp out the liberties it professes to favour. Thus, in the face of free organisations, a government must daily become either less and less dominant or less and less liberal.

Another way of making room, in a great nondescript empire, for various definite moral bodies, was accepted long ago in the East and may have a great future. A Cyrus might conquer vast regions; he would upset only their rulers, substituting his own satraps and slender garrisons; but this domination remained superficial, and little more than tribute levied, and perhaps richly repaid, in view of the protection secured against further invasion or tyranny. The Romans adopted the same system, and afterwards the British in their conquests, as distinct from their settlements.

Under such a Roman Peace, as we call it, a further development is possible. Not only may each nation, within its territory, preserve its language and laws and religion under the imperial insurance, but where different nations have intermingled, as often happens in great cities or in provinces vaguely open to any immigrant, each may preserve all its moral idiosyncrasy, its speech, dress, and domestic life, side by side with the most alien races. Far from mingling, these different nations may abound in hatred and contempt for one another; and they would undoubtedly come to blows till at last only one should remain in the field. But the imperial forces impose peace; and perhaps some division into quarters or villages, each pure, renders it possible for the orthodox of every sect to meet in the market place without contamination.

The Jews are a most wonderful instance of a people preserving its moral identity for two thousand years without any territorial possessions. Their fate has been hard, and the sentiment they have aroused in their gentile neighbours has not been kindly. The prejudice against them, however, has been religious rather than political; and even the difficulty they have encountered in establishing a "National home" in Palestine was due largely to the fact that their Holy City is also a Holy City for Christians and Moslems, with the

# MIGHT WISDOM RULE THE WORLD? 453

two latter in possession, and at first alone disposing of military force.[2] But suppose these circumstances had been different. Nothing would have then prevented the Israelites, scattered all over the world, from maintaining everywhere their religion and language, and preserving in Jerusalem a sanctuary where all the ceremonies of their Law might have been carried out. Round this sacred nucleus of race and religion, a complete body of arts and sciences, manners and domestic laws might then have grown up; and this without army or navy or police or local jurisdiction. It would have sufficed that the common law, in whatever other countries they lived, should have allowed them possession, as private property, of enough land for their synagogues and dwelling-houses: and especially licence to educate their children in their own schools, in their own language, up to the highest studies which they should wish to pursue. And I do not think a truly imperial authority, preserving a Roman Peace all the world over, would have any reason for denying any nation these moral liberties.

## CHAPTER 41

### THROUGH WHOM MIGHT WISDOM RULE THE WORLD?

THE world has several times come in sight of a liberal universal empire, under which every form of moral order might be developed by those communities to which it was native or congenial. Yet neither universality nor stability has ever been achieved. An Alexander, with his young genius and courage, stretched universal dominion to the eastern limits geographically possible in that age: to-day, with the ease and thoroughness of modern intercourse, the world is positively crying for a universal government, and almost creating it against all national wills. And Alexander was not too Hellenic, not too disrespectful of barbarians, to have been accepted by Picts and Ethiopians, by Chinese and American Indians, if he had conquered them all, as their providential overlord. But stability was wholly wanting. Macedon was nothing, and that expedi-

[2] See footnote on p. 1 of this chapter.

tionary force, spread over the continents, was not a power capable of controlling them, or of recruiting itself.

The case of Napoleon was not dissimilar. He had the advantage of representing a revolution, a rational movement that might be welcome and might take root anywhere; and he was not too French, just as Alexander had not been too Greek. But the French Revolution, being intellectual, was speculatively deluded, though Napoleon personally was not: deluded, I mean, in that it disregarded realities, and waved the flag of ideas. It therefore had all the true powers of the world, physical and sanely moral, ranged against it; and it was nothing, and could be nothing, but a convulsion.

In this respect the Empire of the Caliphs and the British Empire were far more fortunate. The religion of a Moslem prince or of an English general, whatever it may be for his private conscience, is nothing for the world except a beautiful code of manners and of manly sentiment. It can leave all other religions free and not be itself offensive. On the contrary, to an intelligent observer it may seem the symbol, as the word Moslem itself indicates, of submission to fact, to the only real public authority in this world, the authority of things. This is the religion or philosophy proper to a universal power; and if any general domination is to be established and successfully maintained over mankind, it must needs be in the name of physical necessities and physical conditions. The universal government must have no arbitrary moral tradition, no gospel of its own; it must nowhere seem, or in fact be, a foreign government.

Here is where the Moslems and the British fail. They possess a sense of superiority, a great indifference, if not contempt, for what is not theirs; and sometimes they seem to wish to impose their manners, if not to preach their ideas. But that is unworthy of a ruler. It renders him odious, and perhaps ridiculous. His subjects may be conscious of having an incomparably deeper and grander religion, an incomparably sweeter and richer morality than he can conceive; his superiority lies in representing and mastering material forces only. That function, when properly exercised, renders him a beneficent governor and physician and engineer; there lies all his authority and all his dignity. If he oversteps those limits, he becomes a fool. And then very likely his subjects will rebel, preferring to lose the material advantages of an imperial government to being overshadowed or insulted by a foreign and inferior quality of life.

## MIGHT WISDOM RULE THE WORLD?

So Islam was finally driven out of Spain and the Balkans, and now the English, almost if not quite, from Ireland and India.

Perhaps the Soviets might be better fitted than any other power to become the guardians of universal peace. In the first place, they are a real power, with an autonomous army, navy, and air force, grown out of the remnants of the old Russian armaments: this is the first prerequisite to accomplish anything. Secondly, the Soviets are theoretically international, and might become thoroughly so if extended further; they might become absolutely neutral in matters of race, nationality, education, and religion. Thirdly, they represent the Dictatorship of the Proletariat, that is, of the nondescript masses of human beings without country, religion, property, or skill. We are all born proletarians, and remain such all our lives long in our physical being and in respect to those radical animal wants which are alone coercive. The dictatorship is therefore not artificial here, but simply a recognition of the fundamental conditions of our existence. At that level, and in those respects, we live under the control of universal material forces; it would be childish not to recognise them and irrational not to confront them with foresight and method. Lastly, such foresight and method are foreshadowed in the Soviet doctrine of Historical Materialism. Supposing the Hegelian verbiage contained in this to be discarded, there would remain an explicit recognition of the physical basis of society. In regard to tenure of land, and to the management of industry and communications, if the management were competent, a universal communism, backed by irresistible armed force, would be a wonderful boon to mankind. Imaginations might still quarrel, but only with the arms of imagination; and the equal and safe possession of one's daily pittance would liberate the mind, where mind existed, for higher flights.

But these higher flights are not easy or arbitrary: it is they, more than the material order of life, that presuppose discipline. The Soviets would therefore have to renounce all control of education, religion, manners, and arts. We are proletarians and unwitting communists only in the absence of these things; in their presence, we all instantly become aristocrats. Everything except the mechanical skeleton of society, all culture in the German sense of this word, must be left to free associations, to inspiration founding traditions and traditions guiding inspiration. The local attachments of such culture are important, and a just universal government would not disturb them. Each nation or religion might occupy, as private property under the common law, its special precincts or tracts of land; or it might live locally intermingled with other nations and religions; but each in its own home would be protected from annoyance, and free to worship its gods with the homage of a complete life fashioned in their image.

This system would also solve the problem of the sporadic individual finding himself ill at ease in his nation: he could secede, or he could be excommunicated, without physical penalties, simply reverting to his fundamental human status of proletarian; or by mutual consent he might pass into another nation. And if anyone born unattached discovered late his moral affinities in some existing society, that society might receive and adopt him; or he might found a fresh institution with persons of a like mind. All this would certainly not happen without heart-burnings and trials and self-deceptions, not to speak of imposture and enthusiasm run mad; but at least the principle of spiritual wealth in spiritual liberty would be vindicated and this without any possible encroachment on the material order established beneath.

## CHAPTER 42

### THE UNITED STATES AS LEADER

THERE is a point in political theory in which events have confirmed the position adopted above. A universal government would have to be a particular government, rooted in the generative order of history, and not an alliance of sovereign states or a universal parliament. The League of Nations was still-born; and when it had been buried, almost the same group of victorious powers that had blindly set it up set up the Organisation of United Nations on the same blind principles. They even introduced the old Polish system of an individual right of veto for each of the Great Powers, as if to make executive impotence not only constitutional but expressly intended and prized.

Yet this impotence had a vital nerve in it. A decision cannot be universally satisfying unless it is unanimous. And Russia had already established at home the ideal of unanimity and the practice of autocratic government to impose that unanimity by education and training or, failing that, by terror. Russia too had been the most brilliant of the victors in this second war; and Stalin at once adopted the policy of vetoing everything that did not conduce to the extension of communist domination.

Here, then, is one living and powerful government, strongly national in its central seat and in its leading members, but theoretically liberal in the treatment of other nationalities and languages. At the same time there is a militant thirst for the political assimilation of all peoples to the social regimen of Russia, which in that claim forfeits all rational authority. Rational authority, according to my analysis, can accrue to governments only in so far as they represent the inescapable *authority of things*, that is to say, of the material conditions of free life and free action. In the Marxist theory this almost seems to be involved in its materialistic character; yet in Russian practice it is not the authority of things but nominally the material class interests and militant Will of the proletariat and really the ambition of the self-appointed inner circle of the Communist party that not only rule absolutely but intend to keep the whole world unanimous by "liquidating" all dissentients. And half by the wonderful power of propaganda and mass-suggestion and half by systematic extermination of all other ways of thinking, this artificial unanimity has actually seemed to cover vast regions of Europe and Asia like a blanket of Siberian snow. The depth of it is unknown, but the silence is impressive.

It is not, then, by the authority of universal physical conditions of existence that the Russian government would exercise control over all nations in military and economic matters; it would be rather by a revolutionary conspiracy fomented everywhere that it would usurp a moral and intellectual domination over all human societies. Such baseless pretensions cancel the right which economic science might have to guide a universal material economy.

What fitness have the United States, which have now come forward as a rival, to become the secular arm of Reason in checking the unreason of the world?

I had not, in 1934, ventured to name the United States as one of the powers that might be entrusted with that universal political duty. The American people had refused to join the League of Nations, more by an instinct of general distrust than by an insight into the folly of expecting an assembly of sovereign powers to possess or to carry out a consistent policy. The prevalence of representative government and the habit of being docile to majorities, when no fundamental interests were at stake, made Americans slow to feel that danger. And it was under this domestic illusion that, in 1946, a replica of the rejected and extinct League of Nations, with the aggravating feature of right of veto for each of the great powers, was established under American leadership on American soil. Except for that veto, which at once paralysed all decisive action, it would have been natural for the United States to have begun to offer its own forces, then very strong and fit, to carry out the decrees of the universal authority. This authority, indeed, would have been little but a chorus to approve, or at most to retard by some accidental scruple, the special foreign policy of the United States.

At the same moment, by the unprecedented election of a President for a third and fourth term of office, and by an immense extension and elaborate organisation of all the departments of State, the American Government was becoming an automatic power, far more intelligent and determined than any floating and temporary majority in Congress; so that a traditional great government, comparable to the Roman, might have arisen in the United States and might have legally, and by general consent, have established its universal jurisdiction.

Would such an American hegemony have operated justly and deserved to endure?

There are several respects in which it would seem eminently capable of doing so. In the first place, the American people are good; their mentality is settled and pervasive; they are devoted and ingenious in improving the instruments and methods of material economy: and it is precisely in this sphere that they would have been called upon to act for the welfare of all mankind. They would have done so honestly, diligently, guided by experts in every department; and while a cumbrous official system, with much pedantry and delay and some false and premature theories, might have intervened, there need not have been, in their government, that open, perhaps unconscious, selfishness which many imperial governments have shown in the past. And this not because Americans are superhumanly unselfish, but because in questions of universal peace and universal trade their self-interest coincides with that of all other nations, or would at least do so if it were clearly understood and strictly confined to material economy.

But would an American management of international affairs be really confined to the economic sphere? It is no doubt the desire to keep American enterprise alive and progressive, by establishing everywhere rational commercial relations advantageous to both sides, that fundamentally inspires what the Russians call American imperialism; but quickness and sagacity in the economic arts are human virtues, and in the human psyche which is the agent in politics, they cannot stand alone. By the obvious well-being which they bring, they breed self-satisfaction and complacency; and the technically just belief that rational trade is profitable even to the less enterprising party excites a pleasing passion for doing good. And there are so many other goods, like education and training, that help to secure prosperity and in turn are favoured by it! The authority that controlled universal economy, if it were in American hands, would irresistibly tend to control education and training also. It might set up, as was done in the American zone in occupied Germany, a cultural department, with ideological and political propaganda. The philanthropic passion for service would prompt social, if not legal, intervention in the traditonal life of all other nations, not only by selling there innumerable American products, but by recommending, if not imposing, American ways of living and thinking.

Now, this is, perhaps unintentionally, to transgress the limits of rational control and to exercise an influence that may be justly resented. If you wish to practice a mechanical art, the expert mechanic can rationally teach you how to do it; but if you wish to think or to practice a liberal art, another man, because he is self-satisfied, must not run up unasked and tell you to do it otherwise than as your vital liberty directs. The restraints that circumstances and the nature of things impose on your Will may be kindly pointed out to you before you commit yourself to a hopeless course; but the choice of your way must be left to you, if the authority that controls society is rational and friendly.

If, for instance, some community preferred not to trade at all, seeing that it could live suitably on native products, the universal government ought to limit its action in regard to that community to preventing their interference with the peace and liberty of their neighbours. It is a government, not a religion with a militant mission, that is demanded. It comes to serve and to keep order, not to dominate where it has no moral roots.

The British Empire, which was not founded or held exclusively for economic reasons, had a way of governing at once more reserved and more spectacular than the American system seems likely to be. There was military pomp and official grandeur about it; and the sportsmen of aristocratic breeding who chiefly carried it on meddled as little as possible with the natives. If the measures dictated to them from Whitehall were sometimes oppressive and designed to maintain British trade, even perhaps in opium, the thoughts of the military men and civil servants who actually governed were fixed rather on national prestige and on home and family affairs. It was as Englishmen that they fought and ruled, not as experts in an impartial and international economy. The very idea of a rational moral regimen for mankind was unknown to them, and they quite naturally associated prosperity rather with brave military enterprise than, as Americans naturally associate it, with a rising volume of irresistible trade. The fruits of monopolist adventure and of incessant mechanical invention have dangled in America before the eyes of ambitious youth and of capitalist old age; it was a world in progress and ulterior repercussions and settlements were not considered. The militancy of trade and of political reform seemed vital and almost normal, and undoubtedly it lent a speed and brilliancy to the growth of industry and of wealth in the nineteenth century which seemed to contemporaries an unmixed good, to be pursued and intensified for ever.

It is only now that the multiplication of mechanisms has become a nightmare, omnipresent advertisements a plague, the overgrown proletariat a quicksand beneath the feet of wealth, and the hierarchy of occupations a reversion to a sort of serfdom. In Europe this tragedy of commercialism is perceived; in America it seems to rumble still invisible below the horizon. And it may be a serious question whether a universal government in American hands would not attempt to revitalise the commercial optimism of the nineteenth century, by the aid of new inventions and better coordination of resources. Or would it face the inevitable limit to industrial expansion, and establish a stable economic order in a world where labour might again merge with self-rewarding arts, and imagination turn from devising machines to cultivating liberal arts and enlarging moral freedom?

## CHAPTER 43

### CONCLUSION

THE reflections gathered together in this book have not been prompted by an innocent desire to proclaim a political creed. Would it not have been a strange impertinence to assert that Julius Caesar should behave like Coriolanus or Hamlet like Henry the Fifth, either on the stage or in the world? Even less should I venture to prophesy the course of history in the future. What wiseacre in the nineteenth century could have considered possible the things we have seen in the twentieth?

This view by no means abandons the distinction between rational and irrational or between right and wrong. It rather insists that they cannot be arbitrary distinctions but must have some natural ground. In pronouncing anything to be rational or right we presuppose an underlying direction of vital energy or endeavour (here called primal Will) which some suggested step would serve to carry out. So a policy proposed at a Cabinet meeting can be judged to be right only by its fitness to further the aims of the government, these aims in turn can be judged only by the interests of the nation, and these interests only by the philosophy of the judge.

Rationality and rightness thus appear to be essentially relative; for it is their relativity that makes them relevant to events in the world. Were they absolute, and irrelevant to human nature and circumstances, they would be pathological fixations, making for militant madness.

In politics conscious rationality begins with the economic arts which would become wholly rational if they were organised exclusively in view of their utility and employed materials, time, and labour as economically as possible. In reality, as already pointed out, there is often a margin of spontaneous interest and initiative in doing things, which makes work partly liberal art; and besides, as men are not machines, they inevitably waste time and materials; both workmen and employers lounge a good deal and are more numerous than necessary, as are the clerks, salesmen, auxiliaries of every description, and hangers-on from senior partners to office boys; for they all think that the business exists to employ them and not they to carry on the business. In this way, while the machine threatens to mechanise mankind, old human nature does its best to humanise the machine.

The automatic equilibrium essential to health also helps in another sphere to soften the severity of reason. For sometimes reason tends to substitute pure method or simplicity or symmetry, with their empty magic, for the natural impulses of the artist; impulses that reason might have enlightened if they were misled by appearances or if they were themselves as yet inarticulate.

Many philosophers and politicians indeed tell us that they already possess *a priori* an adequate knowledge of what human needs and capacities are, and that they are really identical in everybody. The contrasts and conflicts in society, and in each man, they attribute to the absence or perversity of education. All men, they say, *must* find the same moral political and scientific regimen, communism, or constitutional democracy, or the One True Religion, perfectly satisfying. If they hesitate or condemn all such regimens, it *must* be because they are ignorant of the facts and of their own true good.

I think that these philosophers and politicians have good knowledge of themselves. They are born dogmatists and congenitally militant. But this disposition of theirs, at once intolerant and uneasy, blinds them to the actual radical diversity among men. This they cannot admit because, if admitted, it would prove them to be born tyrants. If this word "tyrant" is taken for a term of reproach, they can never be convicted of it in their own courts; but if taken to signify the superman, they will claim it with pride. They say we are all super-animals, either fallen from heaven or about to make a heaven for ourselves on earth.

It is often the boldest minds that, inspired by some political or religious dream, impose needless duties and taboos upon one another. A government that would be rational, on the contrary, would imitate the modesty of the physician that recommends only what can enable us to escape or to overcome the assaults that natural accidents may make upon us. Only that while government imposes instead of recommending its legal diet, it may also invite us to meet opportunities open to our powers. In both directions, however, it only forestalls and discovers for us the dumb beckonings of fortune. All else a rational government would leave to the special genius of each free society and each free individual. In suggesting such a division of moral labour, order where the conditions are known, liberty where imagination makes its own laws, I am far from expecting that such a division will actually be made; nor, if by chance the thousand forces at work ever fell into this arrangement, do I imagine that it would last long. Reason is itself a method of imaginative thought. It insinuates itself with difficulty even into economic arts, by virtue of the regularity of natural processes, to which action has to adapt itself; but it lives happy and safe only in ideal constructions, mathematical or poetical.

Fondly, then, as I might regard a final peace between order and liberty, secured by the rational separation of their spheres, yet I can imagine far more clearly, and not without some merriment, the shouts of joy with which one or another passion or irrepressible faith would hasten to break that agreement.

I picture to myself, almost in the clouds, a many-pavilioned International Institute of Rational Economy, faultless in architecture and appointments, like an Oxford set upon the Rock of Gibraltar. All strength and all learning to keep the world in the right path: what could be more satisfying? But at the foot of this citadel there would have to be a commercial and industrial town, with its own self-government and factions. There might be riots and revolutions there, too insignificant and local to demand international control. And in the spiral roads, or steep stairs, or funiculars that led to the citadel there might sometimes be scuffles between town and gown, or academic arguments, even more dangerous to moral peace. Nor would that be the greatest danger. Little knots of critical spirits would be formed in that high nursery of wisdom itself and would whisper their heresies in corners, or run down to join the demonstrations in the town square; for even supposing justice enforced in international relations, who could prevent local tyranny and deadly stagnation in free cities or free Churches? Moreover, economic order could not be maintained in the great world at long range by the International Institute without expeditionary forces of soldiers, sailors, airmen, and police, and all the holders of scholarships, experts, and young professors at that central nursery of peace would have begun by seeing military and inquisitorial service at the outposts of the Institute all over the world; they would all have seen something of the unregenerate edges of civilisation, and of political conspiracy at the heart of it. Imagination in some of these future guardians of universal peace would have been impressed by the lawless spirit they had come to root out. It may have seemed more human than the rational economy they were going to enforce. The excitement of lawlessness may have visited them in dreams. Why not try it in real life? Why not decamp to the mountains or run away to sea? Good luck might cast them on the smallest of islands in the widest of oceans where they might run about naked under the mangoes or paddle out boldly in double canoes beyond the horizon to capture and bring home each his innocent and loving bride. How much prouder they would be at having been ravished at sight by a young stranger than our spectacled sister-students who, after being wall-flowers on show for years, marry some elderly cousin!

But not all those emancipated minds would have been so selfishly pleasure-loving and, alas! so short-sighted! In rushing down from their Peace-Force Barracks, some of them would not have forgotten to fling open the cages of all the animals in the Zoological Gardens which, as an aid to understanding mankind, studded the flanks of that mountain. What new life they would bring to those unhappy brothers of theirs! Soon the old jungle and the old forests would teem with every sort of free creature, feeding, breeding, and fighting without respite! And the feasts would not be conventional like a dinner after a foxhunt, but truly royal, truly primitive, with the stag or boar or suckling-pigs on the table; and they themselves would sit like Nimrods enthroned and magnificently draped in the skins of their leopards and their lions, or like trappers or archers in a mountain camp, sporting the feathers of their quarry.

Other young pupils of Rational Economy might not have had time to shake off the dulcet diction of their former pedagogues; and they might attempt modestly to change the subject. "But how sad," they might murmur, "how sad to think that for so long we should have done that cruel wrong to our fellow-creatures by condemning them to undeserved captivity in dismal bare cells—so like our own, alas! in that prison!—with no outlook except on an artificial garden, with asphalt walks and arc-lights, when they were meant to range freely over wild and boundless spaces! Yes, and what's worse, we have condemned them to be fed on scanty, horrible, monotonous rations, thrown at them (think of the ignominy of this!) at precisely stated hours, while a crowd of grinning cockneys stare at them and poke them with umbrellas!" As if our common Mother Nature had not commanded them to gorge their fill whenever and wherever they found what they wanted; and as for finding it, to have faith and to trust in *Her*!"

It would be to misread the moral of this fable simply to approve one party, the constitutional and rational, or the other party, the militant and romantic; or to propose a third regimen, no less absolute and universal in intention. The study of human behaviour and opinion would then have taught us nothing, except perhaps that we must put up with them, whatever they choose to be. If we wish to draw some moral from experience we must assume that we are living in a world where our behaviour has causes and consequences that recede in all directions until they become irrelevant to our interests; but at closer quarters they can be traced in terms of the sensations and ideas that events excite in us. In these terms we can observe or learn from history and general report what sort of conduct will further our interests and what sort will ruin them; so that the question at once becomes not what we like best, but whether any part, and how much, of what we think we should like we can possibly secure. In a word, we shall be able to distinguish wisdom from folly.

Knowledge of the world and of what is possible in it, though it may discourage some vices, will not solve for us the question of what is our true good. For what the world can offer, when tried, may seem to us vanity. There is therefore another sphere, that of potential goods, which each man may evoke according to the warmth and richness of his imagination; and if he has any integrity or moral strength he will easily discern where his chosen treasure lies. Whether it is attainable in the world or not will not shake his allegiance: it is based on a native bent in his soul without which he would cease to be himself.

It follows from the evolution of the psyche through plants and animals that its treasure is at each stage different; and in man I think it is generally alien domination that makes anyone mistake his vocation. Strictly there is a complete impossibility, even between brothers, to conceive each other's inner man. The catalogue of possible virtues is limited only by the capacity of the cataloguer. But existence imposes limitation and idiosyncrasy even on the imagination and the Will (which Descartes said is infinite); and how should any of us, with his inevitable bias, pronounce which moral vocation is "the best"? Comparison can only be made with reference to a chosen good, chosen by chance; and wisdom lies not in pronouncing what sort of good is best but in understanding each good within the lives that enjoy it as it actually is in its physical complexion and in its moral essence.

# INDEX

NOTE: ITALICIZED WORDS ARE SUBJECTS OF EXTENDED
DISCUSSION

*Acquiescence*, 415–421, 431
*Agriculture*, 97–101
Agriculture, 25, 91–2, 98
*Aims of government*, 421–5
Alexander, 111, 283, 289, 322, 389, 393, 453
*Allegiance*, 281–4
American colonists, 346, 392–3, 397
American management of international affairs, 459
American people, 458
*Anarchy*, 236–242, 430
Anaxagoras, 11
Animals, mankind a race of, 6; ideas and feelings in, 11; functional unity and spirit in, 13; man among, psyches have feeling, 14; physical powers support or threaten, 23; pursuit of food and mates, 41; stupid martyrs, 43; adjusted to habitat, 69; altruistic, 71; tamed, hunted, exploited, 74; view of world, 75; domestic slavery, 76; impulse and power to seize, 87; taming and breeding, 88; trained and domesticated, 99; breeders and hunters of, 100; caged, 212; will for freedom, 225; vermin and unsympathetic, 231; sentiment toward, 232; sympathy with things, 239; experiments with tongue and claws, 248; spontaneous industry among, 262; egotism of, 268; mask of ferocity, 304; militancy of, 305; special actions, 330; comparative skill and value, 340; men as animals endowed for reproduction, not immortality, 440

Appearance, 19, 191, 193
Architecture, 107, 168–171, 227, 364
Aristides, 211
Aristotle, 14, 39, 119, 177, 196, 289, 337–8
*Art, birth of*, 87–91
Art, economic, 127; fine, 305; art for art's sake, 259; human, 87; in religion, 21; monumental, 259; necessary and optional, 25; of government, 394; of the artizan, 89; liberty of, 138; material and spiritual, 142; official, 170; plastic and decorative, 169; Renaissance, 263; savagery in, 214; useful, 190
*Arts, ambiguity of spirit in*, 96–7; *claims and conflicts in*, 92–5; *dissolution of*, 275–8; *economic*, 86–132; *independence and fusion among*, 118–120; *liberal*, 135–172
Arts, as methods of the psyche, 329; as objects of barter or profit, 262; based on use of fire, 88; bohemian, 276; claims and conflicts of, 92–97; dead, 278; distinguish each civilization, 245; dominations, 94; economic, 8, 59, 411, 413, 424; economic and military uses of, 178; economic and liberal, 101, 120, 430; fine, patrons of, 251; for home market, 261; instruments and methods of, 308; liberal, 93, 121, 141, 177, 189; 271; liberal and useful, 91; liberal discarded, 291; made for the gentleman, 277; mechanical, 265; national, 95; new, 180; of merchant and other specialists, 248; of nomads,

467

101; organized by monarchy, 111; parasitical, 24; place of music in, 139; primitive, 97; rational, 299; serving spirit, 171; transmissible, 340; under material influence, 260; vain and pernicious, e.g. advertising and propaganda, 249
Atom, 18, 46–7
Atomism, 11
*Authority*, 310–315, 321–5
Authority, dubious external, 184; at odds in civilized society, 185; of custom, 311; usurped by freedom, 312; of religious imagination, 313; denied by Reformation, 317; claimed by Communism for primal Will of particular class, 320; of family and tribe in antiquity, 321; a relation not inherent in fact or power, 325; recognized, religious, established, 327; hostility to alien, 329; democratic assumption of absolute moral, 352; "consent of the governed" as source of, 418; of things and of primal Will, 433; of rational government, 435, 457

Babylon, 131
Bergson, 338
British Empire, 454, 460
Buddhism, 18, 166, 368
Burke, Edmund, 389

Caesar, Augustus, 111, 254, 394
Caesar, Julius, 223, 307
Caillaux, Mme., 81
Cain, 75–6
Calderon, 63
Capitalists and bankers, 251
Cattle, 74, 100
Celestial hierarchy, 1
Centres, 12, 13, 239, 369, 408
Chaos, 33, 439
*Chaos and order*, 33–5
Change, 39, 51, 298, 338
Charity, 197, 366–8, 403
Charles I of England, 384
Children, Childhood, The Child, games and sports of, 24; first cry, etc., 35; food and pursuit of by, 37; discovery of primal Will through needs, 40; moral embryo, 41; not acquisitive, 42; obstacles and failures, 43; discovery of primal Will and opposition to it, 44; experience and education, 45; desire for freedom, 47; first distress and curiosity, 56; ignominious, 60; dependence, 61; plural non-ego, 64; relations to parents, 65; growth of home, 68; demands and cruelty, 69; resistance to education, 74; relations to mother, father, home and siblings, 102; harmony with mother, 103; imaginary government of, 106; rebellion against parents as enemies, 115; directive imagination, 124; games and inventions, 135–6; boredom vs. liberty, 237; response to brute force, 418; need for good primary, 422; domination by and escape from routine, 446
*Chivalry*, 204–8, 214, 219, 289
Christianity, Christendom, Christians, called atheists, 17; interpretation of liberty in choosing, 54; wretchedness if faith is vain, 155; early propaganda, 157; morality and liberty, 158; attitude toward sin, 221; effect of French Revolution, 224; claim to universal authority, 286; a revealed and militant religion, 288; assimilation of humanism, 289; no quarrel with gaiety, poetry, refinement and splendour, 290; response to humanism and age of discovery, 318; originally communistic, 320; quarrels and moral unity, 322; heir of Judaism and paganism, 335; equality in charity, 368; imposed by governments, 394; as the *chosen people*, 399; unanimity in propaganda, 410
Church of England, 256
Circumstances, encourage, re-shape or suppress man's capacities, 5; favour or defeat passions, 8; influence success of political agents, 17; control

## INDEX

growth of needs, 43; control Will, 126; as viewed by Nietzsche, 127; with primal Will determine interest of each person, 128; response of vital impulse not mere adaptation, 135; causes of individual character, 147; combinations affecting cycles of history, 219; as test of rational action, 313; identified with authority, 313; judged in reference to action, 314; traditional institutions imposed by, 318; in relation to primal Will, 324; in relation to the psyche, 325; weaker than primal Will, 328; as viewed by Hegel, 334; development of life controlled by, 351; oppose political stability, 362; cooperation with, 414; compromise with, 415; imposed by government, 434; response to crushing and continuous pressure of, 446

Cities, 264–5, 279–282, 322, 400

Classes, in monarchy, 110; bred by trade, 250; upper and middle, 252; commercial, 253; non-commercial, 254; intermingled, 256; interests of, 309; insurrection of lower, 323; class war, 366; enemy classes, 444; sophisticated, 445

Commerce, 251, 253–7, 259–61, 263–6, 283

Commercial class, 253

Commercial society, 258

Communism, revolution in reference to, 254; as standard bearer of humanitarianism and equality, 310; moral inspiration of, 320; class war preached by, 366; the People according to, 399, 401, 427; unanimity by force and propaganda, 411; inner circle of, 457

*Compound units,* 267–271

Compromise, 411–414

Conformity, 45–6, 65, 311

Conscience, 227–9, 254

*Contingency,* 49–52, 53

Cooperation, 352, 374, 379, 431

Country people, 101

*Crime,* 227–233

Crime, 81, 204, 213, 227–230, 232, 329

Cromwell, 117

Cruelty, 69, 432

*Custom,* 67–70, 78–83

Custom, thought based on, 7; diverse and arbitrary, 23; operative in physical and social world, 43; democratic, 44; offensive, 49; marks out lines for freedom, 60; origins of, 68; accidental, characterized by restraint, cruelty and ineptitude, 70; more sacred than law, 78; effect on diversity, 111; people in constitutional democracies governed and inspired by, 124; language and morality imposed by, 126; authority of weakened by contagion, 311; religious authority of government established by, 327; in primitive peoples, 408; as source of acquiescence, 417; break with, 418

Cyrus the great, 452

Dante, 48

Darwin, 178, 358

Death, 217

Defence, 423, 439

*Democracy,* 344–352, 355–9

Democracy, egotism of, 123; unanimity in, 132; men of action in, 276; rise of, 344; brotherly, 345; simplicity and peace in, 346; two kinds, 347; absolute, 348; revolutionary, 350; constitutional, 350; liberty and equality in, 350; instrumental, 350; unanimity in, 351; universal suffrage in, 356; types of in the United States, 359; disregard of minorities, 383; effect of large population on, 385; acting by deputy, 387; dilemma of representatives in, 389; ideal defined by Lincoln, 396; unanimity essential to, 410; in trial by jury, 413

Democritus, 17

Descartes, 47, 49, 439, 466

*Directive imagination,* 125–128, 389

Dictator, ideal, 113
Domination, alien, 225-7
Domination as an art, 271-5
Dominations, distinguished from powers, 1; established by accident, 2; distinguished only in relation to animal instincts, needs, passions or interests, 14; workings of in history, 22; individual dependent on, 23; manifestations in different "Orders," 26; view of Aristotle, 39; derived from arts, 94; element of tyranny in, 220; illustrated by landlord and government, 333; as object of liberalism, 353; by political party, 409; defence as the basis of governmental domination, 423; distinguished from Powers in private lives, 445; illustrated by routine in childhood, 446; abolished by tyranny of things, 447
Domestic animals, 74
Dreyfus, 81

Economic order, 25
Economic units, 443-4
Eddington, 267
Education, by child's experience, 45; defeated by change, relieved by retrospective science, 62; resisted by children, 74; adapted to the machine age, 77; dogmatic, 202; for the upper classes, 266; reforms in, 315; as a means, 424
Egotism, 63, 328
Egyptians, 131
Einstein, 11-13, 46
Elizabeth, Queen, 400
Empire, 280, 449-456
England, 123, 255, 266, 278, 278-9, 378, 381, 384, 400, 436
Enlightenment, 317-8
Enterprise, 244-291, 330
Epicurus, 17
Equality, 365-370
Equality, a battle cry of liberalism, 319; in demand for unanimity, 350; Constitutional, 357; real, 359; spiritual, 368; in misery, 369; as moral identity, 370
Esau, 75, 99
Escape, 65, 445-7
Essence, eternal self-identity of, 11; peaceful realm of, 12; images essences without existence, 21; introduced by notion of free beings, 39; infinitude of pure Being the realm of, 56; spirit apprehends things as, 57; ideas, 198; manifested to independent minds, 269; distinguished by reason internal to spirit, 297; wisdom of understanding goods in moral, 466
Established church, 257
Evolution, 209
Experience, first lessons of, 45; dramatic representation of, 56; capacity of psyche to profit by, 60; narrowed by custom in savages, 70; morality based on, 203; grammatical relations of language imposed on, 297; moral drawn from, 465

Fable of the partridges, 231-2
Faction, 177-242
Faith, 202-4
False beliefs, 192
Fanaticism, 20, 200-1, 443-4
Family, of nature, likeness of children in, 62; in Christian ethics, 68; sense of kinship preserved by, 69; growth of, 104; society based on, 105; degrees of extent and cohesion, 106; growth of monarch out of, 107; father's government of, 108; moral organization generated in, 110; must be controlled by father, 112; result of control by mother or self, 113; position in Orient, 227; religion and morals imposed by tyranny of, 227; in classical antiquity authority attributed to, 321
Feudal system, 76, 117, 224, 399
Fichte, 47, 167
Force, 78-80, 118, 295, 418

# INDEX

Form, of matter determines virtue of spirit, 10; relations determined by matter, 12; intrinsic in images, 21; chaos conquered by and besieging, 33; rational as perceived in universe of stars, 50; determinate, 51; changed by liberty, 60; recognizable in nature, 62; Will strives to preserve and manifest, 154; impossible to create substance out of, 259; introduced into flux of events by material rhythms, 308
France, 123, 254, 416, 452
Free will, 53–4, 74
*Freedom*, 46–49
Freedom, of ideal creations, 10; taken for granted by free creatures, 37; as political ideal surrounding chosen way of life, 48; not whole content of world, 49; as notion of miscellaneous variation or continual reform, 50; from obstacle, when determinate form is presupposed, 51; can be recovered by self, 54; not indetermination, 57; charm and promise of vacancy, 58; in youth controlled by custom and opportunity, 60; normal and noble love of, 63; as originality in individual crushed by society, 64; harmony with necessity gives sense of, 66; material obstacles to, 67; servitude provides means of, 73; for sheep, 75; from government, 119; destroyed only partially, 137; of wild animal, 225; inapplicable when alone, 237; never free while fighting for, 238; dependent on limitation, 241; illusion of complete, 242; legitimate when it does not usurp authority, 312; universe as Spirit in quest of, 334; of mind dependent on freedom to rearrange material conditions, 353; of anonymous crowd contrasted with individual liberty, 358; pure pleasures in sphere of, 420; must be rebellious, 447

French Revolution, 255, 316–7, 377, 390, 392
Freud, 103

*Generative Order of Society*, 32–172
Generative order, 23, 26, 177, 274, 296, 344, 350, 427
Genius, 194
German idealism, 167
Germany, 126, 279
Gettysburg Speech, 396
Gladstone, 429
Goethe, 140, 182–3, 230
Gothic architecture, 170
*Government*, 120–5, 325-334, 370–436, 449–453, 453–461
Government, 1, 2, 4, 22, 25, 78–83, 95, 107, 109, 110, 112, 119–123, 129–30, 141–2, 163–5, 199, 209–210, 220, 222, 225–7, 245, 247, 255–6, 265, 268–270, 272, 274, 278–9, 298, 300, 308–310, 319, 325–330, 333, 354, 362, 365, 367, 376–8, 380, 382, 384, 388–391, 393–9, 401–5, 408–9, 415–20, 422–7, 429–36, 438–39, 442, 445, 451–2, 456, 462–3
*Government, representative*, 370–390
Gracchi, The, 377
Greece, 165–6, 192, 222, 235, 282–3, 301
Greed, 93, 98
Greek oracles, 234–5
Greek philosophers, 26–7, 336
Greeks, 123, 322

Hebrews, 285–6
Hegel, 167, 320, 334, 338–9, 374, 392
Hellenism, 288–290, 393
Henry VIII of England, 114
Heraclitus, 12, 178, 441
Heredity, 59, 201
Herodotus, 283
Hindus, 18, 165
History, 4, 22, 194–7, 303
Holy Roman Empire, 48
Home, 68, 102, 279

Homer, 140, 196, 219
Humanism, 266, 289
Humanitarianism, 320
Humility, 63

*Ideas*, 143–148
Ideas, Platonic, 9; drama of life lends moral colour to, 10; emergence of, 11; found contrary to wishes by egotistical mind, 15; all within sphere of Spirit, 55; things seen and loved as, 57; prophetic, 144; various meanings of, 145; in mind and nature, 146; relation to causes, 147; spontaneous growth of, 148; in the arts, 171; pictorial and mathematical, 186; in speculation, 187; products of human nature, 193; as essences, 198; opposed by propaganda, 199; controlled by physical agencies, 201; false, 209; introduced by evolution into ethics, 209; as temptation to wickedness, 211; number and variety favoured by commerce, 258; in service of politician, 419
Idealism, 392
Ideologies, 15, 17, 22
Idle rich, 253
Illusions, 144
Images, 13, 21, 186, 193, 195, 308
Imagination, religious ideas bred by, 20; as system of signs, produced in animal psyche, 21; private, highly coloured, personally biased, 183; trained to reproduce history, 186; permitted by nature to become dominant because waking sensation is evanescent and harmless, 187; wild and extravagant, 190; fertile and redundant, 191; helps render militant motive clear, 192; constitutes inner music, 193; would drift in natural man left to himself, 203; as opposed to and receptive of propaganda, 273; whole wealth of, 372
Incarnation, 57, 184, 370
India, 394
Individual, 72, 202

Industry, compulsions due to, 66; supplies instruments for demands and subjections, 68; man as raw material of, 77; overpowering mechanism of, 88; play with tools the beginning of, 91; moral function of transformed, 177; mutation in equipment of, 180; momentum of, 207; equipment of as destructive weapons, 208; producing revolution in equipment and mind, 246; trade as abstract form of, 250; rural, 254; knowledge and taste diffused by, 261; a spontaneous habit, 262; character before commerce, 263; militant commercial, 264; elastic theology not contrary to, 267; effect on England, 279; profits of, 379; under government control, 382
Inspiration, 17, 96–7, 170
Instruments, to found new economy, 59; extend functions of teeth and claws, 87; first creation and basic character of, 88; destructive power of, 89; misuse and use of, 91; advantages of physical nature of in economic arts, 94; produced by greed, 98; transformed to weapons, 177; not disembodied and perfect, 268
Integrity, 59, 197, 230–2, 295, 306
Intelligence, 36, 188, 435
Interests, 184, 207, 319
*Interests of government*, 425–431
Intuition, 198
Islam, 283–4, 286, 393, 402, 410, 455
Israel, 150, 392, 397, 427

Jacob, 99, 149–151, 312
Jeans, 267
Jews, 17, 165, 200, 252, 287, 361, 399, 402, 452
Judaism, 287, 335
Justice, 81, 108, 118, 205–7, 428–9

Kant, 127, 325, 428
*Knowledge*, 300–303

# INDEX

Knowledge, rejected by sceptic, 7; growth of widens chasm between Will and action, 60; self-transcendence as consequence of, 62; as ideal record or memory, 186; requires assumption that truth can be found as objective, 187; by use of ideal terms applied to describe existence implies ignorance, 189; moral feelings dependent on, 210; doctrine of Socrates, 300; relativity of, 302; will not solve question of true good, 465

Labour, 380
Labour unions, 390
Land, 89, 92, 105, 207, 255, 422
*Language,* 143–5
Language, thought based on, 7; reveals relations of things to psyche, 16; politicians inspired by, 17; superstitious respect for, 70; spontaneous rise of, 78; prevalence and authority of, 80; hypothesis of all-expressive and exclusive, 108; as instrument of fanaticism, 140; characteristics of, 141; as social institution grafted on instinct, 142; functions of, 143; megalomania of, 207; automatism and irresponsible life of, 267–8; in service of humanities, 274; organization of experience by, 297
Law, of motion, 38; generalizations taken for laws of nature, 51; rash generalizations, 53; forms of government in operation before they are defined by, 79; superseded by judges and juries, 81; true morality deeper than, 82; events falsely attributed to abstract, 94; sense of justice better than, 108; force of appears brutal, 118; language and morality opposed by, 126; religion swallowed by, 161; political religions leave to circumstances enforcement of, 164; rudimentary where political religions took shape, 165; of nature cover moral chaos, 181; of dogma inexorable, 202; of tyranny, 220; of freedom, paradox of, 237; passed by parliament, 365; of government sanctioned by military force, 431; of universal government, 442
League of Nations, 205, 246, 456, 458
Legality, 81
Leibnitz, 10–12
Lenin, 221
Liberalism, elements of reform in, 164; preaching contrasted with interests, 309–10; equality and democracy as battle-cries of, 319; character of supporters, 350; doctrine of police and of individualism, 352; would establish domination, not rational order, 353; tendencies of radical liberalism, 430; kindness and beneficence of, 436; absurdities of, 437; relaxation for peace as the program of, 447–8
*Liberty,* 35–7, 44–6, 49–52, 57–60, 224–5, 436–8
Liberty, first assertion of and experiment in, 35; burdens would compromise, 36; service of liberty only seems to abolish liberty, 37; liberty of monotony monstrous, 38; liberty needs food, station and direction of growth, 39; feeling of safety necessary, 42; first discovery of powers opposing, 45; liberty of God, universe, and reformers, 47; relation to reform, 48; kinds and stages of, 49; to pursue some good, 51; crushed by pursuit of order, 52; its vitality springs from incarnation, 57; form of vital liberty ignored, 58; instruments and skills necessary, 59; changes form, 60; a right of primal Will that needs harmony with the Wills of neighbors, 62–3; confluence of Will from many centres determines measure of, 63–4; society suffocates liberty by merely existing, 65; empty freedom not moral liberty, 66; native liberty in parents, 69; in work of liberal arts, 91; the fortunes of vital liberty, 94; growth

of vital liberty from Jacob's religion, 151; threatened by ambiguity of imagination in politics, 183; ancient institutions as impediments to, 223; rigid form of French Revolutionary liberty, 224; fostered by paternal government, 226; love of liberty as modern motive, 236; love of transformed to hatred, 237; safety and peace required, 238; order of genesis inverted by, 240; limited, 241; liberty of opinion favoured by commerce, 258; integrity a triumph of, 295; vice and virtue both expressions of 304; for the rich and for geniuses, 310; in rhetoric and music, 311; liberalism considers material comfort and moral liberty harmonious, 319; shelter and society under government necessary, 326; versus equality in democracy, 350; assumption of democracy in regard to, 351; vs. cooperation, 352; language at liberty must be spoken, 353; liberty differentiates, 358; of the psyche, 359; of each passion, 428; of the hero and criminal, 429; in each person, 430; of liberals, 431; vocation of vital liberty in all men, 432; protection of liberty first principle of rationality in government, 435; paradox of liberty and peace, 447; final peace between order and liberty, 463
*Liberty of indifference*, 52–4
*Limits of government*, 431–6
Lincoln, Abraham, 396, 425–6
Louis XIV of France, 114, 254
Love, 65, 103, 367–8, 375, 436
Lucretius, 4, 20, 178
Luther, 265
Lycurgus, 272, 362

Machiavelli, 208–9, 211, 232, 271, 425–6
Machines, 77
*Madness*, 231–6, 439
Mankind, 6
Manufacture, 91, 262

Marriage, 60
Masks of vice, 304, 306
Masks of virtue, 305, 306
*Matter*, 10–13
Matter, germ of spirit in, 10; fertility of, 11; determines relations of form, 12; unlimited potentiality of, 13; attempts to define, 18; effects produced by, 21; potentialities the essence of, 40
Materialism, interpretation of politics by, 5; opposite effects of, 6; naturalism most brutal form of, 18; philosophy of characterized, 20; potential vocations of, 21; interest in accidents of existence inspired by, 39; terms not inconsistent with, 143
Matriarchy, 112–3
Means and ends, 208
Merchants, 261, 266
Metanoia, 59
Michelangelo, 97, 260
"Might is right," 313
*Militancy*, 245–7
Militancy, not absent morally from peace, 181; roots of, 181; springs from self-contradiction of animal Will, 183; sophistry a case of, 190; speculative militancy not unprejudiced, 192; enterprise a form of, 245; essence of militancy dominant in prophets of world improvement, 246–7; romantic side of, 247; in enterprises, 261; two kinds compared, 262; in medieval orders, 272; a strand in generative order, 295; involuntary rivalry not militancy, 296; in Plato and in religious orders, 364; Israel and Communism extreme cases of, 427
*Militant order*, 177–291
Militant order, 24, 26, 177
*Mind*, 189–194, 372
Minority, 383
Mohammed, 114, 273
Mohammedans, 165
Monads, 12
*Monarchy*, 107–118

# INDEX 475

Monarchy, tradition of patriarchy preserved in, 108; as government by a single psyche, 109; if good, the ideal, 110; glimpse of caught by Alexander, Caesar and Napoleon, 111; tyranny a travesty of, 220; grows in peace, an instrument of war, 225; difference between European and Oriental, 227; tended to create nationalities, 391
Money, 249–251, 253, 263, 266, 366, 379
Montesquieu, 381
Moral causes, 8
Moral forces, 8
Moral horticulture, 363
Moral societies, 450
Moral units, 443
*Morality,* 102–7, 155–9
Morality, proper to self, 5; sympathy with contrary, 6; defect of in family and tribe, 107; imagination militant in traditional morality, 128; dependent on particular religions, 155; each sanctions special morality, 156; religious morality must adapt to worldly economy, 157; Christian morality has never ruled the world, 158; effect of religious decay, 159; in tribal dogmatism, 201; of natural man left to himself, 203; false morality based on "what is done," 209; reigning notions misguided, 210; cosmos its field of action, 216; imposed by commerce, 256; treated as solemn matter, 257; tightened by fanatics and new rich, 266; of members of government, 269; Roman Catholic, 288; choice of reason marks type, 298; founded on conscience, 301; absolute authority assumed by democracy, 352; artificial morality hated, 363; of fighting animal and social architect, 367; humanitarian, 398; not source of happiness, 430
*Morals,* 99, 300–303
Moslems, 200, 454
Motion, 39, 46, 298

*Music,* 138–9
Music, 101, 136, 138, 139, 171, 186, 258
Myths, 192, 318

Napoleon, 111, 118, 223, 454
*Naturalism,* 6–10, 14, 17–21
*Nature,* 373–5
Nature, vital achievements of, 2; fecundity of, 6; change and rhythm of repose, 9; spirit first begotten child of, 13; poetical illusions true to, 16; shepherds and husbandmen assist, 24; harmony or conflict with, 25; chaos at heart of, 33; order and freedom produced by, 34; as taught by Aristotle, 39; automatism and law of, 41; generative resources, 43; gropings after the impossible, 44; order may be transitory, 52; laws of vs. plasticity, 53; chance events, 54; events fresh products, 59; flux of, 61; learning about, 62; no right in, 63; seedbed of beauty and virtue, 95; rebellion against, 180; repetitions and analogies in, 297; judged by reason, 298; Will controlled by, 328; prepares specific animal for action, 330; does not prearrange circumstances to meet Will, 331; order not condemned or approved, 332; source of demands and aspirations, 355; man one of spontaneous products, 363; militancy opposed to, 364; chance cooperation in, 374; social harmonies of, 376; same in all ages, 440; instability of, 441
*Needs,* 41–4
Negro, 357–8, 360
Newton, 38, 47
Nietzsche, 126–7, 167, 211, 224, 232, 271
Nomads, 100, 391
Non-ego, 61, 64

Officials, 17, 122
Order, 9, 11, 21, 24, 33–4, 39, 49–52, 181, 218, 223, 229, 240, 242, 264,

295, 332, 353, 374, 429, 439, 448, 463
Order of generation, 299
Order of genesis, 321
*Organism*, 370–3
Organization, 360
Original sin, 63

Paganism, 284
Pantheism, 18
Parasites, 24–5, 255, 270
Parents, domination of, 23; authority, disappointments and sympathy of, 65; servitude of, 66; cruelty of, 69; psyches of, 102; enemies of children, 115; sacrifice of firstborn by, 440
*Parliaments*, 384–390
Party, political, source of principles and purposes of, 17; support of individual vs. society, 65; served by politicism, 72; demagogues and dictators leading, 118; blind when in power, 125; in United States, 131; rational, 296; mistakes of, 300; influence of enlightenment on, 318; Conservative, Republican and Liberal, 331; morally representative of people, 378; partially representative, 383; expressed in parliaments, 385; deputies selected by, 387; death of leaders and newspapers, 388; speeches vs. pledges, 390; unanimity in two-party system, 409
Pasteur, 410
Pater, Walter, 168–9
Patriarchal government, 108, 112, 114–6
Patriotism, 129, 130, 279–281
*Peace*, 447–449
*People*, 395–436
People, 391, 392, 395–406, 408–9, 416, 419, 421, 422, 424–7, 431, 433
Perception, 193, 371
Pericles, 254, 282
Physical causes, 4
Physical dependence, 61

Physical forces, 8
Pity, 367–8
Plato, 12, 39, 75, 106, 119, 145, 209, 225, 235, 282, 289, 301, 337, 364, 392, 422
*Play*, 90, 135–7, 154, 446
Police, 204, 442
Political passion, 126, 129, 131, 132
Politicians, 387–8
*Politics*, 3–6, 14–17, 128–132, 160–7, 194–8, 307–310
Politics, 3–5, 14, 15, 23, 26, 40, 47, 48, 51, 55, 58, 61, 79, 119, 120–1, 129, 140, 143–4, 163–4, 177, 183, 194, 196, 209, 222, 236, 262, 270, 295–6, 298, 301, 308–9, 312, 318–9, 326, 373, 385, 390, 392, 404, 416–7, 433–4, 446, 461
Polygamy, 114
Possessions, 89, 90
Poverty, 400–1
Powers, distinguished from dominations, 1; change of, 2; man's determined by psyche, 5; distinguished by reference to springs of animal action, 14; recognised by religion, 19–20; bring images and feelings before spirit, 21; history in terms of, 22; physical and first, 23; of man and nature, 25–6; view of Aristotle, 39; Is child Will a power? 44; contrary powers, 45; natural, 59, 60; non-ego formative of, 61; indifferent or destructive, 182; real powers definite, 241; decline of great political, 278; political in service of reason, 296; no authority in absolute power, 325; "power corrupts," 389; distinction from Dominations moral, 445; harmony with, 447
*Private judgment*, 184–9
Process, 7, 11
Profit, 379
*Progress*, 94, 256, 334–341, 358
Proletarian government, 349
Proletariat, defined, 348–9; glorifies undifferentiated existence, 350; rela-

# INDEX

tion to work, 368; equal in misery, 369; Dictatorship of, 455; militant Will of, 457
*Propaganda*, 198–202, 203, 249, 251
Propagation, 199
Property, 81, 98, 379, 381
Prosperity, 424
Protestantism, relation to politics, 166; source of plutocracy of commerce, 255; a tradesman's religion, 256; American democracy rooted in, 346; secured by territorial domination, 393; imposition on northern countries, 394; free churches, 450; household typical of, 451
*Psyche*, 14–17
Psyche, 5, 7, 14–17, 21, 24, 43, 51, 60, 62–3, 87, 89, 92–6, 98, 109, 127, 135, 139, 179, 182, 194–5, 197, 235, 242, 264, 274, 295–6, 299, 302, 304–6, 324–5, 328–9, 357, 359, 364, 371, 373, 375, 383–4, 414, 428–9, 434–5, 465
*Public feeling*, 382–4
*Public interest*, 382–4
*Public opinion*, 341–4
Public passion, 343
Puritanism, 256

*Rational order of society*, 294–466
Rational order, 25, 26, 296
Rationality, 315–6, 321
*Realpolitik*, 209–212
*Reason*, 295–300, 307–310
Reason, in politics, 295; germ of rational political growth a seedling of, 296; alleged political service of, 296; sheds light on events, 297; choice of as guide marks type of morality, 298; sufferings and joys not in, 299; mistakes and failures of in government, 300; demands integrity, 306; a new harmony in vital forces, 307; place of in politics, 308; banished by militant reform, 321; does not destroy power of Will, 324; effects of eager use of, 333; speculative view, 367; moral harmonies opposed to, 373; cannot define or codify human nature, 382; different status in individual and in political conflict, 428; political discipline, 435; cannot persuade anybody to change his nature, 442; a method of imaginative thought, 463
*Reform*, 315–321, 379
Reformation, 265, 316–8
*Relativity*, 12, 46, 300–3, 307–310
*Religion*, 148–167, 284–291
Religion, principles of naturalism do not banish, 18; defined as recognition of Powers, 19; poetical form lent by, 20; pretenses of, 21; new or foreign, 24; visions of order reduced to terrors by, 52; rise of, 78; force of, 80; becomes province of government, 81; rural formation, 99; participation in life of monarchs a type of, 131; economic and liberal interests in, 149–154; dependence of morality on, 154–159; how religion may become political, 160–167; initial interests and militancy, 190; rejected by absolute Will, 214; kindles disinterested passion, 218; imposed by family tyranny, 227; in commercial society, 256–7; human element in not recognized, 267; error discovered in, 268; militant, 273; change of public attitude toward since 1870's, 274; militant religions, 284–291; modern enlightenment in, 318; establishment and sanction, 327; founded on charity, 366; idealism, sacrifice and relation to People, 392; relation to government, 425
Renaissance, 265, 317
*Representation*, 373–382
Representatives, 383–5, 408
Revolution, 223–4
Rhythm, 9, 128, 308
Rights and liberties, 205
Rivalry, 103, 296, 365
(Roman) Catholicism, Catholic Church,

Catholics, 110, 165, 202, 273, 287–8, 361, 402, 452
Romans, 48
Rome, 105, 227, 282–3, 322, 400
Rousseau, 224, 369
Russia, 202, 349, 401, 457
Russian democracy, 347

Saint Augustine, 338
Saint Francis, 16
Saint John, 362
Saint Paul, 155, 265
Savages, 70, 214
Science, in civilized society no authority on conduct, 185; avoided by philosophers of history, 195; influence of commerce on, 259–60; change since 1870's, 274; effect of findings, 322; validity and invalidity, 440
Schopenhauer, 126, 171
Self-government, 405–7, 409
Self-knowledge, 429
*Selfishness and unselfishness*, 71–3
*Sentimental bandit*, 212–4
*Servitude*, 60–70, 73
Sex, 102–3, 114
Shakespeare, 144, 207
Shareholders, 379
Sheep, 75–6, 104
Shelter, 42
Shepherds, 24, 75, 100
Sin, chosen by free will, 54; of arrogance, 63; Christian attitude toward, 221; in moral tales, 230
*Slavery*, 73–77
Slavery, of compulsory sacrifices due to industry and war, 66; involuntary yet accidental servitude, 73; forms of society, 104
Social harmonies, 376
*Society*, 64–7, 362–4, 376–382
Society, point of view of, 1; owes warmth and vitality to virtues, 3; sets up ideal, 5; spirit abdicating from, 6; complicated by faction, 23; conflict of habits and traditions unknown to, 24; of bandits, 25; effect on individual behavior, 38; ideals rooted in, 40; ancient and complex, 48; has aggravated moral entanglements, 54; slavery to, 64; escape from, or conformity with suffocation of liberty by, 65; social and moral conscience offended by, 66; obstacles to freedom more easily surmounted in, 67; home transformed into, 68; may develop various systems, 69; rules in not established by political institutions, 78; power of artisans over, 90; duties imposed by structure of, 99; slavery but for imitation and custom, 104; based on family, as in Rome, 105; of children, 106; source of monarchical order of in family, 107; in monarchy, 109; moral organization of, 110; how reconciled with peace and order, 111; natural growth not rational, 119; growth of not traced to politics, 120; in realm of matter, 135; if managed by instinct, etc., 140; necessities and utilities subserved by, 141; causes of eruptions of, 144; decency established in, 156; arts part of economic articulation of, 177; opinion in, 188; a conspiracy of psychological forces, 203; has lost soul, 208; criminal against, 213; tyranny an assault on, 220; domination of crime over, 228; order unstable, 240; unnoticed transformations of, 245; dominated by producer, 251; commercial domination superficial, 253; characteristics of commercial society, 257; without foreign commerce, 265; character of officials in, 269; dominated by parasite, 270; rise of urban, 281; loss of liberal arts by, 291; rational order imposed on, 295; in which interests of classes are opposed, 309; breeds superstition, 311; unhinged by liberalism, 319; ruled by vital and imaginative human nature, 323; demands of take shape spontaneously, 330; conditions of political democracy in, 345; as reaction of matter to

# INDEX

circumstances, 351; illusion of voluntary, 354; not predetermined to fulfill primal Will, 362; rests on friendship, 366; morality of vermin in, 367; not being an organism lacks vital unity, 370; material not moral unity, 371; moral harmonies in, 373; representation of, 377; view of virtue in mixed or decadent, 384; government superposed politically on, 403; principles and virtues in, 408; break with custom tends to dissolve, 418; pressure of not felt, 430; controlled by government and cooperation, 431; as proof of benevolent impulses in men, 436; lawgiver of perfect, 449

Socrates, 39, 229, 234–5, 282, 300, 301, 336
Solomon, 165
Sophists, 192, 301, 303, 392
South America, 358
Soviet government, 48, 246, 347, 455
Space, 46–7
Speculation, 62
Spinoza, 18
*Spirit*, 10–13, 55–7
Spirit, view of modern moralists, 9; in incarnation, 10; stupefied by limitations, 11; actualized and individuated, 12; diversified by feelings and images, 13; in singing lark, 16; spirit in power of healing, 19; witnesses and compares, 26; nature produced and left free, 34; ultimate religion of, 39; defined, 55–7; psyche kindled into spirit in us, 62; dominated by non-ego, 64; built up by man's animal nature, 66; turns organism into transcendental centre, 67; pure, 97; realm of relevant to physical life, 141; phenomenology of interests moralist, 144; virtues of intelligence and sympathy, 151; hypothesis of spirit not native to heart, 198; come to birth in death, 218; heroism of, 238; roots in earth, 239; activities of, 240–1; speculative and disinterested, 291; reason internal to, 297; reason chief characteristic of, 298; in sufferings and joys, 299; two thousand years in the wilderness, 301; arises in animals, 302; view of man, 314; man needs to discover, 322; in the jungle, 327; Hegel's doctrine, 334; if spirit suffers, 368; awake in men, 369; incarnation involves dispersion of, 370; as witness of psychic dreams, 428; consistency of its organ, 451

Stalin, 457
Sympathy, of parents with children, 65; partial in living creature, 305; potentiality in primal Will, 306; place in charity, 366; adaptation of, 368

Terence, 289
Terms, 12
Tools (See: Instruments), 88–9, 178, 267, 308
Trade unions, 349, 379, 381, 390
*Trade*, 249–260
Trade, 88, 248–251, 261–2, 411, 460
Trial by jury, 413
Tyranny, 220–3, 227, 240

*Unanimity*, 352–5
Unanimity, 350–2, 355, 409–10, 413
Uniformity, 356–7, 365
United Nations, 246, 456
*United States*, 359–62, 456–61
United States, 123, 131, 162, 347, 355–7, 359, 378, 381, 400–1, 425, 451, 457–8
Unselfishness, 71, 72
Unskilled labourers, 380
Utility, 328–9

Vaihinger, 127
Vauban, 49
*Vice*, 303–7
Victoria, Queen of England, 254
Virgil, 48, 96, 196
*Virtue*, 303–7
Virtues, defined, 2; place in this book, 3; progress as an emergence of, 94;

hypocritical and genuine, 95; propagation of, 209; nature, not convention, standard of, 210; mock virtue, 211; in competition, 228; of enterprise, 245; reason a spiritual virtue, 299; expressed by mask of vice, 304; vital virtue, 305; masks of, 306; variation in different phases of life, 337; various combinations, 354

*War*, 177–184, 215–220, 438–444

War, author's experience of, 22; between man and environment, 26; use of shelter in, 42; compulsory sacrifices of, 66; waste and lack of integrity in, 67; government a modification of, 79; religion an occasion for, 81; in government and in peace, 82; of succession, 83; created by instruments, 88; posture of hunting in, 89; among primitive, scattered and domestic populations, 104; provoked by militant hordes, 105; Rome and war, 105; effect of dangers and spoils on predatory peoples, 117; as department of government, 118; the chase a form of, 137; wars of growth, 117–9; wars of imagination, 179–184; contemporary sentiment about, 204; former view of, 205; chivalrous wars, 206; character of future war, 208; recent savagery in, 214; ravages of, 215–20; monarchy an instrument of, 225–6; destroys liberty to operate in chosen field, 238; bewildering effects of, 245–6; irrational character of, 295; communist wars, 320; effects of victory in, 339; as effect of uniformity, 365; class war, 366; dependent on prosperity, 424; in the psyche, 428; war vs. order, 438–440; suppression of war, 440–4; situation and feeling of liberal peace movement against, 447–8

War of 1939–1945, 22, 323

Watteau, 369

Wealth, 400

Will, Primal, 37–41

Will, primal, fecundity of nature lifts incubus of, 6; agent criticized by spirit, 26; doctrine of Aristotle does not express Will in nature, 39; potentialities of man rooted in, 40; not coextensive with automatism of nature, 41; freed by Vodka, 42; adjustments with opportunity, 43; discovered by child, 44; shock of Will disregarded, 45; blind hope of to find freedom, 49; at work in militant passion, 55; prompting to look, notice, understand, 56; not immutable or identical, 59; elastic in time, 60; animates child to discover dependence, 61; when not frustrated, 62; egotism and liberty of, 63; man's Will divided against self, 66; effect of armaments on, 89; casual effects of, 92; place of the useful in field of, 97; greed manifested by, 98; relation to authority, 104; morality of family and monarchy too social for, 107; not function of Will to reconcile society with peace and order, 111; Will of government vs. Will of subjects, 119; enlightened by the philosopher, 120; must respect Circumstances, 126; Will to dominate, 127; with Circumstances determines true interest, 128; strives to manifest and manifest form, 154; religion the voice of, 163; eclipsed by Idea, 171; omnipotent in fully developed universe, 181; in incarnation limited by families and habits, 182; source of militancy in self-contradiction of, 183; religion as friendship with all Will, 190; fear as economic Will in quandary, 190; Will at a tangent becomes madness, 194; place of in charity, 197–8; absolute Will rejects religion and chivalry, 214; Will of wild animal opposed to authority, 225; unqualified, 229; irrationality of, 236; reversed by liberty of peace, 238; intensity in

# INDEX

faction, 262; view of government, 268; governments as Will, 270; Will to rule, 271; integrity of in militancy, 295; in mask of vice, 304; sympathy of, 306; Will and liberty centrifugal and divergent, 310; Will as force, 313; appeal to by Reformation, 316; authority of Will of class claimed by Communism, 320; authority of in rebellion of classes, 323; effect of reason on, 324; authority defined in reference to, 325; as initiative, 328; relation of nature to, 331; acceptance by reason, 333; purer phases of, 335; moral aspirations despised as instances of, 336; evolution described in terms of, 337–8; moral authority of, 341; of the majority, 353; problem of in suffrage, 356; complex system cannot fulfill, 362; in creation and destruction of political structures, 364; rational animal most inconsistent in, 374; Will to Live, 375; Will of the People, 385–6; fusion of Wills, 404; compromise with fate in economic arts, 411; compromise in service of, 414; irrational plasticity of, 415; positive sovereignty of, 420-1; Will of the governed defined, 421–2; moral distinctions express bias of, 428; authority of, 433; government relation to, 434; individual Will vs. traditional constraints, 448; vital energy or endeavour, 461; existence imposes limitation and idiosycrasy on, 466

Will to live, 209, 329, 375

Will to rule, 271

*Words*, 140–2

Work, defined in reference to play, 90; developed through instruments, 91; for the proletariat, 368–9

Work of God (Acts of God), 215

Xenophanes, 193

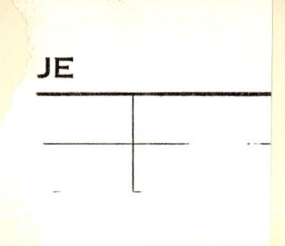